SNOOKER YEAR

EDITED BY CLIVE EVERTON

Best shot of the evening.

Langs Supreme Scottish Masters
Hospitality Inn, Glasgow
18th-21st September 1986

SNOOKER YEAR

EDITED BY CLIVE EVERTON

Virgin

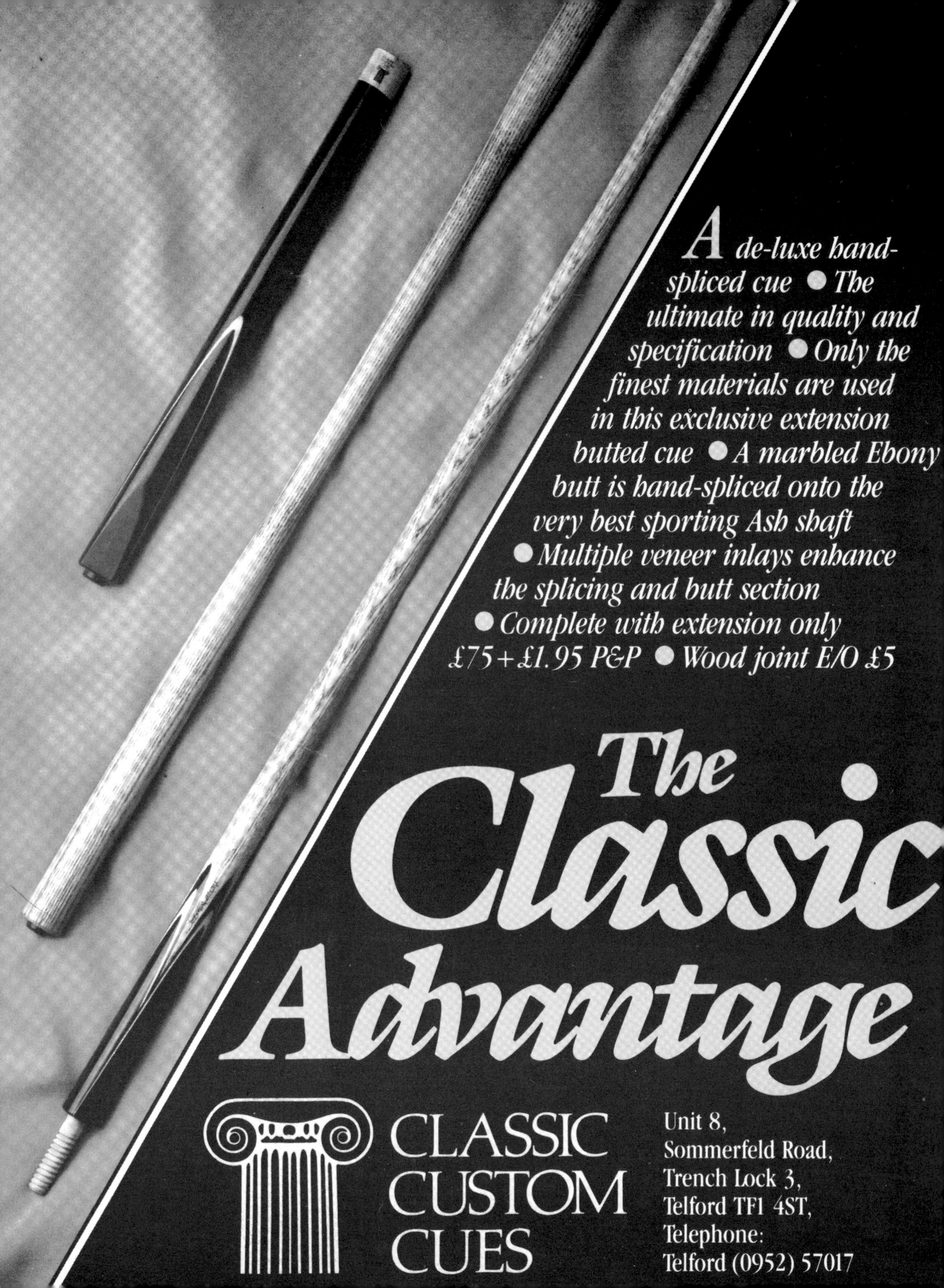
A de-luxe hand-spliced cue ● The ultimate in quality and specification ● Only the finest materials are used in this exclusive extension butted cue ● A marbled Ebony butt is hand-spliced onto the very best sporting Ash shaft ● Multiple veneer inlays enhance the splicing and butt section ● Complete with extension only £75+£1.95 P&P ● Wood joint E/O £5
The Classic Advantage
CLASSIC CUSTOM CUES
Unit 8,
Sommerfeld Road,
Trench Lock 3,
Telford TF1 4ST,
Telephone:
Telford (0952) 57017

The Editor

Clive Everton, snooker's senior and most authoritative journalist, is a BBC Television commentator, snooker correspondent of *The Guardian* and *The Sunday Times* and editor of *Snooker Scene*, the game's leading magazine.

Between winning the British Junior Billiards Championship in 1956 and turning professional in 1981, he was a top amateur at both billiards and snooker, twice reaching the semi-finals of the World Amateur Billiards Championship and winning the Welsh amateur title five times. He was six times a Welsh snooker international and 1976 Midland Amateur Snooker champion.

Contributors

Alexander Clyde is snooker correspondent of the *London Standard*.
John Dee is editor of *Cue World*.
Jane Ennis is a feature writer for *TV Times*.
Alan Green is a member of the BBC sports commentary team and has covered a number of snooker tournaments.
Janice Hale is assistant editor of *Snooker Scene* and snooker correspondent of *The Observer*.
John Martin is snooker correspondent of the *Irish Independent*.
Graham Nickless is snooker correspondent of the *Star*.
Angela Patmore is a freelance journalist who wrote *Playing on Their Nerves*, a study of sportsmen under stress.

Photographs

The editor would like to thank Benson and Hedges, All-Sport (UK) Ltd, David Muscroft Photography, The Lancashire Picture Agency, Simon Weaver Sports, Sportsphoto, BBC Hulton Picture Library and BBC Enterprises for the use of photographic material in this book.

First published in the United Kingdom in 1986 by
Virgin Books Ltd.
328 Kensal Road
London W10 5XJ

ISBN 0 86369 190 0 Export Edition

Printed in Great Britain by Thetford Press Ltd., Thetford
Bound in Great Britain by Skinner & Company, Cambridge

Typeset by Type Generation
Designed by Ray Hyden
Distributed by Arrow Books

Contents

Introduction

The third *Benson and Hedges Snooker Year* chiefly charts the events and personalities of the 1985-86 British season while again furnishing the enthusiast with all the relevant statistics and background of previous seasons.

For the second year in succession, Steve Davis confirmed his status as the game's leading player despite failing in the final of the Embassy World Championship. He chose not to compete in two tournaments but still topped the money list, as we show on pages 12-13, by a considerable margin.

The official world rankings, assessed for the first time on a two- instead of a three-year basis again show (on pages 10-11) Davis well clear of his nearest rival, Cliff Thorburn.

A new feature in the *Benson and Hedges Snooker Year* this year is a compendium of century breaks in major tournaments. It appears on pages 113-114 and to the surprise of no one in snooker reveals Davis to be pre-eminent in yet another sphere of excellence.

During the 1985-86 season, Davis won three of the six world ranking tournaments, the Rothmans Grand Prix, the Coral UK Open and the Dulux British Open and retained the Hofmeister World Doubles with Tony Meo.

But he would undoubtedly be willing to strike a retrospective Faustian bargain to exchange all those first prizes for a fourth world title.

As it was, Joe Johnson, who had started the season a modest 16th in the rankings, brought off an astonishing world title triumph in an incredible climax to the season.

Thorburn won one ranking event, the Goya Trophy, and two non-ranking, the Langs Scottish Masters and the Benson and Hedges Masters; Jimmy White won the remaining ranking tournament, the Mercantile Credit Classic, and retained the Benson and Hedges Irish Masters; Dennis Taylor won two non-ranking invitation events, the BCE Canadian Masters and the Kit Kat Break for World Champions, and Terry Griffiths one, the BCE Belgian Classic. Willie Thorne was king of the runners-up with four second prizes.

The circuit acquired two new events in Canada and Belgium and it is overseas that snooker's main growth is likely to come in the next few seasons if the sponsorship/television equation can be solved as lucratively as it has been on the domestic scene.

In Britain, both live attendances – with isolated exceptions – and television viewing figures remained extremely healthy but with five tournaments nationally shown by BBC, four by ITV and various localised events by BBC Wales, BBC Scotland and Anglia, there would be a real risk of overkill if the World Professional Billiards and Snooker Association, the professional governing body, sanctioned more televised events. This thinking was a factor in the demise of the studio based BBC2 tournament, *Pot Black*, a notable pioneer of television snooker in 1969 but an anachronism in the 1980s.

All aspects of the game's commerce from table sales to snooker centres, from cue endorsements to 'Snooker Loopy' continued to flourish. As in any field where egos and commercial interests clash for high stakes, the game is not without internal strife and the WPBSA itself perhaps needs some reorganisation in the light of fast moving contemporary developments.

Snooker, though, is coping with the problems of success rather than those of failure and the year also brought some notable advances in the women's game, which is now emerging as one of the great growth areas of the eighties, and in billiards, the elder but for half a century overshadowed brother of snooker. This edition increases the amount of coverage devoted to the three-ball game.

Clive Everton

Ranking List

Steve Davis, who won three of the season's world ranking tournaments before his surprise defeat by Joe Johnson in the final of the Embassy World Championship, remains no 1 in the WPBSA official rankings by the massive margin of 18 points. Even if he had lost in the first round at Sheffield, rather than in the final to Joe Johnson, he would still have been top.

It is the first time the list has taken account of performances over only a two-year spread of results rather than three. It will remain in force for the entire 1986–87 season, at the end of which 1984–85 performances, of course, will be disregarded.

In effect, this gives Davis a lead of seven points as he starts next season's campaign hoping not only for the fourth world title which for two years has proved so illusive but also to retain his no 1 ranking for the 1987–88 season.

Conversely, Ray Reardon, who slid spectacularly from 6th to 15th after a 1985–86 season in which he gained only one ranking point, will almost certainly need at least 12 points from 1986–87 if he is to hold on to a place in the top 16, a status which confers two important advantages: exemption from the qualifying section of the Embassy World Championship (thus guaranteeing an appearance at the Crucible) and automatic entry into the 16-man Benson and Hedges Masters.

Even at last year's prize money levels, a place in the top 16 guarantees a player £11,773.50, even if he were to fail to win a match. Players ranked between 17 and 32 were assured £4,570.50 last year.

Rex Williams (up from 27th to 16th) shades John Parrott into 17th place despite having the same number of ranking points (12) and Parrott having *more* merit points (4½ to 4). But under an amendment to the constitution made before the start of last season, where there is an equality of ranking points performances in the immediately preceding season (i.e. 1985–86) decide the placing. Only if these too are equal are merit points then taken into account.

The same system applies lower down the list. If a player has no ranking points and his merit points are thus his primary points, secondary factors (like 'A' points or frames won) come into the reckoning only if performances in 1985–86 are equal.

Neal Foulds entered the top 16 for the first time at 13th, up from 23rd. Spectacular progress was made by Peter Francisco (up to 26th from 59th) and Barry West and Tony Drago, in their first professional seasons, achieved rankings of 30th and 37th respectively. Steve Duggan, largely through reaching the quarter-finals of the Goya Trophy, rose from 70th to 35th; Roger Bales, ranked deceptively low at 100th through a disappointing world championship performance in 1985, rose to 66th, mainly through his Dulux victory over Dennis Taylor.

Steve Davis: top of the rankings again

PLAYER	1984–85 SEASON									
							TOTAL			
	JAMESON	ROTHMANS	CORAL	MERCANTILE	DULUX	WORLD	RANKING	MERIT	GOYA	ROTHMANS
1 (1) Steve Davis	5R	3R ½M	5R	3R	3R ½M	8R	27	1	3R	6R
2 (2) Cliff Thorburn	0	4R ½M	3R	4R	1R ½M	4R	16	1	6R	4R
3 (4) Dennis Taylor	2R	5R ½M	1R	0	2R ½M	10R	20	1	4R	5R
4 (3) Tony Knowles	4R	2R ½M	2R	0	1R ½M	6R	15	1	1R	4R
5 (7) Jimmy White	2R	½M	2R	1R	½M	4R	9	1	5R	2R
6 (9) Alex Higgins	2R	½M	4R	1R	3R ½M	2R	12	1	2R	2R
7 (11) Willie Thorne	2R	1R ½M	2R	5R	½M	0	10	1	2R	1M
8 (16) Joe Johnson	1R ½M	½M	1R ½M	3R ½M	0	1M	5	3	3R	2R
9 (5) Kirk Stevens	0	2R ½M	3R	1R	4R ½M	2R	12	1	1M	3R
10 (8) Terry Griffiths	1R	0	0	2R	½M	4R	7	½	2R	3R
11 (10) Tony Meo	1R	1R ½M	1R	0	2R ½M	2R	7	1	1R	2R
12 (13) Silvino Francisco	3R ½M	1R ½M	½M	½M	5R ½M	1M	9	3½	1M	3R
13 (23) Neal Foulds	½M	3R ½M	0	0	½M	1M	3	2½	4R	1R
14 (15) Doug Mountjoy	0	2R ½M	1R	0	0	2R	5	½	1R	1R
15 (6) Ray Reardon	1R	1R ½M	2R	2R	½M	6R	12	1	1M	1M
16 (27) Rex Williams	½M	½M	1R ½M	1R ½M	0	1M	2	3	1M	1R
17 (18) John Parrott	0	½M	½M	0	½M	4R 1M	4	2½	3R	1M
18 (31) John Campbell	½M	½M	½M	0	0	1M	0	2½	2R	2R
19 (19) John Virgo	1R ½M	½M	0	2R ½M	½M	1M	3	3	1R	1M
20 (21) Eugene Hughes	3R ½M	0	½M	1R ½M	2R ½M	1M	6	3	1M	1R
21 (14) David Taylor	1R	1R ½M	1R	0	0	2R	5	½	2R	1R
22 (26) Murdo Macleod	½M	½M	½M	1R ½M	1R ½M	1M	2	3½	2R	1M
23 (22) Cliff Wilson	0	½M	1R ½M	1R ½M	0	0	2	1½	2R	2R
24 (17) Bill Werbeniuk	0	0	0	0	0	2R	2	0	1R	1M
25 (12) Eddie Charlton	0	1R ½M	1R	0	0	2R	4	½	1M	1R
26 (59) Peter Francisco	0	½M	0	0	0	0	0	½	1A	2R
27 (28) Mike Hallett	0	1R ½M	½M	½M	½M	1M	1	3	1M	1R
28 (29) Dave Martin	0	½M	0	0	1R ½M	0	1	1	1R	1R
29 (24) Dean Reynolds	½M	2R ½M	0	0	½M	1M	2	2½	2R	1M
30 (—) Barry West	0	0	0	0	0	0	0	0	4F	1M
31 (37) Steve Longworth	0	0	0	1R ½M	½M	0	1	1	1M	2R
32 (52) Jim Wych	0	0	0	0	0	0	0	0	1M	1A
33 (55) Danny Fowler	½M	0	½M	0	½M	0	0	1½	1M	1R
34 (20) John Spencer	0	0	0	0	½M	0	0	½	1R	1M
35 (70) Steve Duggan	0	0	0	0	0	0	0	0	3R	1M
36 (30) Perrie Mans	0	0	0	0	0	0	0	0	1M	1M
37 (—) Tony Drago	0	0	0	0	0	0	0	0	2F	2R
38 (39) Marcel Gauvreau	1R ½M	0	½M	½M	0	0	1	1½	1A	1A
39 (32) Dene O'Kane	½M	0	0	0	2R ½M	1M	2	2	1M	1M
40 (34) Steve Newbury	1R ½M	0	0	0	1R ½M	0	2	1	1M	1M
41 (35) Warren King	0	0	½M	2R ½M	0	0	2	1	1R	1A
42 (33) Patsy Fagan	0	0	0	½M	0	2R 1M	2	1½	1M	1A
43 (25) Mark Wildman	0	½M	0	0	½M	0	0	1	1M	1R
44 (41) George Scott	0	0	0	½M	0	0	0	½	1R	1R
45 (66) Bob Harris	0	0	0	0	½M	0	0	½	1R	1R
46 (51) Ray Edmonds	0	0	0	0	0	1M	0	1	1A	1R
47 (56) Fred Davis	0	0	0	0	0	0	0	0	1A	1A
48 (61) Paddy Browne	0	0	0	½M	0	0	0	½	1A	1A
49 (68) Tony Chappel	0	0	½M	0	0	0	0	½	1R	1M
50 (89) Graham Cripsey	0	0	0	0	0	0	0	0	1M	1F
51 (—) Stephen Hendry	0	0	0	0	0	0	0	0	1A	4F
52 (36) Graham Miles	0	½M	0	0	1R ½M	0	1	1	1M	1R
53 (44) Robert Chaperon	0	0	0	0	1R ½M	0	1	½	1R	1A
54 (40) Malcolm Bradley	0	0	0	0	1R ½M	0	1	½	1R	1A

** R denotes ranking points, M denotes merit points.*

55 (50): Tony Jones 1R-7M; **56** (49): Wayne Jones 1R- 6M-1A; **57** (58): Tommy Murphy 1-4½-2; **58** (60): Paul Medati 1-4½-2; **59** (80): Jimmy van Rensburg 1-3-3; **60** (81): Matt Gibson 1-3-2; **61** (81): Bernie Mikkelsen 1-3-2; **62** (67): John Rea 1-2½-3; **63** (65): Vic Harris 1-2½-3; **64** (57): Ian Black 1-2-3; **65** (–): Joe O'Boye 1-2-2-8F; **66** (100): Roger Bales 1-2-1-9; **67** (47): Ian Williamson 1-2½-4; **68** (53): Les Dodd 0-5½-2; **69** (62): Robby Foldvari 0-4½-3; **70** (38): Eddie Sinclair 0-4½-2; **71** (69): Jack McLaughlin 0-4½-2; **72** (–): Dave Gilbert 0-4-1-7; **73** (46): Jim Donnelly 0-3-3; **74** (45): Colin Roscoe 0-3-3; **75** (43): Mario Morra 0-3-3; **76** (74): Jack Fitzmaurice 0-3-3; **77** (42): Mike Watterson 0-3-2; **78** (97): Mike Darrington 0-3-1-4; **79** (48): Geoff Foulds 0-2-4; **80** (–): Sakchai Simngam 0-2-3-2; **81** (99): Des Sheehan 0-2-1-5; **82** (–): Jim Bear 0-2-1-4; **83** (64): John Dunning 0-1½-1; **84** (85): Bill Oliver 0-1-5; **85** (48): Jim Meadowcroft 0-1-5; **86** (77): Gino Rigitano 0-1-5; **87** (54): Mick Fisher 0-1-5; **88** (71):

1985–86 SEASON

TOTAL

CORAL	MERCANTILE	DULUX	WORLD	TOTAL RANKING	TOTAL MERIT	TOTAL 'A' POINTS	TOTAL FRAMES	RANKING	MERIT	'A' POINTS	FRAMES
6R	3R	6R	8R	32	0	0	0	59	1	0	0
2R	5R	2R	6R	25	0	0	0	41	1	0	0
4R	2R	1M	2M	15	3	0	0	35	4	0	0
3R	2R	1R	6R	17	0	0	0	32	1	0	0
4R	6R	1M	4R	21	1	0	0	30	2	0	0
2R	3R	4R	2R	15	0	0	0	27	1	0	0
5R	1M	5R	4R	16	2	0	0	26	3	0	0
1R	3R	1R	10R	20	0	0	0	25	3	0	0
3R	1M	2R	4R	12	2	0	0	24	3	0	0
3R	1M	3R	4R	15	1	0	0	22	1½	0	0
2R	2R	3R	2M	10	2	0	0	17	3	0	0
2R	1M	1R	2R	8	2	0	0	17	5½	0	0
2R	3R	1R	1R	12	0	0	0	15	2½	0	0
1R	4R	1M	2R	9	1	0	0	14	1½	0	0
1R	1M	1M	2M	1	6	0	0	13	7	0	0
2R	4R	2R	1R	10	1	0	0	12	4	0	0
1R	1M	2R	2R	8	2	0	0	12	4½	0	0
1R	2R	2R	2R	11	0	0	0	11	2½	0	0
1R	1R	4R	1R	8	1	0	0	11	4	0	0
1M	2R	1M	2R	5	3	0	0	11	6	0	0
2R	1M	1M	2M	5	4	0	0	10	4½	0	0
2R	1R	2R	2M	7	3	0	0	9	6½	0	0
1M	1M	1R	1R	7	2	0	0	9	3½	0	0
1M	2R	3R	1R	7	2	0	0	9	2	0	0
1M	1M	2R	2R	5	3	0	0	9	3½	0	0
1R	2R	2R	2M	7	2	1	0	7	2½	1	0
1R	1R	1R	2R	6	1	0	0	7	4	0	0
1R	1R	1R	1R	6	0	0	0	7	1	0	0
1R	1R	1M	1R	5	2	0	0	7	4½	0	0
3R	1R	1M	2M	4	4	0	4	4	4	0	4
1M	1A	1R	2M	3	4	1	0	4	5	1	0
1M	1M	3R	2M	3	5	1	0	3	5	1	0
1R	1M	1M	1R	3	3	0	0	3	4½	0	0
1R	1M	1M	1R	3	3	0	0	3	3½	0	0
1A	1A	1M	1M	3	3	2	0	3	3	2	0
1M	1R	1R	1R	3	3	0	0	3	3	0	0
1R	4F	1M	1A	3	1	1	6	3	1	1	6
1A	2R	1A	2M	2	2	4	0	3	3½	4	0
1M	1R	1M	2M	1	6	0	0	3	8	0	0
1M	1A	1R	2M	1	5	1	0	3	6	1	0
1M	1M	1A	2M	1	4	2	0	3	5	2	0
1M	1A	1R	1A	1	2	3	0	3	3½	3	0
1M	1M	1R	2M	2	5	0	0	2	6	0	0
1A	1A	1M	1M	2	2	2	0	2	2½	2	0
1A	1M	1M	1A	2	2	2	0	2	2½	2	0
1M	1A	1A	1R	2	1	3	0	2	2	3	0
1R	1R	1M	1M	2	2	2	0	2	2	2	0
1M	1R	1R	1A	2	1	3	0	2	1½	3	0
1R	1A	1A	1A	2	1	3	0	2	1½	3	0
1R	1R	1A	4F	2	1	1	5	2	1	1	5
2F	1R	1A	1R	2	0	2	6	2	0	2	6
1M	1A	1M	1M	1	4	1	0	2	5	1	0
1A	1M	1M	1M	1	3	2	0	2	3½	2	0
1M	1M	1M	1A	1	3	2	0	2	3½	2	0

Billy Kelly 0-1-5; **89** (–): Omprakesh Agrawal 0-1-4-4; **90** (63): Eddie McLaughlin 0-1-4; **91** (–): Pat Houlihan 0-1-3-9; **92** (102): John Hargreaves 0-1-2-10; **93** (88): Dennis Hughes 0-1-2-10; **94** (–): Martin Smith 0-1-2-7; **95** (–): Greg Jenkins 0-1-1-4; **96** (–): Gerry Watson 0-1-0-8; **97** (–): Paul Thornley 0-1-0; **98** (72): Frank Jonik 0-0-6; **99** (79): Dave Chalmers 0-0-6; **100** (73): Clive Everton 0-0-6; **101** (90): Tony Kearney 0-0-4-9; **102** (–): Glen Wilkinson 0-0-3-10; **103** (76): Jack Rea 0-0-3-0; **104** (86): Pascal Burke 0-0-2-17; **105** (87): Joe Caggianello 0-0-2-0; **106** (93): Paul Watchorn 0-0-1-19; **107** (96): David Greaves 0-0-1-15; **108** (95): Derek Mienie 0-0-1-14; **109** (92): Bert Demarco 0-0-1-13; **110** (–): Jim Rempe 0-0-1-2; **111** (75): Paddy Morgan 0-0-1-0; **112** (–): Robbie Grace 0-0-1-0; **113** (91): Maurice Parkin 0-0-0-12; **114** (94): Bernard Bennett 0-0-0-11; **115**: Mike Hines; **116**: Ian Anderson; **117**: James Giannaros; **118**: Leon Heywood.

Where Snooker's Prize Money Has Gone

		Carlsberg	*Langs*	*Goya*	*Rothmans*	*Canadian*	*Corals*	*Hofmeister*	*Kit Kat*
1.	**Steve Davis**	—	—	5,250.00	50,000.00	9,000.00	24,000.00	20,000.00	6,000.00
2.	**Cliff Thorburn**	5,000.00	10,500.00	35,000.00	15,000.00	5,000.00	1,800.00	6,500.00	1,500.00
3.	**Jimmy White**	11,000.00	3,250.00	21,000.00	3,750.00	3,375.00	7,200.00	875.00	—
4.	**Dennis Taylor**	—	1,750.00	10,500.00	30,000.00	15,000.00	7,200.00	6,500.00	10,000.00
5.	**Joe Johnson**	—	—	5,250.00	3,750.00	—	1,162.50	1,750.00	—
6.	**Willie Thorne**	—	6,500.00	2,625.00	1,093.75	—	14,400.00	6,500.00	—
7.	**Tony Knowles**	—	1,750.00	1,531.00	15,000.00	3,375.00	3,600.00	1,750.00	—
8.	**Terry Griffiths**	—	—	2,625.00	7,500.00	3,375.00	3,600.00	6,500.00	3,500.00
9.	**Alex Higgins**	7,500.00	1,750.00	2,625.00	3,750.00	—	1,800.00	875.00	3,500.00
10.	**Tony Meo**	—	—	1,531.00	3,750.00	—	1,800.00	20,000.00	—
11.	**Kirk Stevens**	—	—	765.50	7,500.00	—	3,600.00	1,750.00	—
12.	**Neal Foulds**	—	—	10,500.00	2,421.87	—	1,800.00	3,250.00	—
13.	**Ray Reardon**	—	—	765.50	1,093.75	5,000.00	1,162.50	11,000.00	1,500.00
14.	**Doug Mountjoy**	—	—	1,531.00	2,421.87	—	1,162.50	3,250.00	—
15.	**Eugene Hughes**	—	—	765.50	2,421.87	—	525.00	1,750.00	—
16.	**John Virgo**	—	—	1,531.00	1,093.75	—	1,162.50	1,750.00	—
17.	**Eddie Charlton**	—	—	765.50	2,421.87	—	525.00	1,750.00	—
18.	**John Campbell**	—	—	2,625.00	3,750.00	—	1,162.50	3,250.00	—
19.	**Silvino Francisco**	—	3,250.00	765.50	7,500.00	—	1,800.00	3,250.00	—
20.	**Rex Williams**	—	—	765.50	2,421.87	—	1,800.00	875.00	—
21.	**Bill Werbeniuk**	—	—	1,531.00	1,093.75	—	525.00	1,750.00	—
22.	**John Parrott**	5,000.00	—	5,250.00	1,093.75	3,375.00	1,162.50	3,250.00	—
23.	**Mike Hallett**	—	—	765.50	2,421.87	—	1,162.50	1,750.00	—
24.	**Cliff Wilson**	—	—	2,625.00	7,500.00	—	525.00	1,750.00	—
25.	**Murdo Macleod**	—	1,750.00	2,625.00	1,093.75	—	1,800.00	875.00	—
26.	**David Taylor**	—	—	2,625.00	2,421.87	—	1,800.00	1,750.00	—
27.	**Tony Jones**	—	—	765.50	1,093.75	—	525.00	11,000.00	—
28.	**Peter Francisco**	—	—	—	3,750.00	—	1,162.50	3,250.00	—
29.	**Dave Martin**	—	—	1,531.00	2,421.87	—	1,162.50	875.00	—
30.	**Dean Reynolds**	—	—	2,625.00	1,093.75	—	1,162.50	875.00	—
31.	**Patsy Fagan**	—	—	765.50	—	—	525.00	875.00	—
32.	**John Spencer**	—	—	1,531.00	1,093.75	—	1,162.50	1,750.00	—
33.	**Perrie Mans**	—	—	765.50	1,093.75	—	525.00	3,250.00	—
34.	**Jim Wych**	—	—	765.50	—	—	525.00	—	—
35.	**Barry West**	—	—	—	1,093.75	—	3,600.00	1,750.00	—
36.	**Mark Wildman**	—	—	765.50	2,421.87	—	525.00	875.00	—
37.	**Danny Fowler**	—	—	765.50	2,421.87	—	1,162.50	1,750.00	—
38.	**Steve Longworth**	—	—	765.50	3,750.00	—	525.00	875.00	—
39.	**Wayne Jones**	—	—	765.50	2,421.87	—	525.00	3,250.00	—
40.	**Warren King**	—	—	1,531.00	—	—	525.00	1,750.00	—
41.	**Tommy Murphy**	—	—	1,531.00	—	—	525.00	875.00	—
42.	**Steve Newbury**	—	—	765.50	1,093.75	—	525.00	1,750.00	—
43.	**Steve Duggan**	—	—	5,250.00	1,093.75	—	—	875.00	—
44.	**Stephen Hendry**	—	—	—	—	—	—	—	—
45.	**Fred Davis**	—	—	—	—	—	1,162.50	875.00	1,500.00
46.	**Ray Edmonds**	—	—	—	2,421.87	—	525.00	875.00	—
47.	**Paddy Browne**	—	—	—	—	—	525.00	875.00	—
48.	**Tony Drago**	—	—	—	3,750.00	—	1,162.50	—	—
49.	**Paul Medati**	—	—	—	—	—	525.00	875.00	—
50.	**Dene O'Kane**	—	—	765.50	1,093.75	—	525.00	—	—
51.	**Graham Miles**	—	—	765.50	2,421.87	—	525.00	875.00	—
52.	**Jim Donnelly**	—	—	—	—	—	—	875.00	—
53.	**John Rea**	—	—	—	—	—	—	875.00	—
54.	**George Scott**	—	—	1,531.00	2,421.87	—	—	—	—
55.	**Matt Gibson**	—	—	1,531.00	1,093.75	—	—	—	—
56.	**Eddie Sinclair**	—	—	765.50	—	—	525.00	—	—
57.	**Roger Bales**	—	—	765.50	1,093.75	—	—	875.00	—
58.	**Bob Harris**	—	—	1,531.00	2,421.87	—	—	—	—
59.	**Malcolm Bradley**	—	—	1,531.00	—	—	525.00	875.00	—
60.	**Graham Cripsey**	—	—	765.50	—	—	1,162.50	875.00	—
61.	**Jack McLaughlin**	—	—	—	1,093.75	—	525.00	875.00	—
62.	**Marcel Gauvreau**	—	—	—	—	—	—	—	—
63.	**Les Dodd**	—	—	765.50	—	—	525.00	875.00	—
64.	**Jimmy van Rensburg**	—	—	—	1,093.75	—	—	—	—
65.	**Ian Black**	—	—	1,531.00	—	—	—	—	—
66.	**Tony Chappel**	—	—	1,531.00	1,093.75	—	1,162.50	875.00	—
67.	**Robbie Foldvari**	—	—	765.50	—	—	—	—	—

MCC	Belgian	Benson and Hedges Masters	Dulux	World Cup	B&H Irish Masters	National	World	Total	Breaks
6,750.00	3,000.00	14,000.00	55,000.00	3,333.33	—	6,000.00	42,000.00	244,333.33	10,750
27,000.00	—	45,000.00	4,125.00	6,666.66	8,035.00	—	21,000.00	192,126.66	3,500
45,000.00	3,000.00	25,000.00	1,203.12	3,333.33	20,089.00	3,000.00	10,500.00	161,575.45	7,125
3,375.00	3,000.00	9,500.00	1,203.12	11,000.00	4,821.00	8,000.00	2,953.12	124,802.24	6,250
6,750.00	—	4,250.00	2,664.06	—	—	3,000.00	70,000.00	98,576.56	—
984.37	—	9,500.00	33,000.00	—	11,607.00	1,500.00	10,500.00	98,210.12	13,332
3,375.00	4,000.00	14,000.00	2,664.06	3,333.33	4,821.00	1,500.00	21,000.00	81,699.39	—
984.37	12,000.00	9,500.00	8,250.00	3,333.33	2,767.00	5,000.00	10,500.00	79,434.70	1,000
6,750.00	4,000.00	4,250.00	16,500.00	11,000.00	2,767.00	5,000.00	5,250.00	77,317.00	400
3,375.00	—	4,250.00	8,250.00	—	4,821.00	18,500.00	2,953.12	69,230.12	2,000
984.37	7,000.00	4,250.00	4,125.00	6,666.66	—	—	10,500.00	47,141.53	—
6,750.50	—	—	2,664.06	—	—	11,000.00	2,953.12	41,339.05	4,400
984.37	3,000.00	4,250.00	1,203.12	3,333.33	2,767.00	750.00	2,953.12	39,762.69	2,500
13,500.00	—	—	1,203.12	3,333.33	—	3,500.00	5,250.00	35,151.82	—
3,375.00	—	—	1,203.12	11,000.00	4,821.00	—	5,250.00	31,111.49	—
2,179.68	—	—	16,500.00	—	—	3,000.00	2,953.12	30,170.05	1,750
984.37	—	9,500.00	4,125.00	2,000.00	—	2,600.00	5,250.00	29,921.74	—
3,375.00	—	—	4,125.00	2,000.00	—	4,250.00	5,250.00	29,787.50	5,000
984.37	—	4,250.00	2,664.06	—	—	—	5,250.00	29,713.93	—
13,500.00	—	—	4,125.00	—	—	1,500.00	2,953.12	27,940.49	—
3,375.00	—	—	8,250.00	6,666.66	—	—	2,953.12	26,144.53	—
984.37	—	—	4,125.00	—	—	1,500.00	5,250.00	25,990.62	—
2,179.68	—	—	2,664.06	—	—	6,000.00	5,250.00	22,192.61	—
984.37	—	—	2,664.06	—	—	1,500.00	2,953.12	20,501.55	—
2,179.68	—	—	4,125.00	2,000.00	—	1,000.00	2,296.87	19,745.30	—
984.37	—	4,250.00	1,203.12	—	—	750.00	2,953.12	18,737.48	—
2,179.68	—	—	1,203.12	—	—	750.00	1,203.12	18,720.17	—
3,375.00	—	—	4,125.00	—	—	—	2,296.87	15,662.50	—
2,179.68	—	—	2,664.06	—	—	1,500.00	2,953.12	15,287.23	1,375
2,179.68	—	—	1,203.12	—	—	3,000.00	2,953.12	15,092.17	13,332
—	—	—	2,664.06	2,000.00	8,035.00	150.00	—	15,014.56	—
984.37	—	—	1,203.12	—	—	1,500.00	2,953.12	13,677.86	—
2,179.68	—	—	2,664.06	—	—	—	2,953.12	13,431.11	—
984.37	—	—	8,250.00	—	—	—	2,296.87	12,821.71	—
2,179.68	—	—	1,203.12	—	—	—	2,296.87	12,123.42	—
984.37	—	—	2,664.06	—	—	1,500.00	2,296.87	12,032.67	—
984.37	—	—	1,203.12	—	—	750.00	2,953.12	11,990.48	—
—	—	—	2,664.06	—	—	750.00	2,269.87	11,626.43	—
—	—	—	1,203.12	—	—	1,500.00	1,203.12	10,898.61	—
984.37	—	—	—	2,000.00	—	1,650.00	2,296.87	10,737.24	—
984.37	—	—	—	2,000.00	—	2,000.00	2,296.87	10,212.24	—
—	—	—	2,664.06	—	—	750.00	2,296.87	9,845.18	—
—	—	—	1,203.12	—	—	—	1,203.12	9,624.99	—
2,179.68	—	—	—	—	—	4,000.00	2,953.12	9,132.80	1,750
2,179.68	—	—	1,203.12	—	—	750.00	1,203.12	8,873.42	—
—	—	—	—	—	—	1,500.00	2,953.12	8,274.99	—
2,179.68	—	—	2,664.06	—	—	150.00	—	8,393.74	—
—	—	—	1,203.12	2,000.00	—	—	—	8,115.62	—
984.37	—	—	2,664.06	—	—	750.00	2,296.87	8,095.30	—
2,179.68	—	—	1,203.12	—	—	—	2,296.87	8,063.92	—
—	—	—	1,203.12	—	—	750.00	1,203.12	7,743.61	—
984.37	—	—	1,203.12	2,000.00	—	1,000.00	1,203.12	7,265.61	—
984.37	—	—	2,664.06	—	—	1,500.00	1,203.12	7,226.55	—
—	—	—	1,203.12	—	—	750.00	1,203.12	7,109.11	—
984.37	—	—	—	—	—	2,000.00	1,203.12	6,812.24	—
984.37	—	—	—	2,000.00	—	1,000.00	1,203.12	6,477.99	—
—	—	—	2,664.06	—	—	750.00	—	6,148.31	—
984.37	—	—	1,203.12	—	—	—	—	6,140.36	—
984.37	—	—	1,203.12	—	—	750.00	—	5,868.49	—
2,179.68	—	—	—	—	—	750.00	—	5,732.68	—
984.37	—	—	1,203.12	—	—	800.00	—	5,481.24	—
3,375.00	—	—	—	—	—	—	2,296.87	5,671.87	—
—	—	—	1,203.12	—	—	—	2,296.87	5,664.99	—
2,179.68	—	—	—	—	—	—	2,296.87	5,570.30	—
—	—	—	1,203.12	—	—	1,500.00	1,203.12	5,437.24	—
—	—	—	—	—	—	750.00	—	5,412.25	—
—	—	—	1,203.12	—	—	875.00	2,296.87	5,140.49	—

The Players

Steve Davis

(England)

BORN: 23.8.57
HOME: ROMFORD
WORLD RANKING: 1

Judged by the same criteria as other players, Steve Davis would have had a marvellously successful season. But he is not so assessed for he created, with his string of titles in the early part of this decade, standards of expectation which make his few failures appear more significant than his many successes.

Between December 1980 – when he won his first major title, the Coral UK – and February 1985, Davis accumulated 24 major titles and reached five other finals.

But it was from one of these losing final appearances that scar tissue began to form in his mind, tissue which cannot be surgically removed.

Once described as 'robotoid' in technique and mental approach, Davis's tuning began to stutter in the 1983 Coral UK final when he was beaten 16-15 by Alex Higgins after leading 7-0.

The 'snatched away' syndrome which this illustrates brought human dimension to the computerised programme. The fear of losing had always been there but now there was a fear of losing after the winning was practically done; it was the live nightmare of the cup within the grasp only for the handle to fall off just as the hand begins to close round it.

Another Irishman, Dennis Taylor, added the next layer to the scar tissue in his psyche.

Taylor's image – somewhat at odds with his highly professional approach to the game – was that of a happy-go-lucky figure, full of quips and good humour. Despite winning the Rothmans Grand Prix earlier in the season, he had not widely been considered a genuine World Championship contender. After all, he had won the Rothmans in extraordinary circumstances.

As the final of the 1985 Embassy World Championship unfolded, the pundits were patting themselves on the back as Davis swept to an 8-0 lead. Taylor grew redder in the face and sank deeper into his chair.

Taylor, though, found inspiration somewhere – perhaps from acknowledging that the worst that could happen would be that he could lose. The final was eventually decided – in Taylor's favour – on the final black in the final frame.

Both handles had now come off the cup for Davis but this did not appear significant as he began the 1985-86 campaign.

After losing to Jimmy White in the quarter-finals of the Goya Matchroom Trophy, Davis won the deciding frame – although this time not on the black – to beat Taylor 10-9 for the Rothmans title. Less than a week later, he lost to an inspired Taylor in the final of the BCE Canadian Masters but won the Coral UK title for the fourth time by beating Willie Thorne 16-14.

With Tony Meo, he regained the Hofmeister World Doubles but then suffered four consecutive losses: to Terry Griffiths in the first round of the BCE Belgian Classic, twice to White in the Benson and Hedges Masters and Mercantile Credit Classic and, for the first time, to Meo, in the Tolly Cobbold English Championship.

He won his third world ranking tournament of the season when he repeated his Coral UK victory over Thorne in the final of the Dulux British Open and then took time off to prepare for the World Championship, declining an invitation to compete in the Benson and Hedges Irish Masters, a title he had won twice previously.

Drawn in what was the tougher half of the draw, Davis began his attempt to win the Embassy World Championship for the fourth time in six attempts with two comfortable victories, 10-4 over Ray Edmonds and 10-5 over Doug Mountjoy, who announced that Davis was playing even better than when he had beaten the Welshman for the title in 1981.

White proved an easier proposition than many had predicted – largely because Davis played so well – and fell 13-5 but Cliff Thorburn, still the equivalent of Beechers Brook in this Grand National of the mind, loomed next.

After a high quality, technically superb game, Davis reached the final for the fourth consecutive year with a 16-12 victory. 'Playing Cliff is the ultimate test,' Davis said afterwards.

He began the final 8-1 on to beat Joe Johnson but although he led 7-4 he was unable – or perhaps in some illogical way afraid – to build up too large a lead. Perhaps again, his matches against White and Thorburn had simply drained him too much.

Even so, when he trailed 13-11 going into the final session, many thought his experience would pull him through. Instead, he won only one frame to Johnson's five as he finished runner-up for the second consecutive year.

This time, there was no handle to come off for no cup has three handles and this time it had never been actually within his grasp.

So Davis had to be content, as they say, with being no 1 in the world rankings and no 1 in the money list – enviable positions both but neither carrying with them either trophy or applause.

Janice Hale

Cliff Thorburn

(Canada)

BORN: 16.1.48
HOME: TORONTO
WORLD RANKING: 2

If genius can reside in the capacity to take infinite pains, Cliff Thorburn falls emphatically into this category. Like a watchmaker he has taken apart every element of his game, adjusted it and put it together again. He is fascinated by technique and motivated by competition. This now comes from tournaments but in his early days on the road in Canada and North America, it came from contests where the winner gathered up all the marbles while the loser held only a bag with a hole in it.

He never concealed his ability but it was not always wise to advertise his identity. One standard ploy was to wear garage mechanics overalls but once, when he had won a sizeable sum, his opponent asked where he worked. He mentioned a gas station he had noticed on his way into town. It turned out that his opponent owned the gas station. 'I have never been so embarrassed in my life,' he recalls.

In those days, he did not realise even that a legit circuit existed. Tournaments in Canada were few and far between but he occasionally played visiting British professionals and learnt from John Spencer the practical steps he needed to take.

He first visited Britain in 1973 and improved steadily each year until he reached the 1977 world final, losing 25-21 to Spencer. He acquired sartorial elegance, a sophisticated image and, above all, a reputation as one of the toughest competitors in the game.

In 1980, he became the first overseas player to win the world title. In that he had lost to Spencer three years earlier from four frames in front it was ironic that he should beat Alex Higgins from four frames behind, 18-16. He decided to live in Britain but felt like a fish out of water. He lacked the managerial backing to cash in on the world title. His style of play made him less in demand for exhibitions than his status as champion had led him to expect and he suffered some frustrating defeats, notably 6-5 to Alex Higgins in the 1981 Benson and Hedges Masters semi-final after leading 5-1. He fought tigerishly in defence of his world title but lost 16-10 to Steve Davis in the semi-finals. The 1981-82 season was an unmitigated disaster and he decided to move home to Toronto even if it meant commuting several times a year.

Gradually, he started to climb again. He took particular satisfaction from captaining Canada to the World Cup in 1982 because he had known his team mates, Bill Werbeniuk and Kirk Stevens, for several years. In less affluent times they had often played for each other's money. Early in 1983, he won the Benson and Hedges Masters – an event he was to win three times in four years – and in a Sheffield spring made history by compiling the so far only 147 maximum in world championship history.

Equally memorable were his marathons, a 3.51 a.m. finish to his 13-12 second-round win over Terry Griffiths after a 6 hour 25 minute final session, a 13-12 quarter-final win over Stevens from two down with three to play and a 16-15 semi-final victory over Tony Knowles from the same position. These three matches drained him dry and he was easy meat for Davis in the final, 18-6.

In 1983-84, he reached only one major final, the Jameson International, beating Griffiths in characteristically gritty fashion from three down with four to play before losing 9-4 to Davis in the final. He sensed there was something amiss with his game and even tried fruitlessly to develop a quicker tempo than comes naturally to him but did not really get anywhere for the rest of the season.

It was a different story in 1984-85 when his 9-7 semi-final victory over Davis in the Rothmans Grand Prix vindicated all the close analysis and purposeful practice which he had invested in his game in the close season.

'I'm a better player now because Steve has set such a high standard,' he said. 'I was just fed up with the way I was playing. I went back to my old style, choking up [shortening his grip] round the pink and black and lengthening the grip for the long shots. I've got a great attitude now. I'm a rejuvenated man. It's good that after playing for 20 years I can still improve. I wake up in the mornings looking forward to playing snooker.'

It was a positive attitude he was able to maintain as he reached the Coral semi-finals, the Hofmeister World Doubles final (with Willie Thorne), the Mercantile Credit Classic final (losing to Thorne) and won his second Benson and Hedges Masters. He was a Dennis Taylor quarter-final victim in the Embassy World Championship but finished the season second in the world rankings.

Robert Winsor, a man of substance from his point-of-sale advertising company, became his manager and remained his golfing companion and all-weather friend. For the first time, Thorburn began to earn serious off-table money featuring in advertising for Scottish Amicable and Creda and signing a BCE cue contract worth a six-figure sum. The added degrees of security and contentment in his life showed in his early season form as he won the Langs Scottish Masters and, with an epic recovery, the Goya Trophy having trailed Jimmy White 0-7 and by 74 with only four reds remaining in the eighth frame.

This 12-10 win was followed by a semi-final loss to Davis in the Rothmans Grand Prix and defeat by Thorne in the last 16 of the Coral UK. He appeared certain to win his second ranking tournament of the season, the Mercantile Credit Classic, but lost 13-12 after White had needed a snooker in the decider with only the pink and black remaining.

He is a player of such consistency that he is hard to beat even when he is well below his best. 'I think I'm probably the best poor-form player on the circuit,' he says.

Many of his matches take a long time but this is usually because he likes to debate the potential risk and gains of all possible options. He is also relatively slow on the shot and does not like to vary the system of addressing and sighting the shot which serves him so well. A standard somewhat below his best was therefore still good enough for him to beat White to retain the Benson and Hedges Masters and he went to Sheffield as one of the favourites for the Embassy World Championship, duly reaching his appointed place against Davis in the semi-finals.

A titanic battle ensued and as the final session started at 11-11 most pundits, erroneously as it turned out, thought they were watching the 'real' final.

Only three balls were potted in the first 17 minutes of this session before Davis's break of 79 decided the opening frame. After a scoreless 12 minutes, Thorburn's 104 decided the next. These two frames epitomised both the quality of the protracted safety exchanges and the deadliness of the break-making once an opening had been created.

Two more long frames went to Davis and Thorburn finally cracked but the effect of this gruelling semi-final made itself felt in the final just as it had three years earlier. Then, an exhausted Thorburn lost to Davis; now Davis, his fine edge blunted, was unable to sharpen his mind and game as he needed to against Joe Johnson.

There was another neat historical reversal. Three years earlier, Thorburn's wife Barbara suffered a miscarriage during the last week of the Championship. This time she was safely delivered of a brother for their four-year-old son, Jamie.

Clive Everton

Dennis Taylor

(Northern Ireland)

BORN: 19.1.49
HOME: BLACKBURN
WORLD RANKING: 3

There was to be no fairy-tale ending to the season, this time, for Dennis Taylor, far from it, but his early demise at Sheffield – beaten 10-6, in the first round, by Mike Hallett – was, on reflection, not the great surprise it seemed to many.

If it is hard to win the world title at the Crucible, it is clearly harder to defend it. Before Taylor, three other champions had been beaten in the first matches back at the venue – John Spencer in 1978, Terry Griffiths in 1980 and Steve Davis in 1982. Davis remains the only man to have retained the title since the Championship moved to Sheffield in 1977.

Taylor, too, had had a miserable time since Christmas. He had won only one tournament match, when he beat Doug Mountjoy 5-2 in the Benson and Hedges Masters at Wembley, and been defeated by Roger Bales, then ranked 100th, in the third round of the Dulux British Open.

Yet the champion went to the Crucible confident from a week's solid practice, 'helped' by another defeat, 5-2 by Willie Thorne in the quarter-finals of the Benson and Hedges Irish Masters. He felt fine. 'However,' he said, 'once I got to the table I suddenly felt very tense.'

It showed in his play. He was 8-1 down at the end of the first session against a player who, in four previous attempts, had not won a match at the Crucible. Taylor pursued a comeback in the evening, reducing the deficit to two frames at one stage, but overall he hardly deserved to win.

It was clear that a hectic year under the management of Barry Hearn had taken a certain toll. Taylor had gained financial security for life but it was inevitable that his form would suffer at some stage.

In the preceding 12 months, he had visited Canada, Thailand, Hong Kong, Singapore, the Middle East and China where, with Steve Davis, he became a snooker pioneer in a country which has

the world's largest population and thus huge potential for the sport.

Also in this period he had collaborated on two books, appeared on most television and radio programmes you might care to mention and done the usual troublesome but lucrative round of personal appearances and exhibitions. Taylor insists he enjoyed it but after defeat at Sheffield he had amply earned his fortnight's golf and long holiday.

Taylor's disappointment with his form in the second half of the season should be tempered by some splendid performances in the first half. Having lost the first round of the Langs Scottish Masters to Willie Thorne, he reached the semi-finals of the Goya Matchroom Trophy before being beaten 9-5 by Cliff Thorburn, the eventual winner.

The next tournament was the Rothmans Grand Prix where he was defending the first major title he had ever won. It was a spirited defence ending in the last frame of the final against Davis. Mercifully for those of a nervous disposition it did not, like their world final, go to the final ball.

In the Coral UK Open, Taylor reached the semi-finals, again confirming his ranking but, on either side of that event, he picked up two first prizes. He won the BCE Canadian Masters in Toronto beating Davis 9-5 in the final. In so doing, he made three century breaks in four frames. Then he won the Kit Kat Break for World Champions at Nottingham. Again Davis was his victim in the final; again the score was 9-5.

There followed two defeats by Alex Higgins in the Mercantile Credit Classic and in the BCE Belgian Classic and then he lost 5-3 in the quarter-finals of the Benson and Hedges Masters to Jimmy White.

The lone success of the barren spell after Christmas came in the Car Care Plan World Cup. Ireland, with Alex Higgins, Eugene Hughes and Taylor, as captain, retained their title, beating Canada in the final.

Dennis Taylor is now judged by the highest standards. Even by those, winning two titles and reaching a final and two semi-finals in ranking tournaments does not represent a bad season, particularly as he retained the Irish cham-

Dennis Taylor with Doug Mountjoy before their match at the 1986 Benson and Hedges Masters

pionship in May. Nor does a final prize money total of £124,802.24.

It is scarcely possible to understand how a couple of seasons ago Taylor was close to dropping out of the world's top 16. The transformation of the vastly popular Ulsterman from being a 'nice guy who loses in the end' to 'major winner' is still considered remarkable by the snooker world.

He has come a long way since at 17 he left Coalisland to live with his aunt in Darwen, Lancashire. Like many others before him, he crossed the Irish Sea looking for a job.

He had been playing snooker in Gervin's Club in the Co. Tyrone town since he was nine. He used to stand on a box so that he could reach the table. By 14 he was good enough to have won the local senior billiards and snooker titles but, leaving for England, he left his cue behind. 'I thought they'd all be so much better. They weren't.'

He got his cue sent over and before long built up a reputation in the North of England, receiving an invitation to play John Spencer, who had already won the first of his three world titles, in a 'Find the Champion' competition run by the *Lancashire Evening Telegraph*.

Taylor feels Spencer was instrumental in his being accepted into the professional ranks at the end of 1972. To begin with he found it hard going but he soon learnt to supplement his snooker skill with his ready wit in the exhibitions round the clubs.

His innate sense of humour endears Taylor to snooker audiences whether live or on television. He employs it in his commentaries for ITV, a role he greatly enjoys. In the unlikely event of his ability on the table deserting him, broadcasting would fit him like a glove.

For the future, you can expect Taylor to stay at or around the top. A summer's rest should allow him to return to the baize for the 1986-87 season, keen and refreshed. Certainly he will continue to be warmed by the genuine affection extended to him by the public. Beaten or not, it is hard to believe we have ever had a more popular world champion.

Alan Green

Tony Knowles

(England)

BORN: 13.6.55
HOME: BOLTON
WORLD RANKING: 4

Three times a semi-finalist in the Embassy World Professional Championship, Tony Knowles knows only too well just how difficult it is to take the last step forward to the final.

In 1983, his first semi-final appearance, Knowles was beaten 16-15 by Cliff Thorburn, leading by two with three to play and missing an easy enough pink on the brink of victory at 15-14 that he probably had nightmares about long afterwards.

Two years later and also last season, Knowles was in the semi-final again but on each occasion he was heavily beaten. Dennis Taylor defeated him 16-5 in 1985 and 12 months later Joe Johnson, Knowles's doubles partner, put him out 16-8.

Significantly, though, Knowles had used the World Championship, with its extra ranking points at stake, yet again to confirm his place among the world's top four players. For someone who has suffered more than once from adverse off-the-table publicity and other troubles that has been quite an achievement.

In 1984-85, Knowles was ranked no 2, outright victories in the 1982 Jameson International and 1983 Professional Players Tournament boosting his ranking points total – at that time calculated over a three-year period. A year later, Knowles had slipped to no 3 and now, with ranking points accumulated over two seasons, he drops a further place to 4.

Below par performances appear to affect him more than most other players but he has only to look at the ranking list if he wants proof of his own ability. He was very critical of some of his performances last season but when it came to an end he had dropped only one place in the ranking list and earned 17 points, a total bettered by just four other players.

This total came from the semi-finals of the Embassy World Championship, and Rothmans Grand Prix, the quarter-finals of the Coral UK, the last 16 of the Mercantile Credit Classic and the last 32 of the Goya Trophy and Dulux British Open.

Ironically, Knowles played some of his best snooker in the Dulux, making five 50 breaks before losing 5-4 to Jim Wych. Yet he went to Derby against doctor's advice, having discharged himself from a hospital where he was being treated for a blood disorder.

In the Goya Trophy, Knowles went on against Neal Foulds having been the subject of a distasteful national newspaper story published that day. He spent the afternoon strongly denying its worst aspects at a press conference, far from ideal preparation for a match.

True or false, the story showed that no longer was anything sacred in the bedroom, if a relationship soured and there was a buyer for 'kiss and tell' stories. Unfortunately, he had to live with such allegations. Deep down he was hurt and angry and the damage could not be repaired overnight.

It was in 1980 that Knowles made his debut in the professional ranks. The following year, he reached the last eight of the Coral UK and within a few months found household fame with a 10-1 victory over Steve Davis, then the holder, in the first round of the Embassy World Championship.

There have been no first prizes in the last two seasons at home but in summer 1985 he won the Winfield Australian Masters and in the 1984-85 home campaign reached the finals both of the Jameson International and the Tolly Cobbold English Championship before losing to Davis.

In 1985-86, he reached two ranking semi-finals – the Rothmans Grand Prix and the World Championships – and two non-ranking – the Benson and Hedges Masters and the BCE Belgian Classic – but a list of losses which included an out-of-form Ray Reardon in the Canadian Masters, Rex Williams in the Mercantile Credit Classic, Mike Hallett in the Tolly Cobbold English Championship, Jim Wych in the Dulux British Open and Patsy Fagan in the Benson and Hedges Irish Masters provided evidence of his inconsistency.

After his World Championship defeat at the hands of Johnson, Knowles observed: 'I'm still not playing to my best form but next season I hope to return to my old attacking style.'

There is an old saying that attack is the best form of defence and Knowles in that sort of form is a very exciting player to watch.

Perhaps the manner in which Joe Johnson won the World Championship provides him with the inspiration he might need for 1986-87.

John Dee

Jimmy White

(England)

BORN: 2.5.62
HOME: WIMBLEDON
WORLD RANKING: 5

With his string of 'youngest evers' now a thing of the past, Jimmy White last season consolidated his position as one of the most outstanding players the game has ever produced.

To the natural flair and talent he possesses in abundance, White has added craft and patience, two qualities which helped him win the Mercantile Credit Classic, retain the Benson and Hedges Irish Masters and reach two other major finals. He beat Steve Davis in three of their five matches during the season.

He began the season by winning the Carlsberg Challenge, a four-man invitation tournament in Dublin which serves as a pipe-opener for the domestic circuit.

He recorded wins over Davis, Neal Foulds and led Cliff Thorburn 7-0 and by 74 with only four reds left in the eighth in the final of the Goya Trophy. Incredibly the Canadian outmanoeuvred him with the aid of penalty points and free balls to win that frame and went on to take the title 12-10.

Many a player would have suffered some reaction from this amazing change of fortune but White does not suffer from a mental approach that indulges in too much analysis. Although he was beaten by Silvino Francisco in the last 16 of the Rothmans Grand Prix he reached the semi-finals of the Coral UK, with Alex Higgins and Tony Knowles among his victims, before losing 9-5 to Davis.

In partnership with Higgins, White was beaten by the unheralded Danny Fowler and Barry West in the Hofmeister World Doubles in their first match in defence of that title but after Christmas came his Mercantile Credit Classic title when he beat Davis in the quarter-finals and Thorburn 13-12 in an extraordinary final after needing a snooker in the deciding frame with only the last two colours still on the table.

Thorburn, though, was to gain revenge in the final of the Benson and Hedges Masters after White had beaten Davis again in the semi-finals. Two bad results for a player of his class followed: the defeat by Peter Francisco which left him with no ranking point to add for the Dulux British Open and a 9-4 hammering by Neal Foulds in the Tolly Cobbold English Championship last 16 where he seemed careless and indifferent.

In the Embassy World Championship, White duly reached his expected place in the quarter-finals. Again as expected, he found Davis waiting for him. The greater number of frames over which the World Championship is played again suited Davis the better – as it had in the Coral UK – and a 13-5 defeat ended White's season.

It had been against Davis in 1984 that White just failed to become the youngest professional champion as he had been the youngest ever English amateur champion (at 16 in 1978), the youngest ever world amateur champion (at 18 in 1980) and the youngest ever winner of a professional tournament (at 19 in the 1981 Langs Scottish Masters).

In that 1984 world final, White trailed 4-12 overnight but attacked with such skill and flair on the second day that Davis only just beat him 18-16.

Perhaps the oft-used phrase 'Danger – genius at work' should now read 'Greater danger – maturing genius at work.'

Janice Hale

Alex Higgins

(Northern Ireland)

BORN: 18.3.49
HOME: MANCHESTER
WORLD RANKING: 6

The 1985-86 season was for Alex Higgins the most traumatic since he turned professional 15 years ago.

It began when his wife, Lynn, left the family home at Mottram St. Andrew in Cheshire's stockbroker belt, taking their two children with her and later instituting divorce proceedings.

What happened afterwards would have tested the mental stability of any man with Higgins accused in the media of drug-taking, molesting various young women, wife-beating and vandalism of his own property.

He himself invented a story which centred around a racehorse named Dreadnought, claiming that early one morning he had been thrown off and suffered a black eye. Later Higgins confessed the story was a fabrication. He had concocted it to relieve the pressure he felt he was under at the Mercantile Credit Classic. Yes, there was a black eye, but he had received it in a far more conventional way than falling off a horse.

As it happened, Higgins – and Dreadnought – received far more publicity than he had bargained for and the whole affair added considerably to the 'harassment' from the media which is one of the heaviest of the crosses he has to bear.

Black eye and all, he beat Dennis Taylor in the Mercantile but, after losing to Rex Williams in the quarter-finals, he erupted in frustration backstage, thus bringing upon himself a summer appearance before a World Professional Billiards and Snooker Association disciplinary tribunal.

Since then, the volatile and often unpredictable Higgins has changed management, leaving Del Simmons to join Framework whose other attractions include Tony Knowles and, most recently, Joe Johnson.

Somehow, the People's Champion survived the season well enough not only to fulfil his commitments but to move up three places in the world ranking list. UK champion in 1983, the year he overturned the 7-0 lead which Steve Davis held at the end of their first session, Higgins last season collected ranking points at every tournament.

His best run was to reach the semi-finals of the Dulux British Open – he was beaten 9-3 by Davis – but for the fifth time in ten World Championship battles at the Crucible, Higgins lost out in the deciding frame when going down 13-12 to Terry Griffiths in the second round.

Arguably, the biggest upset of the season was the 5-4 defeat of Higgins and Jimmy White by Danny Fowler and Barry West as they fell at their first hurdle in defence of their Hofmeister World Doubles title.

World champion in 1972 and 1982 and also twice runner-up, Benson and Hedges Masters titleholder in 1978 and 1981 and runner-up in the two intervening years, Higgins has not won a major event since his UK victory three years ago and as the Irish Championship completed last season for him he was unable to regain that title from Dennis Taylor.

Ireland, for the second consecutive year, held on to the World Cup but the consolation this provided for him only partially offset his concern at his lack of success in individual events. In the build-up to last season, he was convinced another title would come his way but events off the table had their effect.

In various tournaments he beat Dennis Taylor (twice), Neal Foulds and Cliff Thorburn and lost only by a single frame to Kirk Stevens, Terry Griffiths (twice) and Tony Meo. He continued to be a prime box-office attraction and to contribute to a large number of entertaining matches but in the last couple of seasons he has been subdued more often than he ever was when he played every match as if his life depended on it.

His career has produced many memories, notably the 69 clearance with which he saved his 1982 world semi-final against Jimmy White and the 135 clearance with which he clinched the final against Ray Reardon 18-15, and he has good snooker in him as long as he wants to play but for the first time in ten seasons he failed to reach a single individual final.

He still loves the game enough to put in the practice he needs to play his best but the pressures which are special to him and the way the overall standard of play on the circuit is being pushed up through competition are against him.

Frequently in his career, though, he has bounced back from disappointment or adversity. He is a man of moods and if his inspiration is triggered he is capable of anything – as he proved with his 1982 world title after what is one of the worst seasons of his professional career. No one will ever be able to take him lightly and the public will always want to see him.

John Dee

Willie Thorne

(England)

BORN: 4.3.54
HOME: LEICESTER
WORLD RANKING: 7

Willie Thorne reached two ranking and two other major tournament finals during the 1985-86 season, enhancing his reputation as a match player and improving his ranking from 11th to 7th.

The natural fluency of his break-making, always his ace, is now supported by a much tighter safety game than he used to have. He has more patience and control in the tactical exchanges, panics less readily if things go wrong and is much less inclined to underestimate the determination and ruthlessness which are required to knock an opponent out when he has him on the ropes.

The public's memory being what it is, however, his 1985-86 season will be remembered chiefly for a reversion to his bad old habits in the final of the Coral UK after he had played beautifully throughout the tournament.

Corals had quoted him at 40-1 at the start of the tournament and had already paid out £100,000 by the time he reached the final with another £150,000 pay-out due if he had taken the title.

A new tournament record break of 140 marked his 9-6 win over Paddy Browne; in an orgy of break-making which produced five centuries, he beat John Virgo 9-8 with a 112 clearance in the decider; he had a trio of 9-7 wins over Cliff Thorburn, Terry Griffiths and Dennis Taylor.

In the final, he led Steve Davis 4-3 at the first interval, 8-6 at the second and 13-8 going into the final session. He needed only a simple blue to lead 14-8 but instead lost the frame on the black. The turning point of a match has never been more painfully obvious. He lost 16-14.

He lost twice more to Davis. In the quarter-finals of the Benson and Hedges Masters he got the wrong side of the blue in the deciding frame and therefore left himself a slightly more distant pink than he would have liked for what was, with the black over a pocket, effectively the match ball. In the Dulux British Open he came through two 5-4 finishes against Kirk Stevens and Terry Griffiths, swamped Virgo in the semi-finals but was himself well beaten by Davis 12-7 in the final.

His other finals came in the first tournament of the season, the Langs Scottish Masters, when he beat Dennis Taylor and Jimmy White before losing a fine match 9-7 to Thorburn and in the Benson and Hedges Irish Masters when he beat Griffiths, Taylor and Thorburn before losing 9-5 to White.

Set against his achievements in reaching these four finals were some disappointing losses to some players ranked far outside the top 16: to Steve Duggan in the last 16 of the Goya Trophy; to Wayne Jones in the last 64 of the Rothmans Grand Prix and to Tony Jones in the first match in defence of the Mercantile Credit Classic title he had won in the early days of 1985.

It was that 1985 Mercantile success, highlighted by a 9-7 win over Davis and clinched with a 13-8 success over Thorburn, which gave him his first and so far only major title.

He went to Sheffield for the 1986 Embassy World championship realistically discussed as a possible champion for the first time in his career but after beating John Campbell he went out tamely to Thorburn, whom he had beaten two times out of three earlier in the season.

Without being able to put his finger on any reason for it, he did not feel his game was right and his temperament is perhaps moodier than his amiable exterior suggests.

Both in an amateur career in which he became, at 16, England's youngest ever international and in the professional ranks he became notorious for failing to clinch winning positions on big occasions and for following a big win with an anti-climactic loss. Even as he has matured, he has sometimes played poorly against supposedly lesser opponents when he has had more to lose than when he was playing one of his fellow celebrities. Easygoing and genial, he has cause to be confident in his ability but complacency sometimes obscures the small but nevertheless real prospect of losing until he is suddenly under more pressure than ever he had visualised he could be.

The locations of the homes of some leading players are almost irrelevant but Thorne is very much a Leicester man with a whole city behind him and a faithful corps of supporters around him. In his early days these were largely from Osborne's snooker hall in downtown Leicester where he invariably preferred to practise amidst people rather than in isolation on his own table at the Shoulder of Mutton, Braunstone, then the family pub.

In recent years, his base has been the Willie Thorne Snooker Centre, a thriving family concern in the city centre and the rotund figure of 'Racing Raymond' Winterton is invariably at the centre of his non-family support. The England striker Gary Lineker was probably his most regular practice opponent when he was playing for Leicester City and he is still a close friend.

Clive Everton

Joe Johnson

(England)

BORN: 29.7.52
HOME: BRADFORD
WORLD RANKING: 8

One night in Sheffield, the world was his oyster. On the stage of the Crucible Theatre, where sometimes even the tough guys crumble, Joe Johnson overcame Steve Davis, the 8-1 on favourite, to win the £70,000 first prize in the Embassy World Championship.

For Johnson, a 150-1 outsider at the outset, it was, literally, a dream come true. 'I dream all the time,' he said. 'When I'm practising I'm playing for the World Championship. I played at the Crucible like I play in practice.'

He dismissed suggestions that his 18-12 victory over Davis would be an overture to a more high-powered lifestyle. He is quite willing to have more money but is not prepared to put himself out to amass a fortune.

'I won't be doing a lot of exhibitions, whatever the fees,' he said. 'I'll do those I've already arranged but to do them night after night is bad for your game.'

He is the first Yorkshireman to win the world title; he is essentially a Bradford man; he won the title almost exactly a year after the Bradford Football club fire disaster.

'Oh yes, we talked about it,' said Wally Springett, Johnson's manager since 1982. 'I wouldn't say Joe lost a really close pal but he knows most of the Bradford families. You see the sporting public round here come from the working men's clubs, which is Joe's world. We were saying "wouldn't it be great if Joe could win it and in a way reverse the situation." '

He is half Asian by birth. The relationship between his natural father, Malik Farooq, and his mother, Margaret, ended when he was two. His mother married Ken Johnson, a useful Bradford amateur who was to teach him to play.

In 1971 he won the British Junior Championship and while working variously as an apprentice motor mechanic, in the office of a transport firm and as a pipe-layer for the Gas Board, he made the long climb through the amateur ranks, reaching the final of the English Amateur championship in 1978 (losing to Terry Griffiths) and the world amateur championship in Malta later that year (losing to Cliff Wilson).

He won the Yorkshire Championship three times, played for England ten times, losing only twice, and made a break of 140 in the Tyne Tees Television tournament in Middlesbrough in 1978 which still stands as the official world amateur record.

He turned professional in 1979 and for all his steady progression through the professional rankings – 52, 31, 22, 19 and 16 – no one seriously considered him as a potential world champion. Even with maximum ranking points from the Championship, he still stands only eighth in the list.

His first significant impact on the professional game was in the 1983 PPT when he beat Jimmy White, Eddie Charlton, Cliff Thorburn and Tony Meo to reach the final where he trailed Tony Knowles 1-6 but lost only 9-8. His first few television appearances as a professional were unsuccessful, less because of the cameras, he now thinks, than the special lighting installed for television. (A special TV lighting rig has been installed over the table on which he usually practises at Morley Snooker Centre.)

In 1985, he beat Knowles in the Mercantile Credit Classic in reaching the semi-finals before losing to Cliff Thorburn, his best finish in a televised event before his Crucible triumph.

Last season, he consistently accrued ranking points without – until Sheffield – threatening to win a title. In the five preceding ranking tournaments, he reached the quarter-finals of the Goya Trophy, the last 16 of the Rothmans Grand Prix, the last 32 of the Coral UK, the quarter-finals of the Mercantile Credit Classic and the last 32 of the Dulux British Open. In the Tolly Cobbold English Championship, he was a losing quarter-finalist to Mike Hallett, whom he had beaten in the Rothmans and who also became his second victim at Sheffield.

The preliminary handshake for Joe Johnson and Cliff Thorburn before their first-round match in the 1986 Benson and Hedges Masters

Prior to the Embassy World Championship, he had not beaten a single player ranked above him during the season although he was very near to beating Thorburn in the Mercantile quarter-finals. He led 4-3 but did not split the pack favourably with his break of 47. Thorburn snatched the frame with a 51 clearance to the pink and won the decider comfortably.

In contrast to his two losing appearances at the Crucible, Johnson came to Sheffield as a seed. He was thus matched against a qualifier, Dave Martin, whom he beat 10-3. Hallett showed some reaction from his first-round win over Dennis Taylor and Johnson was not really extended in disposing of him 13-6, playing particularly well in the four-frame streak, including breaks of 60, 110, 73 and 85, which took him from 7-4 to 11-4.

He contemplated the quarter-final against Griffiths with some trepidation. 'Terry has murdered me every time he's played me but I think I've improved a bit. I'm playing the balls not the man.'

Johnson led 3-0 and 6-3 and managed to win the last frame of the middle session to go into the final morning's play 9-7 up. He missed a straight black which would have put him 10-7 ahead and when Griffiths won five frames in succession to go three up with four to play at 12-9 the Yorkshireman looked a loser.

Early in the next frame, Griffiths failed at a simple green, screwing back for a choice of easy reds at the top of the table. Within a few minutes, Johnson regained all the confidence which had been slowly drained out of him as he won the frame with a break of 102.

'When someone thinks they've lost, they relax and if you give them a chance, off they go,' says Griffiths afterwards.

Off Johnson went to level the match with frame-winning breaks of 44 and 110. He maintained his inspired form to win the decider with breaks of 54 and 33. He had won the last four frames in only 52 minutes. 'When you feel you can't miss, you go for them,' he said.

His 16-8 semi-final victory over Knowles was in some ways an anti-climax as the world's no 3 player was well short of his best.

Then came his final triumph against all the odds.

Twice on the first day Davis looked as if he might establish a commanding lead but his 3-1 advantage became a 4-3 interval lead for Johnson and his 7-4 lead midway through the evening turned into 8-8 overnight.

The first four frames on the second afternoon put Johnson to 12-8; he was only 13-11 ahead going into the final session but the Davis revival never came as Johnson took the title for the loss of only one further frame.

Clive Everton

Kirk Stevens

(Canada)

BORN: 17.8.58
HOME: TORONTO
WORLD RANKING: 9

Unhappy and confused, Kirk Stevens fell from 5 to 9th in the world rankings in the 1985-86 season. He is so naturally talented that, with a clear mind, no achievement in the game would be beyond him but he has often found overall tranquillity and a fair degree of inner contentment difficult to attain. Easygoing and casual on the surface, he is inwardly screwed up by a variety of pressures.

While Stevens was out playing snooker as a teenager, his mother was killed in a house fire, which was caused by arson. A sister almost died of drug abuse. Strangely, this did not deter Stevens from dabbling in drugs himself. He grew dependent on them and admitted in an exclusive article in the *Daily Star* in June 1985 that he was 'helplessly addicted to cocaine,' a situation which he had drifted into over the previous six years.

His snooker career would have been over had the *Star* not arranged and paid for his treatment in a Toronto drug rehabilitation clinic. Back in Britain, he co-operated keenly in a nationwide Drugwatch campaign warning young people of drug dangers.

He was only 12 when, with a 40 start, he played Cliff Thorburn, already Canada's leading player, for $2 a frame. Two frames later, he was broke but made his first century break the same year and as a teenager went on the road playing for money.

'When I was 15, I looked like 12, so when this little wimp went up to somebody and said: "Like to play for $500" they thought they couldn't lose.'

Amongst various adventures, his car was once pursued out of Dayton, Ohio, by a hail of bullets. He had not stopped to insist on his $10,000 winnings.

'I was beaten up a few times, black eyes and stuff like that.'

In 1978 he became the youngest ever semi-finalist in the World Amateur Championship in Malta and turned professional immediately afterwards.

In 1980 he made a break of 136 in the Embassy World Championship, missing the final black for what would then have been a new Championship record of 143 and became this event's youngest ever semi-finalist too with wins over John Spencer and Eddie Charlton before losing 16-13 to Alex Higgins.

Two years later, Jimmy White, who had already deprived him of one 'youngest ever' distinction in winning the 1980 World Amateur title, deprived him of the other in their 1982 Embassy World Championship quarter-final.

The following season, he reached the semi-finals both of the Jameson International and the Lada Classic and lost in the world quarter-finals to Thorburn only after being two up with three to play.

In the 1984 Benson and Hedges Masters, he compiled a 147 maximum, only to lose a classic semi-final to White 6-4, and lost to White again 16-14 in the world semi-finals.

He was ranked fourth at the end of that season and in March 1985 beat Steve Davis to reach the final of the Dulux British Open before his fateful meeting with Silvino Francisco changed the course of both their careers.

It looked doubtful for a time whether his drug problem could be brought under sufficient control for him to play the circuit at all in 1985-86. For the most part, his results were of a lower quality than would ordinarily be expected from the world's no 5 but he was able to hang on sufficiently well to drop only four places by the end of the season.

But he was always struggling to keep at bay a depression which was altogether more serious than ordinary unhappiness or disappointment. He was shamefully hounded by certain newspapers and so upset by spectators' remarks about his drug history during the deciding frame of his 5-4 Benson and Hedges Masters defeat by Eddie Charlton that he 'simply curled up and died inside.'

His failure to appear for his first-round match against Patsy Fagan in the Benson and Hedges Irish Masters brought an official complaint from the sponsors and the certainty of disciplinary action.

He could not point to a previously unblemished record in this respect. He conceded a walk-over in the 1983 Jameson International when he missed his flight from Toronto and he did not fulfil his commitments in the 12-man Professional Snooker League in 1983-84, when his results were deleted from the league table. His non-appearance for an exhibition match in Jersey in May 1985 brought a High Court judgement against him for £5,000 plus either a further £3,000 or a free exhibition.

He had several changes of management and admitted to severe financial difficulties, notably in taxation areas.

In a difficult season, his best performance in quality was his 5-4 semi-final victory over Alex Higgins before a narrow 9-7 loss to Terry Griffiths in the final of the BCE Belgian Classic. In terms of spirit and determination, it was his victory from two down with three to play against Eddie Charlton before he lost 13-9 to Tony Knowles in the quarter-finals of the Embassy World Championship.

His high state of nervous tension was highlighted in the way in which what would have been two notable wins slipped away from him. He twice missed the final black to lose 5-4 to Knowles in the quarter-finals of the Rothmans Grand Prix and missed a straight brown, screwing back from the only other ball he needed, the blue, in the deciding frame of his 5-4 loss to Willie Thorne in the last 16 of the Dulux.

If innate talent was all that was needed to win snooker matches, Stevens would have no problem, but it can only be hoped that somehow he will find the wherewithal to overcome his personal difficulties and bring his best form back to the table, where newspaper stories should be made.

Janice Hale

Terry Griffiths

(Wales)

BORN: 16.10.47
HOME: LLANELLI
WORLD RANKING: 10

Terry Griffiths rediscovered his old form too late to make a big impact on the 1985-86 season but there were some encouraging signs that the 1979 world champion is not far away from emerging as one of the game's top winners again.

The only first prizes Griffiths had to show for his endeavours were the Welsh national title that had eluded him until he captured it for the first time in 1985 and the inaugural BCE Belgian Classic, in which he beat Steve Davis, Tony Knowles and Kirk Stevens.

In the major world ranking competitions, Griffiths failed to make any real impression until the Embassy World Championship and thus dropped two places in the world ranking list to no 10.

It was at the Crucible Theatre in Sheffield that we saw the Griffiths of old. Had he not suddenly been swept away by Joe Johnson after leading by three frames with four to play, he would probably have reached the final. He had beaten twice world champion Alex Higgins to earn a quarter-final place against Johnson who, before the tournament started, had never won a match in the Crucible.

A semi-final looked assured when he led 12-9 but Johnson suddenly threw caution to the wind and tore away with the next four frames with some of the most incredible snooker ever seen at such a moment.

There was nothing Griffiths could do but ponder over what might have been but when his despondency had subsided he left Yorkshire content in the knowledge that his own game was back on the up.

A couple of months before the end of the season, Griffiths went to Blackpool to seek advice from Frank Callan, the coach who helped Steve Davis perfect his cue action. 'I thought I knew all there was about snooker but this man is in a class of his own,' enthused Griffiths after his victory over Higgins.

'I tried to do the right things myself for three years but a little knowledge can be dangerous. Frank has knitted it all together for me. I didn't think anyone knew that much about snooker.'

Callan, who is a retired fishmonger, observed: 'I have now got Terry in control of his cue. When he won the world title he only knew one cue action but over the years, when he started to study the game, he got so mixed up he didn't know what to do.

'So he came to me and I fixed his method and now he can go to tournaments with confidence. It's not just a case of a player having natural ability but of being able to understand what to do with it.'

As a consolation prize, Griffiths went to Prestatyn to win the Pontins Professional for the third time in six years, beating Willie Thorne in the final.

Griffiths opened the season by losing to John Parrott in the fifth round of the Goya Trophy and to Cliff Thorburn in the quarter-finals of the Rothmans Grand Prix.

A long trip to the Canadian Masters provided only a 5-4 first-round defeat by Davis and at the end of the year there was a quarter-final defeat against Willie Thorne, 9-7, in the Coral UK after beating Silvino Francisco.

After his shock 5-3 reverse to Vic Harris in the third round of the Mercantile Credit Classic he went on holiday – and with no practice won the Belgian Classic.

He lost 5-2 to Cliff Thorburn in the Benson and Hedges Masters at Wembley but retained the Welsh title by beating Doug Mountjoy 9-3 in the final.

He made two centuries but still lost 5-4 to Thorne in the Dulux British Open quarter-finals and lost to him again in the opening round of the Benson and Hedges Irish Masters.

All in all, he had a fair season by most standards but it was nevertheless disappointing in terms of the expectations his early professional record gave him. He won the world title at the first time of asking in 1979, a feat that transformed the former Llanelli postman, bus conductor and insurance salesman into a national celebrity overnight.

In that Championship Griffiths really threw the formbook out of the window in beating Perrie Mans (the previous year's finalist), Alex Higgins, Eddie Charlton and finally Dennis Taylor.

The following season he won the Benson and Hedges Masters and the first of his three consecutive Irish Masters titles.

He lost to Steve Davis in the opening match of his world title defence and Davis was subsequently to throw his career into shadow many times. It was Davis who walloped him 9-0 in the 1980 Coral UK semi-final and 16-3 in the final the following season. The Welshman nudged home on the final black, 9-8, to land the Lada Classic and also beat him in the Irish Masters as they clashed in five consecutive major finals that season.

In the interim between these two successes, Davis beat Griffiths in the Benson and Hedges Masters and Yamaha finals.

At this time, Davis and Griffiths were clearly the two top players but Griffiths' only major first prize on the British circuit since then has been the 1982 Coral UK when he beat Davis in the quarter-finals and Higgins in the final. Davis has beaten him in three world quarter-finals; he has lost several important matches by a single frame; he needs to regain the finest degree of confidence which so often makes the difference between narrowly winning and narrowly losing when it matters most.

Graham Nickless

Tony Meo

(England)

BORN: 4.10.59
HOME: MORDEN
WORLD RANKING: 11

Tony Meo earned over £70,000 in prize money last season but two firsts left the dapper left-hander feeling 'sweet and sour'.

The happy first for the 26-year-old South Londoner with the Italian background was that he at last won his first individual domestic title, the Tolly Cobbold English Professional Championship.

But the unhappy first was that Meo's steady progress up the ranking list came to an abrupt halt. After rising from 24th to 15th and from 15th to 10th, he paid the price for a largely indifferent season in the ranking events by slipping back to 12th.

The enigmatic left-hander – all gritty determination one day and sloppy surrender the next – had a purple patch in February and March. He slew the Ginger Giant, Steve Davis, 9-7 at his eleventh attempt in singles combat in the semi-finals of the English Championship at Ipswich and went on to pocket the title by beating Neal Foulds 9-7 in the final.

Then he reached the quarter-finals of the Dulux British Open at Derby with an impressive 5-3 win over the formidable Canadian Cliff Thorburn, only to go down 5-3 to John Virgo.

Meo's season began and ended with unhappy defeats at the hands of young Liverpudlian John Parrott.

He lost 5-4 in the last 32 of the Goya Matchroom Trophy in September and seven months later it was the same story as he slumped to a bitterly disappointing 10-4 defeat in the first round of the Embassy World Championship. In between, Meo collected some valuable ranking points by reaching the last 16's of three open tournaments – the Rothmans Grand Prix, the Coral UK and the Mercantile Credit Classic.

A large chunk of Meo's prize money came from his share of the Hofmeister World Doubles title which he and his partner, Davis, regained in December. Davis and Meo, champions in 1982 and 1983, suffered their first doubles defeat in 1984 when they lost in the semi-finals to Alex Higgins and Jimmy White. There were no such problems this time as they cruised to victory over outsiders Ray Reardon and Tony Jones in the final.

Meo came to terms a while ago with living in the shadow of his charismatic former schoolmate from Tooting, Jimmy White. The two left-handers are still firm friends despite the fact that they operate from rival management groups.

Meo and his stablemates from the Romford Matchroom were in the charts in the summer with their record 'Snooker Loopy' recorded with Chas and Dave. White and his comrades from the Framework agency – Alex Higgins, Tony Knowles and Kirk Stevens – cut a record called 'The Wanderer' but it failed to wander anywhere near the charts.

White proved to be the master in his battles with his schoolfriend. They met twice last season and White won both encounters – 5-4 in the Benson and Hedges Masters at Wembley in January and 5-2 in the Irish Masters just before the World Championship. Meo had beaten Alex Higgins 5-4 in the previous round but, overall, he was plagued by inconsistency.

His manager, Barry Hearn, remains convinced of his potential. He has, after all, broken through his biggest psychological barrier, beating Davis, and he is English champion. It is not the shakiest of foundations from which to start climbing the rankings once more.

Alexander Clyde

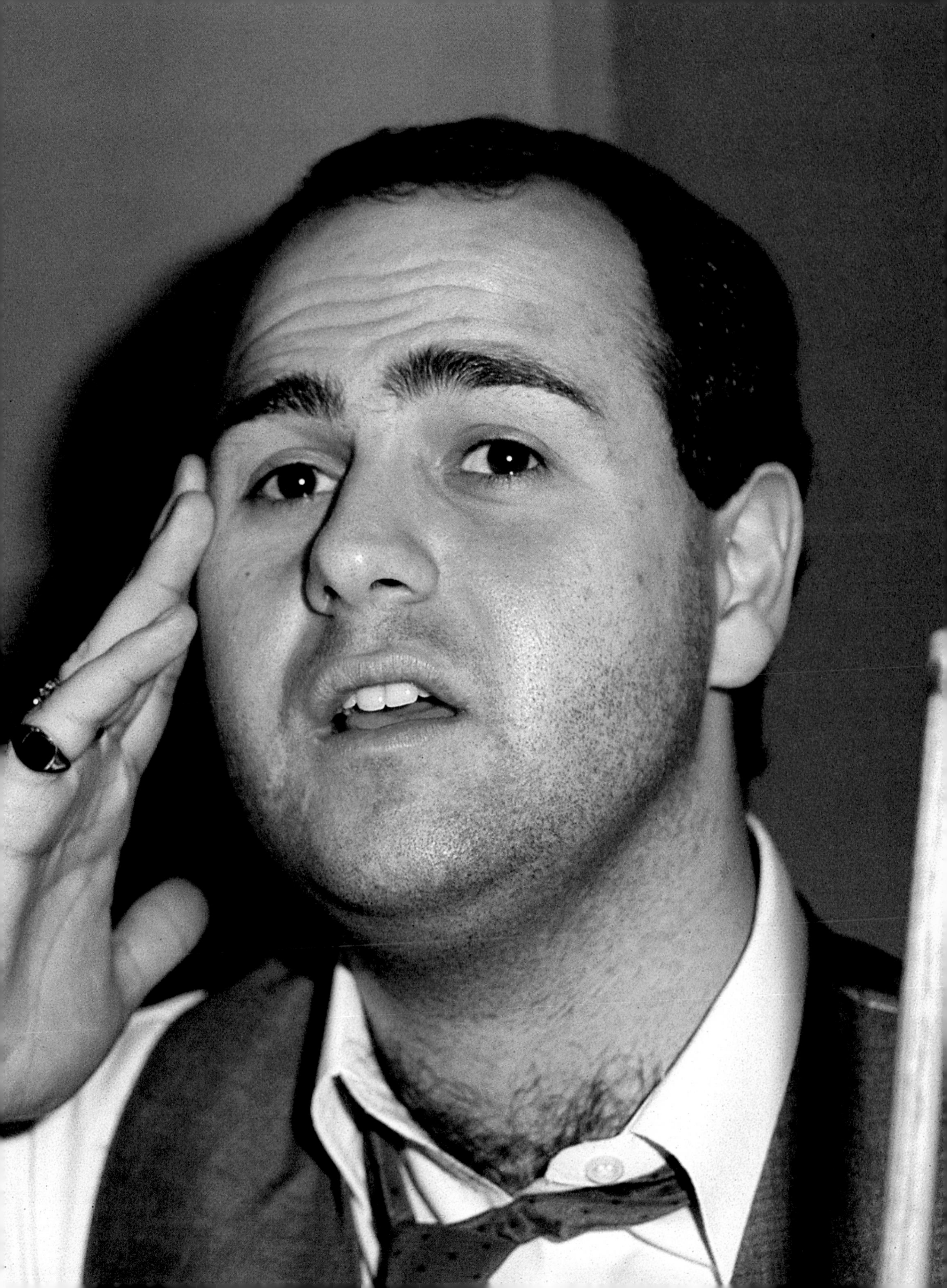

Silvino Francisco

(South Africa)

BORN: 3.5.46
HOME: CHESTERFIELD
WORLD RANKING: 12

If ever there was a poisoned chalice, it was the Dulux British Open trophy which Silvino Francisco won in March 1985. His wins over Jimmy White, Tony Meo, Alex Higgins and, in the final, Kirk Stevens, brought him £50,000 but set in motion a train of events which put him under a year of intense strain, ruining his enjoyment of the game and making it a creditable achievement to hold his place in the top 16.

During the Dulux final, Francisco became convinced that his opponent was playing under the influence of drugs. He made a complaint to a tournament official on the first evening of the match but, when no discernible action was taken, decided on the second afternoon to talk to Stevens personally.

He followed Stevens to the toilets, during a break between frames, and angrily confronted him, gripping him by the shoulders with sufficient force to make him listen to what he had to say. Even after Francisco had won the title he was unhappy with the circumstances. Some of his private remarks were relayed to the *Daily Star*'s chief news reporter, Neil Wallis, who, a few days later, sought to confirm these remarks for a story in his newspaper.

Francisco declined to speak for publication but his unguarded remarks were covertly tape-recorded and he was extensively quoted in a front page article which appeared on the morning of his first match in the 1985 Embassy World Championship on 15 April.

The article contained Francisco's view that his opponent was 'as high as a kite on dope' during the match. At a hastily convened press conference, Francisco ill-advisedly repudiated the *Daily Star*'s story. He had not expected to see it in print, least of all when he was playing Dennis Taylor in the world championship. He lost 10-2.

The *Daily Star* naturally stood by their story. A month later, Francisco was summarily fined a record £6,000 and two world ranking points by the WPBSA for 'not adhering to the tournament rules in speaking directly to the press directly after the Dulux British Open and by his conduct bringing the game into disrepute. The fine also takes into account his admitted misconduct when he physically and verbally abused his opponent at an interval of the final session.'

No disciplinary action had been instituted in the six weeks before the Dulux final and the publication of the *Daily Star* story of 15 April. It appeared Francisco was being made the scapegoat in a situation in which the WPBSA were desperately anxious to convey, particularly to sponsors and commercial interests, that drug-taking had no part in snooker.

The *Daily Star* continued to pursue the story and on 24 June Stevens confessed to them that he had been hooked on cocaine since he was 19 and that he had probably spent £250,000 on the drug in the preceding six years. He denied that he had ever played under the influence in a tournament.

Following publication of this story, the WPBSA issued a statement giving a different emphasis to the basis for their charges against Francisco, elevating physical abuse of his opponent to first place and giving talking to the press only a veiled reference in fourth place.

Chris Nawrat wrote in the *Sunday Times* on 16 June: 'Francisco's life has been made difficult simply because he fell foul of the rulers of the sports which would rather bury their problems than face up to them. Snooker's watchword seems to be: if the news is bad, shoot the messenger.'

Acting on legal advice, Francisco was able to show that his punishment was against the laws of natural justice. The WPBSA gave ground grudgingly but

were compelled to offer a re-trial in the form of an independent tribunal. Francisco's lawyers objected to two members of the proposed three-man tribunal and the case was eventually heard by Gavin Lightman Q.C., sitting alone. In the interim, the WPBSA returned Francisco's £6,000 and restored his two world ranking points.

On 2 March 1986, exactly a year after the original backstage incident had set the whole affair in motion, Lightman adjudged that Francisco be fined £2,000 and be ordered to pay £1,500 towards the costs of Paul Hatherell, the tournament director whose written complaint, six months after the incident, was the only one the WPBSA ever received.

Francisco's own evidence established that he was technically guilty of physical and verbal abuse of his opponent though it seems inconceivable that he would ever have been charged with these offences but for the *Daily Star*'s startling story. The tribunal accepted that Francisco had not intended his remarks for publication but nevertheless found that he had given an unauthorised press interview.

During the whole year that the affair dragged on, Francisco was unable to concentrate on his game. He beat Tony Knowles to reach the semi-finals of the Langs Scottish Masters and also reached the quarter-finals of the Rothmans Grand Prix with a win over Jimmy White but he lost in the last 64 of the Goya Trophy to Robbie Chaperon, at the same stage of the Mercantile Credit Classic to Stephen Hendry and in the last 16 of the Coral UK to Terry Griffiths 9-5 after leading 5-2 at the interval. Suffering from chickenpox he was easily beaten by Knowles in the Benson and Hedges Masters.

After the delivery of the tribunal's verdict, Francisco went on holiday with his wife Denise and their newly born child. Refreshed as he felt, his game was still not in full working order, although he beat Rex Williams 10-4 in the Embassy World Championship before losing 13-10 to Knowles.

Clive Everton

Neal Foulds

(England)

BORN: 13.7.63
HOME: LONDON
WORLD RANKING: 13

There cannot be many sportsmen who would turn down a chance to join Mark McCormack's gigantic IMG agency, as Neal Foulds did in March 1986. Instead, the young Londoner became the sixth man in Barry Hearn's expanding stable of snooker professionals.

'It was flattering that IMG wanted to make Neal their first client from the snooker world,' said Neal's father-cum-mentor, Geoff, who after guiding his career for three years realised that the time had come for him to join an organisation geared to handling big money contracts and promotions.

'John Simpson, from IMG, got as far as sending us a contract,' he continued. 'But we have known Barry Hearn a long time. His track record with his other players and his knowledge and reputation inside snooker convinced Neal that his offer was the best one.'

Hearn was well aware that Foulds, in his third year as a professional, was already certain to clinch a place in the elite top 16 of the rankings for the 1986-87 season. Despite an agonising 10-9 first-round defeat by fourth seed, Tony Knowles, in the subsequent Embassy World Championship at Sheffield, he ended the season as the new no 13 in the ranking, a jump of ten places.

Joe Johnson's dramatic emergence as world champion took everyone outside Bradford by surprise but the arrival of Foulds in snooker's big league was as smooth and steady as everything else about his emerging career.

Ever since his 10-9 victory over Alex Higgins in his debut at the Crucible in April 1984, Foulds had been earmarked as a future champion. He had the game (particularly his lethal long potting), he had the temperament, he had the dedication, he had the ambition. All he lacked was the experience.

Two further seasons on the demanding professional circuit, under the wing of his fiercely protective and highly knowledgeable father – who has largely sacrificed his own professional career to guide Neal's – have provided the experience he needed to make the breakthrough.

The highlights of a season of solid achievement – in contrast to his contemporary and doubles partner John Parrott, whose erratic form has again left him just outside the top 16 – were a semi-final place in the Goya Trophy and the runner-up spot in the Tolly Cobbold English Championship.

The Goya provided him with his second semi-final finish in a ranking tournament, eleven months after he had beaten Tony Knowles and Willie Thorne en route to the last four of the Rothmans Grand Prix at Reading where he lost to the eventual winner, Dennis Taylor.

He beat three men from the top 16 – Knowles, David Taylor and Joe Johnson – on his way to the Goya semi-finals at Stoke before losing 9-5 to Jimmy White.

He went down to Higgins in the last 32 of the Rothmans Grand Prix a few weeks later but reached the last 16 of the Coral UK by beating Johnson 9-8 before losing to Dennis Taylor, and the quarter-finals of the Mercantile Credit Classic. His 5-1 Mercantile win over John Campbell contained breaks of 91, 91 and 102 and the Australian champion said that no one had ever played better against him. He did not play quite as well against Doug Mountjoy and went out 5-3 on a tie-break black in the eighth frame.

Defeat in the last 32 of the Dulux British Open by Terry Griffiths followed but the Tolly Cobbold English Championship provided the Foulds family with two small pieces of snooker history. Geoff beat Fred Davis in the first round and his reward was a match against Neal in professional snooker's first Father v Son confrontation.

Despite light-hearted threats that he would have to find his own way home, Neal ran out the winner 9-3 and went on to reach his first professional final, beating Jimmy White 9-4 and Mike Hallett in the semi-finals 9-8 before going down 9-7 to Tony Meo, who had cleared the major obstacle – Steve Davis – in the other semi.

Neal Foulds' total earnings from the season topped £41,000. A slice of that was earmarked for the deposit on a house in the Ealing area, where he moved after his summer wedding to his long-standing girlfriend, Janet.

One of the perks of winning a place in the top 16 is that Foulds will not have to qualify for the 1987 Embassy World Championship in Sheffield. Another is that he gains an automatic invitation to the Benson and Hedges Masters in January at Wembley Conference Centre, barely a couple of miles from his home.

Neal Foulds has joined the Masters and local boy has made good. At his present rate of progress, he should make a whole lot better.

Alexander Clyde

Doug Mountjoy

(Wales)

BORN: 8.6.42
HOME: EWYAS HAROLD
WORLD RANKING: 14

Doug Mountjoy's position among the world's top 16 ranked players was precarious at the start of last season. He held 15th place on the list but had only five points to carry forward; behind him were several players itching to take his place.

But after a consistent season he was, when the 1986-87 world ranking list was finalised, still in the top 16, having moved up one place to 14th.

Only from the Dulux British Open did Mountjoy fail to collect any ranking points and in the fourth of the season's six ranking events, the Mercantile Credit Classic, he reached the semi-finals.

Of his total of nine ranking points, four came from the Mercantile as he defeated Warren King, Dene O'Kane, Bill Werbeniuk and Neil Foulds before he faced Cliff Thorburn for a place in the final. But the pattern of previous engagements was to follow, for Thorburn, who has never lost to the Welshman, beat him 9-6.

Confirmation of his place in the top 16 for the 1986-87 season came when Mountjoy reached the last 16 of the Embassy World Championship. The two points he received at Sheffield before losing to Steve Davis at least gave him the satisfaction of achieving his seasonal objective.

World amateur champion in 1976 by defeating Silvino Francisco in the semi-finals and Paul Mifsud in the final, Mountjoy turned professional immediately afterwards. He had won the Welsh amateur title both in that year and in 1968.

His impact on the professional scene was immediate for he won on his debut the 1977 Benson and Hedges Masters at Wembley and the following year, the Coral UK Championship.

No one then doubted that Mountjoy was made of world champion material but his best run, marked by what was then a world championship record break of 145, was to the 1981 final. The history books show that Steve Davis defeated him 18-12 but they do not reveal how much psychological damage Mountjoy suffered.

'I still believed I could beat Steve even when he led 14-12. He played something special to win the next four frames but the defeat got to me. It was the start of my problems. I was upset because I didn't feel I had put up a good enough fight in the final session.

'I wouldn't have minded losing but I felt I hadn't given it everything. Afterwards I had the summer off and didn't pick up a cue. That was a silly thing to do and I wouldn't recommend it to anyone.'

At this point, Mountjoy figured at no 6 in the world ranking list but as the pressures got to him, he slipped out of the top 10.

'There was a time when I could have hung up my cue. I was worrying too much about my game. I wanted to win. I probably wanted to win too badly.

'The pressures got to me, I had problems with my neck and shoulder and received regular treatment from an osteopath to help relieve the aches and pains.

'Several players have been affected by pressures – Patsy Fagan and Ray Reardon for instance – but I've recovered and the excitement of each new season is now back with me.'

Welsh champion three times, Mountjoy will this season be seen wearing glasses to prevent eye strain. 'I've suffered from this for some time and glasses appear the best way of overcoming it.'

He wore them for the first time in public in the final session of his second-round match against Davis after he had three times, on the first afternoon, been within a ball of a 5-2 lead. Davis led 11-5 when play resumed on the last morning of the match and Mountjoy did not pot a ball in the two frames with which Davis completed his 13-5 win.

Mountjoy saw the funny side of this but when the new season starts he will be all seriousness as he tries to bridge the eight-year gap since he last won a major title.

John Dee

Ray Reardon

(Wales)

BORN: 8.10.32
HOME: LONDON
WORLD RANKING: 15

Ray Reardon was unrecognisable last season as a player who won six world titles in nine attempts between 1970 and 1978. He won only two matches in the entire season, beating Tony Knowles in the BCE Canadian Masters and Graham Miles in the Coral UK. Among those who defeated him were Steve Duggan, George Scott, Murdo Macleod, Bernie Mikkelsen, Wayne Jones and John Rea, all good players but none of them household names.

His only extended run of the entire season was in the Hofmeister World Doubles when in partnership with Tony Jones, the 1983 English amateur champion, this blend of experience and youth reached the final with a quarter-final win over Perrie Mans and John Campbell and a semi-final victory over Terry Griffiths and Dennis Taylor.

His craft and tactical acumen were amply displayed as Jones did most of the potting but in single combat Reardon could not fulfil both roles to anything like his old standard.

His 1984-85 season had been rescued by a run to the semi-finals of the Embassy World Championship when he reverted to unassisted vision after playing two tournaments in spectacles and one in a green eyeshade.

All players as they grow older take longer to change the focus of their eyes from cue-ball to object-ball. This is why older players tend to pot less consistently well at distance than they did as younger men. A secondary effect is loss of synchronisation between eyes and cue action, a fact which largely explains why in the 1985-86 season Reardon's cue delivery was at distance hurried and jerky.

Too fast a backswing in turn led to too short a pause at the end of the backswing and at distance or when using power he never looked confident. The other chief technical fault, apparent for several years but particularly acute last season, was a compulsive lifting of the head before the shot was completed, a symptom of anxiety, loss of confidence and, at distance, striving to sight the ball properly.

Added to his eyesight problems were the traumas and personal difficulties of the much publicised break-up of his 27-year marriage. There was no way in the world he could achieve the clarity of mind necessary for consistently good play.

Assisting the downward spiral was the self-doubt and perhaps even fear which great players in all sports feel when it becomes clear that they have seen their best days. Some, like Jack Nicklaus in the 1986 US Masters, find new inspiration or possibly a marginal change in technique which enables them to add to their haul of major titles long after most judges have considered this unlikely; others have to come to terms with a lower place in the rankings and a status based on past rather than current results.

Reardon indisputably has the love of the game indispensable for anyone who wants to go on playing at top level but his confidence has been shattered and it will take time and application to rebuild it. The 1986-87 season will be terribly important to him. Having earned only one ranking point in 1985-86, he will be down in the fifties or even sixties in the world rankings if he does no better.

It is the most serious challenge he has ever faced. There was a steady erosion in his effectiveness between his last world title in 1978 and the fierce revival which began through reaching the 1982 final in which he was poised at 15-15 with Alex Higgins before the Irishman took the next three frames for the title.

The 1982-83 season brought him three first prizes (the PPT, the Welsh and the Yamaha International Masters) and second prizes both in the Benson and Hedges Masters and Benson and Hedges Irish Masters before the death of his father prefaced the loss of all the ground he had made up. That bereavement and his shattered marriage perhaps illustrate how emotional upheavals make significant impacts on even the strongest characters.

Clive Everton

Rex Williams

(England)

BORN: 20.7.33
HOME: STOURBRIDGE
WORLD RANKING: 16

When Rex Williams revived the World Professional Championship on the low-key challenge basis which, in 1964, was the limit of its public appeal, he could hardly have foreseen that within 20 years the game would develop into the multi-million pound industry it is today.

Neither could he have envisaged that his pool table business would be a public limited company or that his role as chairman of the World Professional Billiards and Snooker Association would involve both the time and emotional commitment it now does.

Wearing his WPBSA chairman's hat, he has presided at disciplinary hearings and taken a leading role at meetings where million pound contracts have been discussed. He has helped devise the new ranking system and been called upon night and day to give opinions on wildly varying issues.

As these aspects of his life – not to mention his work as an ITV commentator – have become more complex and demanding, it is remarkable that his snooker has actually improved. At the end of last season he stood 16th in the world rankings, a position which guarantees him a place in the Benson and Hedges Masters for the first time since 1977.

After winning the English Amateur Snooker Championship when he was only 17, Williams' early professional years unfortunately coincided with a slump in snooker's fortures. While he might have been winning tournaments, there were very few to play in but he did travel to New Zealand in 1968 to challenge Clark McConachy for the World Professional Billiards title which had been out of circulation for 17 years.

He successfully defended it four times in the next twelve years. Fred Davis beat him for it in 1980 but Williams won it twice more in championship tournaments before announcing his retirement from the event in 1982 following incidents on semi-finals day that year which resulted in him being fined £500 by the WPBSA. He also resigned the WPBSA chairmanship but was again elected to the chair two months later.

When the Snooker Championship was also decided on a challenge basis, he challenged John Pulman twice, without success. After it had been restored to a tournament format in 1969, he reached the semi-finals three times in five years, losing to Alex Higgins only by a single frame in 1972 when the Irishman went on to take the title at his first attempt.

The stresses of his business life and WPBSA responsibilities, added to the strain which all competitive players undergo, affected his cueing rhythm and confidence very badly for most of the seventies and early eighties.

From time to time, though, he produced a good win, notably 9-8 over Terry Griffiths in the qualifying competition of the 1978 Coral UK from six down with seven to play, and he was a quarter-finalist in that event two years later with wins over Doug Mountjoy and David Taylor.

Gradually, his form returned with some consistency as he very rarely lost to players ranked beneath him and began more often to beat those above him including Dennis Taylor (twice), Jimmy White and Bill Werbeniuk.

In 1985-86, he reached two last 16s in ranking tournaments and the semi-finals in a third, the Mercantile Credit Classic, through beating Tony Knowles and Alex Higgins before losing 9-7 to White. He thus rose eleven places in the rankings from 27th.

Janice Hale

John Parrott

(England)

BORN: 11.5.64
HOME: LIVERPOOL
WORLD RANKING: 17

Had John Parrott maintained the fine start to the season which saw him reach the quarter-finals of the Goya Trophy with wins over Tony Meo and Terry Griffiths, a ranking within the top 16 would have been comfortably within his compass.

However, defeats by Steve Longworth in the Rothmans Grand Prix, Jimmy van Rensburg in the Mercantile Credit Classic and Jim Wych in the Dulux British Open, all ranked well below him, and by Cliff Thorburn in the Coral UK left him needing to reach the quarter-finals of the Embassy World Championship to secure his top 16 ranking. He overcame an out-of-sorts Meo 10-4 and led Jimmy White 6-4 but then had to endure a six-frame virtuoso display which left him 6-10 going into the final session and ultimately a 13-8 loser.

Thus another season elapsed without the young Liverpudlian playing to the kind of potential he had suggested in reaching the Lada Classic semi-finals in January 1984 with wins over Doug Mountjoy, Alex Higgins and Tony Knowles. He beat Knowles again in the 1984 Embassy World Championship. At Sheffield a year later he beat Kirk Stevens to reach the quarter-finals and was denied a semi-final place only by a single frame by Ray Reardon.

John Campbell

(Australia)

BORN: 10.4.53
HOME: SYDNEY
WORLD RANKING: 18

In the summer of 1985, John Campbell succeeded Eddie Charlton as Australian Professional Champion, a title the latter had held every year except one since 1964. He also beat Charlton and John Parrott in reaching the final of the Winfield Australian Masters before losing to Tony Meo, and came to Britain for his fourth season on the circuit a more confident and solid player.

With exemplary consistency, he reached the last 16 of five of the six world ranking tournaments with two wins over Doug Mountjoy and one over Ray Reardon as his most notable scalps.

He was Australian amateur champion in 1980 after twice being runner-up and reached the quarter-finals of the 1980 World Amateur Championship before turning professional in 1982.

John Virgo

(England)

BORN: 3.4.46
HOME: GUILDFORD
WORLD RANKING: 19

Although he failed to regain a place in the top 16, John Virgo reached his first major semi-final since the 1982 PPT. His run to the semi-finals of the Dulux British Open included wins over Eddie Charlton and Tony Meo before he went out to Willie Thorne.

In the Embassy World Championship his first-round match at the Crucible against Jimmy White was evenly poised at 7-7 before the left-hander went away to win 10-7 and in the Coral UK Open, much earlier in the season, he had another honourable loss, 9-8 to Thorne, after making three centuries in the course of the match.

While nothing has quite fulfilled the expectations he raised by winning the Coral UK and reaching the semi-finals of the Embassy World Championship in 1979, his form in 1985-86 suggested a possible climb in 1986-87.

Success on the circuit remains his overriding priority but he derives both income and satisfaction from working as a BBC summariser and from the exhibition engagements in which his impressions of his fellow players are a much appreciated feature.

Eugene Hughes

(Republic of Ireland)

BORN: 4.11.55
HOME: LONDON
WORLD RANKING: 20

There is nothing common or garden about his roots. Eugene Hughes is from Monkstown Farm. To put it into a geographical perspective, Monkstown Farm is in Dun Laoighaire which happens to be in the County of Dublin. But one never refers to anyone from Dun Laoighaire as being a Dubliner. They don't like it.

Dun Laoighaire was once a snooty suburb of Dublin and, as its old name of Kingtown implies, was a citadel of British rule. But in the fifties, the Borough of Dun Laoighaire lost its exclusivity. Now the well heeled mix happily with the working classes.

It is a community which boasts a unique (in Irish terms) band of home-grown celebrities including professional golfer John O'Leary and folk singer Ronnie Drew. Boomtown Rat turned Ethiopian fund-raiser Bob Geldof is Dun Laoighaire's most famous son. Now Eugene Hughes has reserved his place in the local council's newly-instituted Hall of Fame.

To mark his achievements to date, Hughes was presented with a tie bearing the Dun Laoighaire coat of arms and he proudly sported it to the second round of the Embassy World Championship in Sheffield in April.

It was inevitable that Dun Laoighaire, and Monkstown Farm in particular, would eventually produce a professional of note. Jack Rogers (Irish Snooker champion on three occasions and twice Irish Billiards champion), internationals Michael Kane, Richard Brennan and Ken Byrne as well as the 1983 Irish champion Jimmy Long, were all either born here or spent their formative years, as did Hughes, and Dun Laoighaire's other professional Patsy Fagan, at the Workmen's Club.

While Geldof was attending the posh Blackrock College, Hughes had finished his education at the St. John the Baptist Primary School. He may, on his own admission, have grasped little of what the teachers were imparting but by the time he was 16 he knew the snooker game, chapter and verse. Soon he was polishing off his opponents at a great rate in open tournaments but not quickly enough for his late father, Mick. Eugene recalls with affection how his father pulled him aside between frames in one final and urged the youngster: 'Finish him off quick and we can go for a pint!'

The crane driver's son – he has four brothers and five sisters – was going up in the world, winning the Irish Junior Championship in 1973, and getting to the semi-finals of the British equivalent where he was beaten by Willie Thorne.

The Irish Junior title was retained and then in 1975 came a unique four-timer when he won the Irish underage titles in snooker and billiards and crossed to Britain to complete the junior double as well.

Eugene Hughes contemplating a shot during his match with Ray Reardon in the 1985 Embassy World Championship.

For a period of more than two years (1977-79) Hughes was to prove virtually unbeatable on home soil in both codes, winning the senior billiards and snooker championships twice. Among his regular opponents in those competitions was Michael Dunne, whose niece Susan was later to become Mrs Hughes and mother of their two children, Stuart and Suzanne.

Having been turned down in 1979 and 1980, he turned professional in January 1981. In his debut year, he was to show the same consistency he displayed as an amateur but his first significant impact was made in 1983 when he beat Terry Griffiths to reach the quarter-finals of the PPT and qualified for the world championship's first round in which he was beaten 10-7 by Ray Reardon.

In 1984, Hughes made further strides by getting to the semi-finals of the Jameson International with wins over Doug Mountjoy, Reardon and Willie Thorne.

He also gained ranking points through reaching the quarter-finals of the Dulux British Open in 1985. His 5-0 win over Reardon in the Benson and Hedges Irish Masters was followed by a narrow 5-4 loss to Steve Davis in the quarter-final but he was disappointingly beaten 10-9 by Reardon in the Embassy World Championship first round at Sheffield.

He secured his financial stability with a lucrative contract with London's King's Cross Club – he lives in East Ham – but apart from a second-round appearance in the Embassy World Championship in 1986 (beating David Taylor 10-7 and then being beaten 13-6 by Cliff Thorburn) he did not do as well in 1985-86 as he had the previous season, a place in the last 16 of the Mercantile Credit Classic with wins over Fred Davis and Jim Wych being his best finish prior to the world championship.

Overall, though, he still did enough to reach 20th place in the rankings and a good 1986-87 season could see him into the elite top 16.

John Martin

David Taylor

(England)

BORN: 29.7.43
HOME: MANCHESTER
WORLD RANKING: 21

After surviving precariously in the top 16 for two seasons, Taylor forfeited this status through only twice reaching the last 16 of the 1985-86 season's six ranking tournaments.

Wins over Tony Jones and Bill Werbeniuk and a narrow 5-4 loss to Neal Foulds got his season off to a deceptively promising start in the Goya Trophy and a win over John Campbell and a 9-7 defeat by Tony Knowles enabled him to come away from the Coral UK not only with some satisfaction but with two more ranking points.

However, defeats by Steve Longworth in the last 32 of the Rothmans Grand Prix and by Marcel Gauvreau and Paul Medati in the last 64s of the Mercantile Credit Classic and the Dulux British Open left him short of confidence for the Embassy World Championship in which he lost his first match at the Crucible to Eugene Hughes.

Taking his career overall, the highlights have been the English and World amateur titles in 1968, second prizes in the Coral UK in 1978, the Yamaha International Masters in 1981 and the Jameson International in 1982, when he beat Steve Davis in the quarter-finals. He was a semi-finalist in the 1980 Embassy World Championship.

He has, in the last two seasons, worn spectacles for competition.

Murdo Macleod

(Scotland)

BORN: 14.1.47
HOME: LIVINGSTONE
WORLD RANKING: 22

Despite having lost all nine of his televised matches, Murdo Macleod has been consistent enough in the pre-televised phases of major tournaments to reach 23rd place in the world rankings, an improvement of three positions on his 1984-85 status.

Twice Scottish professional champion, he was beaten 6-5 on the final black by Stephen Hendry in his first match in defence of that title last season but himself had the distinction of ousting a defending champion, when he beat Silvino Francisco in the last 32 of the Dulux British Open.

He beat two former world champions, Fred Davis and Ray Reardon, in the course of the season and in the past two seasons has only twice lost to players ranked beneath him in ranking tournaments.

Cliff Wilson

(Wales)

BORN: 10.5.34
HOME: CALDICOT
WORLD RANKING: 23

Although Cliff Wilson now only occasionally produces the brilliant potting which made him such a spectacular player in his youth, he can still, on his day, be very difficult to beat, not least because his game is tactically shrewder than is obvious from a casual glance at his apparently open style.

His best run last season was to reach the quarter-finals of the Rothmans Grand Prix beating George Scott (who had eliminated Ray Reardon) and Tony Drago (who had beaten Eddie Charlton) before losing to Dennis Taylor.

Wilson grew up in Tredegar at the same time as Reardon. He was based in

the local billiard hall, Reardon in the Miners Institute. The town was divided into two factions, each prepared to back its hero for money.

In the Welsh Amateur Championship Reardon always won and it was not until he left South Wales that Wilson won the title in 1956. In the Welsh qualifying area of the English Amateur Championship, though, Wilson always won and in 1954 he reached the final of the event.

A loss of interest, however, followed by severe problems with his eyesight, resulted in him retiring for 15 years. When he resumed playing, Wilson won his second Welsh amateur title in 1977, 21 years after his first, so earning him a trip to Malta from which he returned world amateur champion the following year.

He won the Welsh amateur for the third time in 1979 and turned professional, not the player that he was in his youth but still good enough to shake the best. Doug Mountjoy, Jimmy White, Tony Knowles, Willie Thorne, Ray Reardon and Terry Griffiths are among his scalps.

Bill Werbeniuk

(Canada)

BORN: 14.1.47
HOME: WORKSOP
WORLD RANKING: 24

Bill Werbeniuk, inevitably 'Big Bill', is also 'Battling Bill' and emphatically not 'W. Werbeniuk', as he is sometimes mildly irritated to find himself designated in the resultage. He was baptised as Bill but he is no ordinary boy for only extraordinary qualities of heart, mind and, indeed, constitution have kept him in snooker's toughest league.

In terms of heredity, the bad news was a congenital nervous disorder which causes a tremor in his cue-arm. 'I've had it since I was a kid but it came to a head seven or eight years ago,' he said.

The favourable side of his inheritance was a liver and kidneys built to withstand 30 or 40 pints of lager a day (on which he literally has to train to compete) and, pre-eminently, the influence and wisdom of his father, Shorty, who became Canadian champion in the days before there was any official competitive structure there by beating another son of Winnipeg, Conrad Stanbury, who was the first overseas entrant for the world championship in 1935 and who remained in London, chiefly as a coach, until his death a few years ago.

'I learned a whole lot from my dad,' said Werbeniuk, who started playing in a Winnipeg billiard hall when he was nine and made his first century break when he was 13. 'My dad was the original grinder. Maybe this is why he and Cliff [Thorburn] never got along that well. They were too alike.'

Unlike Britain, with its established amateur championships, tournaments, county associations and leagues, Canada offered only one way for a young player to prove himself: he went on the road 'back and right across Canada seeking out the best players.'

Thorburn had gone on the road from Victoria, British Columbia, doing the same when a stranger in a Vancouver bar challenged him on his brother's behalf. This proved to be Eddie Werbeniuk, Bill's brother. They played best of 19 frames for $1,500 and Thorburn led 4-0. Werbeniuk's proposal of a further side-stake of $200 a frame was accepted and he won ten frames in a row to pouch, in all, $3,500.

They became friends, travelling together on many occasions, meeting a few times in the rare tournaments which were like ports in a turbulent sea of money matches.

Werbeniuk reckons he is about 5-5 with Thorburn in tournament head-to-heads but he has beaten him only one time out of four on the pukka tournament circuit. In the 1985 Embassy World Championship, Thorburn beat him 13-3 in the second round after the big man had scored his solitary win of a miserable season; a year later, Thorburn beat him again at the Crucible.

His career was at its peak in 1983 when he reached two major finals, the Lada Classic and the Winfield Australian Masters. His defeat by Thorburn in the latter started his decline because it decided him to change cues.

'I'd had it taken apart and put together again so many times that I thought I couldn't go on using it. I tried several cues until Roger Brecknell of Barracuda Cue Extensions said that he could rebuild it. I didn't think he could but he has and I am playing much better than I was.'

The 1986 Dulux British Open provided him with his first quarter-final finish for two years, and with £26,144 in prize money from the 1985-86 season and 24th place in the rankings, it was, at least, a more satisfactory campaign than his previous two.

'Some people thought that the drinking had got to me but that's not so,' he said in reference to his services to the lager industry. Backstage minions furnish him with a pint per frame in tournaments and he will methodically drink himself into match readiness from early breakfast time if he is involved in a morning session. He used to set off for the snooker in Sydney carrying his day's supply of lager in a milk pail packed with ice. The Inland Revenue briefly agreed to make his lager expenditure tax deductible only to withdraw this concession, aghast at setting such a precedent.

There is no known cure for his condition but he was contemplating acupuncture in the Far East during the summer. Tremor or not, there is nothing wrong with a nerve and match temperament sharpened by years of playing all sorts of cue games for high stakes, a judgement that can also be made of Thorburn.

He overlooked the closing date for entries for the 1977 World Championship so he took himself off to Dayton, Ohio, where, in ten hours, he won $20,000 (US) for playing one James Christopher at Nine Ball Pool.

'The only trouble was I lost it all in the next 20 minutes. But there was a guy there with $200,000 in his briefcase and I figured I could win that as well.'

Clive Everton

Eddie Charlton

(Australia)

BORN: 13.10.29
HOME: SYDNEY
WORLD RANKING: 25

Defeat by Kirk Stevens in the last 16 of the Embassy World Championship after he had led by two frames with three to play marked the end of what was probably Eddie Charlton's last full season on the British circuit.

He is becoming increasingly involved in trade and promotional activities in Australia and even in 1985-86 made several journeys there, back and forth. He is very optimistic that a world ranking tournament will be promoted in Australia in 1987 and, under the aegis of Rothmans, is also looking at possible tournaments in Kuala Lumpur, Singapore, Hong Kong and Auckland.

Since he first won the Australian Professional Championship in 1964, he had only once been deprived of the title – by Warren Simpson in 1968 – before losing it to John Campbell in 1985. In his long professional career, he has reached two world finals and six world semi-finals and become a byword for steadiness and durability.

A brown which would have put him six up with seven to play probably cost him the 1975 world final in which Ray Reardon eventually beat him 31-30. He was also desperately near to winning the World Professional Billiards Championship in 1984 when he lost to Mark Wildman by a mere 33 points.

At snooker, however, two disastrous seasons have seen him plummet to 25th place in the rankings. In last season's five pre-World-Championship ranking tournaments, he was beaten by Matt Gibson, Tony Drago, Peter Francisco (twice) and John Virgo.

Peter Francisco

(South Africa)

BORN: 14.2.62
HOME: CLACTON
WORLD RANKING: 26

In rising from 59th to 26th in his second season as a professional, Peter Francisco established an irrefutable claim to be regarded as the most improved player of the 1985-86 season.

With wins over John Virgo, Eddie Charlton (twice) and, the highlight of his season, Jimmy White, the 24-year-old South African reached the last 16 in three ranking tournaments and was denied his first appearance in the televised phase of the Embassy World Championship only through losing 10-9 to Neal Foulds in the last qualifying round.

As befits a member of South Africa's most famous snooker-playing family, he possesses considerable flair and natural ability. He is the son of Mannie Francisco, who won the South African Amateur Snooker title six times and the Billiards twelve times, and is the nephew of Silvino, now the world's 12th ranked player, who won the South African Amateur Snooker Championship four times and the Billiards three. Peter himself won his domestic amateur championship three times at snooker and once at billiards. He is resident professional at Clacton Snooker Centre.

Mike Hallett

(England)

BORN: 6.7.59
HOME: GRIMSBY
WORLD RANKING: 27

A dramatic 10-6 defeat of Dennis Taylor, the defending champion, provided Mike Hallett with his first ever television victory, a triumph which even a comparatively tame 13-6 defeat by Joe Johnson could not impair.

His professional career has been studded with fine wins, notably over Steve Davis in the 1983 PPT, Alex Higgins in the 1984 Rothmans Grand Prix and Taylor in the 1984 Lada Classic but he has never managed to string a series of good wins together.

He has also shown a distressing tendency to lose from winning positions, notably when he failed to capitalise on a 6-1 lead over Cliff Thorburn in the 1985 Embassy World Championship and was beaten 10-8.

There is, however, no disputing his natural talent and the 1985-86 season saw him beginning to mature as a competitor, not only in being able to clinch victory over Taylor at the Crucible but in beating Tony Knowles and Joe Johnson in consecutive rounds of the Tolly Cobbold English Championship before losing a desperately close 9-8 finish to Neal Foulds in the semi-finals.

Dave Martin

(England)

BORN: 9.5.48
HOME: CHESTERFIELD
WORLD RANKING: 28

Through reaching the last 32 of all six ranking tournaments, Dave Martin marginally improved his world ranking from 29th to 28th. His most memorable moment of the season was his total clearance of 145 in the Dulux British Open.

In 1981, he reached the Jameson International semi-finals after victories over Bill Werbeniuk, Eddie Charlton and Graham Miles. In 1984, in the Yamaha International Masters, he reached the three-player, round-robin final, taking second place behind Steve Davis. He has, however, yet to reach the quarter-finals of a ranking tournament.

Dean Reynolds

(England)

BORN: 11.1.63
HOME: GRIMSBY
WORLD RANKING: 29

For the second consecutive year, Dean Reynolds reached the quarter-finals of the Tolly Cobbold English Championship by beating Willie Thorne and he has beaten this highly ranked player on all three occasions that he has played him.

In view of this, his lack of success against other leading players is surprising though he did beat Silvino Francisco to reach the quarter-finals of the 1984 Rothmans Grand Prix, his best finish in a ranking tournament.

He reached only one last 16 in last season's ranking tournaments but was within a ball of reaching this stage in the Mercantile Credit Classic before Dennis Taylor cleared the table with 47 to beat him 5-4 on the final black.

British Junior Champion in 1981, he reached the last 16 of the Embassy World Championship at his first attempt the following year but since then has not won a match at the Crucible.

Barry West

(England)

BORN: 24.10.58
HOME: ROTHERHAM
WORLD RANKING: 30

After his first three applications for professional status had been inexplicably rejected, Barry West secured 30th place in the world rankings in his first professional season, largely through beating Eugene Hughes, Doug Mountjoy and Murdo Macleod in reaching the quarter-finals of the Coral UK Open.

During his amateur career, he played 15 times for England, losing only twice, and was twice runner-up in the Northern section of the English Amateur Championship.

Steve Longworth

(England)

BORN: 27.7.48
HOME: BLACKBURN
WORLD RANKING: 31

Steve Longworth was recognised as a useful player long before he won an amateur title of any great significance. He was part of what in retrospect appears to be an all-star trio, along with Dennis Taylor and Jim Meadowcroft; together they won the Lancashire team title in the late sixties but it was not until Longworth began to play full-time that he became a consistent tournament winner, notably of the 1984 English Amateur Championship.

The following season, his first as a professional, he reached 37th place in the rankings, beating Neal Foulds and David Taylor in qualifying for the last 16 of the Mercantile Credit Classic before losing to Cliff Thorburn. He also reached the semi-finals of the Tolly Cobbold English Championship with a win over Jimmy White.

In the 1985-86 season, his best run was to the last 16 of the Rothmans Grand Prix with wins over John Parrott and David Taylor and he was consistent enough overall for his season's work to represent a rise of six places in the rankings.

Jim Wych

(Canada)

BORN: 11.1.55
HOME: CALGARY
WORLD RANKING: 32

When Jim Wych beat Rex Williams, John Pulman and Dennis Taylor to reach the quarter-finals of the Embassy World Professional Championship at his first attempt in 1980 before losing to Cliff Thorburn, it appeared very much on the cards that he would soon establish a place in the world's top 10.

However, he did not commit himself to the circuit full-time, preferring to complete his Physical Education degree at Calgary University and establish himself in a snooker club business in Edmonton. He did not achieve anything of any great note in his intermittent appearances on the circuit in the next few years but again played full-time in 1985-86.

The highlight of his season was to reach the quarter-finals of the Dulux British Open in which he lost to Steve Davis after beating Dean Reynolds, Tony Knowles and John Parrott in the three previous rounds.

This was enough for him to achieve the 32nd place in the rankings, which commits him to only one qualifying round in the 1986-87 season's ranking tournaments and which also assures him of prize money each time he plays in these events.

The Circuit

Langs Scottish Masters

TOTAL PRIZE MONEY: £31,000
FIRST PRIZE: £10,500
ENTRIES: Eight invited
TELEVISION: BBC Scotland

Cliff Thorburn played snooker just about as well as the game can be played in beating Silvino Francisco in six straight frames in the semi-finals before beating Willie Thorne in a splendid final 9-7.

Thorburn's semi-final performance included two total clearances of 133 and 142, each in turn a new tournament record, and further breaks of 70, 49, 46 and 62.

The final saw Thorburn avenge the 13-8 defeat Thorne had inflicted on him in the Mercantile Credit Classic final the previous January, though only after his 5-2 interval lead had become a 6-7 deficit.

Thorne began so impressively that he was 2-0 up before Thorburn had potted a ball but, completely unaffected by this, the Canadian dominated the rest of the afternoon so thoroughly that Thorne scored only 12 in five frames.

Thorne dominatingly won five of the first six frames of the evening to lead 7-6 and looked poised to lead 8-6 but Thorburn turned the match with a frame-winning 60 to level at 7-7 and took the next two frames as well for the match.

First round: Cliff Thorburn (Canada) beat Murdo Macleod (Scotland) 5-1; Jimmy White (England) beat Alex Higgins (Northern Ireland) 5-0; Silvino Francisco (South Africa) beat Tony Knowles (England) 5-4; Willie Thorne (England) beat Dennis Taylor (Northern Ireland) 5-3

Semi-finals: Thorburn beat Francisco 6-0; Thorne beat White 6-2

Final: Thorburn beat Thorne 9-7

Steve Davis completed a hat-trick of Langs Scottish Masters titles between 1982 and 1984

Cliff Thorburn, Langs Scottish Masters titleholder

Previous Years

In its five-year existence, Scotland's leading international snooker event has gained each season in prestige and presentation. In its debut year, in the echoing vastness of the Kelvin Hall, Glasgow, it experienced all sorts of teething problems, although these were partly redeemed by the excitement of Jimmy White becoming the youngest ever winner of a professional tournament at the age of 19.

To achieve this, White beat three world champions, Ray Reardon, Steve Davis and Cliff Thorburn. He was to repeat his win over Davis, then the reigning world champion, in the final of the Northern Ireland Classic, a one-off event staged at the Ulster Hall, Belfast, two weeks later.

In 1982, the event was more effectively staged at the Holiday Inn, Glasgow. In 1983/4/5 this standard was maintained and there were large crowds for all sessions, with some full to capacity, at the Skean Dhu Hotel, Glasgow.

Steve Davis recorded a hat-trick of titles in 1982-84 with a tournament record break of 137 in 1983 for good measure.

All four days of the event are televised by BBC Scotland.

1981

TOTAL PRIZE MONEY: £20,500
FIRST PRIZE: £8,000

Qualifying: Vic Harris (England) beat Ian Black (Scotland) 4-0

First round: Jimmy White (England) beat Ray Reardon (Wales) 5-4; Steve Davis (England) beat Doug Mountjoy (Wales) 5-0; Cliff Thorburn (Canada) beat Kirk Stevens (Canada) 5-1; Alex Higgins (Northern Ireland) beat Harris 5-3

Semi-finals: White beat Davis 6-5; Thorburn beat Higgins 6-2

Final: White beat Thorburn 9-4

1982

TOTAL PRIZE MONEY: £23,000
FIRST PRIZE: £9,000

First round: Dennis Taylor (Northern Ireland) beat Jimmy White (England) 5-4; Steve Davis (England) beat Tony Knowles (England) 5-4; Terry Griffiths (Wales) beat Ray Reardon (Wales) 5-3; Alex Higgins (Northern Ireland) beat Eddie Sinclair (Scotland) 5-1

Semi-finals: Davis beat Taylor 6-1; Higgins beat Griffiths 6-5

Final: Davis beat Higgins 9-4

1983

TOTAL PRIZE MONEY: £25,000
FIRST PRIZE: £10,000

First round: Cliff Thorburn (Canada) beat Terry Griffiths (Wales) 5-1; Steve Davis (England) beat Murdo Macleod (Scotland) 5-1; Tony Knowles (England) beat Tony Meo (England) 5-4; Alex Higgins (Northern Ireland) beat Jimmy White (England) 5-3

Semi-finals: Knowles beat Thorburn 6-2; Davis beat Higgins 6-2

Final: Davis beat Knowles 9-6

1984

TOTAL PRIZE MONEY: £28,500
FIRST PRIZE: £10,000

First round: Tony Knowles (England) beat Terry Griffiths (Wales) 5-3; Jimmy White (England) beat Murdo Macleod (Scotland) 5-0; Steve Davis (England) beat Cliff Thorburn (Canada) 5-2; Alex Higgins (Northern Ireland) beat Kirk Stevens (Canada) 5-2

Semi-finals: White beat Knowles 6-5; Davis beat Higgins 6-4

Final: Davis beat White 9-4

Goya Matchroom Trophy

TOTAL PRIZE MONEY: £175,000
FIRST PRIZE: £35,000
ENTRIES: Open to all professionals
TELEVISION: ITV

Cliff Thorburn made an epic recovery to win the first world ranking tournament of the season.

He trailed Jimmy White 0-7 and was 0-74 behind with only four reds remaining in the first frame of the second session.

Incredibly, he recovered to win the frame on the black and took six of the seven frames of that session to trail only 6-8 overnight.

White led 9-6 but Thorburn's 113 clearance in the next frame was the start of a five-frame winning sequence which took him to 11-9 before he clinched victory at 12-10.

White had reached the final with the aid of a 5-3 quarter-final victory over Steve Davis who had won the corresponding tournament, the Jameson International, three times in four years. He then overcame Neal Foulds, who was appearing in his second major semi-final, 9-5.

In the other semi-final, Thorburn avenged his Embassy World Championship defeat by beating Dennis Taylor 9-5.

Steve Duggan, who had begun the season in 70th place in the ranking list, reached his first major quarter-final with the aid of victories over Ray Reardon 5-4 and Willie Thorne 5-4.

Cliff Thorburn holds the Goya Matchroom trophy

Jimmy White, runner-up in the Goya Matchroom Trophy

1985

First round: Mike Darrington (England) beat Dave Gilbert (England) 5-2; Omprekesh Agrawal (India) beat Paul Watchorn (Republic of Ireland) 5-2; Martin Smith (England) beat Dessie Sheehan (Republic of Ireland) 5-2; Sakchai Simnagm (Thailand) beat David Greaves (England) 5-2; Glen Wilkinson (Australia) beat Bert Demarco (Scotland) 5-2; Jim Rempe (USA) beat Pascal Burke (Republic of Ireland) 5-3; Stephen Hendry (Scotland) beat Barry West (England) 5-4; Jim Bear (Canada) beat Pat Houlihan (England) 5-2; Joe Caggianello (Canada) beat John Hargreaves (England) 5-2; Derek Mienie (South Africa) w.o. Gerry Watson (Canada); Joe O'Boye (Rep. of Ireland) beat Maurice Parkin (England) 5-3; Roger Bales (England) beat Tony Drago (Malta) 5-2; Dennis Hughes (England) beat Anthony Kearney (Republic of Ireland) 5-1; Graham Cripsey (England) beat Bernard Bennett (England) 5-3

Second round: Bernie Mikkelsen (Canada) beat Mick Fisher (England) 5-3; Matt Gibson (Scotland) beat Peter Francisco (South Africa) 5-4; Patsy Fagan (Republic of Ireland) beat Mienie 5-4; Warren King (Australia) beat Caggianello 5-0; Robert Chaperon (Canada) beat Dave Chalmers (England) 5-2; Bales beat Ray Edmonds (England) 5-0; Graham Miles (England) beat O'Boye 5-2; Jack Fitzmaurice (England) beat Mike Watterson (England) 5-2; Tony Chappel (Wales) beat Jim Meadowcroft (England) 5-2; Colin Roscoe (Wales) beat Geoff Foulds (England) 5-3; Eddie McLaughlin (Scotland) beat Hendry 5-3; Bear beat Jim Donnelly (Scotland) 5-2; Tony Jones (England) beat Billy Kelly (Republic of Ireland) 5-3; Malcolm Bradley (England) beat John Rea (Scotland) 5-1; Les Dodd (England) beat Simnagm 5-4; Ian Williamson (England) beat Jack McLaughlin (Northern Ireland) 5-3; John Dunning (England) beat Clive Everton (Wales) 5-2; Mario Morra (Canada) beat Bill Oliver (England) 5-1; Danny Fowler (England) beat Agrawal 5-2; Jim Wych (Canada) beat Rempe 5-1; Eddie Sinclair (Scotland) beat Darrington 5-0; Steve Longworth (England) beat Wilkinson 5-0; Cripsey beat Paul Medati (England) 5-2; Steve Newbury (Wales) beat Frank Jonik (Canada) 5-4; Steve Duggan (England) beat Fred Davis (England) 5-1; Ian Black (Scotland) beat Gino Rigitano (Canada) 5-4; Robbie Foldvari (Australia) beat Vic Harris (England) 5-4; George Scott (England) beat Jimmy van Rensburg (South Africa) 5-4; Tommy Murphy (Northern Ireland) beat Jack Rea (Northern Ireland) 5-1; Bob Harris (England) beat Paddy Browne (Republic of Ireland) 5-3; Wayne Jones (Wales) beat Smith 5-3; D. Hughes beat Marcel Gauvreau (Canada) 5-4

Third round: Doug Mountjoy (Wales) beat Wych 5-1; Cliff Thorburn (Canada) beat Longworth 5-3; Jimmy White (England) beat Fagan 5-2; Dean Reynolds (England) beat Mikkelsen 5-0; Chappel beat Kirk Stevens (Canada) 5-3; David Taylor (England) beat T. Jones 5-4; Tony Knowles (England) beat E. McLaughlin 5-1; Joe Johnson (England) beat Bear 5-1; Murdo Macleod (Scotland) beat Fitzmaurice 5-1; John Virgo (England) beat Miles 5-2; Chaperon beat Silvino Francisco (South Africa) 5-3; Dave Martin (England) beat Sinclair 5-1; B. Harris beat Dene O'Kane (New Zealand) 5-3; King beat Rex Williams (England) 5-3; Gibson beat Eddie Charlton (Australia) 5-4; John Parrott (England) beat W. Jones 5-3; Steve Davis (England) beat Bales 5-2; Willie Thorne (England) beat Fowler 5-1; Alex Higgins (Northern Ireland) beat D. Hughes 5-1; Bill Werbeniuk (Canada) beat Williamson 5-2; Neal Foulds (England) beat Dodd 5-3; Dennis Taylor (Northern Ireland) beat Cripsey 5-1; Bradley beat Mike Hallett (England) 5-4; Cliff Wilson (Wales) beat Roscoe 5-1; Duggan beat Ray Reardon (England) 5-3; Scott beat Mark Wildman (England) 5-1; Black beat Perrie Mans (South Africa) 5-4; John Spencer (England) beat Foldvari 5-4; Tony Meo (England) beat Dunning 5-0; Murphy beat Eugene Hughes (Northern Ireland) 5-3; Terry Griffiths (Wales) beat Newbury 5-2; Campbell beat Mario Morra (Canada) 5-2

Fourth round: S. Davis beat Virgo 5-1; Macleod beat Chaperon 5-4; Reynolds beat Gibson 5-0; White beat King 5-2; Wilson beat Chappel 5-0; Johnson beat Bradley 5-2; David Taylor beat Werbeniuk 5-4; N. Foulds beat Knowles 5-3; Thorburn beat Martin 5-3; Campbell beat Mountjoy 5-1; Thorne beat Scott 5-1; Duggan beat Black 5-1; Griffiths beat Spencer 5-1; Parrott beat Meo 5-4; Higgins beat Murphy 5-2; Dennis Taylor beat B. Harris 5-3

Fifth round: S. Davis beat Macleod 5-1; White beat Reynolds 5-1; Johnson beat Wilson 5-1; N. Foulds beat Dave Taylor 5-4; Thorburn beat Campbell 5-0; Duggan beat Thorne 5-4; Parrott beat Griffiths 5-1; Dennis Taylor beat Higgins 5-1

Quarter-finals: White beat S. Davis 5-3; N. Foulds beat Johnson 5-2; Thorburn beat Duggan 5-2; Dennis Taylor beat Parrott 5-1

Semi-finals: White beat N. Foulds 9-5; Thorburn beat Dennis Taylor 9-5

Final: Thorburn beat White 12-10

Previous Years

ITV's desire to compete seriously with BBC on the snooker front was an important factor in the establishment of the Jameson International in 1981. A couple of promoters, whose events ITV had covered, had been unable to maintain continuity of sponsorship or a high level of efficiency, two deficiencies which were overcome at a stroke through the involvement of Snookasport, who at that time had the Embassy World Championship, the State Express World Team Classic and the Coral UK Championship in their promotional portfolio.

To these events, Snookasport added not only the Jameson International but the Yamaha International Masters, both of which were covered by ITV.

In its second year, the Jameson became the first tournament other than the Embassy World Championship to be taken into consideration for ranking purposes, thus adding another incentive to the substantial prize money already at stake.

Steve Davis has won the first prize twice in three years. In 1981, his first win, he whitewashed Dennis Taylor 9-0 in the final after surviving very perilously 9-8 against Alex Higgins in the semi-finals.

He was beaten by David Taylor in the 1982 quarter-finals, when Tony Knowles came through to win his first major title. But Davis again dominated in 1983 and 1984 when the event was moved to a new venue, Eldon Square Recreational Centre, Newcastle.

After the 1984 event, Jameson withdrew from sponsorship and were replaced by Goya with the event moving to a new venue, Trentham Gardens, Stoke. However, Goya themselves withdrew from the sponsorship after only a one-year involvement.

The continuance of the event, the first world ranking tournament of the year, was assured as financial backing was available from the WPBSA's own funds. As we went to press, a new sponsor was being sought.

1981

TOTAL PRIZE MONEY: £66,000
FIRST PRIZE: £20,000

First round: Joe Johnson (England) beat Jim Wych (Canada) 5-2; Dave Martin (England) beat John Dunning (England) 5-2; Rex Williams (England) beat Jimmy White (England) 5-1; Tony Knowles (England) beat Mike Hallett (England) 5-2; Ray Edmonds (England) beat Eugene Hughes (Rep. of Ireland) 5-4; Jim Meadowcroft (England) beat Cliff Wilson (Wales) 5-4; Tony Meo (England) beat Eddie McLaughlin (Scotland) 5-2

Second round: Graham Miles (England) beat Johnson 5-3; Martin beat Bill Werbeniuk (Canada) 5-2; Williams beat Fred Davis (England) 5-0; Alex Higgins (Northern Ireland) beat Patsy Fagan (Rep. of Ireland) 5-3; John Spencer (England) beat Edmonds 5-3; John Virgo (England) beat Knowles 5-2; Kirk Stevens (Canada) beat Meadowcroft 5-1; Perrie Mans (South Africa) beat Meo 5-3

Third round: Miles beat Cliff Thorburn (Canada) 5-0; Martin beat Eddie Charlton (Australia) 5-2; Virgo beat Ray Reardon (Wales) 5-3; David Taylor (England) beat Stevens 5-0; Dennis Taylor (Northern Ireland) beat Williams 5-1; Higgins beat Doug Mountjoy (Wales) 5-1; Terry Griffiths (Wales) beat Spencer 5-2; Steve Davis (England) beat Mans 5-3

Quarter-finals: Martin beat Miles 5-1; Higgins beat Griffiths 5-2; Dennis Taylor beat Virgo 5-2; Davis beat David Taylor 5-1

Semi-finals: Dennis Taylor beat Martin 9-1; Davis beat Higgins 9-8

Final: Davis beat Dennis Taylor 9-0

1982

TOTAL PRIZE MONEY: £75,000
FIRST PRIZE: £22,000

Qualifying

Group 1: Ray Edmonds (England) beat Dennis Hughes (England) 5-0; Edmonds beat Graham Miles (England) 5-1

Group 2: Vic Harris (England) beat Dessie Sheehan (Rep. of Ireland) 5-3; John Virgo (England) beat Harris 5-2

Group 3: Mick Fisher (England) beat Tommy Murphy (Northern Ireland) 5-1; Fisher beat Fred Davis (England) 5-3

Group 4: Bernard Bennett (England) beat Marcus Owen (Wales) 5-2; Jim Wych (Canada) beat Bennett 5-0

Group 5: Mario Morra (Canada) beat Bert Demarco (Scotland) 5-2; Dean Reynolds (England) beat Morra 5-1

Group 6: Mike Watterson (England) beat Clive Everton (Wales) 5-1; Watterson beat Patsy Fagan (Rep. of Ireland) 5-1

Group 7: Eddie Sinclair (Scotland) beat Ian Anderson (Australia) 5-2; Sinclair beat Tony Meo (England) 5-3

Group 8: George Scott (England) beat Bob Harris (England) 5-4; Scott w.o. John Bear (Canada) scr

Group 9: Joe Johnson (England) w.o. John Phillips (Scotland) scr; Cliff Wilson (Wales) beat Johnson 5-4

Group 10: Eugene Hughes (Rep. of Ireland) beat Maurice Parkin (England) 5-2; Hughes beat Dave Martin (England) 5-4

Group 11: Chris Ross (Scotland) w.o. David Greaves (England) scr; Jim Meadowcroft (England) beat Ross 5-0

Group 12: Ian Williamson (England) beat Jim Donnelly (Scotland) 5-3; Billy Kelly (Rep. of Ireland) beat Geoff Foulds (England) 5-4; Kelly beat Williamson 5-1

Group 13: Colin Roscoe (Wales) beat John Dunning (England) 5-2; Doug French (England) beat Graham Cripsey (England) 5-1; Roscoe beat French 5-2

Group 14: Mike Hallett (England) beat Frank Jonik (Canada) 5-2; Mark Wildman (England) beat Matt Gibson (Scotland) 5-1; Wildman beat Hallett 5-2

Group 15: Jack Fitzmaurice (England) beat Ian Black (Scotland) 5-3; Les Dodd (England) beat Murdo Macleod (Scotland) 5-1; Dodd beat Fitzmaurice 5-3

Group 16: Rex Williams (England) beat Paul Medati (England) 5-3; Eddie McLaughlin (Scotland) beat Pat Houlihan (England) 5-2; Williams beat McLaughlin 5-1

Competition Proper

First round: Tony Knowles (England) beat Sinclair 5-2; Reynolds beat Willie Thorne (England) 5-3; Steve Davis (England) beat Roscoe 5-0; Bill Werbeniuk (Canada) beat Wych 5-3; David Taylor (England) beat Fisher 5-1; Kirk Stevens (Canada) beat Watterson 5-3; Terry Griffiths (Wales) beat Williams 5-2; John Spencer (England) beat Edmonds 5-2; Dennis Taylor (Northern Ireland) beat Wildman 5-2; Virgo beat Eddie Charlton (Australia) 5-4; Perrie Mans (South Africa) beat Dodd 5-3; Jimmy White (England) beat Meadowcroft 5-1; Ray Reardon (Wales) beat Hughes 5-3; Cliff Thorburn (Canada) beat Scott 5-1; Alex Higgins (Northern Ireland) beat Kelly 5-3; Wilson beat Doug Mountjoy (Wales) 5-4

Second round: Davis beat Reynolds 5-0; David Taylor beat Werbeniuk 5-2; Stevens beat Mans 5-2; Griffiths beat Higgins 5-2; Dennis Taylor beat Thorburn 5-2; Wilson beat White 5-2; Virgo beat Spencer 5-4; Knowles beat Reardon 5-2

Quarter-finals: Virgo beat Dennis Taylor 5-3; David Taylor beat Davis 5-3; Knowles beat Wilson 5-4; Stevens beat Griffiths 5-3

Semi-finals: Knowles beat Stevens 9-3; David Taylor beat Virgo 9-5

Final: Knowles beat David Taylor 9-6

1983

TOTAL PRIZE MONEY: £85,000
FIRST PRIZE: £24,000

Qualifying

Group 1: Mike Watterson (England) beat Bert Demarco (Scotland) 5-3; Watterson beat Perrie Mans (South Africa) 5-4

Group 2: Tommy Murphy (Northern Ireland) beat Dessie Sheehan (Rep. of Ireland) 5-2; Willie Thorne (England) beat Murphy 5-2

Group 3: Rex Williams (England) beat Doug French (England) 5-1; Dean Reynolds (England) beat Williams 5-3

Group 4: Jim Donnelly (Scotland) beat Bernard Bennett (England) 5-1; Donnelly beat Cliff Wilson (Wales) 5-1

Steve Davis was a quarter-final loser to Jimmy White in the Goya Matchroom Trophy

Group 5: Mike Darrington (England) beat Ian Williamson (England) 5-3; Silvino Francisco (South Africa) beat Darrington 5-2

Group 6: Warren King (Australia) beat Ian Black (Scotland) 5-3; Graham Miles (England) beat King 5-3

Group 7: Dennis Hughes (England) beat Maurice Parkin (England) 5-0; Joe Johnson (England) beat Hughes 5-1

Group 8: Bob Harris (England) beat John Dunning (England) 5-3; Mark Wildman (England) beat Harris 5-2

Group 9: Dave Martin (England) beat David Greaves (England) 5-1; Martin beat Patsy Fagan (Rep. of Ireland) 5-0

Group 10: Roy Andrewartha (Wales) beat Clive Everton (Wales) 5-1; Eddie Sinclair (Scotland) beat Andrewartha 5-4

Group 11: Paul Medati (England) beat Vic Harris (England) 5-0; Murdo Macleod (Scotland) beat Medati 5-3

Group 12: Fred Davis (England) beat Billy Kelly (Rep. of Ireland) 5-1; Paddy Morgan (Australia) beat Jack Fitzmaurice (England) 5-4; Morgan beat Davis 5-3

Group 13: Mike Hallett (England) beat Colin Roscoe (Wales) 5-2; Mario Morra (Canada) beat Paul Watchorn (Rep. of Ireland) 5-3; Morra beat Hallett 5-3

Group 14: Geoff Foulds (England) beat Pascal Burke (Rep. of Ireland) 5-2; Eugene Hughes (Rep. of Ireland) beat Mick Fisher (England) 5-4; Hughes beat Foulds 5-1

Group 15: Matt Gibson (Scotland) beat Les Dodd (England) 5-1; George Scott (England) beat Pat Houlihan (England) 5-0; Scott beat Gibson 5-3

Group 16: Eddie McLaughlin (Scotland) beat John Campbell (Australia) 5-2; Ray Edmonds (England) beat Jack Rea (Northern Ireland) 5-1; Edmonds beat McLaughlin 5-1

Intermediate round

Dennis Taylor (Northern Ireland) beat Reynolds 5-3; Ray Reardon (Wales) beat Macleod 5-2; Thorne beat John Virgo (England) 5-2; Morra beat Jimmy White (England) 5-3; Doug Mountjoy (Wales) beat Wildman 5-4; Martin beat Alex Higgins (Northern Ireland) 5-2; Watterson beat Tony Meo (England) 5-3; Scott beat Bill Werbeniuk (Canada) 5-3; Terry Griffiths (Wales) beat Miles 5-2; Steve Davis (England) beat E. Hughes 5-1; Donnelly beat David Taylor (England) 5-3; Francisco w.o. Kirk Stevens (Canada) scr; Eddie Charlton (Australia) beat Johnson 5-2; Cliff Thorburn (Canada) beat Sinclair 5-0; John Spencer (England) beat Morgan 5-1; Tony Knowles (England) beat Edmonds 5-1

Competition Proper

First round: Griffiths beat Scott 5-0; Spencer beat Knowles 5-4; Thorburn beat Dennis Taylor 5-3; Mountjoy beat Martin 5-0; Charlton beat Morra 5-3; Thorne beat Reardon 5-0; Francisco beat Donnelly 5-1; Davis beat Watterson 5-0

Quarter finals: Griffiths beat Spencer 5-4; Thorburn beat Mountjoy 5-2; Charlton beat Thorne 5-0; Davis beat Francisco 5-1

Semi-finals: Thorburn beat Griffiths 9-8; Davis beat Charlton 9-2

Final: Davis beat Thorburn 9-4

1984

TOTAL PRIZE MONEY: £150,000
FIRST PRIZE: £30,000

Qualifying

Group A: Geoff Foulds (England) beat Peter Francisco (South Africa) 5-4; Ian Williamson (England) beat Vic Harris (England) 5-0; Foulds beat Williamson 5-4; Foulds beat Jim Donnelly (Scotland) 5-3; John Campbell (Australia) beat Foulds 5-3

Group B: Wayne Jones (Wales) beat Paul Watchorn (Rep. of Ireland) 5-0; Matt Gibson (Scotland) beat Paul Medati (England) 5-3; Jones beat Gibson 5-2; Jones beat George Scott (England) 5-0; Jones beat Mark Wildman (England) 5-0

Group C: Tony Jones (England) beat Doug French (England) 5-1; Steve Duggan (England) beat Jones 5-2; Eddie Sinclair (Scotland) beat Duggan 5-0; Sinclair beat Perrie Mans (South Africa) 5-2

Group D: Bernard Bennett (England) beat Bert Demarco (Scotland) 5-1; Bennett w.o. Paddy Morgan (Australia) scr; Bennett w.o. Jim Wych (Canada) scr; Neal Foulds (England) beat Bennett 5-0

Group E: Robbie Foldvari (Australia) beat Gino Rigitano (Canada) 5-2; Foldvari beat Ray Edmonds (England) 5-1; Les Dodd (England) beat Foldvari 5-3; Dodd beat Cliff Wilson (Wales) 5-1

Group F: Bernie Mikkelsen (Canada) beat Tony Chappel (Wales) 5-4; Mikkelsen beat Clive Everton (Wales) 5-0; Colin Roscoe (Wales) beat Mikkelsen 5-1; Eugene Hughes (Rep. of Ireland) beat Roscoe 5-1

Group G: Dene O'Kane (New Zealand) beat Maurice Parkin (England) 5-2; O'Kane beat Eddie McLaughlin (Scotland) 5-1; O'Kane beat Jack Fitzmaurice (England) 5-4; O'Kane beat Mike Hallett (England) 5-4

Group H: Jack McLaughlin (Northern Ireland) beat David Greaves (England) 5-3; Frank Jonik (Canada) beat McLaughlin 5-2; Marcel Gauvreau (Canada) beat Jonik 5-4; Gauvreau beat John Parrott (England) 5-4

Group I: Graham Cripsey (England) beat Paul Thornley (Canada) 5-3; John Dunning (England) beat Cripsey 5-3; Fred Davis (England) beat Dunning 5-4; John Virgo (England) beat Davis 5-3

Group J: John Hargreaves (England) beat Pat Houlihan (England) 5-2; Billy Kelly (Northern Ireland) beat Hargreaves 5-2; Kelly beat Warren King (Australia) 5-4; Silvino Francisco (South Africa) beat Kelly 5-3

Group K: Danny Fowler (England) beat Robert Chaperon (Canada) 5-0; Fowler w.o. Paul Mifsud (Malta) scr; Fowler beat Roy Andrewartha (Wales) 5-0; Fowler beat Dave Martin (England) 5-0

Group L: Malcolm Bradley (England) beat Mike Darrington (England) 5-3; Bradley beat Jack Rea (Northern Ireland) 5-2; Mario Morra (Canada) beat Bradley 5-3; Joe Johnson (England) beat Morra 5-0

Group M: Dave Chalmers (England) w.o. Lou Condo (Australia) scr; Bill Oliver (England) beat Dennis Hughes (England) 5-4; Chalmers beat Oliver 5-4; Jim Meadowcroft (England) beat Chalmers 5-1; Rex Williams (England) beat Meadowcroft 5-4

Group N: Paddy Browne (Rep. of Ireland) beat John Rea (Scotland) 5-2; Ian Black (Scotland) beat Browne 5-4; Black beat Mike Watterson (England) 5-3; Murdo Macleod (Scotland) beat Black 5-3

Group O: Steve Newbury (Wales) beat Steve Longworth (England) 5-4; Pascal Burke (Eire) beat Tony Kearney (Rep. of Ireland) 5-4; Newbury beat Burke 5-0; Newbury beat Patsy Fagan (Rep. of Ireland) 5-0; Newbury beat Graham Miles (England) 5-1

Group P: Roger Bales (England) beat Dessie Sheehan (Rep. of Ireland) 5-2; Bales beat Tommy Murphy (Northern Ireland) 5-4; Bales beat Mick Fisher (England) 5-3; Dean Reynolds (England) beat Bales 5-4

Competition Proper

First round: David Taylor (England) beat W. Jones 5-4; E. Hughes beat Doug Mountjoy (Wales) 5-1; Newbury beat Bill Werbeniuk (Canada) 5-2; Gauvreau beat Kirk Stevens (Canada) 5-1; Johnson beat Eddie Charlton (Australia) 5-1; Jimmy White (England) beat Williams 5-3; Tony Knowles (England) beat Reynolds 5-1; S. Francisco beat John Spencer (England) 5-2; Willie Thorne (England) beat O'Kane 5-3; Alex Higgins (Northern Ireland) beat Sinclair 5-1; Ray Reardon (Wales) beat Dodd 5-4; Dennis Taylor (Northern Ireland) beat Fowler 5-0; Tony Meo (England) beat Macleod 5-1; Virgo beat Cliff Thorburn (Canada) 5-0; Steve Davis (England) beat Campbell 5-1; Terry Griffiths (Wales) beat Foulds 5-3

Second round: Davis beat David Taylor 5-1; Higgins beat Griffiths 5-4; Hughes beat Reardon 5-1; Thorne beat Gauvreau 5-3; Francisco beat Virgo 5-2; White beat Meo 5-1; Dennis Taylor beat Johnson 5-2; Knowles beat Newbury 5-4

Quarter-finals: Davis beat Higgins 5-1; Hughes beat Thorne 5-2; Francisco w.o. Dennis Taylor scr; Knowles beat White 5-4

Semi-finals: Davis beat Hughes 9-3; Knowles beat Francisco 9-6

Final: Davis beat Knowles 9-2

Jimmy White waits his turn

Rothmans Grand Prix

TOTAL PRIZE MONEY: £250,000
FIRST PRIZE: £50,000
ENTRIES: Open to all professionals
TELEVISION: BBC

Steve Davis, who had waited six months to avenge his dramatic final black defeat by Dennis Taylor in the 1985 world final, managed to do so but only after a 10 hour, 21 minute struggle which prolonged their match to 2.14 a.m., the latest ever finish to a major final.

Davis led 6-1 at the interval but fell behind 7-8 before winning 10-9.

Taylor, defending the title, beat Tony Knowles in the semi-finals after Knowles had prevailed 5-4 on the final black over Kirk Stevens in the quarters. Davis's semi-final against Cliff Thorburn saw his 6-2 lead dwindle to 6-5 before he pulled away to win 9-5.

Among the early upsets, Wayne Jones defeated Willie Thorne and George Scott ousted Ray Reardon. Tony Drago, Malta's only professional, beat Murdo Macleod and Eddie Charlton to reach his first professional last 16.

First round: Barry West (England) beat Bert Demarco (Scotland) 5-2; Pat Houlihan (England) w.o. Gordon Robinson (Australia) scr; Sakchai Simnagm (Thailand) beat Derek Mienie (South Africa) 5-3; Tony Drago (Malta) beat Paul Watchorn (Rep. of Ireland) 5-2; Roger Bales (England) beat Martin Smith (England) 5-1; Gerry Watson (Canada) beat Dessie Sheehan (Rep. of Ireland) 5-1; John Hargreaves (England) beat Graham Cripsey (England) 5-1; Tony Kearney (Rep. of Ireland) beat Jim Bear (Canada) 5-3; Dave Gilbert (England) beat Glen Wilkinson (Australia) 5-4; Joe O'Boye (Rep. of Ireland) beat Stephen Hendry (Scotland) 5-4; Dennis Hughes (England) beat Bernard Bennett (England) 5-4; Mike Darrington (England) beat David Greaves (England); Omprakesh Agrawal (India) beat Jim Rempe USA 5-2

Second round: West beat Jim Meadowcroft (England) 5-2; Mike Watterson (England) beat Joe Caggianello (Canada) 5-1; Tony Jones (England) beat Houlihan 5-4; Simnagm beat Fred Davis (England) 5-2; Geoff Foulds (England) beat Ian Black (Scotland) 5-3; Drago beat Warren King (Australia) 5-4; George Scott (England) beat Dave Chalmers (England) 5-2; Bales beat Mick Fisher (England) 5-3; Watson beat Colin Roscoe (Wales) 5-2; Graham Miles (England) beat Gino Rigitano (Canada) 5-4; Steve Newbury (Wales) beat Pascal Burke (Rep.of Ireland) 5-3; Steve Longworth (England) beat Hargreaves 5-2; Tony Chappel (Wales) beat Les Dodd (England) 5-2; Jimmy van Rensburg (South Africa) beat Eddie McLaughlin (Scotland) 5-4; Matt Gibson (Scotland) beat Malcolm Bradley (England) 5-4; Ray Edmonds (England) beat Kearney 5-2; Bill Oliver (England) beat Patsy Fagan (Rep. of Ireland) 5-4; Steve Duggan (England) beat Marcel Gauvreau (Canada) 5-4; Gilbert beat Ian Williamson (England) 5-4; Bernie Mikkelsen (Canada) beat Tommy Murphy (Northern Ireland) 5-4; Wayne Jones (Wales) beat John Rea (Scotland) 5-0; Peter Francisco (South Africa) beat Clive Everton (Wales) 5-0; Jack McLaughlin (Northern Ireland) beat Paul Medati (England) 5-2; Bob Harris (England) beat Paddy Browne (Rep. of Ireland) 5-3; Jack Fitzmaurice (England) beat Eddie Sinclair (Scotland) 5-3; O'Boye beat Robbie Chaperon (Canada) 5-3; Billy Kelly (Rep. of Ireland) beat Jim Donnelly (Scotland) 5-4; Mario Morra beat D. Hughes 5-2; Vic Harris (England) beat Jim Wych (Canada) 5-3; Darrington beat Robbie Foldvari (Australia) 5-3; Agrawal beat John Dunning (England) 5-0; Danny Fowler (England) beat Frank Jonik (Canada) 5-4

Third round: Dennis Taylor (Northern Ireland) beat West 5-1; Rex Williams (England) beat Watterson 5-2; Tony Meo (England) beat T. Jones 5-2; Eugene Hughes (Rep. of Ireland) beat Simnagm 5-1; Eddie Charlton (Australia) beat G. Foulds 5-1; Drago beat Murdo Macleod (Scotland) 5-3; Scott beat Ray Reardon (Wales) 5-4; Cliff Wilson (Wales) beat Bales 5-1; Kirk Stevens (Canada) beat Watson 5-0; Miles beat Dean Reynolds (England) 5-3; David Taylor (England) beat Newbury 5-2; Longworth beat John Parrott (England) 5-2; Doug Mountjoy (Wales) beat Chappel 5-1; John Campbell (Australia) beat van Rensburg 5-4; Tony Knowles (England) beat Gibson 5-1; Edmonds beat Dene O'Kane (New Zealand) 5-2; Cliff Thorburn (Canada) beat Oliver 5-0; Mark Wildman (England) beat Duggan 5-4; Joe Johnson (England) beat Gilbert 5-2; Mike Hallett (England) beat Mikkelsen 5-3; W. Jones beat Willie Thorne (England) 5-0; P. Francisco beat John Virgo (England) 5-4; Terry Griffiths (Wales) beat J. McLaughlin 5-4; B. Harris beat John Spencer (England) 5-2; Jimmy White (England) beat Fitzmaurice 5-0; O'Boye beat Perrie Mans (South Africa) 5-3; Silvino Francisco (South Africa) beat Kelly 5-2; Dave Martin (England) beat Morra 5-2; Alex Higgins (Northern Ireland) beat V. Harris 5-1; Neal Foulds (England) beat Darrington 5-0; Steve Davis (England) beat Agrawal 5-0; Fowler beat Bill Werbeniuk (Canada) 5-1

Fourth round: Dennis Taylor beat Williams 5-2; Meo beat E. Hughes 5-3; Drago beat Charlton 5-3; Wilson beat Scott 5-3; Stevens beat Miles 5-2; Longworth beat David Taylor 5-1; Campbell beat Mountjoy 5-2; Knowles beat Edmonds 5-3; Thorburn beat Wildman 5-2; Johnson beat Hallett 5-4; P. Francisco beat W. Jones 5-3; Griffiths beat B. Harris 5-3; White beat O'Boye 5-4; S. Francisco beat Martin 5-3; Higgins beat N. Foulds 5-3; S. Davis beat Fowler 5-1

Fifth round: Dennis Taylor beat Meo 5-3; Wilson beat Drago 5-2; Stevens beat Longworth 5-3; Knowles beat Campbell 5-2; Thorburn beat Johnson 5-1; Griffiths beat P. Francisco 5-2; S. Francisco beat White 5-4; S. Davis beat Higgins 5-0

Quarter-finals: Dennis Taylor beat Wilson 5-2; Knowles beat Stevens 5-4; Thorburn beat Griffiths 5-1; S. Davis beat S. Francisco 5-2

Semi-finals: Dennis Taylor beat Knowles 9-6; S. Davis beat Thorburn 9-5

Final: S. Davis beat Dennis Taylor 10-9

Previous Years

The Rothmans Grand Prix grew out of the Professional Players Tournament which was inaugurally staged in 1982 in the match arenas of two Birmingham clubs, the International Snooker Club, Aston, and the La Reserve Club, Sutton Coldfield.

It was indifferently supported by the public but Ray Reardon won his first major prize since the 1978 Embassy World Championship by defeating Jimmy White in the final.

Tony Knowles, who had won the Jameson International in 1982, took his second major first prize on the professional circuit by beating Joe Johnson 9-8 in the 1983 PPT final. Such a desperately close finish had seemed highly unlikely when Knowles led 6-1.

The WPBSA had created the tournament as a means of redistributing to its members in the form of prize money some of the income it would otherwise have had to pay away in tax.

The major contribution to this income was television fees but the second PPT at Redwood Lodge Country Club, Bristol, was so successful in terms of the drama it provided that it cried out for television coverage and thus became highly viable in its own right.

Rothmans came into snooker to sponsor the event and its final phase at the Hexagon in 1984 received nine days television coverage. This has been made possible through the withdrawal from all sports sponsorship of State Express, who had thus released the nine days television which had been devoted to their world team championship at the same venue.

The climax of the first Rothmans Grand Prix helped establish it as one of the game's major events as Dennis Taylor took his first major title in 13 years as a professional.

His 10-2 triumph over Cliff Thorburn gave him what was then snooker's record first prize of £45,000 and gave the snooker world one of its most memorably emotional evenings. His success was all the more remarkable since it came only three weeks after the death of his mother.

'I don't think I'll ever feel the pressure that I did in the past,' he said. 'When something like this happens, you realise that snooker comes a poor second to your family.'

Steady wins over Ray Reardon and Kirk Stevens enabled him to advance to the semi-finals, at which point Neal Foulds, who had done splendidly to get so far with wins over Willie Thorne and Tony Knowles, blew up and was unable to offer significant resistance.

He also had the advantage of catching Cliff Thorburn in the immediate aftermath of his 9-7 victory over Steve Davis in the previous day's semi-final, in quality and drama certainly the match of the tournament.

In the final, Taylor played like a man possessed, reeling off eight frames in succession from 2-2.

1982

TOTAL PRIZE MONEY: £32,000
FIRST PRIZE: £5,000

First round: Eddie Sinclair (Scotland) beat Fred Davis (England) 5-2; Jim Meadowcroft (England) beat Bernard Bennett (England) 5-4; Mike Watterson (England) beat Jim Donnelly (Scotland) 5-4; Terry Griffiths (Wales) beat Colin Roscoe (Wales) 5-1; Alex Higgins (Northern Ireland) beat Doug French (England) 5-3; Ray Reardon (Wales) beat Tommy Murphy (Northern Ireland) 5-0; Bill Werbeniuk (Canada) beat Paddy Morgan (Australia) 5-3; Clive Everton (Wales) beat Patsy Fagan (Rep. of Ireland) 5-2; Cliff Thorburn (Canada) beat Paul Medati (England) 5-1; David Taylor (England) beat Ian Anderson (Australia) 5-1; Dennis Taylor (Northern Ireland) beat Ray Edmonds (England) 5-4; Jim Wych (Canada) beat Billy Kelly (Rep. of Ireland) 5-0; Rex Williams (England) beat Chris Ross (Scotland) 5-0; Perrie Mans (South Africa) beat Eddie McLaughlin (Scotland) 5-2; Willie Thorne (England) beat Bert Demarco (Scotland) 5-3; Mark Wildman (England) beat John Dunning (England) 5-4; Joe Johnson (England) beat Graham Miles (England) 5-1; Eddie Charlton (Australia) beat Dennis Hughes (England) 5-2; Frank Jonik (Canada) beat Doug Mountjoy (Wales) 5-3; Kirk Stevens (Canada) beat Eugene Hughes (Rep. of Ireland) 5-2; Tony Meo (England) beat Marcus Owen (Wales) 5-4; Cliff Wilson (Wales) beat Mario Morra (Canada) 5-2; Tony Knowles (England) beat Pat Houlihan (England) 5-4; John Virgo (England) beat Ian Black (Scotland) 5-2; Mike Hallett (England) beat Vic Harris (England) 5-3; Dave Martin (England) beat Matt Gibson (Scotland) 5-2; Jack Fitzmaurice (England) beat Dessie Sheehan (Rep. of Ireland) 5-1; John Spencer (England) beat Geoff Foulds (England) 5-1

Second round: Werbeniuk beat Jack Rea (Northern Ireland) 5-2; Sinclair beat Meadowcroft 5-3; Thorburn beat Everton 5-2; Griffiths beat Watterson 5-2; Reardon beat Higgins 5-2; Dennis Taylor beat David Taylor 5-1; Wildman beat Mans 5-4; Charlton beat Wiliams 5-2; Macleod beat Thorne 5-4; White beat Wych 5-0; Johnson beat Stevens 5-1; Meo beat Jonik 5-0; Wilson beat Knowles 5-4; Virgo beat Hallett 5-2; Spencer beat Martin 5-3; Reynolds beat Fitzmaurice 5-0

Third round: Werbeniuk beat Thorburn 5-2; Johnson beat Wildman 5-4; Reynolds beat Wilson 5-1; Virgo beat Spencer 5-1; Charlton beat Meo 5-3; White beat Dennis Taylor 5-3; Griffiths beat Sinclair 5-3; Reardon beat Macleod 5-2

Quarter-finals: White beat Griffiths 5-2; Virgo beat Johnson 5-1; Reardon beat Werbeniuk 5-3; Charlton beat Reynolds 5-2

Semi-finals: White beat Virgo 10-4; Reardon beat Charlton 10-7

Final: Reardon beat White 10-5

1983

TOTAL PRIZE MONEY: £60,000
FIRST PRIZE: £12,500

Qualifying: George Ganim Jr (Australia) beat Graham Cripsey (England) 5-4; Steve Duggan (England) beat Mike Darrington (England) 5-4; Tony Jones (England) beat Bill Oliver (England) 5-2; Doug French (England) beat Neal Foulds (England) 5-2; Bernard Bennett (England) beat Bert Demarco (Scotland) 5-4; Pascal Burke (Rep. of Ireland) beat Geoff Foulds (England) 5-4; Vic Harris (England) w.o. Paul Mifsud (Malta) scr; Paul Medati (England) beat Dennis Hughes (England) 5-1; Tommy Murphy (Northern Ireland) beat Paddy Browne (Rep. of Ireland) 5-2; John Parrott (England) beat Paul Watchorn (Rep. of Ireland) 5-0; Dessie Sheehan (Rep. of Ireland) beat Paul Houlihan (England) 5-2; Mario Morra (Canada) beat John Hargreaves (England) 5-0; David Greaves (England) beat Roy Andrewartha (Wales) 5-2; Warren King (Australia) beat Bob Harris (England) 5-3; Paddy Morgan (Australia) beat Matt Gibson (Scotland) 5-4

First round: Ray Reardon (Wales) beat Ganim 5-4; Cliff Thorburn (Canada) beat V. Harris 5-1; Jim Meadowcroft (England) beat Colin Roscoe (Wales) 5-4; Duggan beat John Dunning (England) 5-2; John Virgo beat French 5-4; John Spencer (England) beat Ian Black (Scotland) 5-2; Willie Thorne (England) beat Clive Everton (Wales) 5-1; Cliff Wilson (Wales) beat Bennett 5-1; Terry Griffiths (Wales) beat Les Dodd (England) 5-3; Jimmy White (England) beat Ian Williamson (England) 5-2; Parrott beat Patsy Fagan (Rep. of Ireland) 5-2; Joe Johnson (England) beat Burke 5-3; Eugene Hughes (Rep. of Ireland) beat Eddie Sinclair (Scotland) 5-4; Mick Fisher (England) beat Fred Davis (England) 5-4; Bill Werbeniuk (Canada) beat Tony Jones (England) 5-4; Eddie Charlton (Australia) beat Eddie McLaughlin (Scotland) 5-0; Mike Watterson (England) beat Alex Higgins (Northern Ireland) 5-2; Kirk Stevens (Canada) beat Ray Edmonds (England) 5-1; Dave Martin (England) beat Jack Fitzmaurice (England) 5-0; Tommy Murphy (Northern Ireland) beat Murdo Macleod (Scotland) 5-0; John Campbell (Australia) beat Doug Mountjoy (Wales) 5-3; David Taylor (England) beat Paddy Morgan (Australia) 5-3; Graham Miles (England) beat Marcel Gauvreau (Canada) 5-3; Mark Wildman (England) beat Frank Jonik (Canada) 5-4; T. Knowles (England) beat P. Medati (England) 5-1; Rex Williams (England) beat D. Sheehan (Rep. of Ireland) 5-1; Silvino Francisco (South Africa) beat Morra (Canada) 5-3; Dean Reynolds (England) beat David Greaves (England) 5-1; Tony Meo (England) beat Warren King (Australia) 5-2

Second round: Reardon beat Duggan 5-2; Thorburn beat Meadowcroft 5-1; Thorne beat Spencer 5-1; Wilson beat Virgo 5-2; Griffiths beat Parrott 5-1; Johnson beat White 5-3; E. Hughes beat Werbeniuk 5-0; Charlton beat Fisher 5-4; Stevens beat Murphy 5-1; Martin beat Watterson 5-4; Wildman beat David Taylor 5-3; Campbell beat Miles 5-2; Meo beat Reynolds 5-0; Francisco beat Scott 5-1; Knowles beat Williams 5-4; Hallett beat Davis 5-2

Third round: Thorne beat Reardon 5-3; Thorburn beat Wilson 5-3; E. Hughes beat Griffiths 5-2; Johnson beat Charlton 5-0; Stevens beat Wildman 5-0; Campbell beat Martin 5-0; Knowles beat Francisco 5-0; Meo beat Hallett 5-3

Quarter-finals: Johnson beat Thorburn 5-1; Thorne beat E. Hughes 5-1; Meo beat Stevens 5-3; Knowles beat Campbell 5-3

Semi-finals: Knowles beat Thorne 9-7; Johnson beat Meo 9-6

Final: Knowles beat Johnson 9-8

1984

TOTAL PRIZE MONEY: £225,000
FIRST PRIZE: £45,000

Qualifying (At Sheffield Snooker Centre): Ian Williamson (England) beat Paul Thornley (Canada) 5-2; Jim Donnelly (Scotland) beat John Hargreaves (England) 5-4; Bert Demarco (Scotland) w.o. Patsy Fagan (Rep. of Ireland) scr; Vic Harris (England) beat Fred Davis (England) 5-1; John Dunning (England) beat Dennis Hughes (England) 5-0; Dene O'Kane (New Zealand) beat Billy Kelly (Northern Ireland) 5-4; Marcel Gauvreau (Canada) beat Robbie Foldvari (Australia) 5-2; Eddie McLaughlin (Scotland) beat Steve Longworth (England) 5-2; Mario Morra (Canada) beat Graham Cripsey (England) 5-3; Steve Duggan (England) beat Paddy Browne (Rep. of Ireland) 5-2; Dessie Sheehan (Rep. of Ireland) w.o. Lou Condo (Australia) scr; Sheehan beat Bernie Mikkelsen (Canada) 5-3; Pascal Burke (Rep. of Ireland) beat Mike Darrington (England) 5-3; Dave Chalmers (England) beat Roy Andrewartha (Wales) 5-2; Warren King (Australia) beat David Greaves (England) 5-0; Paul Medati (England) beat Les Dodd (England) 5-4

(At Masters Club, Stockport): Robert Chaperon (Canada) beat Tony Kearney (Rep. of Ireland) 5-1; Chaperon beat Matt Gibson (Scotland) 5-4; Peter Francisco (South Africa) beat Ian Black (Scotland) 5-4; Gino Rigitano (Canada) beat Ray Edmonds (England) 5-3; Malcolm Bradley (England) beat Frank Jonik (Canada) 5-1; Wayne Jones (Wales) beat Mike Watterson (England) 5-3; John Rea (Scotland) beat Jack Fitzmaurice (England) 5-2

(At Hatton Garden Snooker Centre, London): Steve Newbury (Wales) beat Mick Fisher (England) 5-0; Bill Oliver (England) beat Bernard Bennett (England) 5-3; Clive Everton (Wales) beat Pat Houlihan (England) 5-3; Jack McLaughlin (Northern Ireland) beat Jim Meadowcroft (England) 5-1; Tony Chappel (Wales) beat George Scott (England) 5-1; Tommy Murphy (Northern Ireland) beat Geoff Foulds (England) 5-1; Tony Jones (England) beat Eddie Sinclair (Scotland) 5-4; Colin Roscoe (Wales) beat Doug French (England) 5-0; Paul Watchorn (Rep. of Ireland) w.o. Paddy Morgan (Australia) scr; Danny Fowler (England) w.o. Paul Mifsud (Malta) scr

First round (At Redwood Lodge Country Club, Bristol): Tony Knowles (England) beat V. Harris 5-1; Dunning beat Perrie Mans (South Africa) 5-4; Williamson beat Bill Werbeniuk (Canada) 5-2; Joe Johnson (England) beat Medati 5-1; Willie Thorne (England) beat Newbury 5-2; Murdo Macleod (Scotland) beat King 5-4; Neal Foulds (England) beat Demarco 5-2; T. Jones beat Terry Griffiths (Wales) 5-3; Ray Reardon (Wales) beat Roscoe 5-1; Cliff Wilson (Wales) beat Donnelly 5-2; Dennis Taylor (Northern Ireland) beat Watchorn 5-1; John Virgo (England) beat Bradley 5-0; Alex Higgins (Northern Ireland) beat Bales 5-1; Mike Hallett (England) beat Sheehan 5-1; Rex Williams (England) beat Chalmers 5-0; Kirk Stevens (Canada) beat Chappel 5-3; Cliff Thorburn (Canada) beat Rigitano 5-4; John Campbell (Australia) beat W. Jones 5-4; Tony Meo (England) beat Burke 5-1; Dave Martin (England) beat Chaperon 5-4; Doug Mountjoy (Wales) beat E. McLaughlin 5-4; Mark Wildman (England) beat J. McLaughlin 5-3; John Parrott (England) beat Gauvreau 5-3; Eddie Charlton (Australia) beat Everton 5-1; Jimmy White (England) beat Oliver 5-1; Silvino Francisco (South Africa) beat Duggan 5-3; Peter Francisco beat John Spencer (England) 5-2; Dean Reynolds (England) beat Fowler 5-2; David Taylor (England) beat O'Kane 5-1; Rea beat Eugene Hughes (Rep. of Ireland) 5-4; Graham Miles (England) beat Murphy 5-3; Steve Davis (England) beat Morra 5-2

Second round: Knowles beat Dunning 5-1; Williamson beat Johnson 5-4; Thorne beat Macleod 5-3; N. Foulds beat T. Jones 5-0; Reardon beat Wilson 5-4; Dennis Taylor beat Virgo 5-3; Hallett beat Higgins 5-3; Stevens beat Williams 5-3; Thorburn beat Campbell 5-1; Meo beat Martin 5-4; Mountjoy beat Wildman 5-0; Charlton beat Parrott 5-1; S. Francisco beat White 5-1; David Taylor beat Rea 5-1; S. Davis beat Miles 5-0; Reynolds beat P. Francisco 5-4

Third round: Knowles beat Williamson 5-2; N. Foulds beat Thorne 5-1; Dennis Taylor beat Reardon 5-3; Stevens beat Hallett 5-3; Thorburn beat Meo 5-4; Mountjoy beat Charlton 5-4; Reynolds beat S. Francisco 5-1; Davis beat David Taylor 5-1

Quarter-finals: Foulds beat Knowles 5-2; Dennis Taylor beat Stevens 5-2; Thorburn beat Mountjoy 5-3; Davis beat Reynolds 5-0

Semi-finals: Taylor beat Foulds 9-3; Thorburn beat Davis 9-7

Final: Dennis Taylor beat Thorburn 10-2

Dennis Taylor won the 1985 Rothmans Grand Prix

BCE Canadian Masters

TOTAL PRIZE MONEY: £50,000
FIRST PRIZE: £15,000
ENTRIES: Eight invited
TELEVISION: CBC

Dennis Taylor made three centuries in four frames, the first such sequence since John Spencer achieved it in the 1970 world final, in beating Steve Davis 9-5 in the final of an event which marked the first attempt to present snooker in Canada along the lines so familiar from Britain's snooker success story.

The Canadian Broadcasting Corporation staged the event in its own Toronto studios with one hour's late night transmission on each of the first four days supplemented by extensive afternoon and evening coverage of the final.

The viewing figures exceeded CBC's most optimistic expectations and hinted that, in time, the WPBSA might be able to build an overseas circuit, as they have in Britain, financed by television and sponsorship interest.

The final reversed the result of the Rothmans Grand Prix final a week earlier but only after Davis had led 3-0.

Then came Taylor's three centuries in four frames and there were later centuries, both from Taylor and Davis, before the world champion concluded the match with a run of 89 comprising the first twelve reds and eleven blacks.

First round: Dennis Taylor (Northern Ireland) beat John Parrott (England) 5-1; Ray Reardon (Wales) beat Tony Knowles (England) 5-2; Cliff Thorburn (Canada) beat Jimmy White (England) 5-3; Steve Davis (England) beat Terry Griffiths (Wales) 5-4

Semi-finals: Dennis Taylor beat Reardon 8-3; S. Davis beat Thorburn 8-1

Final: Dennis Taylor beat S. Davis 9-5

Dennis Taylor made three centuries in four frames in winning the BCE Canadian Masters

Coral UK Open Championship

TOTAL PRIZE MONEY: £120,000
FIRST PRIZE: £24,000
ENTRIES: Open to all professionals
TELEVISION: BBC

Having failed to beat Alex Higgins in the 1983 final after leading 7-0, Steve Davis recovered from 6-12 to beat Willie Thorne 16-14 at Preston Guild Hall to win the title for the fourth time in six attempts.

Thorne led 13-8 going into the final session and looked certain to go six up with nine to play until a simple blue from its spot eluded him. This error completely changed the psychological balance of the match and Thorne won only one further frame.

Corals almost marked the completion of their sponsorship agreement with a record pay-out in their betting shops. Having quoted Thorne at 40-1 for the title, they had paid out £100,000 to various appreciative punters and stood to lose another £150,000 if Thorne had won the final.

From his opening match, in which he set a new tournament record break of 140 in beating Paddy Browne 9-6, through his run of fine wins over John Virgo (9-8) (seizing victory with a 112 clearance in the decider), Cliff Thorburn (9-7), Terry Griffiths (9-7), and Dennis Taylor (9-7), Thorne had been the man of the tournament until he stumbled fatally within sight of the winning post.

Barry West, a Yorkshireman in his first season as a professional, displayed admirable consistency and steadiness of temperament in reaching the quarter-finals with wins over Eugene Hughes, Doug Mountjoy and Murdo Macleod before falling to Davis.

Preliminary round: Dessie Sheehan (Rep. of Ireland) beat Paul Watchorn (Rep. of Ireland) 9-7; Tony Drago (Malta) beat Dave Gilbert (England) 9-5; Glen Wilkinson (Australia) beat Martin Smith (England) 9-4; Omprakesh Agrawal (India) beat Stephen Hendry (Scotland) 9-2; Barry West (England) w.o. Gordon Robinson (Australia) scr; Greg Jenkins (Australia) beat Pascal Burke (Rep. of Ireland) 9-5; Joe O'Boye (Rep. of Ireland) beat Bernard Bennett (England) 9-3; Mike Darrington (England) w.o. Maurice Parkin (England) scr; Pat Houlihan (England) beat Gerry Watson (Canada) 9-4; John Hargreaves (England) beat Derek Mienie (South Africa) 9-7; Dennis Hughes (England) beat Tony Kearney (Rep. of Ireland) 9-8; Sakchai Simnagm (Thailand) beat Roger Bales (England) 9-2; Jim Bear (Canada) beat Bert Demarco (Scotland) 9-1; Graham Cripsey (England) beat David Greaves (England) 9-4

Qualifying round: Sheehan beat George Scott (England) 9-6; Drago beat Jim Donnelly (Scotland) 9-8; Steve Longworth (England) beat Matt Gibson (Scotland) 9-2; Danny Fowler (England) beat Wilkinson 9-6; Mario Morra (Canada) beat Agrawal 9-8; West beat Colin Roscoe (Wales) 9-5; Graham Miles (England) beat Bill Oliver (England) 9-4; Tommy Murphy (Northern Ireland) beat Clive Everton (Wales) 9-4; Malcolm Bradley (England) beat Jenkins 9-3; Tony Chappel (Wales) w.o Eddie McLaughlin (Scotland) scr; Ray Edmonds (England) beat Jimmy van Rensburg (South Africa) 9-5; Fred Davis (England) beat John Rea (Scotland) 9-8; Bernie Mikkelsen (Canada) beat Ian Williamson (England) 9-3; Paul Medati (England) beat Billy Kelly (Rep. of Ireland) 9-1; O'Boye beat Marcel Gauvreau (Canada) 9-5; Vic Harris (England) beat Ian Black (Scotland) 9-3; Les Dodd (England) w.o. Jack Rea (Northern Ireland) scr; Eddie Sinclair (Scotland) beat Geoff Foulds (England) 9-4; Paddy Browne (Rep. of Ireland) beat Dave Chalmers (England) 9-4; Wayne Jones (Wales) beat Jack Fitzmaurice (England) 9-3; Jim Wych (Canada) beat Steve Duggan (England) 9-5; Darrington beat Robbie Foldvari (Australia) 9-6; Tony Jones (England) beat Frank Jonik (Canada) 9-4; Jack McLaughlin (Northern Ireland) beat Robbie Chaperon (Canada) 9-5; Steve Newbury (Wales) beat Houlihan 9-3; Jim Meadowcroft (England) beat Hargreaves 9-8; Peter Francisco (South Africa) w.o. Gino Rigitano (Canada) scr; Warren King (Australia) beat Dennis Hughes (England) 9-0; Simnagm beat Mick Fisher (England) 9-4; Patsy Fagan (Rep. of Ireland) beat Bob Harris (England) 9-2; Jim Bear (Canada) beat Mike Watterson (England) 9-0; Cripsey w.o. John Dunning (England) scr

First round: Steve Davis (England) beat Sheehan 9-1; Drago beat Mark Wildman (England) 9-5; Tony Meo (England) beat Longworth 9-5; Fowler beat Perrie Mans (South Africa) 9-2; Doug Mountjoy (Wales) beat Morra 9-2; West beat Eugene Hughes (Rep. of Ireland) 9-3; Ray Reardon (Wales) beat Miles 9-4; Murdo Macleod (Scotland) beat Murphy 9-7; Jimmy White (England) beat Bradley 9-4; Chappel beat Dene O'Kane (New Zealand) 9-5; Alex Higgins (Northern Ireland) beat Edmonds 9-8; F. Davis beat Bill Werbeniuk (Canada) 9-7; David Taylor (England) beat Mikkelsen 9-6; John Campbell (Australia) beat Medati 9-7; Tony Knowles (England) beat O'Boye 9-5; John Spencer (England) beat V. Harris 9-5; Cliff Thorburn (Canada) beat Dodd 9-4; John Parrott (England) beat Sinclair 9-2; Willie Thorne (England) beat Browne 9-6; John Virgo (England) beat W. Jones 9-7; Silvino Francisco (South Africa) beat Wych 9-8; Dave Martin (England) beat Darrington 9-3; Terry Griffiths (Wales) beat T. Jones 9-5; Dean Reynolds (England) beat J. McLaughlin 9-7; Kirk Stevens (Canada) beat Newbury 9-7; Mike Hallett (England) beat Meadowcroft 9-1; P. Francisco beat Eddie Charlton (Australia) 9-5; Rex Williams (England) beat King 9-5; Joe Johnson (England) beat Simnagm 9-4; Neal Foulds (England) beat Fagan 9-5; Dennis Taylor (Northern Ireland) beat Jim Bear 9-3; Cripsey beat Cliff Wilson (Wales) 9-7

Second round: S. Davis beat Drago 9-2; Meo beat Fowler 9-2; West beat Mountjoy 9-4; Macleod beat Reardon 9-5; White beat Chappel 9-5; Higgins beat F. Davis 9-2; David Taylor beat Campbell 9-4; Knowles beat Spencer 9-7; Thorburn beat Parrott 9-6; Thorne beat Virgo 9-8; S. Francisco beat Martin 9-6; Griffiths beat Reynolds 9-7; Stevens beat Hallett 9-5; Williams beat P. Francisco 9-7; N. Foulds beat Johnson 9-8; Dennis Taylor beat Cripsey 9-2

Third round: S. Davis beat Meo 9-5; West beat Macleod 9-4; White beat Higgins 9-6; Knowles beat David Taylor 9-7; Thorne beat Thorburn 9-7; Griffiths beat S. Francisco 9-5; Stevens beat Williams 9-7; Dennis Taylor beat N. Foulds 9-5

Quarter-finals: S. Davis beat West 9-1; White beat Knowles 9-4; Thorne beat Griffiths 9-7; Dennis Taylor beat Stevens 9-1

Semi-finals: S. Davis beat White 9-5; Thorne beat Dennis Taylor 9-7

Final: S. Davis beat Thorne 16-14

Previous Years

Mike Watterson's Snookasport Promotions, fresh from their successful and innovative staging of the 1977 Embassy World Championship, initiated an important new event at Blackpool Tower Circus with sponsorship from the manufacturers of Super Crystalate balls and BBC television coverage of the final.

Despite poor attendances, not all that surprising at Blackpool in December, the event clearly possessed potential and the following year Coral Racing offered almost twice as much as Super Crystalate's £7,000.

With a prize fund increased to £12,500, television coverage of the semi-finals as well as the final and a move to a prestigious new venue, Preston Guild Hall, the event blossomed.

Doug Mountjoy's and John Virgo's names fell in beneath that of the first champion, Patsy Fagan, in the list of winners and in 1980 the Coral UK gave Steve Davis his first major title.

The prize money increased in stages to 1983's £60,000, and television coverage was extended to the last eight and then the last nine days. Davis won again in 1981 and Terry Griffiths and Alex Higgins in turn succeeded him, both in finals which went the full distance of 31 frames.

After two unsuccessful appearances in the final, Higgins beat Davis in extraordinary fashion, 16-15, to win the 1983 title.

Davis, who had beaten Higgins with a session to spare in their world semi-final the previous spring, looked as if he was about to do the same when he whitewashed the Irishman 7-0 on the first afternoon.

With immense grit, Higgins won seven of the eight frames on the first evening, levelled at 11-11 the following afternoon and ultimately took the last two frames on the second evening to win the title.

Thus ended a modern fairy tale. Throughout the season Higgins had been desperately out of touch. His wife had instituted divorce proceedings and the threat of separation from the two children to whom he is devoted cast him into the depths of despair. It was only when reconciliation with his wife started to appear a definite possibility that his form began to improve.

Having dropped the first four frames to the Scottish champion, Murdo Macleod, in the first round, Higgins was watched by his wife in the evening session as he took the match 9-6.

He looked an altogether different player when he beat Paul Medati 9-1, Tony Knowles 9-5 and Terry Griffiths 9-4 to earn his place in the final.

So well did Davis play in the opening session of the final that Higgins could do little about it; but as soon as the world champion started to play like an ordinary mortal, Higgins regained his form and met the challenge.

In spite of losing 9-4 to Davis in the quarter-finals, Tony Meo equalled the championship break record of 139, set by Graham Miles in 1978, and history was made in the first round when two survivors of the qualifying competition, Geoff and Neal Foulds, became the first father and son combination ever to compete in a major professional tournament.

In 1984, the event was thrown open to all professionals instead of merely those holding a UK passport and the event became eligible for ranking points.

Davis earned the five points available to the winner by beating Higgins 16-8 in the final after his 8-2 lead had dwindled to 9-8.

Davis had been seriously threatened by Tony Meo in the second round, trailing 4-7 but taking the match with a five-frame winning streak in which he aggregated 474-30 in the last four frames.

There was another notable recovery by Cliff Thorburn who beat Ray Reardon from four down with five to play in the quarter-finals before losing to Higgins 9-7 in the semis.

Steve Davis on his way to winning the 1985 Coral UK title

1977

(Super Crystalate UK Championship)

TOTAL PRIZE MONEY: £7,000
FIRST PRIZE: £2,000

First round: John Virgo (England) w.o. John Barrie (England) scr; Chris Ross (Scotland) beat Jack Karnehm (England) 5-4; Patsy Fagan (Rep. of Ireland) beat Jack Rea (Northern Ireland) 5-1; Jim Meadowcroft (England) beat Pat Houlihan (England) 5-1; Doug Mountjoy (Wales) beat Roy Andrewartha (Wales) 5-2; Willie Thorne (England) beat Bernard Bennett (England) 5-1; John Dunning (England) beat Maurice Parkin (England) 5-4; David Taylor (England) beat David Greaves (England) 5-4

Second round: Virgo beat Dennis Taylor (Northern Ireland) 5-2; Graham Miles (England) beat Ross 5-1; Fagan beat Fred Davis (England) 5-0; Meadowcroft beat Ray Reardon (Wales) 5-4; Mountjoy beat John Spencer (England) 5-3; Thorne beat Rex Williams (England) 5-4; Dunning w.o. John Pulman (England) scr; Alex Higgins (Northern Ireland) beat David Taylor 5-4

Quarter-finals: Virgo beat Miles 5-2; Fagan beat Meadowcroft 5-4; Mountjoy beat Thorne 5-4; Higgins beat Dunning 5-0

Semi-finals: Fagan beat Virgo 9-8; Mountjoy beat Higgins 9-2

Final: Fagan beat Mountjoy 12-9

1978

TOTAL PRIZE MONEY: £12,500
FIRST PRIZE: £3,500

Qualifying: Willie Thorne (England) beat Bernard Bennett (England) 9-4; Roy Andrewartha (Wales) beat Pat Houlihan (England) 9-3; Doug Mountjoy (Wales) beat John Barrie (England) 9-5; Rex Williams (England) beat Terry Griffiths (Wales) 9-8; John Dunning (England) beat David Greaves (England) 9-3; John Virgo (England) beat Ray Edmonds (England) 9-4; David Taylor (England) beat Maurice Parkin (England) 9-2; Jim Meadowcroft (England) beat Jack Rea (Northern Ireland) 9-5

First round: David Taylor beat Fagan 9-7; Virgo beat John Pulman (England) 9-3; Fred Davis (England) beat Dunning 9-2; Alex Higgins (Northern Ireland) beat Meadowcroft 9-6; Thorne beat Ray Reardon (Wales) 9-6; Graham Miles (England) beat Williams 9-8; Mountjoy beat Dennis Taylor (Northern Ireland) 9-4; Andrewartha beat John Spencer (England) 9-8

Quarter-finals: David Taylor beat Virgo 9-2; Higgins beat Davis 9-4; Miles beat Thorne 9-1; Mountjoy beat Andrewartha 9-4

Semi-finals: David Taylor beat Higgins 9-5; Mountjoy beat Miles 9-1

Final: Mountjoy beat David Taylor 15-9

1979

TOTAL PRIZE MONEY: £15,000
FIRST PRIZE: £4,500

First round: Jack Rea (Northern Ireland) beat Bernard Bennett (England) 9-8; Mike Hallett (England) beat Maurice Parkin (England) 9-1; John Dunning (England) beat David Greaves (England) 9-8

Second round: Willie Thorne (England) beat Roy Andrewartha (Wales) 9-4; Pat Houlihan (England) beat Rea 9-3; Steve Davis (England) beat Dunning 9-3; Patsy Fagan (Rep. of Ireland) beat Hallett 9-4; Bill Werbeniuk (Canada) beat Joe Johnson (England) 9-3; Ray Edmonds (England) beat Jim Meadowcroft (England) 9-3; Tony Meo (England) beat David Taylor (England) 9-7; Cliff Wilson (Wales) beat John Pulman (England) 9-7

Third round: Steve Davis beat Doug Mountjoy (Wales) 9-5; Terry Griffiths (Wales) beat Wilson 9-4; Alex Higgins (Northern Ireland) beat Houlihan 9-3; Fagan beat Graham Miles (England) 9-5; Werbeniuk beat John Spencer (England) 9-8; Dennis Taylor (Northern Ireland) beat Thorne 9-8; John Virgo (England) beat Meo 9-6; Edmonds beat Fred Davis (England) 9-6

Quarter-finals: Werbeniuk beat Edmonds 9-8; Dennis Taylor beat Fagan 9-6; Virgo beat Steve Davis 9-7; Griffiths beat Higgins 9-7

Semi-finals: Virgo beat Dennis Taylor 9-4; Griffiths beat Werbeniuk 9-3

Final: Virgo beat Griffiths 14-13

1980

TOTAL PRIZE MONEY: £22,500
FIRST PRIZE: £6,000

Qualifying

First round: Mike Hallett (England) beat Bernard Bennett (England) 9-4; Sid Hood (England) beat Chris Ross (Scotland) 9-3

Second round: Hallett beat Ray Edmonds (England) 9-8; Eddie Sinclair (Scotland) beat Kingsley Kennerley (England) 9-1; Mark Wildman (England) beat Cliff Wilson (Wales) 9-8; Jim Meadowcroft (England) beat David Greaves (England) 9-1; Roy Andrewartha (Wales) beat Tony Knowles (England) 9-8; Rex Williams (England) beat John Barrie (England) 9-1; Joe Johnson (England) beat John Dunning (England) 9-6; Tony Meo (England) beat Hood 9-5

Competition Proper

First round: Meo beat Pat Houlihan (England) 9-1; Steve Davis (England) beat Hallett 9-1; Patsy Fagan (Rep. of Ireland) beat Johnson 9-4; Sinclair beat Graham Miles (England) 9-5; Willie Thorne (England) beat Meadowcroft 9-1; Wildman beat John Spencer (England) 9-7; Williams beat Doug Mountjoy (Wales) 9-8; Andrewartha beat John Pulman (England) 9-6

Second round: Meo beat John Virgo (England) 9-1; S. Davis beat Bill Werbeniuk (Canada) 9-3; Dennis Taylor (Northern Ireland) beat Sinclair 9-6; Terry Griffiths (Wales) beat Fagan 9-8; Alex Higgins (Northern Ireland) beat Thorne 9-7; Fred Davis (England) beat Wildman 9-6; Ray Reardon (Wales) beat Andrewartha 9-3; Williams beat David Taylor (England) 9-7

Quarter-finals: S. Davis beat Meo 9-5; Griffiths beat Dennis Taylor 9-2; Higgins beat F. Davis 9-6; Reardon beat Williams 9-4

Semi-finals: S. Davis beat Griffiths 9-0; Higgins beat Reardon 9-7

Final: S. Davis beat Higgins 16-6

1981

TOTAL PRIZE MONEY: £40,000
FIRST PRIZE: £10,000

Qualifying

Group 1: Paul Medati (England) beat Eddie McLaughlin (Scotland) 9-5; Medati beat Jim Donnelly (Scotland) 9-7; Willie Thorne (England) beat Medati 9-6

Group 2: Mike Hallett (England) beat Vic Harris (England) 9-4; Hallett beat Dennis Hughes (England) 9-6; Hallett beat Patsy Fagan (Rep. of Ireland) 9-5

Group 3: Matt Gibson (Scotland) beat Jack Fitzmaurice (England) 9-6; Clive Everton (Wales) beat Gibson 9-7; Jimmy White (England) beat Everton 9-4

Group 4: Joe Johnson (England) beat Tommy Murphy (Northern Ireland) 9-1; Mike Watterson (England) beat Bernard Bennett (England) 9-4; Johnson beat Watterson 9-3; Johnson beat Cliff Wilson (Wales) 9-5

Group 5: Pat Houlihan (England) beat Kingsley Kennerley (England) 9-1; Houlihan beat Ian Black (Scotland) 9-4; Houlihan beat Jim Meadowcroft (England) 9-4

Group 6: Geoff Foulds (England) beat Billy Kelly (Rep. of Ireland) 9-7; Tony Knowles (England) beat Foulds 9-1

Group 7: Eddie Sinclair (Scotland) beat Mark Wildman (England) 9-8; Sinclair beat Sid Hood (England) 9-0; Dave Martin (England) beat Sinclair 9-7

Group 8: Rex Williams (England) beat Doug French (England) 9-3; Colin Roscoe (Wales) beat Murdo Macleod (Scotland) 9-7; Williams beat Roscoe 9-4; Williams beat John Dunning (England) 9-4

Competition Proper

First round: Thorne beat Ray Edmonds (England) 9-4; Kirk Stevens (Canada) beat Hallett 9-4; White beat John Virgo (England) 9-6; Johnson beat John Spencer (England) 9-5; Graham Miles (England) beat Houlihan 9-5; Knowles beat Fred Davis (England) 9-6; Alex Higgins (Northern Ireland) beat Martin 9-7; Tony Meo (England) beat Williams 9-8

Second round: Steve Davis (England) beat Thorne 9-2; Bill Werbeniuk (Canada) beat Stevens 9-7; White beat Dennis Taylor (Northern Ireland) 9-5; Ray Reardon (Wales) beat Johnson 9-7; Terry Griffiths (Wales) beat Miles 9-4; Knowles beat Doug Mountjoy (Wales) 9-6; Higgins beat David Taylor (England) 9-5; Meo beat Cliff Thorburn (Canada) 9-6

Quarter-finals: Davis beat Werbeniuk 9-5; White beat Reardon 9-8; Griffiths beat Knowles 9-5; Meo beat Higgins 9-4

Semi-finals: Davis beat White 9-0; Griffiths beat Meo 9-3

Final: Davis beat Griffiths 16-3

1982

TOTAL PRIZE MONEY: £50,000
FIRST PRIZE: £11,000

Qualifying

Group 1: Tony Meo (England) beat George Scott (England) 9-5

Group 2: Cliff Wilson (Wales) beat Eddie McLaughlin (Scotland) 9-6

Group 3: Dave Martin (England) beat Murdo Macleod (Scotland) 9-6

Group 4: Jim Meadowcroft (England) beat Dennis Hughes (England) 9-8

Group 5: Jim Donnelly (Scotland) beat Chris Ross (Scotland) 9-5

Group 6: Pat Houlihan w.o. John Dunning (England) scr

Group 7: Mike Hallett (England) beat Bert Demarco (Scotland) 9-1

Group 8: Billy Kelly (Rep. of Ireland) beat Jack Fitzmaurice (England) 9-0

Group 9: Geoff Foulds (England) beat Matt Gibson (Scotland) 9-3; Rex Williams (England) beat Foulds 9-7

Group 10: Vic Harris (England) beat Marcus Owen (Wales) 9-4; Joe Johnson (England) beat Harris 9-8

Group 11: Tommy Murphy (Northern Ireland) beat Clive Everton (Wales) 9-4; Eddie Sinclair (Scotland) beat Murphy 9-5

Group 12: Bob Harris (England) beat Graham Cripsey (England) 9-6; Harris beat Mike Watterson (England) 9-3

Group 13: Mick Fisher (England) beat Ian Black (Scotland) 9-3; Fisher beat Ray Edmonds (England) 9-8

Group 14: Les Dodd (England) beat Ian Williamson (England) 9-1; Dodd beat Doug French (England) 9-7

Group 15: Bernard Bennett (England) w.o. John Phillips (Scotland) scr; Paul Medati (England) beat Bennett 9-1

Group 16: Colin Roscoe (Wales) beat Jack Rea (Northern Ireland) 9-6; Mark Wildman (England) beat Roscoe 9-4

Competition Proper

First round: Steve Davis (England) beat Williams 9-6; Patsy Fagan (Rep. of Ireland) beat B. Harris 9-6; Terry Griffiths (Wales) beat Johnson 9-1; Dennis Taylor (Northern Ireland) beat Meadowcroft 9-7; David Taylor (England) beat Dodd 9-7; Meo beat Graham Miles (England) 9-4; John Virgo (England) beat Kelly 9-2; Doug Mountjoy (Wales) beat Houlihan 9-3; Ray Reardon (Wales) beat Wildman 9-5; Hallett beat Fred Davis (England) 9-7; Wilson beat Willie Thorne (England) 9-7; Jimmy White (England) beat Medati 9-7; John Spencer (England) beat Sinclair 9-8; Tony Knowles (England) beat Donnelly 9-6; Dean Reynolds (England) beat Fisher 9-6; Alex Higgins (Northern Ireland) beat Martin 9-7

Second round: S. Davis beat Fagan 9-3; Griffiths beat Dennis Taylor 9-7; Meo beat David Taylor 9-6; Virgo beat Mountjoy 9-5; Reardon beat Hallett 9-8; White beat Wilson 9-5; Spencer beat Knowles 9-6; Higgins beat Reynolds 9-8

Quarter-finals: Griffiths beat S. Davis 9-6; Meo beat Virgo 9-6; Reardon beat White 9-8; Higgins beat Spencer 9-5

Semi-finals: Griffiths beat Meo 9-7; Higgins beat Reardon 9-6

Final: Griffiths beat Higgins 16-15

1983

TOTAL PRIZE MONEY: £60,000
FIRST PRIZE: £12,000

Qualifying

Group 1: Joe Johnson (England) beat Matt Gibson (Scotland) 9-6

Group 2: Tony Jones (England) beat Eddie Sinclair (Scotland) 9-3

Group 3: Mark Wildman (England) beat David Greaves (England) 9-5

Group 4: Murdo Macleod (Scotland) beat Bernard Bennett (England) 9-0

Group 5: Mike Watterson (England) beat Clive Everton (Wales) 9-6; Watterson beat Fred Davis (England) 9-6

Group 6: Mike Darrington (England) beat Graham Cripsey (England) 9-3; Mike Hallett (England) beat Darrington 9-1

Group 7: Neal Foulds (England) beat Colin Roscoe (Wales) 9-2; Foulds beat Jim Meadowcroft (England) 9-2

Group 8: Vic Harris (England) beat Pat Houlihan (England) 9-6; Rex Williams (England) beat Harris 9-6

Group 9: Doug French (England) beat Jack Rea (Northern Ireland) 9-5; Dave Martin (England) beat French 9-3

Group 10: Geoff Foulds (England) beat Steve Duggan (England) 9-8; Foulds beat Les Dodd 9-7

Group 11: John Parrott (England) beat George Scott (England) 9-7; Parrott beat Mick Fisher (England) 9-0

Group 12: Roy Andrewartha (Wales) beat Bill Oliver (England) 9-1; John Dunning (England) beat Andrewartha 9-2

Group 13: Tommy Murphy (Northern Ireland) beat Bert Demarco (Scotland) 9-4; Murphy beat Jim Donnelly (Scotland) 9-4

Group 14: Paul Medati (England) beat Dennis Hughes (England) 9-3; Medati beat Ray Edmonds (England) 9-7

Group 15: Bob Harris (England) beat Eddie McLaughlin (Scotland) 9-8; Harris beat Jack Fitzmaurice (England) 9-3

Group 16: Ian Williamson (England) beat John Hargreaves (England) 9-4; Ian Black (Scotland) beat Williamson 9-6

Competition proper

First round: Terry Griffiths (Wales) beat Martin 9-4; Hallett beat Graham Miles (England) 9-4; Johnson beat John Virgo (England) 9-6; David Taylor (England) beat N. Foulds 9-4; Tony Knowles (England) beat Jones 9-5; Doug Mountjoy (Wales) beat Watterson 9-2; Alex Higgins (Northern Ireland) beat Macleod (Scotland) 9-6; Medati beat Dean Reynolds (England) 9-3; Cliff Wilson (Wales) beat Williams 9-4; Ray Reardon (Wales) beat Harris 9-7; Dennis Taylor (Northern Ireland) beat Murphy 9-6; Jimmy White (England) beat Black 9-1; John Spencer (England) beat Dunning 9-7; Tony Meo (England) beat Parrott 9-7; Willie Thorne (England) beat Wildman 9-5; Steve Davis (England) beat G. Foulds 9-1

Second round: Griffiths beat Hallett 9-5; Johnson beat David Taylor 9-3; Knowles beat Mountjoy 9-5; Higgins beat Medati 9-1; Reardon beat Wilson 9-4; White beat Dennis Taylor 9-4; Meo beat Spencer 9-5; Davis beat Thorne 9-3; White beat Reardon 9-4; Griffiths beat Johnson 9-2; Higgins beat Knowles 9-5; Davis beat Meo 9-4

Semi-finals: Higgins beat Griffiths 9-4; Davis beat White 9-4

Final: Higgins beat Davis 16-15

1984

TOTAL PRIZE MONEY: £100,000
FIRST PRIZE: £20,000

Qualifying

Group 1: Tony Jones (England) beat Robert Chaperon (Canada) 9-1; Jones beat Patsy Fagan (Rep. of Ireland) 9-2; Jones beat Mark Wildman (England) 9-2

Group 2: Paul Watchorn (Rep. of Ireland) beat Bob Harris (England) 9-7; Watchorn beat Clive Everton (Wales) 9-6; Mick Fisher (England) beat Watchorn 9-5; Rex Williams (England) beat Fisher 9-8

Group 3: Robbie Foldvari (Australia) beat David Greaves (England) 9-5; Graham Cripsey (England) beat Foldvari 9-7; Jack Fitzmaurice (England) beat Cripsey 9-8; John Parrott (England) beat Fitzmaurice 9-6

Group 4: Peter Francisco (South Africa) beat Dessie Sheehan (Rep. of Ireland) 9-5; P. Francisco beat Ian Williamson (England) 9-2; Eddie Sinclair (Scotland) beat P. Francisco 9-8; Silvino Francisco (South Africa) beat Sinclair 9-4

Group 5: Danny Fowler (England) beat Bert Demarco (Scotland) 9-3; Fowler beat Bill Oliver (England) 9-3; Fowler beat Fred Davis (England) 9-4; Fowler beat Neal Foulds (England) 9-6

Group 6: Dene O'Kane (New Zealand) beat Wayne Jones (Wales) 9-7; O'Kane beat Steve Duggan (England) 9-6; George Scott (England) beat O'Kane 9-7; Murdo Macleod (Scotland) beat Scott 9-5

Group 7: Steve Newbury (Wales) beat Gino Rigitano (Canada) 9-6; Newbury beat Frank Jonik (Canada) 9-3; Les Dodd (England) beat Newbury 9-6; Cliff Wilson (Wales) beat Dodd 9-8

Group 8: Jack McLaughlin (Northern Ireland) beat Doug French (England) 9-3; McLaughlin w.o. Paddy Morgan (Australia) scr; McLaughlin beat Colin Roscoe (Wales) 9-8; McLaughlin beat Graham Miles (England) 9-8

Group 9: Roger Bales (England) beat Dave Chalmers (England) 9-2; Bales beat Eddie McLaughlin (Scotland) 9-4; Marcel Gauvreau (Canada) beat Bales 9-8; Gauvreau beat Perrie Mans (South Africa) 9-6

Group 10: Geoff Foulds (England) beat Dennis Hughes (England) 9-7; Paddy Browne (Rep. of Ireland) beat Foulds 9-5; Warren King (Australia) beat Browne 9-5; King beat John Virgo (England) 9-4

Group 11: John Rea (Scotland) beat Bernard Bennett (England) 9-5; Rea beat John Dunning 9-3; Rea beat Ray Edmonds (England) 9-6; Joe Johnson (England) beat Rea 9-6

Group 12: Tony Chappel (Wales) beat Pat Houlihan (England) 9-3; Chappel beat Ian Black (Scotland) 9-3; Chappel w.o. Roy Andrewartha (Wales) scr; Chappel beat Dean Reynolds 9-6

Group 13: John Hargreaves (England) beat Paul Medati (England) 9-6; Matt Gibson (Scotland) beat Hargreaves 9-8; Jim Donnelly (Scotland) beat Matt Gibson 9-6; John Campbell (Australia) beat Donnelly 9-6

Group 14: Malcolm Bradley (England) beat Vic Harris (England) 9-8; Bradley beat Billy Kelly (Northern Ireland) 9-6; Bradley beat Jim Meadowcroft (England) 9-7; Mike Hallett (England) beat Bradley 9-8

Group 15: Steve Longworth (England) beat Mike Darrington (England) 9-5; Longworth beat Pascal Burke (Rep. of Ireland) 9-4; Mario Morra (Canada) beat Longworth 9-1; Eugene Hughes (Rep. of Ireland) beat Morra 9-8

Group 16: Tommy Murphy (Northern Ireland) beat Tony Kearney (Rep. of Ireland) 9-2; Murphy beat Mike Watterson (England) 9-4; Murphy beat Dave Martin (England) 9-8

Competition Proper

First round: Alex Higgins (Northern Ireland) beat T. Jones 9-7; Steve Davis (England) beat Murphy 9-1; Jimmy White (England) beat Campbell 9-7; Williams beat Bill Werbeniuk (Canada) 9-1; Willie Thorne (England) beat Parrott 9-7; Eddie Charlton (Australia) beat S. Francisco 9-4; Doug Mountjoy (Wales) beat Hallett 9-2; Tony Meo (England) beat E. Hughes 9-4; Ray Reardon (Wales) beat Fowler 9-2; Kirk Stevens (Canada) beat Chappel 9-7; Dennis Taylor beat King 9-5; Wilson beat Terry Griffiths (Wales) 9-6; Johnson beat John Spencer (England) 9-6; David Taylor (England) beat Macleod 9-6; Tony Knowles (England) beat Gauvreau 9-5; Cliff Thorburn (Canada) beat J. McLaughlin 9-4

Second round: Thorne beat Charlton 9-7; White beat Mountjoy 9-2; Higgins beat Williams 9-7; Stevens beat Johnson 9-2; Reardon beat David Taylor 9-4; Knowles beat Dennis Taylor 9-2; Thorburn beat Wilson 9-3; Davis beat Meo 9-7

Quarter-finals: Higgins beat Thorne 9-5; Davis beat White 9-4; Thorburn beat Reardon 9-8; Stevens beat Knowles 9-7

Semi-finals: Higgins beat Thorburn 9-7; Davis beat Stevens 9-7

Final: Davis beat Higgins 16-8

Steve Davis: Coral UK champion

Hofmeister World Doubles Championship

TOTAL PRIZE MONEY: £175,000
FIRST PRIZE: £40,000
ENTRIES: Open to all professionals
TELEVISION: ITV

Steve Davis and Tony Meo won the title for the third time in four years although the impact of the event on the public was much diminished by the industrial action which prevented a single ball of the final being shown on ITV. Earlier coverage of the event had also been disrupted.

The defending champions, Alex Higgins and Jimmy White, failed to reach the televised phase of the championship at the Derngate Centre, Northampton. They were beaten 5-4 in the preliminary phase at the Ladbroke International Hotel, Birmingham, by Barry West and Danny Fowler who, on television, recovered from 0-4 to 4-4 against Perrie Mans and John Campbell before the South African/Australian combination won the deciding frame.

By this time, however, snooker coverage had yielded to darts and the climax of the match was not shown, an example of the lack of flexibility in ITV's sports coverage as opposed to the BBC's.

There was one exceptionally exciting match in the last 16 in which the Welsh mentor/protégé combination of Doug Mountjoy and Wayne Jones prevailed 5-4 only on the final black over Tony Knowles and Joe Johnson after leading by 30 with only the last four colours remaining in the decider.

Eddie Charlton and Bill Werbeniuk, who had helped set a new record duration for a professional tournament frame of 76 minutes in their 5-4 victory over Jim Bear and Les Dodd at Birmingham, were involved in another marathon at Northampton against Neal Foulds and John Parrott with the younger pair recovering from 1-4 to win 5-4 after 4 hours 20 minutes play.

However, the heroes of the competition proved to be a new combination, Ray Reardon and Tony Jones. Reardon, so out of form that he had won only one match in five British tournaments, played the tactical containing role while Jones, talented but inexperienced at this level, did most of the scoring.

Their run to the final included a 5-4 quarter-final victory over Mans and Campbell and a surprise 9-6 defeat of Dennis Taylor and Terry Griffiths in the semi-finals before Davis and Meo proved too strong for them in what was largely a sedate final.

Finalists in the 1985 Hofmeister World Doubles: Tony Jones (left) and Ray Reardon v Steve Davis and Tony Meo (right). The referee is Peter Koniotes

First round: Paul Watchorn (Rep. of Ireland) and Dessie Sheehan (Rep. of Ireland) beat David Greaves (England) and Greg Jenkins (Australia) 5-4; Graham Cripsey (England) and Glen Wilkinson (Australia) beat Pat Houlihan (England) and Bernard Bennett (England) 5-2; Roger Bales (England) and Jack McLaughlin (Northern Ireland) beat Sakchai Simnagm (Thailand) and Omprakesh Agrawal (India) 5-3; John Hargreaves (England) and Pascal Burke (Rep. of Ireland) beat Tony Drago (Malta) and Joe O'Boye (Rep. of Ireland) 5-3

Second round: Danny Fowler (England) and Barry West (England) beat Robert Chaperon (Canada) and Marcel Gauvreau (Canada) 5-4; Perrie Mans (South Africa) and John Campbell (Australia) beat Watchorn and Sheehan 5-1; Paul Medati (England) and Paddy Browne (Rep. of Ireland) beat Robbie Foldvari (Australia) and Mick Fisher (England) 5-3; Cripsey and Wilkinson beat Matt Gibson (Scotland) and Dene O'Kane (New Zealand) 5-4; Tommy Murphy (Northern Ireland) and Patsy Fagan (Rep. of Ireland) beat Tony Kearney (Rep. of Ireland) and Dennis Hughes (England) 5-2; Malcolm Bradley (England) and Dave Chalmers (England) beat Bill Oliver (England) and Mike Darrington (England) 5-4; Bales and J. McLaughlin beat Bernie Mikkelsen (Canada) and Jim Meadowcroft (England) 5-4; Mark Wildman (England) and Ray Edmonds (England) beat Stephen Hendry (Scotland) and Gino Rigitano (Canada) 5-3; Tony Chappel (Wales) and Frank Jonik (Canada) beat Eddie Sinclair (Scotland) and Ian Black (Scotland) 5-1; Ian Williamson (England) and Steve Duggan (England) beat Dave Gilbert (England) and Bob Harris (England) 5-1; Mike Watterson (England) and Fred Davis (England) w.o Jack Fitzmaurice (England) and Vic Harris (England) scr; Dean Reynolds (England) and Steve Longworth (England) beat Jimmy van Rensburg (South Africa) and Derek Mienie (South Africa) 5-4; Jim Bear (Canada) and Les Dodd (England) beat Mario Morra (Canada) and Jim Wych (Canada) 5-1; Jim Donnelly (Scotland) and Colin Roscoe (Wales) beat Hargreaves and Burke 5-4; John Rea (Scotland) and Eddie McLaughlin (Scotland) beat George Scott (England) and Geoff Foulds (England) 5-0; Rex Williams (England) and Graham Miles (England) w.o. John Dunning (England) and Bert Demarco (Scotland) scr

Third round: Fowler and West beat Alex Higgins (Northern Ireland) and Jimmy White (England) 5-4; Mans and Campbell beat Dave Martin (England) and Murdo Macleod (Scotland) 5-3; Mike Hallett (England) and David Taylor (England) beat Medati and Browne 5-4; Tony Jones (England) and Ray Reardon (Wales) beat Cripsey and Wilkinson 5-3; Tony Knowles (England) and Joe Johnson (England) beat Murphy and Fagan 5-2; Wayne Jones (Wales) and Doug Mountjoy (Wales) beat Bradley and Chalmers 5-2; John Spencer (England) and Steve Newbury (Wales) beat Bales and J. McLaughlin 5-4; Terry Griffiths (Wales) and Dennis Taylor (Northern Ireland) beat Wildman and Edmonds 5-4; Cliff Thorburn (Canada) and Willie Thorne (England) beat Chappel and Jonik 5-1; Warren King (Australia) and Cliff Wilson (Wales) beat Williamson and Duggan 5-3; Peter Francisco (South Africa) and Silvino Francisco (South Africa) beat Watterson and Davis 5-0; John Virgo (England) and Kirk Stevens (Canada) beat Reynolds and Longworth 5-0; Eddie Charlton (Australia) and Bill Werbeniuk (Canada) beat Jim Bear and Dodd 5-4; Neal Foulds (England) and John Parrott (England) beat Donnelly and Roscoe 5-1; Eugene Hughes (Rep. of Ireland) and Martin Smith (England) beat John Rea and E. McLaughlin 5-4; Steve Davis (England) and Tony Meo (England) beat Williams and Miles 5-2

Fourth round: Mans and Campbell beat Fowler and West 5-4; T. Jones and Reardon beat Hallett and David Taylor 5-0; W. Jones and Mountjoy beat Knowles and Johnson 5-4; Griffiths and Dennis Taylor beat Spencer and Newbury 5-0; Thorburn and Thorne beat King and Wilson 5-2; P. Francisco and S. Francisco beat Virgo and Stevens 5-3; N. Foulds and Parrott beat Charlton and Werbeniuk 5-4; S. Davis and Meo beat E. Hughes and Smith 5-1

Quarter-finals: T. Jones and Reardon beat Mans and Campbell 5-4; Griffiths and Dennis Taylor beat W. Jones and Mountjoy 5-2; Thorburn and Thorne beat P. Francisco and S. Francisco 5-3; S. Davis and Meo beat N. Foulds and Parrott 5-3

Semi-finals: T. Jones and Reardon beat Griffiths and Dennis Taylor 9-6; S. Davis and Meo beat Thorburn and Thorne 9-6

Final: S. Davis and Meo beat T. Jones and Reardon 12-5

Previous Years

Doubles (or pairs) snooker has always been popular at amateur level but, apart from a couple of week-long challenge matches in the fifties featuring Joe and Fred Davis, John Pulman and Walter Donaldson, the four best players at that time, it was an unknown quantity in terms of a professional tournament.

Sports Sponsorship International, promoters new to snooker, sensed that the rapid growth in the number of active professionals, from around a couple of dozen in 1978 to almost 100, made a world doubles championship a realistic possibility.

ITV, seeking some variant of single combat/knock-out tournaments in the pursuit of a wider involvement in professional snooker, agreed an authentic new world championship was worth a try and sponsorship was quickly forthcoming from Hofmeister.

The inaugural championship suffered from small crowds and an inappropriate venue, but its second and third years provided enough compensating success to assure it of maintaining a valued place in the calendar.

A change of venue from the National Sports Centre, Crystal Palace, a vast, remote, cold sports hall inaccessibly sited on the outskirts of London, to the plush, modern, theatrical setting of the Derngate Centre, Northampton, made all the difference.

On the table, the mixture was as before: Steve Davis and Tony Meo retained their title by beating Tony Knowles and Jimmy White 10-2, just as emphatically as they had won it the year before when they beat Terry Griffiths and Doug Mountjoy 13-2; but in every other respect the second championship was a class apart from the first.

In their 9-1 semi-final defeat of Eddie Charlton and Bill Werbeniuk, a total clearance of 140 by Davis and a 56 clearance by Meo made the combined highest breaks by partners in the same match and fetched a £2,000 prize.

Runners-up, Tony Knowles and Jimmy White, beat Cliff Thorburn and John Virgo 9-7 in their semi-finals, which turned on an unusual incident. At 7-7 Knowles committed a foul and was asked by Virgo, who was due to play next, to play again. This in some way confused the Virgo/Thorburn partnership. Thorburn took the next shot, was penalized for playing out of turn and from the position left White won the frame with a break of 74.

With another partner, Alex Higgins, White went one better the following year by taking the title with an overwhelming 10-2 victory over another new partnership, Thorburn and Willie Thorne, in the final.

Davis and Meo's two-year tenure of the title was ended in the semi-finals by Higgins and White, a virtuoso display from Higgins carrying his side from 6-6 to victory at 9-6.

1982

TOTAL PRIZE MONEY: £60,000
FIRST PRIZE: £24,000

Qualifying

Group 1: Joe Johnson (England) and Cliff Wilson (Wales) w.o. Mario Morra (Canada) and Frank Jonik (Canada) scr; Johnson and Wilson beat

Ray Edmonds (England) and Jim Meadowcroft (England) 6-4; Ray Reardon (Wales) and John Spencer (England) beat Johnson and Wilson 6-2

Group 2: Dave Martin (England) and Dennis Taylor (Northern Ireland) beat Les Dodd (England) and Doug French (England) 6-2; Terry Griffiths (Wales) and Doug Mountjoy (Wales) beat Martin and Dennis Taylor 6-0

Group 3: Fred Davis (England) and Paul Medati (England) beat John Dunning (England) and Bert Demarco (Scotland) 6-0; Alex Higgins (Northern Ireland) and Eddie Charlton (Australia) beat Davis and Medati 6-3

Group 4: Pat Houlihan (England) and Bernard Bennett (England) beat Eddie Sinclair (Scotland) and Ian Black (Scotland) 6-2; Dean Reynolds (England) and Mike Watterson (England) beat Houlihan and Bennett 6-3; Steve Davis (England) and Tony Meo (England) beat Reynolds and Watterson 6-3

Group 5: Mike Hallett (England) and Graham Cripsey (England) beat Murdo Macleod (Scotland) and Eddie McLaughlin (Scotland) 6-3; Hallett and Cripsey beat Patsy Fagan (Rep. of Ireland) and Geoff Foulds (England) 6-2; Kirk Stevens (Canada) and Jim Wych (Canada) beat Hallett and Cripsey 6-4

Group 6: Vic Harris (England) and Ian Williamson (England) beat Tommy Murphy (Northern Ireland) and Eugene Hughes (Rep. of Ireland) 6-1; Rex Williams (England) and Jack Fitzmaurice (England) beat Harris and Williamson 6-1; Graham Miles (England) and Bill Werbeniuk (Canada) beat Williams and Fitzmaurice 6-5

Group 7: Jimmy White (England) and Tony Knowles (England) beat George Scott (England) and Dennis Hughes (England) 6-2; White and Knowles beat David Taylor (England) and Willie Thorne (England) 6-1

Steve Davis (left) and Tony Meo have won the Hofmeister World Doubles title three times in four years

Group 8: Mick Fisher (England) and Mark Wildman (England) beat Clive Everton (Wales) and Colin Roscoe (Wales) 6-3; Fisher and Wildman beat Jim Donnelly (Scotland) and Matt Gibson (Scotland) 6-5; Cliff Thorburn (Canada) and John Virgo (England) beat Fisher and Wildman 6-2

Quarter-finals: Griffiths and Mountjoy beat Stevens and Wych 6-1; Davis and Meo beat Thorburn and Virgo 6-2; White and Knowles beat Reardon and Spencer 6-2; Higgins and Charlton beat Miles and Werbeniuk 6-3

Semi-finals: Griffiths and Mountjoy beat Charlton and Higgins 10-7; David and Meo beat White and Knowles 10-5

Final: Davis and Meo beat Griffiths and Mountjoy 13-2

1983

TOTAL PRIZE MONEY: £75,000
FIRST PRIZE: £25,000

Pre-qualifying: Bernard Bennett (England) and Pat Houlihan (England) beat Matt Gibson (Scotland) and Murdo Macleod (Scotland) 5-2; Steve Duggan (England) and John Hargreaves (England) beat Bill Oliver (England) and Paddy Browne (Rep. of Ireland) 5-1; George Scott (England) and John Parrott (England) beat Geoff Foulds (England) and Neal Foulds (England) 5-4; Bob Harris (England) and Mario Morra (Canada) beat Dessie Sheehan (Rep. of Ireland) and Eddie McLaughlin (Scotland) 5-2

Qualifying: Tommy Murphy (Northern Ireland) and Paddy Morgan (Australia) beat Pascal Burke (Rep. of Ireland) and Dave Martin (England) 5-4; Jack Fitzmaurice (England) and Vic Harris (England) beat Bennett and Houlihan 5-4; Jim Donnelly (Scotland) and Colin Roscoe (Wales) beat Warren King (Australia) and John Campbell (Australia) 5-3; Duggan and Hargreaves beat Dennis Hughes (England) and Billy Kelly (Rep. of Ireland) 5-0; John Dunning (England) and Bert Demarco (Scotland) beat Mike Hallett (England) and Graham Cripsey (England) 5-4; Ray Edmonds (England) and Jim Meadowcroft (England) beat Doug French (England) and Clive Everton (Wales) 5-2; Eugene Hughes (Rep. of Ireland) and Les Dodd (England) beat Scott and Parrott 5-2; B. Harris and Morra beat Mike Darrington (England) and Ian Williamson (England) 5-1

First round: Murphy and Morgan beat Ian Black (Scotland) and Eddie Sinclair (Scotland) 5-1; Dennis Taylor (Northern Ireland) and Rex Williams (England) beat Fitzmaurice and V. Harris 5-1; Tony Jones (England) and Silvino Francisco (South Africa) beat Donnelly and Roscoe 5-2; Graham Miles (England) and George Ganim Jr (Australia) beat Duggan and Hargreaves 5-3; Fred Davis (England) and Mike Watterson (England) beat Dunning and Demarco 5-3; Dean Reynolds (England) and Patsy Fagan (Rep. of Ireland) beat Edmonds and Meadowcroft 5-0; Hughes and Dodd beat Cliff Wilson (Wales) and Joe Johnson (England) 5-1; B. Harris and Morra beat Mick Fisher (England) and Mark Wildman (England) 5-2

Second round: Steve Davis (England) and Tony Meo (England) beat Murphy and Morgan 5-2; David Taylor (England) and Willie Thorne (England) beat Dennis Taylor and Williams 5-4; Eddie Charlton (Australia) and Bill Werbeniuk (Canada) beat Jones and Francisco 5-3; Alex Higgins (Northern Ireland) and Kirk Stevens (Canada) w.o. Miles and Ganim scr; Ray Reardon (Wales) and John Spencer (England) beat Davis and Watterson 5-2; John Virgo (England) and Cliff Thorburn (Canada) beat Reynolds and Fagan 5-2; Doug Mountjoy (Wales) and Terry Griffiths (Wales) beat Hughes and Dodd 5-3; Tony Knowles (England) and Jimmy White (England) beat B. Harris and Morra 5-4

Quarter-finals: Davis and Meo beat Taylor and Thorne 5-3; Charlton and Werbeniuk beat Higgins and Stevens 5-1; Thorburn and Virgo beat Reardon and Spencer 5-0; Knowles and White beat Mountjoy and Griffiths 5-0

Semi-finals: Davis and Meo beat Charlton and Werbeniuk 9-1; Knowles and White beat Thorburn and Virgo 9-7

Final: Davis and Meo beat Knowles and White 10-2

Tony Jones and Ray Reardon pulled off a surprise semi-final victory over Dennis Taylor and Terry Griffiths. Len Ganley was the referee

1984

TOTAL PRIZE MONEY: £150,000
FIRST PRIZE: £34,500

Qualifying: Jim Donnelly (Scotland) and Colin Roscoe (Wales) beat Steve Longworth (England) and Doug French (England) 5-3; Dave Chalmers (England) and Jack McLaughlin (Northern Ireland) beat Patsy Fagan (Rep. of Ireland) and Bob Harris (England) 5-0; Mario Morra (Canada) and Malcolm Bradley (England) beat Ian Williamson (England) and Mike Darrington (England) 5-1; Graham Miles (England) and Peter Francisco (South Africa) beat John Hargreaves (England) and Steve Duggan (England) 5-1; Tony Chappel (Wales) and Steve Newbury (Wales) beat Gino Rigitano (Canada) and George Scott (England) 5-0; Marcel Gauvreau (Canada) and Danny Fowler (England) beat Bernard Bennett (England) and Pat Houlihan (England) 5-1; Roger Bales (England) and Bill Oliver beat John Rea (Scotland) and Eddie McLaughlin (Scotland) 5-2; Jim Meadowcroft (England) and Ray Edmonds (England) beat Frank Jonik (Canada) and Robert Chaperon (Canada) 5-4; Vic Harris (England) and Jack Fitzmaurice (England) beat Pascal Burke (Eire) and Billy Kelly (Northern Ireland) 5-2; Dessie Sheehan (Rep. of Ireland) and Paul Watchorn (Rep. of Ireland) beat Murdo Macleod (Scotland) and Matt Gibson (Scotland) 5-0; Mike Watterson (England) and Fred Davis (England) beat Clive Everton (Wales) and Robbie Foldvari (Australia) 5-3; Paul Medati (England) and Paddy Browne (Rep. of Ireland) beat Ian Black (Scotland) and Eddie Sinclair (Scotland) 5-1; Dennis Hughes (England) and Tony Kearney (Rep. of Ireland) w.o. John Dunning (England) and Bert Demarco (Scotland) scr

First round: Doug Mountjoy (Wales) and Wayne Jones (Wales) beat Chappel and Newbury 5-1; Silvino Francisco (South Africa) and Tony Jones (England) beat John Campbell (Australia) and Warren King (Australia) 5-4; Alex Higgins (Northern Ireland) and Jimmy White (England) beat Dave Martin (England) and Graham Cripsey (England) 5-2; David Taylor (England) and Mike Hallett (England) beat Eugene Hughes (Rep. of Ireland) and Les Dodd (England) 5-3; P. Francisco and Miles beat Cliff Wilson (Wales) and Joe Johnson (England) 5-4; Dean Reynolds (England) and Dene O'Kane (New Zealand) beat Gauvreau and Fowler 5-4; Dennis Taylor (Northern Ireland) and Rex Williams (England) beat Medati and Browne 5-0; Bales and Oliver beat Geoff Foulds (England) and Neal Foulds (England) 5-2; Steve Davis (England) and Tony Meo (England) beat Hughes and Kearney 5-2; Ray Reardon (Wales) and Tommy Murphy (Northern Ireland) beat Watterson and F. Davis 5-2; Mark Wildman (England) and Mick Fisher (England) beat Edmonds and Meadowcroft 5-3; Eddie Charlton (Australia) and Bill Werbeniuk (Canada) beat Sheehan and Watchorn 5-2; Terry Griffiths (Wales) and John Parrott (England) beat Chalmers and J. McLaughlin 5-0; John Virgo (England) and Kirk Stevens (Canada) beat Donnelly and Roscoe 5-0; Cliff Thorburn (Canada) and Willie Thorne (England) beat Morra and Bradley 5-1; Tony Knowles (England) and John Spencer (England) beat V. Harris and Fitzmaurice 5-2

Second round: Davis and Meo beat Miles and Francisco 5-2; Virgo and Stevens beat Dennis Taylor and Williams 5-3; Higgins and White beat Reynolds and O'Kane 5-4; Thorburn and Thorne beat Mountjoy and Jones 5-3; Reardon and Murphy beat S. Francisco and T. Jones 5-3; Griffiths and Parrott beat Bales and Oliver 5-4; David Taylor and Hallett beat Charlton and Werbeniuk 5-4; Knowles and Spencer beat Fisher and Wildman 5-4

Quarter-finals: Knowles and Spencer beat Reardon and Murphy 5-4; Higgins and White beat Griffiths and Parrott 5-2; Thorburn and Thorne beat Virgo and Stevens 5-3; Davis and Meo beat Hallett and David Taylor 5-1

Semi-finals: Thorburn and Thorne beat Knowles and Spencer 9-1; Higgins and White beat Davis and Meo 9-6

Final: Higgins and White beat Thorburn and Thorne 10-2

Kit Kat Break for World Champions

As television cannot screen snooker every day of the winter, there is clearly scope for non-televised tournaments. The Kit Kat Break for World Champions, the brainchild of Roger Lee, brought together the eight winners of the world professional title still playing professionally and a ninth, John Pulman, was at the East Midlands Conference Centre, Nottingham, in a public relations role.

The prize money – £30,000, with £10,000 going to the winner – was substantial by non-televised standards but neither the money nor the title generated quite the incentive, in a demanding season, of a world ranking or televised event. This is hardly a criticism of the players, merely a statement of the realities.

Dennis Taylor's 9-5 win over Steve Davis in the final therefore generated a mere fraction of the tension that had been in the air in their two previous finals since the 1985 world final, Davis winning the Rothmans Grand Prix 10-9 and Taylor prevailing in the Canadian Masters 9-5.

The sponsorship was not renewed for the 1986-87 season.

First round: Dennis Taylor (Northern Ireland) beat Fred Davis (England) 5-0; Terry Griffiths (Wales) beat Ray Reardon (Wales) 5-2; Steve Davis (England) beat John Spencer (England) 5-2; Alex Higgins (Northern Ireland) beat Cliff Thorburn (Canada) 5-4

Semi-finals: Dennis Taylor beat Griffths 6-4; S. Davis beat Higgins 6-1

Final: Dennis Taylor beat S. Davis 9-5

The nine living world champions assembled for this unique picture at the Kit Kat Break For World Champions. From left to right: John Williams (referee), Fred Davis, John Pulman, John Spencer, Roger Lee (organiser), Ray Reardon, Alex Higgins, Robert Winsor, Terry Griffiths, Cliff Thorburn, Steve Davis, Dennis Taylor, and Jim Thorpe (referee). Joe Johnson added his name to the World trophy four months later

Mercantile Credit Classic

TOTAL PRIZE MONEY: £225,000
FIRST PRIZE: £45,000
ENTRIES: Open to all professionals
TELEVISION: ITV

Jimmy White captured the £45,000 first prize in unlikely circumstances at the Spectrum Arena, Warrington, by beating Cliff Thorburn 13-12 after needing a snooker with only pink and black remaining in the deciding frame.

White had led 4-0 but trailed 4-6 after conceding the eighth frame, the first of the evening, through late arrival.

Thorburn led 8-5 but from 7-9 White won four frames in a row to lead 11-9 before the match came to its memorable climax.

Off the table, Alex Higgins made the headlines not so much through beating Dennis Taylor 5-4 in the last 16 but by sporting a black eye as he did so. He claimed on ITV that he had been kicked by a horse called Dreadnought but it transpired that he had been involved in a fist fight. All this happened in the context of the final disintegration of his turbulent marriage, reported in graphic detail by the tabloid press.

After losing 5-2 to Rex Williams, chairman of the WPBSA, in the quarter-finals, Higgins erupted in a childish tantrum but with a man's vehemence in threatening to 'take the lid off snooker' if the price was right. He later withdrew this threat but this and other backstage incidents resulted in him being hauled before a WPBSA disciplinary tribunal.

Meanwhile, Williams, who had earlier beaten Tony Knowles, went on to extend White to 9-7 in the semi-finals after White had beaten Davis in the quarters.

Willie Thorne fell at the first fence in defence of his title to Tony Jones in the pre-televised phase of the competition. Dennis Taylor earned his appearance in the televised last 16 only by virtue of the 48 clearance which gave him a black ball deciding-frame victory over Dean Reynolds.

First round: Dave Gilbert (England) beat Gerry Watson (Canada) 5-4; Tony Kearney (Rep. of Ireland) beat Jim Bear (Canada) 5-0; Stephen Hendry (Scotland) beat Dessie Sheehan (Rep. of Ireland) 5-2; Bert Demarco (Scotland) beat Omprakesh Agrawal (India) 5-4; Martin Smith (England) beat Derek Mienie (South Africa) 5-1; Joe O'Boye (Rep. of Ireland) beat Glen Wilkinson (Australia) 5-1; Barry West (England) beat Mike Darrington (England) 5-0; Pascal Burke (Rep. of Ireland) beat Dennis Hughes (England) 5-3; Roger Bales (England) beat Maurice Parkin (England) 5-0; David Greaves (England) beat Paul Watchorn (Rep. of Ireland) 5-4; Greg Jenkins (Australia) w.o Gordon Robinson (Australia) scr; Graham Cripsey (England) beat Tony Drago (Malta) 5-4; Pat Houlihan (England) beat Bernard Bennett (England) 5-0

Second round: Tony Jones (England) beat Gilbert 5-3; Geoff Foulds (England) beat Ian Black (Scotland) 5-2; Warren King (Australia) beat Steve Duggan (England) 5-2; Paul Medati (England) beat Kearney 5-2; Hendry beat Graham Miles (England) 5-1; Malcolm Bradley (England) beat Bill Oliver (England) 5-3; Bernie Mikkelsen (Canada) beat George Scott (England) 5-1; Jim Donnelly (Scotland) beat Dave Chalmers (England) 5-0; Fred Davis (England) beat Billy Kelly (Rep. of Ireland) 5-3; Jim Wych (Canada) beat Demarco 5-0; Bob Harris (England) beat Mario Morra (Canada) 5-3; Smith beat Ray Edmonds (England) 5-2; O'Boye beat Steve Longworth (England) 5-1; West beat Jim Meadowcroft (England) 5-0; Jack McLaughlin (Northern Ireland) beat Eddie McLaughlin (Scotland) 5-2; John Rea (Scotland) beat Ian Williamson (England) 5-4; Robert Chaperon (Canada) beat Burke 5-2; Jimmy van Rensburg (South Africa) beat Wayne Jones (Wales) 5-4; Peter Francisco (South Africa) beat Frank Jonik (Canada) 5-2; Tommy Murphy (Northern Ireland) beat Tony Chappel (Wales) 5-4; Marcel Gauvreau (Canada) beat Sakchai Simnagm (Thailand) 5-1; Paddy Browne (Rep. of Ireland) beat Clive Everton (Wales) 5-0; Danny Fowler (England) beat Bales 5-4; Matt Gibson (Scotland) w.o. John Dunning (England) scr; Gino Rigitano (Canada) beat Les Dodd (England) 5-3; Eddie Sinclair (Scotland) beat Greaves 5-1; Vic Harris (England) beat Colin Roscoe (Wales) 5-1; Mike Watterson (England) beat Jenkins 5-2; Mick Fisher (England) beat Jack Rea (Northern Ireland) 5-3; Cripsey beat Steve Newbury (Wales) 5-4; Jack Fitzmaurice (England) beat Patsy Fagan (Rep. of Ireland) 5-3; Houlihan beat Robbie Foldvari (Australia) 5-4

Third round: T. Jones beat Willie Thorne (England) 5-3; Bill Werbeniuk (Canada) beat G. Foulds 5-3; Doug Mountjoy (Wales) beat King 5-4; Dene O'Kane (New Zealand) beat Medati 5-0; Hendry beat Silvino Francisco (South Africa) 5-4; Neal Foulds (England) beat Bradley 5-3; Mikkelsen beat Ray Reardon (Wales) 5-3; John Campbell (Australia) beat Donnelly 5-2; F. Davis beat Kirk Stevens (Canada) 5-2; Eugene Hughes (Rep. of Ireland) beat Wych 5-2; Joe Johnson (England) beat B. Harris 5-4; Perrie Mans (South Africa) beat Smith 5-4; Tony Meo (England) beat O'Boye 5-3; West beat Mark Wildman (England) 5-2; Cliff Thorburn (Canada) beat J. McLaughlin 5-1; Mike Hallett (England) beat John Rea 5-2; Steve Davis (England) beat Chaperon 5-1; van Rensburg beat John Parrott (England) 5-3; P. Francisco beat Eddie Charlton (Australia) 5-1; D. Martin (England) beat Murphy 5-3; Gauvreau beat David Taylor (England) 5-3; Browne beat Cliff Wilson (Wales) 5-3; Jimmy White (England) beat Fowler 5-1; John Virgo (England) beat Gibson 5-3; Tony Knowles (England) beat Rigitano 5-4; Murdo Macleod (Scotland) beat Sinclair 5-2; V. Harris beat Terry Griffiths (Wales) 5-3; Rex Williams (England) beat Watterson 5-0; Alex Higgins (Northern Ireland) beat Fisher 5-0; Cripsey beat John Spencer (England) 5-1; Dennis Taylor (Northern Ireland) beat Fitzmaurice 5-1; Dean Reynolds (England) beat Houlihan 5-1

Fourth round: Werbeniuk beat T. Jones 5-3; Mountjoy beat O'Kane 5-3; N. Foulds beat Hendry 5-4; Campbell beat Mikkelsen 5-2; E. Hughes beat F. Davis 5-3; Johnson beat Mans 5-2; Meo beat West 5-1; Thorburn beat Hallett 5-3; S. Davis beat van Rensburg 5-3; P. Francisco beat Martin 5-2; Gauvreau beat Browne 5-3; White beat Virgo 5-2; Knowles beat Macleod 5-4; Williams beat V. Harris 5-1; Higgins beat Cripsey 5-2; Taylor beat Reynolds 5-4

Fifth round: Mountjoy beat Werbeniuk 5-3; N. Foulds beat Campbell 5-1; Johnson beat E. Hughes 5-1; Thorburn beat Meo 5-1; S. Davis beat P. Francisco 5-0; White beat Gauvreau 5-2; Williams beat Knowles 5-2; Higgins beat Dennis Taylor 5-4

Quarter-finals: Mountjoy beat N. Foulds 5-3; Thorburn beat Johnson 5-4; White beat S. Davis 5-2; Williams beat Higgins 5-2

Semi-finals: Thorburn beat Mountjoy 9-6; White beat Williams 9-7

Final: White beat Thorburn 13-12

Previous Years

Granada's wish to show its own home-produced tournament in its own area led to the promotion of the first Wilson's Classic in January 1980, which was won by John Spencer, and the second in December that year, which was won by Steve Davis.

The event was packaged into a seven-part series for weekly showing but press coverage of the matches, inevitable from any venue where the public is charged for admission, lessened its dramatic impact compared with tournaments which received live or, at least, same-day television coverage.

There was also a growing feeling that the event might appropriately be shown in other regions but Wilson's, the Lancashire brewers, had nothing to gain from the tournament being shown outside Granada-land and decided not to renew their sponsorship.

Only at the eleventh hour were Lada, the Russian car company, secured as sponsors for the January 1982 event.

The precise extent of coverage outside Granada's area was uncertain when Lada agreed a sponsorship of £15,000, an arrangement which turned into the bargain of the year when Steve Davis, jet-lagged from a round-the-world trip, compiled against John Spencer the first 147 maximum (fifteen reds, fifteen blacks and all the colours) to be seen in a television tournament.

(By a supreme irony, Spencer had made a 147 in the Holsten Lager tournament, at Slough in January 1979, but during a period when the camera crew was absent owing to union regulations over hours. It is for this reason that camera crews have sufficient manpower now to cover every frame.)

Davis's history-making break made the tournament's name and there was another bonus when Terry Griffiths beat Davis 9-8 on the final black in a memorable final.

The following year, as ITV decided to network the whole eight days of the event, Lada increased the prize money to £65,000 and extended the field from eight to sixteen. In 1984 this was further increased to £75,000 and the event was thrown open to all professionals, thus enabling players to earn world ranking points from it.

Steve Davis beat Bill Werbeniuk in the 1983 final and Tony Meo 9-8 in a highly dramatic 1984 final at the Spectrum Arena, Warrington.

In the decider, Meo needed only a straightforward yellow to pink clearance to clinch his first major individual title but was cruelly distracted as he attempted the yellow by a spectator's untimely shout of 'Come on, Tony.'

Davis was also forced to deciding frames in order to beat Terry Griffiths 5-4 in the quarter-finals and John Parrott, the 19-year-old Merseysider, 5-4 in an epic semi-final, for which 2,000 spectators crammed into the event's magnificent venue.

Parrott, in his first season as a professional, made his name with the television public with his victories over Doug Mountjoy, Alex Higgins and Tony Knowles.

In 1985, in the first year of Mercantile Credit's sponsorship, Willie Thorne captured the £40,000 first prize by following his dramatic 9-8 semi-final victory over Davis with a 13-8 final success over Thorburn.

1982

TOTAL PRIZE MONEY: £15,000
FIRST PRIZE: £5,000

First round: Terry Griffiths (Wales) beat Cliff Thorburn (Canada) 5-1; Alex Higgins (Northern Ireland) beat Dennis Taylor (Northern Ireland) 5-1; Ray Reardon (Wales) beat David Taylor (England) 5-1; Steve Davis (England) beat John Spencer (England) 5-2

Semi-finals: Griffiths beat Higgins 5-1; Davis beat Reardon 5-4

Final: Griffiths beat Davis 9-8

1983

TOTAL PRIZE MONEY: £65,000
FIRST PRIZE: £16,000

First round: Eddie Charlton (Australia) beat John Virgo (England) 5-2; John Spencer (England) beat Ray Reardon (Wales) 5-3; Cliff Thorburn (Canada) beat Cliff Wilson (Wales) 5-3; Doug Mountjoy (Wales) beat Terry Griffiths (Wales) 5-1; David Taylor (England) beat Jimmy White (England) 5-3; Bill Werbeniuk (Canada) beat Alex Higgins (Northern Ireland) 5-4; Kirk Stevens (Canada) beat Tony Knowles (England) 5-0; Steve Davis (England) beat Dennis Taylor (Northern Ireland) 5-2

Quarter-finals: Spencer beat David Taylor 5-2; Werbeniuk beat Mountjoy 5-2; Stevens beat Thorburn 5-3; Davis beat Charlton 5-4

Semi-finals: Davis beat Spencer 5-4; Werbeniuk beat Stevens 5-2

Final: Davis beat Werbeniuk 9-5

1984

TOTAL PRIZE MONEY: £75,000
FIRST PRIZE: £18,000

Qualifying

First round: Geoff Foulds (England) beat Marcel Gauvreau (Canada) 5-2; Bert Demarco (Scotland) beat Matt Gibson (Scotland) 5-2; Neal Foulds (England) beat Pat Houlihan (England) 5-3; Mario Morra (Canada) beat Pascal Burke (Rep. of Ireland) 5-2; George Ganim Jr (Australia) beat Dennis Hughes (England) 5-2; Ian Williamson (England) beat Doug French (England) 5-1; John Hargreaves (England) beat Warren King (Australia) 5-3; Bill Oliver (England) beat Dessie Sheehan (Rep. of Ireland) 5-3; Paddy Morgan (Australia) beat Mike Darrington (England) 5-3; Tony Jones (England) beat Paul Mifsud (Malta) 5-3; Graham Cripsey (England) beat Vic Harris (England) 5-4; John Parrott (England) beat Bernard Bennett (England) 5-0; Paddy Browne (Rep. of Ireland) beat David Greaves (England) 5-2; Paul Watchorn (Rep. of Ireland) beat Roy Andrewartha (Wales) 5-2; Steve Duggan (England) beat Bob Harris (England) 5-2; Paul Medati (England) beat Tommy Murphy (Northern Ireland) 5-4

Second round: Eddie McLaughlin (Scotland) beat G. Foulds 5-1; George Scott (England) beat Demarco 5-2; N. Foulds beat Jack Rea (Northern Ireland) 5-1; Morra beat Clive Everton (Wales) 5-0; Colin Roscoe (Wales) beat Ganim 5-3; Frank Jonik (Canada) beat Williamson 5-1; Hargreaves beat Billy Kelly (Rep. of Ireland) 5-4; Oliver beat Jim Donnelly (Scotland) 5-4; Morgan beat Mike Watterson (England) 5-3; Jones beat Ian Black (Scotland) 5-0; John Campbell (Australia) beat Cripsey 5-3; Parrott beat Jack Fitzmaurice (England) 5-2; Ray Edmonds (England) beat Browne 5-1; Mick Fisher (England) beat Watchorn 5-4; Les Dodd (England) beat Duggan 5-2; Eugene Hughes (Rep. of Ireland) beat Medati 5-1

Third round: McLaughlin beat Willie Thorne (England) 5-3; Dean Reynolds (England) beat Scott 5-3; Cliff Wilson (Wales) beat N. Foulds 5-4; Silvino Francisco (South Africa) beat Morra 5-1; Roscoe beat Graham Miles (England) 5-2; Joe Johnson (England) beat Jonik 5-2; Mark Wildman (England) beat Hargreaves 5-1; Patsy Fagan (Rep. of Ireland) beat Oliver 5-1; Eddie Sinclair (Scotland) beat Morgan 5-2; Murdo Macleod (Scotland) beat Jones 5-2; Campbell beat Fred Davis (England) 5-0; Parrott beat Dave Martin (England) 5-1; Rex Williams (England) beat Edmonds 5-1; Jim Meadowcroft (England) beat Fisher 5-0; Mike Hallett (England) beat Dodd 5-1; E. Hughes beat John Dunning (England) 5-4

Competition Proper

First round: Kirk Stevens (Canada) beat McLaughlin 5-4; Terry Griffiths (Wales) beat Reynolds 5-2; Eddie Charlton (Australia) beat Wilson 5-0; Francisco beat Cliff Thorburn (Canada) 5-1; Roscoe beat Bill Werbeniuk (Canada) 5-4; John Spencer (England) beat Johnson 5-4; Wildman beat

John Virgo (England) 5-2; Alex Higgins (Northern Ireland) beat Fagan 5-3; Steve Davis (England) beat Sinclair 5-2; Macleod beat David Taylor (England) 5-4; Jimmy White (England) beat Campbell 5-1; Parrott beat Doug Mountjoy (Wales) 5-4; Williams beat Ray Reardon (Wales) 5-4; Tony Meo (England) beat Meadowcroft 5-1; Hallett beat Dennis Taylor (Northern Ireland) 5-4; Tony Knowles (England) beat E. Hughes 5-1

Second round: Davis beat Spencer 5-1; Charlton beat White 5-3; Wildman beat Francisco 5-1; Knowles beat Hallett 5-3; Stevens beat Macleod 5-1; Griffiths beat Roscoe 5-2; Meo beat Williams 5-3; Parrott beat Higgins 5-2

Quarter-finals: Wildman beat Charlton 5-4; Davis beat Griffiths 5-4; Meo beat Stevens 5-2; Parrott beat Knowles 5-1

Semi-finals: Meo beat Wildman 5-3; Davis beat Parrott 5-4

Final: Davis beat Meo 9-8

1985

TOTAL PRIZE MONEY: £200,000
FIRST PRIZE: £40,000

Preliminary round: Paul Watchorn (Rep. of Ireland) beat Dennis Hughes (England) 5-0; Bernie Mikkelsen (Canada) beat Dave Chalmers (England) 5-1

Qualifying 'A': Tony Jones (England) beat David Greaves (England) 5-2; James Giannaros (Australia) beat Tony Chappel (Wales) 5-2; Steve Newbury (Wales) beat Vic Harris (England) 5-3; Geoff Foulds (England) beat Robert Chaperon (Canada) 5-3; Dessie Sheehan (Rep. of Ireland) beat John Rea (Scotland) 5-2; Roger Bales (England) beat Bernard Bennett (England) 5-1; Robbie Foldvari (Australia) beat Pat Houlihan (England) 5-1; Paul Medati (England) beat Graham Cripsey (England) 5-4; Jack McLaughlin (Northern Ireland) beat Bert Demarco (Scotland) 5-1; Steve Longworth (England) beat Peter Francisco (South Africa) 5-4; Tony Kearney (Rep. of Ireland) beat Doug French (England) 5-1; Paddy Browne (Rep. of Ireland) beat Malcolm Bradley (England) 5-1; Wayne Jones (Wales) beat Dene O'Kane (New Zealand) 5-0; Danny Fowler (England) beat Gino Rigitano (Canada) 5-0; John Hargreaves (England) beat Mike Darrington (England) 5-2

Qualifying 'B': T. Jones beat Matt Gibson (Scotland) 5-0; Newbury beat Pascal Burke (Rep. of Ireland) 5-1; G. Foulds beat Frank Jonik (Canada) 5-2; Eddie McLaughlin (Scotland) beat Sheehan 5-2; Bales beat Billy Kelly (Rep. of Ireland) 5-3; Foldvari beat Jack Rea (Northern Ireland) 5-4; J. McLaughlin beat Ian Black (Scotland) 5-0; Longworth beat Bill Oliver (England) 5-1; Watchorn beat Mikkelsen 5-1; Ian Williamson (England) beat Kearney 5-3; Browne beat Clive Everton (Wales) 5-0; Steve Duggan (England) beat W. Jones 5-0; Fowler beat Tommy Murphy (Northern Ireland) 5-0; Ray Edmonds (England) beat Hargreaves 5-2

Qualifying 'C': T. Jones beat Les Dodd (England) 5-1; Marcel Gauvreau (Canada) beat Giannaros 5-3; Newbury beat Mario Morra (Canada) 5-2; G. Foulds beat J. Fitzmaurice (England) 5-1; E. McLaughlin beat Fred Davis (England) 5-1; Medati beat Colin Roscoe (Wales) 5-4; George Scott (England) beat J. McLaughlin 5-4; Longworth beat M. Fisher (England) 5-1; Jim Donnelly (Scotland) beat Watchorn 5-1; Patsy Fagan (Rep. of Ireland) beat Williamson 5-1; Warren King (Australia) beat Duggan 5-4; Fowler beat Jim Meadowcroft (England) 5-2; Edmonds beat Mike Watterson (England) 5-2

Qualifying 'D': S. Francisco beat T. Jones 5-1; Fagan beat Mark Wildman (England) 5-3; Mike Hallett (England) beat G. Foulds 5-4; Murdo Macleod (Scotland) beat E. McLaughlin 5-4; Medati beat John Parrott (England) 5-3; Cliff Wilson (Wales) beat Fowler 5-4; Gauvreau beat Eddie Sinclair (Scotland) 5-1; Joe Johnson (England) beat Edmonds 5-4; Scott beat John Campbell (Australia) 5-4; Eugene Hughes (Rep. of Ireland) beat Newbury 5-3; King beat Dean Reynolds (England) 5-2; Rex Williams (England) beat Donnelly 5-3; John Virgo (England) beat Bales 5-1; Longworth beat N. Foulds (England) 5-3; Foldvari beat Dave Martin (England) 5-2; Browne beat Graham Miles (England) 5-3

Competition Proper

First round: Longworth beat David Taylor (England) 5-4; Johnson beat Tony Knowles (England) 5-1; Cliff Thorburn (Canada) beat Scott 5-1; King beat John Spencer (England) 5-2; Terry Griffiths (Wales) beat Fagan 5-0; Jimmy White (England) beat Browne 5-2; E. Hughes beat Tony Meo (England) 5-4; Macleod beat Eddie Charlton (Australia) 5-1; Alex Higgins (Northern Ireland) beat Gauvreau 5-3; Virgo beat Bill Werbeniuk (Canada) 5-2; Wilson beat Doug Mountjoy (Wales) 5-4; Williams beat Dennis Taylor (Northern Ireland) 5-3; Ray Reardon (Wales) beat Hallett 5-3; S. Davis (England) beat S. Francisco 5-0; Willie Thorne (England) beat Foldvari 5-2; Kirk Stevens (Canada) beat Medati 5-4

Second round: Reardon beat E. Hughes 5-1; S. Davis beat Higgins 5-2; Virgo beat Macleod 5-0; Thorne beat Stevens 5-1; Thorburn beat Longworth 5-3; Griffiths beat Williams 5-3; Johnson beat Wilson 5-0; King beat White 5-2

Quarter-finals: S. Davis beat Reardon 5-1; Thorburn beat Griffiths 5-4; Johnson beat King 5-3; Thorne beat Virgo 5-1

Semi-finals: Thorne beat S. Davis 9-8; Thorburn beat Johnson 9-2

Final: Thorne beat Thorburn 13-8

Cliff Thorburn and Jimmy White in the final of the 1986 Mercantile Credit Classic

BCE Belgian Classic

TOTAL PRIZE MONEY: £40,000
FIRST PRIZE: £12,000
ENTRIES: Top eight in world rankings who were available
TELEVISION: Belgian Television Service

A remarkable 96 per cent of Belgian viewers switched to the BBC's coverage of the final session of the 1985 world final, a figure which has much to do with clinching 15 hours coverage by BTV of the first BCE Belgian Classic at Ostend Casino.

Snooker, virtually unknown in Belgium three years ago, has become, through its popularity with television viewers, a rapidly expanding sport with all the commercial opportunities for club owners and equipment manufacturers that this implies.

Bizarrely, Terry Griffiths won the tournament despite not having held a cue in his hand for the previous three weeks while he went on holiday. His 5-2 win over Steve Davis contained a break of 121, the highest of the tournament, and with wins over Tony Knowles and Kirk Stevens he secured the £12,000 first prize.

Stevens' 5-4 semi-final win over Higgins was the match of the tournament and one of the best of the season. Having trailed 1-3, Stevens levelled at 3-3 with the aid of a break of 120. He fell behind 3-4 to the Irishman's 70 break but ran away with the remaining two frames with breaks of 111 and 74.

First round: Alex Higgins (Northern Ireland) beat Dennis Taylor (Northern Ireland) 5-1; Kirk Stevens (Canada) beat Ray Reardon (Wales) 5-1; Tony Knowles (England) beat Jimmy White (England) 5-4; Terry Griffiths (Wales) beat Steve Davis (England) 5-2

Semi-finals: Stevens beat Higgins 5-4; Griffiths beat Knowles 5-2

Final: Griffiths beat Stevens 9-7

Tony Knowles in play against Terry Griffiths in the semi-final of the BCE Belgian Classic

Benson and Hedges Masters

TOTAL PRIZE MONEY: £175,000
FIRST PRIZE: £45,000
ENTRIES: Top 16 in world rankings
TELEVISION: BBC

In retaining the Benson and Hedges Masters title at Wembley Conference Centre, Cliff Thorburn took the first prize – in this case £45,000 – for the third time in four years. His 9-5 final defeat of Jimmy White gave him a 2-1 edge in their meetings in major finals during the season.

'I can't try to pot him off the table. I've no chance,' said Thorburn reflecting on his solid, cagey performance which had succeeded where Steve Davis, a 6-3 semi-final loser to White, had failed.

Thorburn made his psychologically killing thrust in the final at 7-5 when his 52 clearance gave him the black ball win which put him three up with four to play.

No fewer than seven of the tournament's fifteen matches ran the full distance.

Eddie Charlton and Kirk Stevens had to return to the arena at midnight for their deciding frame after it had taken from 2 o'clock to 7.22 to reach 4-4; White recovered from 1-4 to beat Tony Meo with a run of four straight frames; Ray Reardon missed a tiddler of a black which would have given him a 5-2 win over Willie Thorne; and Thorne himself got within the last two colours of snatching the deciding frame of his quarter-final against Davis from 0-61.

First round: Cliff Thorburn (Canada) beat Joe Johnson (England) 5-3; Terry Griffiths (Wales) beat Alex Higgins (Northern Ireland) 5-4; Eddie Charlton (Australia) beat Kirk Stevens (Canada) 5-4; Tony Knowles (England) beat Silvino Francisco (South Africa) 5-1; Steve Davis (England) beat David Taylor (England) 5-4; Willie Thorne (England) beat Ray Reardon (Wales) 5-4; Jimmy White (England) beat Tony Meo (England) 5-4; Dennis Taylor (Northern Ireland) beat Doug Mountjoy (Wales) 5-2

Quarter-finals: Thorburn beat Griffiths 5-2; Knowles beat Charlton 5-4; Davis beat Thorne 5-4; White beat Dennis Taylor 5-3

Semi-finals: Thorburn beat Knowles 6-4; White beat Davis 6-3

Final: Thorburn beat White 9-5

Previous Years

The inaugural Benson and Hedges Masters, which was staged at the West Centre Hotel, London, in 1975, was not its parent company Gallaher's first major venture into snooker sponsorship. Under the banner of another Gallaher brand, Park Drive, four four-man round-robin tournaments were staged in 1971 and 1972 with the top two finishers in each meeting in a play-off recorded by the BBC. Another Park Drive event was televised by Yorkshire TV.

All these events strengthened television sports departments' conviction that authentic competitive snooker over a reasonable spread of frames could make entertaining viewing.

The 1973 and 1974 Park Drive World Professional Championships had an even more dramatic long term effect on the game. The decision to compress the 1973 Championship into a fortnight, instead of allowing it to ramble on for an entire season according to established practice, revitalised the whole event. There was television coverage only of the two finals but even this was, at the time, a substantial step forward for professional snooker.

Cliff Thorburn: three times Benson and Hedges Masters champion

The WPBSA chose to award the 1975 Championship to Australia and Park Drive never returned as sponsors, but the Benson and Hedges Masters very quickly established its own distinctive identity. It was played at the West Centre Hotel only once – in the era in which tournaments were won by Ray Reardon and John Spencer with the occasional intervention of Alex Higgins.

Reardon looked like winning the first Masters when he went two up on Spencer with three to play but the score moved to 8-8 and into a deciding frame.

The standard of play had deteriorated as the match reached its final phase partly through tension perhaps but also because the table had become uncontrollably fast.

Although only the final was televised in those days, it was thought beneficial to the players to reduce the problems of adjustment by playing the whole tournament under television lighting.

But as the television lighting was much less sophisticated then than it is now, no one realized that a week's heat from the lights would increase the speed of the cloth so dramatically. Certain shots became either very difficult or even impossible to control because the cue-ball seemed to run on for ever.

With each player losing position in turn, winning chances were cast away on both sides until the final frame ended in a tie with an extra black thus needed to decide it.

Reardon had first chance but Spencer sank it with one of the best pots of the day to take the £2,000 first prize. It is still the only Masters final to go the ultimate distance.

Even in that first event, the distinctive identity of the Masters – one of its great strengths – had been established. It was enhanced the following year when it moved to the New London Theatre, Drury Lane, snooker's first but by no means last association with a theatre-in-the-round. The Masters became established as the great London showcase event of the season and Reardon disposed comfortably of Graham Miles in the final.

There was a new name in 1977: Doug Mountjoy – invited as a late replacement for Eddie Charlton, who has played in every other Masters – had turned professional the day following his capture of the World Amateur Championship in Johannesburg a couple of months previously and in storybook fashion went on to win the Masters, his first professional tournament, by beating Reardon 7-6 on the final pink.

Such a scenario cannot be re-enacted under present circumstances. Entry to the Masters is no longer by invitation – the only feasible method in those days – but strictly by world ranking. A world amateur champion would not possibly have time to accrue the professional ranking points to make the top 16 to which the Masters field is restricted.

Alex Higgins won the 1978 Masters, the last to be staged at the New London Theatre, and also reached the 1979 final, the first at Wembley Conference Centre. But Perrie Mans, who did not make a 50 break in any of his matches, proved that it is not always necessary to make big breaks to win by beating him 8-4 for the title.

Higgins extended his run to four consecutive Masters finals, losing in 1980 to Terry Griffiths and in 1981 regaining the title by beating Griffiths 9-6, despite the Welshman's new tournament record break of 136.

This brought to a close a vintage tournament. After capturing his first major title, the Coral UK, two months earlier, Steve Davis was expected to win the Masters at his first attempt but was beaten 5-2 by Mans in the first round; Higgins made an extraordinary recovery to beat Cliff Thorburn 6-5 in one semi-final after the Canadian had led 5-1; and Griffiths, trailing Spencer 2-5 and needing two snookers in the eighth, made one no less extraordinary to win 6-5 also. Attendance figures soared into the stratosphere with new records of 18,742 for the event's six-day run and 2,422 for the final session.

No less than six sessions in the 1982 Masters exceeded this figure with 2,686 the new record – and the total attendance was 23,270. Tony Meo equalled the tournament break record of 136 and gave Davis a fright by extending him to 6-4 in their semi-final after losing the first five frames.

The other semi-final also provided another dramatic 6-4 finish – for Griffiths over Higgins – but Davis took what has so far been his only Masters title by winning the final 9-5.

The seventies' steady build-up of public interest in the Masters and of the prestige attaching to it had exploded into a success story of an altogether different dimension in the eighties.

This trend was maintained in 1983 by a Masters extended from 12 to 16 players and from six to eight days. 'This is the Big Daddy after the world championship,' said Thorburn, with every justification after beating Reardon 9-7 in the final. Attendances totalled 28,297. Mountjoy came from behind to beat Davis 5-4 in the quarter-finals; Thorburn beat Charlton 6-5 from three down with four to play in the semi-finals.

So to the 1984 Masters which produced possibly the greatest match – certainly the greatest in terms of potting and break building – in the history of the event.

The semi-final in which Jimmy White beat Kirk Stevens 6-4 provided three centuries in five frames, two typically dazzling efforts of 113 and 119 from the winner and a 147 maximum from the loser.

For Stevens the 147 – which earned him a £10,000 jackpot plus £1,500 for a new and unchallengeable tournament break record – followed his 5-3 quarter-final defeat of Davis. To have achieved two such feats and still not reached the final shows just how hard the competition had become.

In the almost inevitable anti-climax which followed such a contest, White beat Griffiths 9-5 for the £35,000 first prize.

The highlight of Thorburn's capture of the Masters title for the second time was his 6-4 semi-final win over White after the defending titleholder had quickly led 3-0.

The most dramatic match of the tournament, Alex Higgins' 5-4 first round win over Steve Davis unhappily featured a new problem for snooker: persistent crowd misbehaviour.

Quite unacceptably for the standards expected of snooker spectators, Davis was booed both at his first appearance and before the commencement of the deciding frame, as the ugly behaviour of a minority in Wembley's vast arena impaired the enjoyment of everyone else.

The merit of Higgins' win was also obscured when in his moment of victory he let slip a swear-word to his supporters which was recorded by BBC cameras. In a television interview the following day, he also admitted his personal dislike of Davis. For his part in these two incidents, Higgins was fined, excessively some thought, £1,500.

All this brouhaha may also have affected his performance in his next match against Griffiths as the Welshman had little difficulty in beating him 5-1 before himself falling away 6-2 to Mountjoy in the semi-finals. Thorburn then beat Mountjoy 9-6 in the final.

1975

TOTAL PRIZE MONEY: £5,000
FIRST PRIZE: £2,000

First round: John Pulman (England) beat Cliff Thorburn (Canada) 5-3; Alex Higgins (Northern Ireland) beat Bill Werbeniuk (Canada) 5-0

Quarter-finals: Eddie Charlton (Australia) beat Fred Davis (England) 5-3; John Spencer (England) beat Pulman 5-3; Ray Reardon (Wales) beat Graham Miles (England) 5-3; Rex Williams (England) beat Higgins 5-3

Semi-finals: Spencer beat Charlton 5-2; Reardon beat Williams 5-4

Final: Spencer beat Reardon 9-8

1976

TOTAL PRIZE MONEY: £5,200
FIRST PRIZE: £2,000

First round: Fred Davis (England) beat Cliff Thorburn (Canada) 4-2; John Pulman (England) beat Dennis Taylor (Northern Ireland) 4-2

Quarter-finals: Graham Miles (England) beat Alex Higgins (Northern Ireland) 4-1; Ray Reardon (Wales) beat Pulman 4-1; John Spencer (England) beat Davis 4-0; Eddie Charlton (Australia) beat Rex Williams (England) 4-1

Semi-finals: Miles beat Spencer 5-4; Reardon beat Charlton 5-4

Final: Reardon beat Miles 7-3

1977

TOTAL PRIZE MONEY: £5,200
FIRST PRIZE: £2,000

First round: Doug Mountjoy (Wales) beat John Pulman (England) 4-2; John Spencer (England) beat Dennis Taylor (Northern Ireland) 4-2

Quarter-finals: Ray Reardon (Wales) beat Rex Williams (England) 4-1; Graham Miles (England) beat Spencer 4-1; Alex Higgins (Northern Ireland) beat Perrie Mans (South Africa) 4-2; Mountjoy beat Fred Davis (England) 4-2

Semi-finals: Mountjoy beat Higgins 5-3; Reardon beat Miles 5-2

Final: Mountjoy beat Reardon 7-6

1978

TOTAL PRIZE MONEY: £8,000
FIRST PRIZE: £3,000

First round: John Pulman (England) beat Patsy Fagan (Rep. of Ireland) 4-2; Graham Miles (England) beat Fred Davis (England) 4-3

Quarter-finals: John Spencer (England) beat Pulman 4-2; Alex Higgins (Northern Ireland) beat Dennis Taylor (Northern Ireland) 4-3; Cliff Thorburn (Canada) beat Doug Mountjoy (Wales) 4-2; Ray Reardon (Wales) beat Miles 4-1

Semi-finals: Higgins beat Reardon 5-1; Thorburn beat Spencer 5-3

Final: Higgins beat Thorburn 7-5

1979

TOTAL PRIZE MONEY: £8,000
FIRST PRIZE: £3,000

First round: Doug Mountjoy (Wales) beat Fred Davis (England) 5-2; David Taylor (England) beat Patsy Fagan (Rep. of Ireland) 5-4

Quarter-finals: Alex Higgins (Northern Ireland) beat Eddie Charlton (Australia) 5-2; Perrie Mans (South Africa) beat Cliff Thorburn (Canada) 5-4; Mountjoy beat John Spencer (England) 5-0; Ray Reardon (Wales) beat Taylor 5-2

Semi-finals: Higgins beat Mountjoy 5-1; Mans beat Reardon 5-3

Final: Mans beat Higgins 8-4

Cliff Thorburn and Jimmy White: finalists in the 1986 Benson and Hedges Masters

1980

TOTAL PRIZE MONEY: £14,000
FIRST PRIZE: £4,500

First round: Cliff Thorburn (Canada) beat John Virgo (England) 5-3; Alex Higgins (Northern Ireland) beat Fred Davis (England) 5-1

Quarter-finals: Ray Reardon (Wales) beat Dennis Taylor (Northern Ireland) 5-3; Terry Griffiths (Wales) beat Thorburn 5-3; John Spencer (England) beat Eddie Charlton (Australia) 5-2; Higgins beat Perrie Mans (South Africa) 5-1

Semi-finals: Griffiths beat Spencer 5-0; Higgins beat Reardon 5-2

Final: Griffiths beat Higgins 9-5

1981

TOTAL PRIZE MONEY: £20,500
FIRST PRIZE: £6,000

First round: Perrie Mans (South Africa) beat Steve Davis (England) 5-3; Doug Mountjoy (Wales) beat Eddie Charlton (Australia) 5-0; Fred Davis (England) beat Kirk Stevens (Canada) 5-4; John Spencer (England) beat Dennis Taylor (Northern Ireland) 5-2

Quarter-finals: Alex Higgins (Northern Ireland) beat Mountjoy 5-1; Cliff Thorburn (Canada) beat Mans 5-4; John Spencer (England) beat Ray Reardon (Wales) 5-1; Terry Griffiths (Wales) beat F. Davis 5-2

Semi-finals: Higgins beat Thorburn 6-5; Griffiths beat Spencer 6-5

Final: Higgins beat Griffiths 9-6

Cliff Thorburn holds the Benson and Hedges Masters trophy aloft

1982

TOTAL PRIZE MONEY: £27,250
FIRST PRIZE: £8,000

First round: Ray Reardon (Wales) beat Dennis Taylor (Northern Ireland) 5-3; Doug Mountjoy (Wales) beat John Spencer (England) 5-4; Tony Meo (England) beat David Taylor (England) 5-2; Eddie Charlton (Australia) beat Jimmy White (England) 5-4

Quarter-finals: Meo beat Cliff Thorburn (Canada) 5-0; Steve Davis (England) beat Mountjoy 5-2; Alex Higgins (Northern Ireland) beat Charlton 5-1; Terry Griffiths (Wales) beat Reardon 5-3

Semi-finals: Davis beat Meo 6-4; Griffiths beat Higgins 6-5

Final: Davis beat Griffiths 9-5

1983

TOTAL PRIZE MONEY: £55,250
FIRST PRIZE: £16,000

First round: Bill Werbeniuk (Canada) beat Alex Higgins (Northern Ireland) 5-4; Eddie Charlton (Australia) beat Tony Meo (England) 5-3; Terry Griffiths (Wales) beat Kirk Stevens (Canada) 5-3; Cliff Thorburn (Canada) beat Joe Johnson (England) 5-2; Ray Reardon (Wales) beat Dean Reynolds (England) 5-1; Doug Mountjoy (Wales) beat John Virgo (England) 5-1; Steve Davis (England) beat Mark Wildman (England) 5-2; J. White (England) beat David Taylor (England) 5-2

Quarter-finals: Charlton beat Werbeniuk 5-3; Thorburn beat Griffiths 5-3; Reardon beat White 5-2; Mountjoy beat Davis 5-4

Semi-finals: Thorburn beat Charlton 6-5; Reardon beat Mountjoy 6-3

Final: Thorburn beat Reardon 9-7

1984

TOTAL PRIZE MONEY: £115,000
FIRST PRIZE: £35,000

First round: Tony Knowles (England) beat Dennis Taylor (Northern Ireland) 5-2; Ray Reardon (Wales) beat John Virgo (England) 5-3; John Spencer (England) beat Cliff Thorburn (Canada) 5-4; Terry Griffiths (Wales) beat Bill Werbeniuk (Canada) 5-1; Jimmy White (England) beat Eddie Charlton (Australia) 5-2; Alex Higgins (Northern Ireland) beat Doug Mountjoy (Wales) 5-2; Kirk Stevens (Canada) beat David Taylor (England) 5-1; Steve Davis (England) beat Tony Meo (England) 5-0

Quarter-finals: Griffiths beat Spencer 5-4; Knowles beat Higgins 5-1; White beat Reardon 5-3; Stevens beat Davis 5-3

Semi-finals: Griffiths beat Knowles 6-4; White beat Stevens 6-4

Final: White beat Griffiths 9-5

1985

TOTAL PRIZE MONEY: £150,000
FIRST PRIZE: £37,000

First round: Cliff Thorburn (Canada) beat Dennis Taylor (Northern Ireland) 5-3; Doug Mountjoy (Wales) beat Tony Knowles (England) 5-3; Ray Reardon (Wales) beat David Taylor (England) 5-1; Jimmy White (England) beat Willie Thorne (England) 5-2; John Spencer (England) beat Eddie Charlton (Australia) 5-3; Tony Meo (England) beat Kirk Stevens (Canada) 5-2; Terry Griffiths (Wales) beat Bill Werbeniuk (Canada) 5-2; Alex Higgins (Northern Ireland) beat Steve Davis (England) 5-4

Quarter-finals: Thorburn beat Reardon 5-0; White beat Spencer 5-2; Mountjoy beat Meo 5-4; Griffiths beat Higgins 5-1

Semi-finals: Mountjoy beat Griffiths 6-2; Thorburn beat White 6-4

Final: Thorburn beat Mountjoy 9-6

Dulux British Open

TOTAL PRIZE MONEY: £275,000
FIRST PRIZE: £55,000
ENTRIES: Open to all professionals
TELEVISION: ITV

Steve Davis won his third ranking tournament of the season in most convincing style, only Willie Thorne, whom he beat 12-7, avoiding the indignity of being beaten by a frame ratio of more than 2:1.

In Davis's half, the most outstanding deeds were done by Jim Wych, a Canadian left-hander who had appeared only intermittently on the circuit since reaching the world quarter-finals at his first attempt in 1980.

After his 5-4 win over Tony Knowles, during which the loser made five breaks over 50, Wych again upset common prediction by beating John Parrott 5-4 and held Davis for the first half of the match before going down 5-2 in their quarter-final.

Thorne led a charmed life in beating Kirk Stevens 5-4 in the last 16, the Canadian incredibly missing a straight brown from its spot screwing back for the only other ball he needed in the deciding frame, the blue.

He was also taken the distance by Terry Griffiths in the quarter-finals but quelled John Virgo 9-4 in the semi-finals with the aid of an 87-minute, six-frame winning streak which gave him a 6-1 interval lead.

Breaks of 104, 100, 95, 83 and 83 featured in this virtuoso display but Virgo was able to take consolation from beating both Tony Meo and Eddie Charlton from behind in reaching his first major semi-final since the 1982 PPT.

Silvino Francisco's troubled reign as champion came to an end with his 5-1 defeat by Murdo Macleod in the last 32 in his first match at Derby. Taken with Thorne's failure in the last 64 of the Mercantile Credit Classic and the last 32 defeat for Alex Higgins and Jimmy White in the Hofmeister World Doubles, this completed for ITV the unhappy hat-trick of having the defending champion lose before the televised phase was reached.

The preliminary phase of the competition at Solihull Civic Centre was notable for a 145 total clearance by Dave Martin and the defeat of Dennis Taylor, the reigning world champion, by Roger Bales, a little known professional from Birmingham.

First round: Joe O'Boye (Rep. of Ireland) beat Jim Bear (Canada) 5-1; John Hargreaves (England) w.o. Gerry Watson (Canada) scr; Omprakesh Agrawal (India) beat Dave Greaves (England) 5-3; Dave Gilbert (England) beat Pascal Burke (Rep. of Ireland) 5-1; Stephen Hendry (Scotland) beat Dennis Hughes (England) 5-1; Glen Wilkinson (Australia) beat Paul Watchorn (Rep. of Ireland) 5-4; Dessie Sheehan (Rep. of Ireland) beat Sakchai Simnagm (Thailand) 5-2; Greg Jenkins (Australia) beat Bert Demarco (Scotland) 5-1; Barry West (England) beat Bernard Bennett (England) 5-1; Graham Cripsey (England) beat Mike Darrington (England) 5-4; Pat Houlihan (England) w.o. Gordon Robinson (Australia) scr; Tony Kearney (Rep. of Ireland) beat Martin Smith (England) 5-2; Roger Bales (England) beat Maurice Parkin (England) 5-1; Tony Drago (Malta) w.o. Derek Mienie (South Africa) scr

Second round: Tony Jones (England) beat O'Boye 5-2; Fred Davis (England) beat Billy Kelly (Rep. of Ireland) 5-4; George Scott (England) beat Dave Chalmers (England) 5-1; Hargreaves beat Ray Edmonds (England) 5-3; Les Dodd (England) beat Frank Jonik (Canada) 5-4; Wayne Jones (Wales) beat Gino Rigitano (Canada) 5-1; Graham Miles (England) beat Agrawal 5-4; Robbie Chaperon (Canada) beat Vic Harris (England) 5-0; John Rea (Scotland) beat Warren King (Australia) 5-1; Danny Fowler (England) beat Tony Chappel (Wales) 5-4; Gilbert beat Mario Morra (Canada) 5-4; Paddy Browne (Rep. of Ireland) beat Hendry 5-0; Jim Donnelly (Scotland) beat Wilkinson 5-4; Steve Newbury (Wales) beat Bill Oliver (England) 5-2; Dessie Sheehan (Rep. of Ireland) w.o. Mike Watterson (England) scr; Jenkins beat Jim Meadowcroft (England) 5-2; Ian Black (Scotland) beat Matt Gibson (Scotland) 5-0; Bob Harris (England) beat Eddie Sinclair (Scotland) 5-3; West beat Eddie McLaughlin (Scotland) 5-3; Patsy Fagan (Rep. of Ireland) beat Jack Fitzmaurice (England) 5-4; Colin Roscoe (Wales) beat Bernie Mikkelsen (Canada) 5-4; Ian Williamson (England) beat Cripsey 5-4; Jim Wych (Canada) beat Jimmy van Rensburg (South Africa) 5-0; Peter Francisco (South Africa) beat Geoff Foulds (England) 5-2; Steve Longworth (England) beat Houlihan 5-3; Malcom Bradley (England) beat Jack Rea (Northern Ireland) 5-1; Steve Duggan (England) beat Tommy Murphy (Northern Ireland) 5-1; Jack McLaughlin (Northern Ireland) beat Mike Fisher (England) 5-3; Robbie Foldvari (Australia) beat Kearney 5-2; Bales w.o. John Dunning (England) scr; Drago beat Marcel Gauvreau (Canada) 5-3

Third round: Silvino Francisco (South Africa) beat T. Jones 5-2; Murdo Macleod (Scotland) beat F. Davis 5-4; Terry Griffiths (Wales) beat Scott 5-3; Neal Foulds (England) beat Hargreaves 5-4; Willie Thorne (England) beat Dodd 5-2; Perrie Mans (South Africa) beat Jones 5-2; Kirk Stevens (Canada) beat Miles 5-3; Cliff Wilson (Wales) beat Chaperon 5-3; John Rea beat Ray Reardon (Wales) 5-3; John Virgo (England) beat Fowler 5-1; Eddie Charlton (Australia) beat Gilbert 5-2; Browne beat John Spencer (England) 5-0; Tony Meo (England) beat Donnelly 5-3; Newbury beat Dene O'Kane (New Zealand) 5-3; Cliff Thorburn (Canada) beat Sheehan 5-0; Mark Wildman (England) beat Jenkins 5-4; Steve Davis (England) beat Black 5-2; Dave Martin (England) beat B. Harris 5-1; Medati beat David Taylor (England) 5-1; John Campbell (Australia) beat West 5-4; Fagan beat Doug Mountjoy (Wales) 5-1; John Parrott (England) beat Roscoe 5-2; Tony Knowles (England) beat Williamson 5-1; Wych beat Dean Reynolds (England) 5-3; P. Francisco beat Jimmy White (England) 5-4; Longworth beat Eugene Hughes (Rep. of Ireland) 5-4; Alex Higgins (Northern Ireland) beat Bradley 5-3; Mike Hallett (England) beat Duggan 5-3; Joe Johnson (England) beat J. McLaughlin 5-2; Bill Werbeniuk (Canada) beat Foldvari 5-4; Bales beat Dennis Taylor (Northern Ireland) 5-4; Rex Williams (England) beat Drago 5-1

Fourth round: Macleod beat S. Francisco 5-1; Griffiths beat N. Foulds 5-3; Thorne beat Mans 5-1; Stevens beat Wilson 5-0; Virgo beat John Rea 5-0; Charlton beat Browne 5-1; Meo beat Newbury 5-0; Thorne beat Wildman 5-1; S. Davis beat Martin 5-1; Campbell beat Medati 5-4; Parrott beat Fagan 5-0; Wych beat Knowles 5-4; P. Francisco beat Longworth 5-2; Higgins beat Hallett 5-1; Werbeniuk beat Johnson 5-3; Williams beat Bales 5-4

Fifth round: Griffiths beat Macleod 5-2; Thorne beat Stevens 5-4; Virgo beat Charlton 5-4; Meo beat Thorburn 5-3; S. Davis beat Campbell 5-0; Wych beat Parrott 5-4; Higgins beat P. Francisco 5-2; Werbeniuk beat Williams 5-3

Quarter-finals: Thorne beat Griffiths 5-4; Virgo beat Meo 5-3; S. Davis beat Wych 5-2; Higgins beat Werbeniuk 5-1

Semi-finals: Thorne beat Virgo 9-4; S. Davis beat Higgins 9-3

Final: S. Davis beat Thorne 12-7

Previous Years

As the tournament circuit developed, variants of the traditional single combat straight knock-out format were sought. One such, the Yamaha International Masters, grew out of the British Gold Cup, which was instituted in 1980 by Snookasport and sponsored by three concerns within the industry, E.J. Riley (tables), Strachan (cloth) and Super Crystalate (balls).

With four four-man round-robin groups producing the qualifiers for the knock-out semi-finals, Alex Higgins had to beat Terry Griffiths 3-0 to win his group. He did so with the aid of breaks of 135 and 134 in the last two frames and went on to make a break of 132 in beating Ray Reardon 5-1 for the £4,000 first prize.

Between his round robin group and his semi-final, Higgins won the Tolly Cobbold Classic at Ipswich, travelling overnight from that success to reach Derby at 6.00 a.m., only five hours before beating Tony Meo 4-0 in the Gold Cup semi-final.

Such a scenario helped to establish the tournament's commercial potential and in 1981 the event returned to the Derby Assembly Rooms with a major sponsor, Yamaha Organs, who contributed a £30,000 prize fund and won four days' coverage by ITV. This, in fact, was the first major tournament to be fully networked by ITV on a daily basis, programming which had already produced impressive viewing figures for BBC.

Steve Davis won the event, retained the title in 1982 and regained it in 1984 after Ray Reardon had taken first prize in 1983.

The format underwent various changes. Four-man groups spread over two sessions were replaced by three-man groups concluded in a single session and the group format itself was extended to the semi-finals and then, in 1984, to the final itself.

The event became a firm fixture at Derby and ITV covered the seven-day action in its entirety. Overall, however, it proved more popular with the public than with the players who felt that prize money and television exposure of such magnitude should not be devoted to such short matches.

With the WPBSA's asking price for major sponsorships rising in relation to the value of television coverage, Yamaha withdrew from the 1985 event and the WPBSA felt a change of sponsor provided a suitable juncture to institute a ranking tournament on traditional lines. The Dulux British Open thus made its first appearance in 1985 when Silvino Francisco took the £50,000 first prize through beating Jimmy White, Tony Meo and Alex Higgins before his 12-9 final victory over Kirk Stevens.

Stevens earned his place in a major final for the first time through beating Steve Davis 9-7 in the semis, Davis having been pressed to a 6-5 decision in the pre-televised phase of the competition by a young Welshman, Tony Chappel.

Strangely, first and second round matches were of the best of eleven frames before reverting to best of nine for the third round and quarter-finals, ITV having forcibly made the point that both early starts and potentially late finishes were financially injurious to them.

1985

TOTAL PRIZE MONEY: £250,000
FIRST PRIZE: £50,000

Qualifying: Tony Chappel (Wales) beat Ian Williamson (England) 6-5; Dave Chalmers (England) beat Pascal Burke (Rep. of Ireland) 6-5; John Rea (Scotland) beat Mick Fisher (England) 6-0; Warren King (Australia) beat Paul Medati (England) 6-4; Danny Fowler (England) beat Clive Everton (Wales) 6-1; Tommy Murphy (Northern Ireland) beat Dessie Sheehan (Rep. of Ireland) 6-3; Robbie Foldvari (Australia) beat Steve Duggan (England) 6-4; Vic Harris (England) beat Les Dodd (England) 6-1; Tony Jones (England) beat Geoff Foulds (England) 6-0; Peter Francisco (South Africa) beat Billy Kelly (Rep. of Ireland) 6-3; Dene

Steve Davis beat Willie Thorne to win the Dulux British Open trophy in 1986

The Dulux British Open was the occasion for some dogged performances from Steve Davis and Willie Thorne

O'Kane (New Zealand) beat Graham Cripsey (England) 6-4; Steve Newbury (Wales) beat Paddy Browne (Rep. of Ireland) 6-0; Malcolm Bradley (England) beat Mario Morra (Canada) 6-2; Tony Kearney (Rep. of Ireland) beat Mike Watterson (England) 6-4; Doug French (England) beat Eddie McLaughlin (Scotland) 6-0; Robert Chaperon (Canada) beat Patsy Fagan (Rep. of Ireland) 6-5; Bob Harris (England) beat Jim Meadowcroft (England) 6-1; Steve Longworth (England) beat Fred Davis (England) 6-1; Bernie Mikkelsen (Canada) beat Dennis Hughes (England) 6-0; George Scott (England) beat Mike Darrington (England) 6-3; James Giannaros (Australia) beat Colin Roscoe (Wales) 6-1; Frank Jonik (Canada) beat Jack McLaughlin (Northern Ireland) 6-2; Roger Bales (England) beat Ian Black (Scotland) 6-4; Marcel Gauvreau (Canada) beat David Greaves (England) 6-3; Matt Gibson (Scotland) beat Bert Demarco (Scotland) 6-1; Ray Edmonds (England) beat Derek Mienie (South Africa) 6-1

First round: Dean Reynolds (England) beat Giannaros 6-3; Murdo Macleod (Scotland) beat Murphy 6-5; Eugene Hughes (Rep. of Ireland) beat Watchorn 6-4; Longworth beat C. Wilson (Wales) 6-3; W. Jones beat Joe Johnson (England) 6-5; Mike Hallett (England) w.o. Mikkelsen scr; Cliff Thorburn (Canada) beat Rigitano 6-3; Alex Higgins (Northern Ireland) beat Bales 6-3; Chaperon beat Bill Werbeniuk (Canada) 6-1; Silvino Francisco (South Africa) beat Kearney 6-4; Tony Meo (England) beat Foldvari 6-0; Willie Thorne (England) beat Oliver 6-3; B. Harris beat Eddie Charlton (Australia) 6-3; Jimmy White (England) beat T. Jones 6-5; Tony Knowles (England) beat French 6-2; Neal Foulds (England) beat Hargreaves 6-1; Newbury beat Eddie Sinclair (Scotland) 6-3; Mark Wildman (England) beat Gibson 6-1; John Spencer (England) beat Jonik 6-0; V. Harris beat Doug Mountjoy (Wales) 6-5; O'Kane beat John Campbell (Australia) 6-4; Graham Miles (England) beat Edmonds 6-1; Terry Griffiths (Wales) beat Chalmers 6-0; Ray Reardon (Wales) beat King 6-5; John Parrott (England) beat John Rea 6-4; John Virgo (England) beat P. Francisco 6-2; Fowler beat Rex Williams (England) 6-4; Dave Martin (England) beat Bennett 6-0; Steve Davis (England) beat Chappel 6-5; Dennis Taylor (Northern Ireland) beat Scott 6-2

Second round: Newbury beat Griffiths 5-3; Bradley beat Fowler 5-4; S. Davis beat Virgo 5-2; Knowles beat Longworth 5-2; O'Kane beat V. Harris 5-3; Thorburn beat Reynolds 5-3; Higgins beat N. Foulds 5-1; Dennis Taylor beat Parrott 5-2; Macleod beat Thorne 5-0; Martin beat Reardon 5-4; Miles beat Spencer 5-3; S. Francisco beat White 5-4; Meo beat Hallett 5-4; E. Hughes beat B. Harris 5-4; Stevens beat Wildman 5-2; Chaperon beat W. Jones 5-2

Third round: Meo beat Knowles 5-2; S. Davis beat Bradley 5-2; O'Kane beat Martin 5-4; S. Francisco beat Chaperon 5-2; Dennis Taylor beat Newbury 5-3; E. Hughes beat Macleod 5-2; Stevens beat Miles 5-2; Higgins beat Thorburn 5-2

Quarter-finals: Stevens beat Dennis Taylor 5-2; S. Davis beat O'Kane 5-1; S. Francisco beat Meo 5-4; Higgins beat E. Hughes 5-2

Semi-finals: Stevens beat S. Davis 9-7; S. Francisco beat Higgins 9-6

Final: S. Francisco beat Stevens 12-9

Car Care Plan World Cup

TOTAL PRIZE MONEY: £100,000
FIRST PRIZE: £33,000
ENTRIES: National teams of three
TELEVISION: BBC

Ireland's trio of Alex Higgins, Dennis Taylor and Eugene Hughes retained professional snooker's world team title by beating Canada (Cliff Thorburn, Kirk Stevens, Bill Werbeniuk) 9-7 in the final at the Bournemouth International Centre.

First round: Ireland 'A' (Dennis Taylor, Alex Higgins, Eugene Hughes) beat Ireland 'B' (Patsy Fagan, Tommy Murphy, Paddy Browne) 5-0; Wales (Ray Reardon, Terry Griffiths, Doug Mountjoy) beat Scotland (Murdo Macleod, Eddie Sinclair, Jim Donnelly) 5-1; Canada (Cliff Thorburn, Kirk Stevens, Bill Werbeniuk) beat Rest of World (Tony Drago, Omprakesh Agrawal, Sakchai Simnagm) 5-0; England (Steve Davis, Tony Knowles, Jimmy White) beat Australia (Eddie Charlton, John Campbell, Warren King) 5-2

Semi-finals: Ireland 'A' beat Wales 5-2; Canada beat England 5-3

Final: Ireland 'A' beat Canada 9-7

Previous Years

The State Express World Team Classic was created in 1979 as a result of the developing relationship between snooker and television. Its format was devised with television's requirements very much in mind and it received nine days' BBC coverage from the outset.

Team snooker, a new concept in the professional game, provided good entertainment and attracted highly respectable viewing figures. But it was felt that to spend the first six days painstakingly reducing the six teams to four for the knock-out semi-finals was an inappropriately prodigious use of television time.

The withdrawal of State Express from its British sports sponsorship commitments provided a suitable juncture for the WPBSA to review the situation on behalf of the sport. The WPBSA and BBC agreed to transfer the early season nine-day slot to the new Rothmans tournament (formerly the Professional Players Tournament) but to continue to televise the team event under a new four-day format with a new sponsor, Guinness.

However, Guinness chose not to renew their sponsorship and were only belatedly replaced by Car Care Plan, who contributed £50,000 to the £100,000 prize fund with the WPBSA making up the balance, the first televised tournament for which this had ever proved necessary. Even so, this represented a significant reduction on the 1985 prize fund of £125,000.

Eugene Hughes, Alex Higgins and Dennis Taylor enabled Ireland to retain the Car Care Plan World Cup in 1986

1979

TOTAL PRIZE MONEY: £27,500
FIRST PRIZE: £7,500

Group A: England (Fred Davis, Graham Miles, John Spencer) beat Rest of World (Perrie Mans, Jimmy van Rensburg, Patsy Fagan) 8-7; England beat Northern Ireland (Jack Rea, Alex Higgins, Dennis Taylor) 8-7; Northern Ireland beat Rest of World 8-7

Group B: Wales (Ray Reardon, Terry Griffiths, Doug Mountjoy) beat Canada (Cliff Thorburn, Kirk Stevens, Bill Werbeniuk) 9-6; Australia (Eddie Charlton, Gary Owen, Paddy Morgan) beat Canada 8-7; Wales beat Australia 9-6

Final: Wales beat England 14-3

1980

TOTAL PRIZE MONEY: £31,555
FIRST PRIZE: £9,000

Group A: Wales (Ray Reardon, Terry Griffiths, Doug Mountjoy) beat Canada (Cliff Thorburn, Kirk Stevens, Bill Werbeniuk) 10-5; Canada beat Rest of World (Jim Rempe, Eddie Sinclair, Perrie Mans) 9-6; Wales beat Rest of World 13-2

Group B: England (Fred Davis, John Virgo, David Taylor) beat Ireland (Alex Higgins, Dennis Taylor, Patsy Fagan) 11-4; Australia (Eddie Charlton, Ian Anderson, Paddy Morgan) beat England 8-7; Ireland beat Australia 10-5

Semi-finals: Wales beat Ireland 8-7; Canada beat England 8-5

Final: Wales beat Canada 8-5

1981

TOTAL PRIZE MONEY: £40,555
FIRST PRIZE: £12,000

Group 1: England (Steve Davis, John Spencer, David Taylor) beat Australia (Ian Anderson, Eddie Charlton, Paddy Morgan) 4-3; Northern Ireland (Tommy Murphy, Dennis Taylor, Alex Higgins) beat Australia 4-1; England beat Northern Ireland 4-3

Group 2: Wales (Ray Reardon, Doug Mountjoy, Terry Griffiths) beat Canada (Kirk Stevens, Cliff Thorburn, Bill Werbeniuk) 4-2; Wales beat Republic of Ireland (Patsy Fagan, Eugene Hughes, Dessie Sheehan) 4-0; Canada beat Republic of Ireland 4-2

Semi-finals: England beat Canada 4-2; Wales beat Northern Ireland 4-3

Final: England beat Wales 4-3

1982

TOTAL PRIZE MONEY: £50,555
FIRST PRIZE: £16,500

Group A: England (Tony Knowles, Steve Davis, Jimmy White) beat Northern Ireland (Alex Higgins, Tommy Murphy, Dennis Taylor) 4-3; Scotland (Eddie Sinclair, Jim Donnelly, Ian Black) beat Northern Ireland 4-1; England beat Scotland 4-1

Group B: Canada (Cliff Thorburn, Bill Werbeniuk, Kirk Stevens) beat Wales (Terry Griffiths, Doug Mountjoy, Ray Reardon) 4-3; Canada beat Australia (Eddie Charlton, Paddy Morgan, Ian Anderson) 4-0; Wales beat Australia 4-1

Semi-finals: England beat Wales 4-2; Canada beat Scotland 4-0

Final: Canada beat England 4-2

1983

TOTAL PRIZE MONEY: £60,000
FIRST PRIZE: £20,000

Group A

Wales beat Canada 4-3
Doug Mountjoy lost to Cliff Thorburn 0-2; Ray Reardon lost to Bill Werbeniuk 0-2; Terry Griffiths beat Kirk Stevens 2-1; Mountjoy beat Stevens 2-1; Griffiths beat Werbeniuk 2-1; Reardon lost to Thorburn 0-2; Tie-break: Reardon beat Thorburn

Canada beat Australia 4-2
Werbeniuk lost to Eddie Charlton 1-2; Thorburn lost to Warren King 1-2; Stevens beat Campbell 2-1; Werbeniuk beat Campbell 2-0; Stevens beat King 2-1; Thorburn beat Charlton 2-1

Wales beat Australia 4-0
Reardon beat King 2-0; Mountjoy beat Charlton 2-1; Griffiths beat Campbell 2-1; Griffiths beat King 2-0

Group B

England beat Northern Ireland 4-1
Tony Meo beat Alex Higgins 2-1; Steve Davis beat Tommy Murphy 2-1; Tony Knowles beat Dennis Taylor 2-0; Meo lost to Taylor 0-2; Knowles beat Murphy 2-0

Northern Ireland beat Scotland 4-3
Murphy lost to Eddie Sinclair 0-2; Higgins lost to Ian Black 0-2; Taylor beat Murdo Macleod 2-0; Murphy beat Macleod 2-1; Taylor beat Black 2-0; Higgins lost to Sinclair 1-2; Tie-break: Higgins beat Sinclair

England beat Scotland 4-0
Davis beat Black 2-0; Meo beat Sinclair 2-1; Knowles beat Macleod 2-0; Knowles beat Black 2-0

Semi-finals

Wales beat Northern Ireland 4-1
Mountjoy beat Higgins 4-1; Reardon beat Murphy 2-1; Griffiths beat Taylor 2-0; Mountjoy lost to Taylor 0-2; Griffiths beat Murphy 2-1

England beat Canada 4-2
Meo beat Thorburn 2-0; Davis beat Werbeniuk 2-0; Knowles lost to Stevens 1-2; Meo beat Stevens 2-1; Knowles lost to Werbeniuk 1-2; Davis beat Thorburn 2-1

Final

England beat Wales 4-2
Davis lost to Mountjoy 0-2; Meo beat Reardon 2-0; Knowles beat Griffiths 2-1; Knowles beat Mountjoy 2-1; Meo lost to Griffiths 0-2; Davis beat Reardon 2-0

1984

TOTAL PRIZE MONEY: £125,000
FIRST PRIZE: £40,000

First round: Wales (Terry Griffiths, Doug Mountjoy, Ray Reardon) beat Australia (Eddie Charlton, John Campbell, Warren King) 5-4; England (Steve Davis, Tony Knowles, Tony Meo) beat Scotland (Eddie Sinclair, Murdo Macleod, Jim Donnelly) 5-4; England 'B' (Jimmy White, Willie Thorne, John Spencer) beat Rest of World (Silvino Francisco, Jim Rempe, Dene O'Kane) 5-2; Ireland (Dennis Taylor, Alex Higgins, Eugene Hughes) beat Canada (Cliff Thorburn, Kirk Stevens, Bill Werbeniuk) 5-2

Semi-finals: Ireland beat Wales 5-3; England beat England 'B' 5-2

Final: Ireland beat England 9-7

Benson and Hedges Irish Masters

TOTAL PRIZE MONEY: IR£90,000
FIRST PRIZE: IR£22,500
ENTRIES: Twelve invited
TELEVISION: RTE

Jimmy White retained the Benson and Hedges Irish Masters title in a thoroughbred manner appropriate to its setting, Goffs Sale Ring at Kill, Co. Kildare, where millions of pounds worth of bloodstock is auctioned each year.

White's break-building skills burst into full flower not only in beating Patsy Fagan in six straight frames in their semi-final but in the five-frame winning streak at the start of the evening session of the final against Willie Thorne which put him four up with five to play.

White's 9-5 victory left Thorne with second prize for the fourth time in the 1985-86 season.

Thorne progressed to the final through beating Terry Griffiths, Dennis Taylor and Cliff Thorburn, the latter bringing his record against the Canadian during the season to three wins in four matches.

Kirk Stevens achieved notoriety by choosing a later flight than arranged from London to Dublin and then missing the last possible one which would have ensured prompt arrival. This gave Fagan, one of the sponsors' two wild-card entries, free passage to the quarter-finals, where he sprang a major surprise by beating Tony Knowles 5-4 on the final pink after losing a 4-1 lead.

Stevens's non-arrival was the subject of an official complaint to the WPBSA from the sponsors.

First round: Eugene Hughes (Rep. of Ireland) beat Ray Reardon (Wales) 5-2; Willie Thorne (England) beat Terry Griffiths (Wales) 5-2; Tony Meo (England) beat Alex Higgins (Northern Ireland) 5-4; Patsy Fagan (Rep. of Ireland) w.o. Kirk Stevens (Canada) scr

Quarter-finals: Cliff Thorburn (Canada) beat Hughes 5-1; Thorne beat Dennis Taylor (Northern Ireland) 5-2; Jimmy White (England) beat Meo 5-2; Fagan beat Tony Knowles (England) 5-4

Semi-finals: Thorne beat Thorburn 6-4; White beat Fagan 6-0

Final: White beat Thorne 9-5

Previous Years

The Benson and Hedges Irish Masters, which receives extensive coverage from Radio Telefis Eireann, provides a unique mixture of tournament play and relaxed social atmosphere which makes it, for the top players, a popular last port of call on the circuit before the rigours of the Embassy World Championship.

Its venue, the sales ring at Goffs, Kill, Co. Kildare, just outside Dublin, might have been tailor-made for snooker rather than bloodstock sales. Its 744 plush seats are set nearer the table than they are in many major tournament arenas, thus creating a specially intimate atmosphere.

Founded in 1978, the tournament initially comprised a combination of round robin groups and play-off semi-finals and final until a straight knock-out format was introduced in 1981.

John Spencer and Doug Mountjoy were the first two titleholders before Terry Griffiths achieved a hat-trick of successes in 1980-82. Steve Davis won first prize in 1983 and 1984.

A Davis hat-trick was prevented by his 6-2 loss to Higgins in the 1985 semi-finals, at which stage Jimmy White beat Tony Knowles 6-4 with a run of five straight frames.

White then took the title with a 9-5 win over Higgins after they had gone into the final session level at 4-4.

1978

TOTAL PRIZE MONEY: £3,000
FIRST PRIZE: £1,000

Final: John Spencer (England) beat Doug Mountjoy (Wales) 5-3

1979

TOTAL PRIZE MONEY: £6,000
FIRST PRIZE: £2,000

Final: Doug Mountjoy (Wales) beat Ray Reardon (Wales) 6-5

1980

TOTAL PRIZE MONEY: £8,000
FIRST PRIZE: £2,500

Final: Terry Griffiths (Wales) beat Doug Mountjoy (Wales) 9-8

Patsy Fagan scored a notable victory over Tony Knowles to reach the semi-finals of the 1986 Benson and Hedges Irish Masters

Jimmy White: twice Benson and Hedges Irish Masters champion

1981

TOTAL PRIZE MONEY: IR£15,000
FIRST PRIZE: IR£5,000

First round: Dennis Taylor (Northern Ireland) beat John Spencer (England) 4-2; Steve Davis (England) beat John Virgo (England) 4-3

Quarter-finals: Terry Griffiths (Wales) beat Kirk Stevens (Canada) 4-0; Cliff Thorburn (Canada) beat Doug Mountjoy (Wales) 4-0; Ray Reardon (Wales) beat Davis 4-2; Alex Higgins (Northern Ireland) beat Taylor 4-2

Semi-finals: Griffiths beat Thorburn 6-5; Reardon beat Higgins 6-5

Final: Griffiths beat Reardon 9-7

1982

TOTAL PRIZE MONEY: IR£25,000
FIRST PRIZE: IR£7,500

First round: Dennis Taylor (Northern Ireland) beat Dessie Sheehan (Rep. of Ireland) 5-3; Tony Meo (England) beat John Spencer (England) 5-3; Alex Higgins (Northern Ireland) beat Jim Wych (Canada) 5-3; Doug Mountjoy (Wales) beat Eugene Hughes (Rep. of Ireland) 5-4

Quarter-finals: Terry Griffiths (Wales) beat Meo 5-3; Ray Reardon (Wales) beat Taylor 5-4; Steve Davis (England) beat Mountjoy 5-2; Higgins beat Cliff Thorburn (Canada) 5-4

Semi-finals: Griffiths beat Reardon 6-3; Davis beat Higgins 6-2

Final: Griffiths beat Davis 9-5

1983

TOTAL PRIZE MONEY: IR£35,000
FIRST PRIZE: IR£12,000

First round: Jimmy White (England) beat Dennis Taylor (Northern Ireland) 5-4; Tony Meo (England) beat Pascal Burke (Rep. of Ireland) 5-0; Doug Mountjoy (Wales) beat Tony Knowles (England) 5-1; Eddie Charlton (Australia) beat David Taylor (England) 5-4

Quarter-finals: Ray Reardon (Wales) beat Meo 5-4; Alex Higgins (Northern Ireland) beat White 5-2; Steve Davis (England) beat Charlton 5-1; Terry Griffiths (Wales) beat Mountjoy 5-4

Semi-finals: Reardon beat Higgins 6-3; Davis beat Griffiths 6-2

Final: Davis beat Reardon 9-2

1984

TOTAL PRIZE MONEY: IR£45,000
FIRST PRIZE: IR£15,000

First round: Terry Griffiths (Wales) beat Bill Werbeniuk (Canada) 5-2; Dennis Taylor (Northern Ireland) beat Eugene Hughes (Rep. of Ireland) 5-1; Tony Meo (England) beat Jimmy White (England) 5-4; Alex Higgins (Northern Ireland) beat Eddie Charlton (Australia) 5-2

Quarter-finals: Taylor beat Cliff Thorburn (Canada) 5-2; Griffiths beat Tony Knowles (England) 5-0; Higgins beat Ray Reardon (Wales) 5-2; Steve Davis (England) beat Meo 5-4

Semi-finals: Griffiths beat Taylor 6-5; Davis beat Higgins 6-4

Final: Davis beat Griffiths 9-1

1985

TOTAL PRIZE MONEY: IR£80,000
FIRST PRIZE: IR£20,000

First round: Eddie Charlton (Australia) beat Dennis Taylor (Northern Ireland) 5-4; Jimmy White (England) beat Tony Meo (England) 5-1; Eugene Hughes (Rep. of Ireland) beat Ray Reardon (Wales) 5-0; Alex Higgins (Northern Ireland) beat Terry Griffiths (Wales) 5-2

Quarter-finals: Tony Knowles (England) beat Charlton 5-3; White beat Cliff Thorburn (Canada) 5-3; Steve Davis (England) beat E. Hughes 5-4; Higgins beat Kirk Stevens (Canada) 5-3

Semi-finals: White beat Knowles 6-4; Higgins beat Davis 6-2

Final: White beat Higgins 9-5

Embassy World Championship

TOTAL PRIZE MONEY: £350,000
FIRST PRIZE: £70,000
ENTRIES: Open to all professionals
TELEVISION: BBC

Joe Johnson's capture of the record first prize of £70,000 in the Embassy World Championship at the Crucible Theatre, Sheffield, maintained the reputation of snooker's blue riband event as a provider of drama and surprises.

Johnson was certainly the most unexpected champion since Terry Griffiths in 1979. Ironically, it was his quarter-final victory over Griffiths from three down with four to play which was the key to his success.

Much as he had a year earlier, Steve Davis looked a racing certainty for his fourth world title until the last lap. He did not in the 1986 final lose an eight-frame lead as he had against Dennis Taylor in 1985 but after he had played so well to beat Jimmy White 13-6 and Cliff Thorburn 16-12 in the quarter and semi-finals, it seemed inconceivable that he could fade, as he did against Johnson, to an 18-12 defeat.

That he did so was partly attributable to the world title carrying so much more prestige and thus so much more pressure than any number of other tournaments put together. Conversely, Johnson's inspiration was that of a man seizing the chance of a lifetime.

The absence of confidence and inspiration accounted for the exit of a jaded Taylor, the defending champion, beaten 10-6 in the first round by Mike Hallett, who himself played in deflated fashion against Johnson.

Tony Knowles, who had been seeded to meet Taylor in the semi-finals, was also out of sorts but creditably battled his way past Neal Foulds 10-9, Silvino Francisco 13-10 and Kirk Stevens 13-9 to reach his appointed place.

Alex Higgins, who at the Crucible has won a disappointingly low proportion of the dramatic contests in which he has so often figured, was a 13-12 second-round loser to Griffiths, a stage at which Stevens required the full distance to beat Eddie Charlton from two down with three to play.

In the bottom half of the draw, Stephen Hendry, the 17-year-old Scottish Professional champion, who had already become the youngest competitor in the history of the event, followed his notable run in the qualifying competition, in which he won five matches and made the highest break, 141, by leading Willie Thorne 7-6 and was beaten only 10-8 after one of the Crucible's most exciting first-round matches.

John Campbell, the Australian champion, made Ray Reardon, who had been struggling all season, a first-round loser at the Crucible for the first time but lost 13-9 to Thorne, who in turn lost to Thorburn 13-6.

John Parrott ousted Tony Meo 10-4 but faded against White 13-8. White was outplayed by Davis and in quality Davis's semi-final defeat of Thorburn provided the match of the Championship.

Davis also made the highest break of the televised phase of the competition, 134.

Neither attendances nor BBC viewing figures gave any support to those who felt that snooker might have passed its peak in public appeal.

The final averaged 11.3m viewers with a peak of 16.6m in comparison to the record 18.5m for the incredible Taylor v Davis climax in 1985.

Evening transmissions attracted between 5-7m, the main afternoon transmission 5m and even mornings 2m. Snooker filled 19 of the top 20 BBC2 slots in viewing terms during the two weeks of the Championship.

First round: Dave Gilbert (England) beat Roger Bales (England) 10-7; Omprakesh Agrawal (India) beat Dennis Hughes (England) 10-6; Tony Kearney (Rep. of Ireland) beat Glen Wilkinson (Australia) 10-5; Bill Oliver (England) beat Joe O'Boye (Rep. of Ireland) 10-8; Dessie Sheehan (Rep. of Ireland) beat Pat Houlihan (England) 10-7; Matt Gibson (Scotland) beat Greg Jenkins (Australia) 10-4; Sakchai Simnagm (Thailand) beat Bernard Bennett (England) 10-0; Jim Bear (Canada) beat Pascal Burke (Rep. of Ireland) 10-8; Tony Drago (Malta) beat Graham Cripsey (England) 10-4; Martin Smith (England) beat David Greaves (England) 10-4; Barry West (England) w.o. James Giannaros (Australia) scr; Paul Thornley (Canada) beat Derek Mienie (South Africa) 10-3; Robbie Grace (South Africa) beat Maurice Parkin (England) 10-8; Stephen Hendry (Scotland) beat Bert Demarco (Scotland) 10-7; Paul Watchorn (Rep. of Ireland) w.o. Jim Rempe (USA) scr; Bernie Mikkelsen (Canada) beat John Hargreaves (England) 10-7; Mike Darrington (England) w.o. Wayne Sanderson (Canada) scr

Second round: Jim Wych (Canada) beat Tony Chappel (Wales) 10-6; Steve Duggan (England) beat Mick Fisher (England) 10-3; Tony Jones (England) beat Vic Harris (England) 10-7; Gilbert beat Malcolm Bradley (England) 10-7; Steve Newbury (Wales) beat Agrawal 10-5; Ian Black (Scotland) beat Bob Harris (England) 10-8; George Scott (England) beat Kearney 10-8; Danny Fowler (England) beat Oliver 10-8; Colin Roscoe (Wales) beat Geoff Foulds (England) 10-3; Warren King (Australia) beat Sheehan 10-4; Gibson beat Mario Morra (Canada) 10-9; Paul Medati (England) beat Simnagm 10-9; Robby Chaperon (Canada) beat Frank Jonik (Canada) 10-8; Marcel Gauvreau (Canada) beat Bear 10-5; Fred Davis (England) beat Dave Chalmers (England) 10-6; Peter Francisco (South Africa) beat Drago 10-4; Jim Donnelly (Scotland) beat Smith 10-6; West beat John Dunning (England) 10-3; Tommy Murphy (Northern Ireland) beat Jack McLaughlin (Northern Ireland) 10-7; Thornley beat Patsy Fagan (Rep. of Ireland) 10-7; Wayne Jones (Wales) beat Grace 10-3; Hendry beat Paddy Browne (Rep. of Ireland) 10-9; Eddie Sinclair (Scotland) beat Paddy Morgan (Australia) 10-8; Jimmy van Rensburg (South Africa) beat Ian Williamson (England) 10-9; John Rea (Scotland) beat Eddie McLaughlin (Scotland) 10-6; Steve Longworth (England) beat Watchorn 10-7; Graham Miles (England) beat Clive Everton (Wales) 10-3; Robby Foldvari (Australia) beat Gino Rigitano (Canada) 10-6; Mike Watterson (England) beat Mikkelsen 10-2; Les Dodd (England) beat Jack Fitzmaurice (England) 10-6; Darrington beat Jim Meadowcroft (England) 10-6; Ray Edmonds (England) beat Billy Kelly (Rep. of Ireland) 10-0

Third round: Wych beat Duggan 10-5; Gilbert beat T. Jones 10-7; Newbury beat Black 10-2; Fowler beat Scott 10-7; King beat Roscoe 10-5; Medati beat Gibson 10-6; Gauvreau beat Chaperon 10-8; P. Francisco beat F. Davis 10-1; West beat Donnelly 10-5; Murphy beat Thornley 10-3; Hendry beat W. Jones 10-8; van Rensburg beat Sinclair 10-2; Longworth beat Rea 10-4; Foldvari beat Miles 10-7; Dodd beat Watterson 10-1; Edmonds beat Darrington 10-5

Fourth round: Mike Hallett (England) beat Wych 10-7; Dave Martin (England) beat Gilbert 10-5; John Spencer (England) beat Newbury 10-7; Fowler beat Murdo Macleod (Scotland) 10-6; Dean Reynolds (England) beat King 10-7; Cliff Wilson (Wales) beat Medati 10-6; Rex Williams (England) beat Gauvreau 10-3; Neal Foulds (England) beat P. Francisco

10-9; Bill Werbeniuk (Canada) beat West 10-8; Eugene Hughes (Rep. of Ireland) beat Murphy 10-7; Hendry beat O'Kane (New Zealand) 10-9; John Campbell (Australia) beat van Rensburg 10-6; John Virgo (England) beat Longworth 10-8; John Parrott (England) beat Foldvari 10-6; Perrie Mans (South Africa) beat Dodd 10-7; Edmonds beat Mark Wildman (England) 10-9

Fifth round: Hallett beat Dennis Taylor (Northern Ireland) 10-6; Joe Johnson (England) beat Martin 10-3; Alex Higgins (Northern Ireland) beat Spencer 10-7; Terry Griffiths (Wales) beat Fowler 10-2; Kirk Stevens (Canada) beat Reynolds 10-6; Eddie Charlton (Australia) beat Wilson 10-6; E. Hughes beat David Taylor (England) 10-7; Tony Knowles (England) beat N. Foulds 10-9; Cliff Thorburn (Canada) beat Werbeniuk 10-5; Silvino Francisco (South Africa) beat Williams 10-4; Willie Thorne (England) beat Hendry 10-8; Campbell beat Ray Reardon (Wales) 10-8; Jimmy White (England) beat Virgo 10-7; Parrott beat Tony Meo (England) 10-4; Doug Mountjoy (Wales) beat Mans 10-3; Steve Davis (England) beat Edmonds 10-4

Sixth round: Johnson beat Hallett 13-5; Griffiths beat Higgins 13-12; Stevens beat Charlton 13-12; Knowles beat Francisco 13-10; Thorburn beat Hughes 13-6; Thorne beat Campbell 13-9; White beat Parrott 13-8; Davis beat Mountjoy 13-5

Quarter-finals: Johnson beat Griffiths 13-12; Knowles beat Stevens 13-9; Thorburn beat Thorne 13-6; Davis beat White 13-5

Semi-finals: Johnson beat Knowles 16-8; Davis beat Thorburn 16-12

Final: Johnson beat Davis 18-12

Previous Years

Snooker's blue riband event could hardly have been less pretentious in its beginnings. The Billiards Association and Control Council (BA & CC), the then governing body, was sceptical of snooker's public appeal but Joe Davis, who was then world professional billiards champion, and his friend Bill Camkin, a Birmingham billiard trader, both knew that snooker was becoming extremely popular in billiard halls and clubs and between them brought the Championship into being.

The first final, in May 1927, was staged in one of Camkin's public billiard halls in John Bright Street, Birmingham, and attracted little attention. Few of the early Championships, which included one in which the final was played in a back room of a Nottingham public house, were much more prestigious.

In the mid-thirties, snooker started first to share with billiards and later to monopolise the schedule at Thurston's, the showcase venue of the game in Leicester Square.

Whatever the venue, Joe Davis won the Championship annually and with ease. It was not until he beat his younger

A champion moment for Joe Johnson, the 1986 Embassy World Champion

John Parrott, who often produces his best at the Crucible

brother Fred by only 37-36 in the week-long 1940 final that it looked conceivable that he might lose.

After the war, the Championship continued to be played on a season-long basis with each match lasting at least three days. The 1946 final, in which Joe Davis won the fourteenth, and last, of the titles which made up his 20-year reign as world champion, was played over a fortnight at the Horticultural Hall, Westminster, for the very simple and commercial reason that public support, it was calculated, made such a long match the best paying proposition.

For the next few years, all matches in the Championship proper were of a week's duration with the final over a fortnight, usually in the vast arena of Blackpool Tower Circus. Apart from a couple of years when it was sponsored by the now defunct Empire News, the Championship was financed solely by gate money.

What now seems extraordinary is that the public was prepared to watch not only session after session long before a result was in sight, but many sessions after one or other player held a winning lead.

Such long matches were a very reliable test of skill but made relatively little demand on nerve, a supreme quality in modern snooker when matches are frequently no more than the best of nine frames. Even the world final today is only the best of 35.

Fred Davis, with eight wins, and Walter Donaldson with two, monopolised the title in the decade after Joe's last success, but the appeal of the Championship waned with that of professional snooker in general. Despite his retirement from the Championship, Joe continued to play in other events and was universally regarded as no 1, so the Championship itself, without the best player in it, came to be regarded as hollow.

Other professional events, which were contested on a handicap basis partly because the extended length of matches tended to emphasise even small differences of class between players, suffered because the cast did not change often enough.

Fred did not think it worthwhile to enter in 1957 and John Pulman became champion in a field of four. No promoter came forward to stage the Championship for seven years and it required an initiative from Rex Williams to get it going again on a challenge basis in 1964.

Pulman made seven successful title defences and through his exhibition contract with John Player managed to interest them in sponsoring the 1968-69 Championship on the old season-long knock-out formula with eight entries. John Spencer won the title; in 1970 Ray Reardon took it, again with John Player sponsorship.

An offer to stage the Championship six months later in Australia, the first time it had gone overseas, was accepted, so Reardon was champion only for six months before Spencer regained the title.

No sponsor was obtained for the 1971-72 Championship which straggled on for fourteen months before Alex Higgins won the title in February 1972.

The excitement which Higgins generated at a time when sports sponsorships were beginning to be managed in the highly professional way which has now become so familiar led to West Nally, a West End firm specialising in such matters, enlisting the sponsorship of Park Drive. The 1973 Championship was staged, Wimbledon-fashion, on eight tables at the City Exhibition Halls, Manchester, the whole event being streamlined into a fortnight.

Television coverage was obtained for the two Saturdays of the Championship, the first television exposure it had ever received, and it was clear that the new, modern format was more to the public's liking than the discontinuous method of running the Championship which had been standard in the past.

The 1974 Championship at Belle Vue, Manchester, was not quite so successful, particularly as the final was somewhat one-sided. Park Drive also disappeared as sponsors when the World Professional Billiards and Snooker Association, which had taken over from the amateur-based Billiards and Snooker Control Council (formerly the BA & CC) as the professional governing body in 1971, awarded the 1975 Championship to Australia. This multi-venue event provided Reardon with his fourth title.

The first Embassy World Championship was held in 1976, when a new promoter, Maurice Hayes, secured almost out of the blue the sponsorship of W. D. and H. O. Wills. The top half of the draw was played at Middlesbrough Town Hall and the bottom half at Wythenshawe Forum, Manchester, where the final was also staged.

Organisational disasters, ranging from imperfect tables to the absence of blackouts for the vast windows and of telephones for the press, did not prevent Reardon retaining the title but it did hasten the departure of Hayes from the sport.

Embassy also had every reason to flee from snooker at high speed but the persuasion of the WPBSA, added to the ideas put forward by a new promoter, Mike Watterson, saw the name not only remain in the sport but go on to be associated with one of the great, modern sporting success stories.

Inspired by his wife's suggestion after she had seen a play there, Watterson booked the Crucible Theatre, Sheffield, for the 1977 Championship. Nick Hunter, who had the previous year managed to distinguish the dramatic quality of the matches from the organisational imperfections with which they were staged, persuaded the BBC to cover the semi-finals and final, the first time a professional tournament, apart from the studio produced *Pot Black,* had been shown outside the Saturday afternoon *Grandstand* slot.

So successful was the Championship that the 1978 event carried, for the first time, daily BBC coverage of the fortnight's action (then, as now, Nick Hunter was executive producer) as Ray Reardon regained the title from John Spencer to become champion for the sixth time.

Since then, the Championship has remained firmly at the Crucible, with Embassy's sponsorship and the BBC's hours of transmission increasing year by year. Spencer, the first champion to be crowned at the Crucible, pocketed a first prize of £6,000 from a total prize fund of £17,000 in 1977. Steve Davis, in winning the title for the third time in 1984, took £44,000 from the total prize money of £200,000.

Stephen Hendry: the youngest ever World Championship competitor

The Embassy World Championship, which now receives over 100 hours of television coverage during its 17-day Championship proper, has long since transcended the world of snooker to become, like the Cup Final, the Grand National and Wimbledon, one of the nation's great annual sporting occasions. Terry Griffiths took the title at his first attempt in 1979, and was followed in turn by Cliff Thorburn, the first overseas champion, Steve Davis, Higgins and Davis twice more. Davis seemed certain to complete a hat-trick in 1985 when he led Dennis Taylor 8-0 in the final only to lose 18-17 on the final black.

But behind the necessary summary of who won and who lost lies snooker's collective store of memories: Thorburn's 147 maximum in 1983; the 69 clearance in the penultimate frame which helped Higgins beat Jimmy White from two down with three to play in the 1982 semi-final; the emotional scenes after Higgins's victory that year when his wife and baby daughter emerged from backstage to share his moment of triumph; the mixture of pride and incredulity with which Griffiths, then in his first professional season, said to the nation at 1.40a.m.: 'I'm in the final now you know,' after beating Eddie Charlton in their marathon 1979 semi-final and will there ever be a more dramatic climax than Dennis Taylor provided in 1985 when 18.5m BBC viewers, the biggest British television audience ever recorded for any sporting event, saw him pot the last black of the last frame to beat Steve Davis for the title.

1927

First round: M. Inman beat T. Newman 8-5; T. Carpenter beat N. Butler 8-3

Second round: T. A. Dennis beat F. Lawrence 8-7; A. Cope beat A. Mann 8-6; J. Davis beat J. Brady 10-5; Carpenter beat Inman 8-3

Semi-finals: J. Davis beat Cope 16-7; Dennis beat Carpenter 12-10

Final: J. Davis beat Dennis 20-11

1928

First round: T. Newman beat F. Smith 12-6; A. Mann beat A. Cope 14-9

Second round: Newman beat T. A. Dennis 12-5; F. Lawrence beat Mann 12-11

Third round: Lawrence beat Newman 12-7

Final: J. Davis beat Lawrence 16-13

1929

First round: F. Lawrence beat A. Mann 13-12

Semi-finals: J. Davis beat Lawrence 13-10; T. A. Dennis beat K. Prince 14-6

Final: J. Davis beat Dennis 19-14

1930

First round: F. Lawrence beat A. Mann 13-11; N. Butler beat T. Newman 13-11

Semi-finals: J. Davis beat Lawrence 13-2; T. A. Dennis beat Butler 13-11

Final: J. Davis beat Dennis 25-12

1931

Final: J. Davis beat T. A. Dennis 25-21

1932

First round: C. McConachy beat T. A. Dennis 13-11

Final: J. Davis beat McConachy 30-19

1933

First round: W. Donaldson beat W. Leigh 13-11

Semi-finals: J. Davis beat Donaldson 13-1; W. Smith beat T.A. Dennis 16-9

Final: J. Davis beat Smith 25-18

1934

Final: J. Davis beat T. Newman 25-23

1935

First round: W. Smith beat C. Stanbury 13-12

Semi-finals: Smith beat A. Mann 13-4; J. Davis beat T. Newman 15-10

Final: J. Davis beat Smith 25-20

1936

First round: C. O'Donnell beat S. Lee 16-15; H. Lindrum beat H. Terry 20-11; J. Davis beat T. Newman 29-2; W. Smith beat S. Smith 16-15; C. Stanbury beat A. Mann 22-9

Second round: Alec Brown beat Stanbury 16-15; Lindrum beat O'Donnell 19-6 (retired); J. Davis beat W. Smith 22-9; S. Newman w.o.

Semi-finals: J. Davis beat Alec Brown 21-10; Lindrum beat S. Newman 29-2

Final: J. Davis beat Lindrum 34-27

1937

First round: W.A. Withers beat F. Davis 17-14

Second round: J. Davis beat Withers 30-1; H. Lindrum beat S. Lee 20-11; W. Smith beat T. Newman 16-15; S. Smith beat Alec Brown 18-13

Semi-finals: Lindrum beat W. Smith 20-11; J. Davis beat S. Smith 18-13

Final: J. Davis beat Lindrum 32-29

1938
Qualifying

First round: H. Holt beat C.W. Read 21-10

Second round: F. Davis beat Holt 23-8

Competition Proper

First round: F. Davis beat Alec Brown 14-6 (retired ill); S. Smith beat C. Stanbury 27-4; J. Davis beat S. Lee 24-7; W. Smith beat T. Newman 16-15

Semi-finals: J. Davis beat W. Smith (n.r.s.); S. Smith beat F. Davis (n.r.s.)

Final: J. Davis beat S. Smith 37-24

1939
Qualifying

First round: W. Donaldson beat H. Holt 18-13; H.W. Laws beat S. Newman 19-12

Second round: Donaldson beat Laws 18-13

Competition Proper

First round: S. Smith beat S. Lee 21-10; W. Donaldson beat C. Falkiner 21-10; T. Newman beat A. Mann 19-12; F. Davis beat C. Stanbury 19-12

Second round: J. Davis beat W. Smith 19-12; F. Davis beat T. Newman 20-11; Alec Brown beat H. Lindrum 17-14; S. Smith beat Donaldson 16-15

Semi-finals: J. Davis beat F. Davis 17-14; S. Smith beat Alec Brown 20-11

Final: J. Davis beat S. Smith 43-30

1940
Qualifying

H. Holt beat C. Stanbury 18-13

Competition Proper

First round: W. Donaldson beat Holt 24-7; J. Davis beat Alec Brown 20-11; F. Davis beat S. Lee 20-11; S. Smith beat T. Newman 22-9

Semi-finals: J. Davis beat Donaldson 22-9; F. Davis beat S. Smith 17-14

Final: J. Davis beat F. Davis 37-36

1946
Qualifying

First round: K. Kennerley beat F. Lawrence 22-9; C. Stanbury beat J. Barrie 18-13; S. Newman beat W. Leigh 16-15

Second round: Kennerley beat T. Reece 8-2 (retired); S. Newman beat Stanbury 17-14

Third round: S. Newman beat Kennerley 21-10

Competition Proper

First round: J. Davis beat W. Donaldson 21-10; S. Newman beat S. Lee 19-12; F. Davis beat Alec Brown 24-7; H. Lindrum beat H. Holt 17-14

Semi-finals: J. Davis beat S. Newman 21-10; Lindrum beat F. Davis 16-12

Final: J. Davis beat Lindrum 78-67

1947
Qualifying

First round: Albert Brown beat J. Pulman 21-14; W. Leigh beat H.F. Francis 19-16; S. Lee beat J. Lees 19-16; K. Kennerley beat C. Stanbury 23-12; E. Newman w.o. H. Holt

Second round: J. Barrie beat F. Lawrence 25-10; Albert Brown beat Newman 28-7; Kennerley beat A. Mann 23-12; Leigh beat Lee 25-10

Third round: Albert Brown beat Barrie 24-11; Kennerley beat Leigh 21-14

Fourth round: Albert Brown beat Kennerley 21-14

Competition Proper

First round: H. Lindrum beat Albert Brown 39-34; S. Smith beat Alec Brown 43-28; W. Donaldson beat S. Newman 46-25; F. Davis beat C. McConachy 53-20

Semi-finals: Donaldson beat Lindrum 39-32; F. Davis beat Smith 39-32

Final: Donaldson beat F. Davis 82-63

1948
Qualifying

First round: C. Stanbury beat E. Newman 26-9; W. Leigh beat H. Holt 18-17; J. Barrie beat H.F. Francis 19-16; J. Pulman w.o. S. Lee.

Second round: Leigh beat Barrie 21-14; Pulman beat Stanbury 19-16

Third round: Pulman beat Leigh 18-17

Competition Proper

First round: F. Davis beat Alec Brown 43-28; C. McConachy beat J. Pulman 42-29; Albert Brown beat S. Smith 36-35; W. Donaldson beat K. Kennerley 46-25

Semi-finals: F. Davis beat McConachy 43-28; Donaldson beat Alec Brown 40-31

Final: F. Davis beat Donaldson 84-61

1949
Qualifying

First round: C. Stanbury beat H.F. Francis 18-17

Second round: Stanbury beat J. Rea 18-17

Third round: Stanbury beat H. Holt 18-17

Steve Davis and Jimmy White between frames in their 1986 Embassy World Championship quarter-final

Competition Proper

First round: W. Donaldson beat Stanbury 58-13; J. Pulman beat Albert Brown 42-29; S. Smith beat Alec Brown 41-30; F. Davis beat K. Kennerley 50-21

Semi-finals: Donaldson beat Pulman 49-22; F. Davis beat Smith 42-29

Final: F. Davis beat Donaldson 80-65

1950
Qualifying

First round: W. Smith beat W.A. Withers 28-7; H. Holt beat H.W. Laws 26-9; S. Lee beat C. Stanbury 20-15; K. Kennerley beat J. Barrie 21-14

Second round: Kennerley beat Smith 22-13; Lee beat Holt 16-8 (retired ill)

Third round: Kennerley beat Lee 21-14

Competition Proper

First round: Albert Brown beat J. Pulman 37-34; W. Donaldson beat K. Kennerley 42-29; G. Chenier beat P. Mans 37-34; F. Davis beat Alec Brown 44-27

Semi-finals: Donaldson beat Albert Brown 37-34; F. Davis beat Chenier 43-28

Final: Donaldson beat F. Davis 51-46

1951
Qualifying

First round: J. Barrie beat S. Lee 23-12

Second round: Barrie beat H.W. Laws 28-7

Competition Proper

First round: F. Davis beat Barrie 42-29; H. Lindrum beat Albert Brown 43-28; W. Donaldson beat K. Kennerley 41-30; J. Pulman beat S. Smith 38-33

Semi-finals: Donaldson beat Lindrum 41-30; F. Davis beat Pulman 22-14 (retired ill)

Final: F. Davis beat Donaldson 58-39

1952

First round: Alec Brown beat R. Williams 39-22; J. Rea beat J. Lees 38-32; Albert Brown beat J. Pulman 32-27 (records incomplete)

Semi-finals: W. Donaldson beat Albert Brown 31-30

Final: F. Davis beat Donaldson 38-35

1953
Qualifying

First round: W. Smith beat J. Lees 21-14; K. Kennerley beat R. Williams 25-12

Second round: Kennerley beat Smith 42-29

Competition Proper

First round: Albert Brown beat Alec Brown 35-26; J. Pulman beat J. Rea 36-25; W. Donaldson beat Kennerley 42-19; F. Davis beat J. Barrie 32-29

Semi-finals: Donaldson beat Brown n.r.s.; F. Davis beat Pulman 36-25

Final: F. Davis beat Donaldson 37-34

1954

First round: J. Pulman beat J. Rea 31-30

Semi-finals: W. Donaldson beat Alec Brown 36-25; F. Davis beat Pulman 32-29

Final: F. Davis beat Donaldson 39-21

1955

First round: J. Pulman beat R. Williams 22-15; J. Rea beat H. Stokes n.r.s.

Semi-finals: F. Davis beat Rea 36-25; Pulman beat Alec Brown n.r.s.

Final: F. Davis beat Pulman 37-34

1956

Semi-finals: J. Pulman beat J. Rea 36-25; F. Davis beat R. Williams 35-26

Final: Davis beat Pulman 38-35

1957

Semi-finals: J. Pulman beat R. Williams 21-16; J. Rea beat K. Kennerley 25-12

Final: Pulman beat Rea 39-34

Through lack of public support no championship was organised between 1957 and 1964. After a truce with the BA & CC a new system was adopted whereby the champion defended his title against a series of single challengers. These matches resulted as follows:

1964

J. Pulman beat F. Davis 19-16
J. Pulman beat R. Williams 40-33

1965

J. Pulman beat F. Davis 37-36
J. Pulman beat R. Williams 25-22 (matches)
J. Pulman beat F. van Rensburg 39-12

1966

J. Pulman beat F. Davis 5-2 (matches)

1968

J. Pulman beat E. Charlton 39-34

1969

First round: John Spencer (England) beat John Pulman (England) 25-18; Rex Williams (England) beat Bernard Bennett (England) 25-4; Gary Owen (England) beat Jack Rea (Northern Ireland) 25-17; Fred Davis (England) beat Ray Reardon (Wales) 25-24

Semi-finals: Spencer beat Williams 37-12; Owen beat Davis 37-24

Final: Spencer beat Owen 37-24

Tony Meo lines up a shot in the 1986 Embassy World Championship

1970 (April)

First round: David Taylor (England) beat Bernard Bennett (England) 11-8

Quarter-finals: John Pulman (England) beat Taylor 31-20; Gary Owen (England) beat Rex Williams (England) 31-11; Ray Reardon (Wales) beat Fred Davis (England) 31-26; John Spencer (England) beat Jack Rea (Northern Ireland) 31-15

Semi-finals: Pulman beat Owen 37-12; Reardon beat Spencer 37-33

Final: Reardon beat Pulman 37-33

1970 (November)

Round robin: John Spencer (England) beat Perrie Mans (South Africa) 20-17; beat Norman Squire (Australia) 27-10; beat John Pulman (England) 23-14
Ray Reardon (Wales) beat Mans 22-15; beat Eddie Charlton (Australia) 21-16; beat Spencer 21-16
Warren Simpson (Australia) beat Gary Owen (England) 19-18; beat Pulman 21-16; beat Mans 19-18
Charlton beat Squire 27-10; beat Mans 26-11; beat Owen 23-14
Owen beat Paddy Morgan (Australia) 26-11; beat Squire 26-11; Morgan beat Simpson 21-16

Semi-finals: Spencer beat Reardon 34-15; Simpson beat Charlton 27-22

Final: Spencer beat Simpson 37-29

1972 Qualifying

First round: Alex Higgins (Northern Ireland) beat Ron Gross (England) 15-6; Maurice Parkin (England) beat Geoffrey Thompson (England) 11-10; Graham Miles (England) beat Bernard Bennett (England) 15-6; John Dunning (England) beat Pat Houlihan (England) 11-10

Second round: Higgins beat Parkin 11-3; Dunning beat Miles 11-5

Competition Proper

First round: John Pulman (England) beat Dunning 19-7; Higgins beat Jack Rea (Northern Ireland) 19-11

Quarter-finals: John Spencer (England) beat Fred Davis (England) 31-21; Eddie Charlton (Australia) beat David Taylor (England) 31-25; Higgins beat Pulman 31-23; Rex Williams (England) beat Ray Reardon (Wales) 25-23

Semi-finals: Higgins beat Williams 31-30; Spencer beat Charlton 37-32

Final: Higgins beat Spencer 37-32

1973

First round: Pat Houlihan (England) beat Jack Rea (Northern Ireland) 9-2; David Greaves (England) beat Bernard Bennett (England) 9-8; Graham Miles (England) beat Geoffrey Thompson (England) 9-5; Perrie Mans (South Africa) beat Ron Gross (England) 9-2; Warren Simpson (Australia) beat Maurice Parkin (England) 9-3; Cliff Thorburn (Canada) beat Dennis Taylor (Northern Ireland) 9-8; David Taylor (England) beat John Dunning (England) 9-4

Second round: Fred Davis (England) beat Greaves 16-1; Miles beat John Pulman (England) 16-10; Eddie Charlton (Australia) beat Mans 16-8; Gary Owen (Australia) beat Simpson 16-14; Ray Reardon (Wales) beat Jim Meadowcroft (England) 16-10; Rex Williams (England) beat Thorburn 16-15; John Spencer (England) beat David Taylor 16-5; Alex Higgins (Northern Ireland) beat Houlihan 16-3

Quarter-finals: Higgins beat Davis 16-14; Spencer beat Williams 16-7; Charlton beat Miles 16-6; Reardon beat Owen 16-6

Semi-finals: Charlton beat Higgins 23-9; Reardon beat Spencer 23-22

Final: Reardon beat Charlton 38-32

1974

Qualifying: John Dunning (England) beat David Greaves (England) 8-2; Warren Simpson (Australia) beat Jack Rea (Northern Ireland) 8-3; Jim Meadowcroft (England) beat Pat Houlihan (England) 8-5; Cliff Thorburn

(Canada) beat Alan McDonald (Australia) 8-3; John Pulman (England) beat Jack Karnehm (England) 8-0; David Taylor (England) beat Ron Gross (England) 8-7; Marcus Owen (Wales) beat Dennis Taylor (Northern Ireland) 8-1

First round: Bernard Bennett (England) beat Simpson 8-2; Bill Werbeniuk (Canada) beat Geoffrey Thompson (England) 8-3; Meadowcroft beat Kingsley Kennerley (England) 8-5; M. Owen beat Maurice Parkin (England) 8-5; Perrie Mans (South Africa) beat Ian Anderson (Australia) 8-1; Pulman beat Sydney Lee (England) 8-0; Dunning beat David Taylor 8-6; Paddy Morgan (Australia) beat Thorburn 8-4

Second round: Mans beat John Spencer (England) 15-13; Dunning beat Eddie Charlton (Australia) 15-13; M. Owen beat Gary Owen (Australia) 15-8; Alex Higgins (Northern Ireland) beat Bennett 15-4; Graham Miles (England) beat Morgan 15-7; Rex Williams (England) beat Pulman 15-12; Fred Davis (England) beat Werbeniuk 15-5; Ray Reardon (Wales) beat Meadowcroft 15-3

Quarter-finals: Williams beat Mans 15-4; Miles beat Dunning 15-13; F. Davis beat Higgins 15-14; Reardon beat M. Owen 15-11

Semi-finals: Miles beat Williams 15-7; Reardon beat F. Davis 15-3

Final: Reardon beat Miles 22-12

1975

Qualifying: Phil Tarrant (Australia) beat Bernard Bennett (England) 15-8; Lou Condo (Australia) beat Maurice Parkin (England) 15-8; David Greaves (England) beat Jim Charlton (Australia) 15-14

First round: Warren Simpson (Australia) beat Ron Mares (Australia) 15-5; John Pulman (England) beat Tarrant 15-5; David Taylor (England) beat Rex King (Australia) 15-8; Ian Anderson (Australia) beat Condo 15-8; Dennis Taylor (Northern Ireland) beat Perrie Mans (South Africa) 15-12; Gary Owen (Australia) beat Greaves 15-3; Bill Werbeniuk (Canada) beat Jim Meadowcroft (England) 15-9; Cliff Thorburn (Canada) beat Paddy Morgan (Australia) 15-6

Second round: Ray Reardon (Wales) beat Simpson 15-11; John Spencer (England) beat Pulman 15-10; Alex Higgins (Northern Ireland) beat David Taylor 15-2; Rex Williams (England) beat Anderson 15-4; Dennis Taylor beat Fred Davis (England) 15-14; Owen beat John Dunning (England) 15-8; Eddie Charlton (Australia) beat Werbeniuk 15-11; Thorburn beat Graham Miles (England) 15-2

Quarter-finals: Reardon beat Spencer 19-17; Higgins beat Williams 19-12; Dennis Taylor beat Owen 19-9; Charlton beat Thorburn 19-12

Semi-finals: Charlton beat Dennis Taylor 19-12; Reardon beat Higgins 19-14

Final: Reardon beat Charlton 31-30

1976 Qualifying

First round: Jack Rea (Northern Ireland) beat Ian Anderson (Australia) 8-5; David Greaves (England) beat Jim Charlton (Australia) 8-5; Jim Meadowcroft (England) beat Dennis Wheelwright (Australia) 8-1; Ron Gross (England) beat Maurice Parkin (England) 8-5; Lou Condo (Australia) beat Marcus Owen (Wales) 8-6

Second round: Rea beat Bernard Bennett (England) 8-5; David Taylor (England) beat Greaves 8-1; Meadowcroft beat Gross 8-4; Willie Thorne (England) beat Condo 8-3

Competition Proper

First round: Ray Reardon (Wales) beat John Dunning (England) 15-7; Dennis Taylor (Northern Ireland) beat Gary Owen (Australia) 15-9; Perrie Mans (South Africa) beat Graham Miles (England) 15-10; Meadowcroft beat Rex Williams (England) 15-7; Eddie Charlton (Australia) beat John Pulman (England) 15-9; Fred Davis (England) beat Bill Werbeniuk (Canada) 15-12; Alex Higgins (Northern Ireland) beat Cliff Thorburn (Canada) 15-14; John Spencer (England) beat David Taylor (England) 15-5

Quarter-finals: Reardon beat Dennis Taylor 15-2; Mans beat Meadowcroft 15-8; Charlton beat F. Davis 15-13; Higgins beat Spencer 15-14

Semi-finals: Reardon beat Mans 20-10; Higgins beat Charlton 20-18

Final: Reardon beat Higgins 27-16

1977 Qualifying

First round: John Virgo (England) beat Roy Andrewartha (Wales) 11-1

Second round: Patsy Fagan (Rep. of Ireland) beat Jim Meadowcroft (England) 11-9; Virgo beat John Dunning (England) 11-6; Willie Thorne (England) beat Bernard Bennett (England) 11-4; John Pulman (England) w.o. M. Parkin (England) scr; David Taylor (England) beat David Greaves (England) 11-0; Cliff Thorburn (Canada) beat Chris Ross (Scotland) 11-0; Dennis Taylor (Northern Ireland) beat Jack Karnehm (England) 11-0; Doug Mountjoy (Wales) beat Jack Rea (Northern Ireland) 11-9

Competition Proper

First round: Ray Reardon (Wales) beat Fagan 13-7; John Spencer (England) beat Virgo 13-9; Graham Miles (England) beat Thorne 13-4; Pulman beat Fred Davis (England) 13-12; Eddie Charlton (Australia) beat David Taylor (England) 13-5; Thorburn beat Rex Williams (England) 13-6; Dennis Taylor beat Perrie Mans (South Africa) 13-11; Mountjoy beat Alex Higgins (Northern Ireland) 13-12

Quarter-finals: Spencer beat Reardon 13-6; Pulman beat Miles 13-10; Thorburn beat Charlton 13-12; Dennis Taylor beat Mountjoy 13-11

Semi-finals: Spencer beat Pulman 18-16; Thorburn beat Dennis Taylor 18-16

Final: Spencer beat Thorburn 25-21

Perrie Mans: runner-up in the 1978 Embassy World Championship

1978
Qualifying

First round: Maurice Parkin (England) beat Bernard Bennett (England) 9-4; Roy Andrewartha (Wales) beat Jack Karnehm (England) 9-0; John Barrie (England) beat David Greaves (England) 9-3; Pat Houlihan (England) beat Chris Ross (Scotland) 9-1

Second round: Doug Mountjoy (Wales) beat Andrewartha 9-3; Patsy Fagan (Rep. of Ireland) beat John Dunning (England) 9-5; Willie Thorne (England) beat Rex Williams (England) 9-3; Bill Werbeniuk (Canada) beat Maurice Parkin (England) 9-2; Perrie Mans (South Africa) beat Barrie 9-6; David Taylor (England) beat Paddy Morgan (Australia) 9-7; Houlihan beat Jim Meadowcroft 9-6; Fred Davis (England) beat John Virgo (England) 9-8

Competition Proper

First round: Mans beat John Spencer (England) 13-8; Graham Miles (England) beat David Taylor (England) 13-10; Fagan beat Alex Higgins (Northern Ireland) 13-12; Davis beat Dennis Taylor (Northern Ireland) 13-9; Eddie Charlton (Australia) beat Thorne 13-12; Cliff Thorburn (Canada) beat Houlihan 13-8; Werbeniuk beat John Pulman (England) 13-4; Ray Reardon (Wales) beat Mountjoy 13-9

Quarter-finals: Mans beat Miles 13-7; Davis beat Fagan 13-10; Charlton beat Thorburn 13-12; Reardon beat Werbeniuk 13-6

Semi-finals: Mans beat Davis 18-16; Reardon beat Charlton 18-14

Final: Reardon beat Mans 25-18

1979
Qualifying

First round: Doug Mountjoy (Wales) beat Derek Mienie (South Africa) 9-1; Terry Griffiths (Wales) beat Bernard Bennett (England) 9-2; Pat Houlihan (England) beat John Barrie (England) 9-5; Willie Thorne (England) beat Jim Charlton (Australia) 9-3; John Virgo (England) beat Maurice Parkin (England) 9-0; John Dunning (England) beat Jack Rea (Northern Ireland) 9-5; Rex Williams (England) beat David Greaves (England) 9-2; Jim Meadowcroft (England) beat Jimmy van Rensburg (South Africa) 9-7; Roy Andrewartha (Wales) beat Ray Edmonds (England) 9-8; Steve Davis (England) beat Ian Anderson (Australia) 9-1; Kirk Stevens (Canada) beat Roy Amdor (South Africa) 9-1

Second round: Virgo beat Thorne 9-8; Bill Werbeniuk (Canada) beat Andrewartha 9-2; David Taylor (England) beat Dunning 9-8; Mountjoy beat Houlihan 9-6; S. Davis beat P. Fagan (Rep. of Ireland) 9-2; Griffiths beat Meadowcroft 9-6; Stevens beat John Pulman (England) 9-0; Graham Miles (England) beat Williams 9-5

Competition Proper

First round: Eddie Charlton (Australia) beat Mountjoy 13-6; Werbeniuk beat John Spencer (England) 13-11; Virgo beat Cliff Thorburn 13-10; F. Davis beat Stevens 13-8; Dennis Taylor (Northern Ireland) beat S. Davis 13-11; Alex Higgins (Northern Ireland) beat David Taylor 13-5; Griffiths beat Perrie Mans (South Africa) 13-8; Ray Reardon (Wales) beat Miles 13-8

Quarter-finals: Charlton beat F. Davis 13-4; Dennis Taylor beat Reardon 13-8; Virgo beat Werbeniuk 13-9; Griffiths beat Higgins 13-12

Semi-finals: Griffiths beat Charlton 19-17; Dennis Taylor beat Virgo 19-12

Final: Griffiths beat Dennis Taylor 24-16

1980
Qualifying

Group 1: Jack Rea (Northern Ireland) beat Bernard Bennett (England) 9-1; Willie Thorne (England) beat Kevin Robitaille (Canada) 9-4; Thorne beat Rea 9-1

Bill Werbeniuk: always a popular figure at the Embassy World Championship

Group 2: Steve Davis (England) beat Chris Ross (Scotland) 9-3; Paddy Morgan (Australia) beat Paul Thornley (Canada) 9-4; S. Davis beat Morgan 9-0

Group 3: Mike Hallett (England) beat Kingsley Kennerley (England) 9-2; Kirk Stevens (Canada) beat David Greaves (England) 9-3; Stevens beat Hallett 9-3

Group 4: Joe Johnson (England) beat Roy Andrewartha (Wales) 9-5; Pat Houlihan (England) beat Johnson 9-6; Tony Meo (England) beat Jimmy van Rensburg (South Africa) 9-1; Meo beat Houlihan 9-1

Group 5: Roy Amdor (South Africa) beat Bernie Mikkelsen (Canada) 9-7; Rex Williams (England) beat Amdor 9-4; Jim Wych (Canada) beat John Bear (Canada) 9-5; Wych beat Williams 9-7

Group 6: Frank Jonik (Canada) beat Mark Wildman (England) 9-7; Cliff Wilson (Wales) beat Jonik 9-6

Group 7: Ray Edmonds (England) beat Maurice Parkin (England) 9-2; Sid Hood (England) beat John Dunning (England) 16-7; Edmonds beat Hood 9-6

Group 8: Eddie Sinclair (Scotland) beat Mario Morra (Canada) 9-5; Sinclair beat Derek Mienie (South Africa) 9-7; Jim Meadowcroft (England) beat Sinclair 9-1

Competition Proper

First round: S. Davis beat Patsy Fagan (Rep. of Ireland) 10-6; Alex Higgins (Northern Ireland) beat Meo 10-9; Doug Mountjoy (Wales) beat Wilson 10-6; Wych beat John Pulman (England) 10-5; John Virgo (England) beat Meadowcroft 10-2; Stevens beat Graham Miles (England) 10-3; David Taylor (England) beat Edmonds 10-3; Bill Werbeniuk (Canada) beat Thorne 10-9

Second round: S. Davis beat Terry Griffiths (Wales) 13-10; Higgins beat Perrie Mans (South Africa) 13-6; Stevens beat John Spencer (England) 13-8; Eddie Charlton (Australia) beat Virgo 13-12; Cliff Thorburn (Canada) beat Mountjoy 13-10; Wych beat Dennis Taylor (Northern Ireland) 13-10; Ray Reardon (Wales) beat Werbeniuk 13-6; David Taylor beat Fred Davis (England) 13-5

Quarter-finals: David Taylor beat Reardon 13-11; Thorburn beat Wych 13-6; Stevens beat Charlton 13-7; Higgins beat S. Davis 13-9

Semi-finals: Thorburn beat David Taylor 16-7; Higgins beat Stevens 16-13

Final: Thorburn beat Higgins 18-16

1981 Qualifying

Group 1: Willie Thorne (England) beat Mario Morra (Canada) 9-5; David Greaves (England) beat Maurice Parkin (England) 9-5; Thorne beat Greaves 9-3

Group 2: Jimmy White (England) beat Bernie Mikkelsen (Canada) 9-4; White beat Jim Meadowcroft (England) 9-8

Group 3: Ray Edmonds (England) beat Mark Wildman (England) 9-3; Rex Williams (England) beat Sid Hood (England) 9-4; Edmonds beat Williams 9-7

Group 4: Tony Meo (England) beat Joe Johnson (England) 9-8; Mike Hallett (England) beat Frank Jonik (Canada) 9-1; Meo beat Hallett 9-4

Group 5: John Dunning (England) beat Bernard Bennett (England) 9-6; Dunning beat Patsy Fagan (Rep. of Ireland) 9-7

Group 6: Dave Martin (England) beat Ian Anderson (Australia) 9-3; Martin beat John Pulman (England) 9-2

Group 7: Cliff Wilson (Wales) beat Roy Andrewartha (Wales) 9-4; Eddie Sinclair (Scotland) beat Paddy Morgan (Australia) 9-8; Wilson beat Sinclair 9-4

Group 8: Tony Knowles (England) beat Chris Ross (Scotland) 7-0 (retired); Knowles beat Jim Wych (Canada) 9-3

Competition Proper

First round: Graham Miles (England) beat Knowles 10-8; David Taylor (England) beat Wilson 10-6; Doug Mountjoy (Wales) beat Thorne 10-6; Kirk Stevens (Canada) beat Dunning 10-4; Meo beat John Virgo (England) 10-6; Steve Davis (England) beat White 10-8; Bill Werbeniuk (Canada) beat Martin 10-4; John Spencer (England) beat Edmonds 10-9

Second round: Cliff Thorburn (Canada) beat Miles 13-2; David Taylor beat Fred Davis (England) 13-3; Terry Griffiths (Wales) beat Meo 13-6; S. Davis beat Alex Higgins (Northern Ireland) 13-8; Mountjoy beat Eddie Charlton (Australia) 13-7; Dennis Taylor (Northern Ireland) beat Stevens 13-11; Werbeniuk beat Perrie Mans (South Africa) 13-5; Ray Reardon (Wales) beat Spencer 13-11

Quarter-finals: Thorburn beat David Taylor 13-6; S. Davis beat Griffiths 13-9; Mountjoy beat Dennis Taylor 13-8; Reardon beat Werbeniuk 13-10

Semi-finals: Davis beat Thorburn 16-10; Mountjoy beat Reardon 16-10

Final: Davis beat Mountjoy 18-22

1982 Qualifying

Group 1: John Bear (Canada) beat Frank Jonik (Canada) 9-4; Bear beat Jim Wych (Canada) 9-4

Group 2: Dennis Hughes (England) beat Clive Everton (Wales) 9-4; Tony Meo (England) beat Hughes 9-4

Group 3: Dean Reynolds (England) beat Dessie Sheehan (Rep. of Ireland) 9-5; Reynolds beat Ray Edmonds (England) 9-6

Group 4: Eugene Hughes (Rep. of Ireland) w.o. Derek Mienie (South Africa) scr; Tony Knowles (England) beat Hughes 9-7

Group 5: Mark Wildman (England) beat Geoff Foulds (England) 9-8; Jimmy White (England) beat Wildman 9-4

Group 6: Colin Roscoe (Wales) beat Bernie Mikkelsen (Canada) 9-6; Willie Thorne (England) beat Roscoe 9-1

Group 7: Paul Medati (England) beat John Phillips (Scotland) 9-3; Cliff Wilson (Wales) beat Medati 9-5

Group 8: Pat Houlihan (England) beat Ian Anderson (Australia) 9-5; Dave Martin (England) beat Houlihan 9-3

Group 9: Murdo Macleod (Scotland) beat Eddie McLaughlin (Scotland) 9-8; John Dunning (England) beat Macleod 9-4

Group 10: Mike Watterson (England) beat Bert Demarco (Scotland) 9-6; Jim Meadowcroft (England) beat Watterson 9-7

Group 11: Doug French (England) beat Bernard Bennett (England) 9-3; Patsy Fagan (Rep. of Ireland) beat French 9-6

Group 12: Ian Black (Scotland) beat Maurice Parkin (England) 9-6; Rex Williams (England) beat Black 9-2

Group 13: Joe Johnson (England) beat Vic Harris (England) 9-4; Mike Hallett (England) beat Johnson 9-8

Group 14: Jim Donnelly (Scotland) beat Matt Gibson (Scotland) 9-8; Eddie Sinclair (Scotland) beat Billy Kelly (Rep. of Ireland) 9-8; Donnelly beat Sinclair 9-8

Group 15: Paddy Morgan (Australia) beat David Greaves (England) 9-2; Silvino Francisco (South Africa) beat Chris Ross (Scotland) 9-0; Francisco beat Morgan 9-1

Group 16: Mario Morra (Canada) beat Tommy Murphy (Northern Ireland) 9-5; Jack Fitzmaurice (England) w.o. John Pulman (England) scr; Fitzmaurice beat Morra 9-7

Mike Hallett scored a notable victory over defending champion Dennis Taylor in the 1986 Embassy World Championship

Competition Proper

First round: Knowles beat S. Davis (England) 10-1; Graham Miles (England) beat Martin 10-5; Bill Werbeniuk (Canada) beat Bear 10-7; Eddie Charlton (Australia) beat Wilson 10-5; Francisco beat Dennis Taylor (Northern Ireland) 10-7; Reynolds beat Fred Davis (England) 10-7; John Virgo (England) beat Hallett 10-4; Ray Reardon (Wales) beat Donnelly 10-5; Thorne beat Griffiths 10-6; John Spencer (England) beat Dunning 10-4; Alex Higgins (Northern Ireland) beat Meadowcroft 10-5; Doug Mountjoy (Wales) beat Williams 10-3; Fagan beat David Taylor (England) 10-9; Kirk Stevens (Canada) beat Fitzmaurice 10-4; Perrie Mans (South Africa) beat Meo 10-8; White beat Cliff Thorburn (Canada) 10-4

Second round: Knowles beat Miles 13-7; Charlton beat Werbeniuk 13-5; Francisco beat Reynolds 13-8; Reardon beat Virgo 13-8; Thorne beat Spencer 13-5; Higgins beat Mountjoy 13-12; Stevens beat Fagan 13-7; White beat Mans 13-6

Quarter-finals: Charlton beat Knowles 13-11; Reardon beat Francisco 13-8; Higgins beat Thorne 13-10; White beat Stevens 13-9

Semi-finals: Reardon beat Charlton 16-11; Higgins beat White 16-15

Final: Higgins beat Reardon 18-15

1983 Qualifying

Group 1: Billy Kelly (Rep. of Ireland) beat Bert Demarco (Scotland) 10-4; Silvino Francisco (South Africa) beat Kelly 10-5

Group 2: Paddy Morgan (Australia) beat Pascal Burke (Rep. of Ireland) 10-9; Graham Miles (England) beat Morgan 10-6

Group 3: Tommy Murphy (Northern Ireland) beat Pat Houlihan (England) 10-9; John Virgo (England) beat Murphy 10-8

Group 4: Rex Williams (England) beat Mike Darrington (England) 10-0; Williams beat Fred Davis (England) 10-1

Group 5: Mark Wildman (England) beat Bob Harris (England) 10-7; Wildman w.o. Jim Wych (Canada) scr

Group 6: Ray Edmonds (England) beat Frank Jonik (Canada) 10-4; Dean Reynolds (England) beat Edmonds 10-6

Group 7: Mick Fisher (England) beat Patsy Fagan (Rep. of Ireland) 10-8; Eddie McLaughlin (Scotland) beat David Greaves (England) 10-7; Fisher beat McLaughlin 10-9

Group 8: Tony Meo (England) beat Vic Harris (England) 10-0; Geoff Foulds (England) beat Matt Gibson (Scotland) 10-6; Meo beat Foulds 10-4

Group 9: Ian Black (Scotland) beat Mario Morra (Canada) 10-9; Paul Medati (England) beat John Bear (Canada) 10-7; Black beat Medati 10-4

Group 10: Cliff Wilson (Wales) beat Clive Everton (Wales) 10-1; Joe Johnson (England) beat Paul Watchorn (Rep. of Ireland) 10-0; Wilson beat Johnson 10-8

Group 11: Murdo Macleod (Scotland) beat Marcus Owen (Wales) 10-5; Dave Martin (England) beat Maurice Parkin (England) 10-1; Martin beat Macleod 10-7

Group 12: Jim Meadowcroft (England) beat Bernard Bennett (England) 10-3; Graham Cripsey (England) beat Dennis Hughes (England) 10-2; Meadowcroft beat Cripsey 10-6

Group 13: Jim Donnelly (Scotland) beat Dessie Sheehan (Rep. of Ireland) 10-6; John Campbell (Australia) beat Mike Watterson (England) 10-6; Campbell beat Donnelly 10-2

Group 14: Les Dodd (England) w.o. John Dunning (England) scr; Ian Williamson (England) beat Doug French (England) 10-8; Dodd beat Williamson 10-9

Group 15: Mike Hallett (England) beat Roy Andrewartha (Wales) 10-7; Warren King (Australia) beat Ian Anderson (Australia) 10-6; Hallett beat King 10-6

Group 16: Eugene Hughes (Rep. of Ireland) beat Jack Fitzmaurice (England) 10-7; Eddie Sinclair (Scotland) beat Colin Roscoe (Wales) 10-2; Hughes beat Sinclair 10-8

Competition Proper

First round: Alex Higgins (Northern Ireland) beat Reynolds 10-4; Willie Thorne (England) beat Virgo 10-3; Bill Werbeniuk (Canada) beat Martin 10-4; David Taylor (England) beat Meadowcroft 10-2; Eddie Charlton (Australia) beat Dodd 10-7; John Spencer (England) beat Hallett 10-7; Dennis Taylor (Northern Ireland) beat Francisco 10-9; Steve Davis (England) beat Williams 10-4; Cliff Thorburn (Canada) beat Campbell 10-5; Terry Griffiths (Wales) beat Wildman 10-8; Perrie Mans (South Africa) beat Black 10-3; Kirk Stevens (Canada) beat Fisher 10-2; Doug Mountjoy (Wales) beat Wilson 10-2; Meo beat Jimmy White (England) 10-8; Tony Knowles (England) beat Miles 10-3; Ray Reardon (Wales) beat Hughes 10-7

Second round: Higgins beat Thorne 13-8; Werbeniuk beat David Taylor 13-10; Charlton beat Spencer 13-11; Davis beat Dennis Taylor 13-11; Thorburn beat Griffiths 13-12; Meo beat Mountjoy 13-11; Knowles beat Reardon 13-12; Stevens beat Mans 13-3

Quarter-finals: Higgins beat Werbeniuk 13-11; Davis beat Charlton 13-5; Thorburn beat Stevens 13-12; Knowles beat Meo 13-9

Semi-finals: Thorburn beat Knowles 16-15; Davis beat Higgins 16-5

Final: Davis beat Thorburn 18-6

1984 Qualifying

Group 1: John Parrott (England) beat Dennis Hughes (England) 10-3; Parrott beat Clive Everton (Wales) 10-2; Parrott beat Perrie Mans (South Africa) 10-0

Group 2: Bernie Mikkelsen (Canada) beat Paul Medati (England) 10-8; Mikkelsen beat Frank Jonik (Canada) 10-9; Willie Thorne (England) beat Mikkelsen 10-3

Group 3: Mario Morra (Canada) beat Geoff Foulds (England) 10-2; Tommy Murphy (Northern Ireland) beat Jack Fitzmaurice (England) 10-8; Morra beat Murphy 10-5; Morra beat Dean Reynolds (England) 10-7

Group 4: Wayne Sanderson (Canada) beat Paddy Morgan (Australia) 10-8; Paul Mifsud (Malta) beat Eugene Hughes (Rep. of Ireland) 10-5; Mifsud beat Sanderson 10-5; Mifsud beat Cliff Wilson (Wales) 10-8

Group 5: Jimmy van Rensburg (South Africa) beat Vic Harris (England) 10-7; Ray Edmonds (England) beat David Greaves (England) 10-0; van Rensburg beat Edmonds 10-9; Silvino Francisco (South Africa) beat van Rensburg 10-3

Group 6: Ian Williamson (England) beat Pat Houlihan (England) 10-5; Mike Hines (South Africa) beat Ian Black (Scotland) 10-5; Williamson beat Hines 10-6; Graham Miles (England) beat Williamson 10-6

Group 7: Matt Gibson (Scotland) beat Gino Rigitano (Canada) 10-7; Mick Fisher (England) beat Paul Thornley (Canada) 10-8; Gibson beat Fisher 10-7; Joe Johnson (England) beat Gibson 10-3

Cliff Thorburn about to play in his epic Embassy World Championship semi-final in 1986 against Steve Davis

Group 8: Eddie McLaughlin (Scotland) beat John Hargreaves (England) 10-5; Roy Andrewartha (Wales) w.o. John Bear (Canada) scr; Andrewartha beat McLaughlin 10-8; Andrewartha beat Mark Wildman (England) 10-9

Group 9: Jim Wych (Canada) beat George Ganim Jr (Australia) 10-1; George Scott (England) beat Leon Heywood (Australia) 10-7; Wych beat Scott 10--6; Wych beat Patsy Fagan (Rep. of Ireland) 10-3

Group 10: Paddy Browne (Rep. of Ireland) beat Steve Duggan (England) 10-9; Colin Roscoe (Wales) beat Bert Demarco (Scotland) 10-7; Browne beat Roscoe 10-4; Eddie Sinclair (Scotland) beat Browne 10-1

Group 11: Marcel Gauvreau (Canada) beat John Campbell (Australia) 10-7; Graham Cripsey (England) beat Maurice Parkin (England) 10-4; Gauvreau beat Cripsey 10-1; Gauvreau beat Murdo Macleod (Scotland) 10-6

Group 12: Ian Anderson (Australia) beat Gerry Watson (Canada) 10-4; Jim Donnelly (Scotland) beat Paul Watchorn (Rep. of Ireland) 10-7; Donnelly beat Anderson 10-6; Fred Davis (England) beat Donnelly 10-5

Group 13: Warren King (Australia) beat Tony Jones (England) 10-9; Mike Watterson (England) beat Bernard Bennett (England) 10-5; King beat Watterson 10-8; King beat Dave Martin (England) 10-8

Group 14: Joe Caggianello (Canada) beat Mike Darrington (England) 10-7; Bill Oliver (England) beat John Dunning (England) 10-3; Oliver beat Caggianello 10-7; Rex Williams (England) beat Oliver 10-8

Group 15: Neal Foulds (England) beat Doug French (England) 10-5; Les Dodd (England) beat James Giannaros (Australia) 10-1; N. Foulds beat Dodd 10-4; N. Foulds beat Jim Meadowcroft (England) 10-2

Group 16: Bob Harris (England) beat Dessie Sheehan (Rep. of Ireland) 10-3; Pascal Burke (Rep. of Ireland) beat Billy Kelly (Rep. of Ireland) 10-7; Burke beat Harris 10-4; Mike Hallett (England) beat Burke 10-5

Competition Proper

First round: Steve Davis (England) beat King 10-3; John Spencer (England) beat Miles 10-3; Terry Griffiths (Wales) beat Mifsud 10-2; Bill Werbeniuk (Canada) beat F. Davis 10-4; N. Foulds beat Alex Higgins (Northern Ireland) 10-9; Doug Mountjoy (Wales) beat Hallett 10-4; Dennis Taylor (Northern Ireland) beat Johnson 10-1; Parrott beat Tony Knowles (England) 10-7; Cliff Thorburn (Canada) beat Morra 10-3; Thorne beat John Virgo (England) 10-9; Jimmy White (England) beat Williams 10-6; Eddie Charlton (Australia) beat Andrewartha 10-4; Kirk Stevens (Canada) beat Sinclair 10-1; David Taylor (England) beat Gauvreau 10-5; Francisco beat Tony Meo (England) 10-5; Ray Reardon (Wales) beat Wych 10-7

Second round: S. Davis beat Spencer 13-5; Griffiths beat Werbeniuk 13-5; Mountjoy beat N. Foulds 13-6; Dennis Taylor beat Parrott 13-11; Thorburn beat Thorne 13-11; White beat Charlton 13-7; Stevens beat David Taylor 13-10; Reardon beat Francisco 13-8

Quarter-finals: Davis beat Griffiths 13-10; Dennis Taylor beat Mountjoy 13-8; White beat Thorburn 13-8; Stevens beat Reardon 13-2

Semi-finals: Davis beat Dennis Taylor 16-9; White beat Stevens 16-14

Final: Davis beat White 18-16

1985 Qualifying

First round: Gino Rigitano (Canada) beat Dessie Sheehan (Rep. of Ireland) 10-9; Dene O'Kane (New Zealand) w.o. Jack McLaughlin (Northern Ireland) scr; Steve Longworth (England) beat James Giannaros (Australia) 10-1; Robert Chaperon (Canada) beat Roger Bales (England) 10-7; Dennis Hughes (England) beat Doug French (England) 10-5; Mike Hines (South Africa) beat Tony Chappel (Wales) 10-8; Danny Fowler (England) beat John Hargreaves (England) 10-1

Second round: Rigitano beat Bob Harris (England) 10-4; O'Kane beat Vic Harris (England) 10-5; Longworth beat Graham Cripsey (England) 10-8; Chaperon beat Leon Heywood (Australia) 10-1; Steve Newbury (Wales) beat D. Hughes 10-9; Hines beat Paul Watchorn (Rep. of Ireland) 10-4; Fowler w.o. Gerry Watson (Canada) scr; Dave Chalmers (England) beat David Greaves (England) 10-3; Geoff Foulds (England) beat Maurice Parkin (England) 10-6; Paul Medati (England) beat Bernard Bennett (England) 10-4; Ian Anderson (Australia) beat Tony Kearney (Rep. of Ireland) 10-8; Wayne Jones (Wales) beat John Rea (Scotland) 10-3; Malcolm Bradley (England) beat Derek Mienie (South Africa) 10-4; Peter Francisco (South Africa) beat Bert Demarco (Scotland) 10-4; Tony Jones (England) beat Mike Darrington (England) 10-2

Third round: Matt Gibson (Scotland) beat Hines 10-7; Fowler w.o. Joe Caggianello (Canada) scr; Robbie Foldvari (Australia) beat Bill Oliver (England) 10-3; Chalmers beat Eddie McLaughlin (Scotland) 10-9; G. Foulds beat Clive Everton (Wales) 10-2; Medati beat Ian Williamson (England) 10-8; Rigitano beat Bill Kelly (Rep. of Ireland) 10-6; O'Kane beat Frank Jonik (Canada) 10-5; Jimmy van Rensburg (South Africa) beat Longworth 10-7; Chaperon beat Paddy Morgan (Australia) 10-3; Newbury beat Pascal Burke (Rep. of Ireland) 10-3; Paddy Browne (Rep. of Ireland) beat Anderson 10-5; W. Jones beat John Dunning (England) 10-6; Bradley beat Bernie Mikkelsen (Canada) 10-9; P. Francisco beat Tommy Murphy (Northern Ireland) 10-4; T. Jones beat Steve Duggan (England) 10-8

Fourth round: Rigitano beat Mick Fisher (England) 10-2; O'Kane beat Les Dodd (England) 10-7; Marcel Gauvreau (Canada) beat van Rensburg 10-9; Fred Davis (England) beat Chaperon 10-9; Newbury beat George Scott (England) 10-2; Patsy Fagan (Rep. of Ireland) beat Gibson 10-8; Fowler beat Jim Donnelly (Scotland) 10-0; Ray Edmonds (England) beat Foldvari 10-3; Chalmers beat Ian Black (Scotland) 10-4; G. Foulds beat Colin Roscoe (Wales) 10-7; Medati beat Warren King (Australia) 10-9; Mario Morra (Canada) beat Browne 10-6; W. Jones beat Mike Watterson (England) 10-5; Jim Wych (Canada) beat Bradley 10-7; P. Francisco beat Jim Meadowcroft (England) 10-5; T. Jones beat Jack Fitzmaurice (England) 10-4

Steve Davis and Joe Johnson exchange a preliminary handshake before their 1986 Embassy World Championship final

Fifth round: Neal Foulds (England) beat Rigitano 10-8; O'Kane beat Dave Martin (England) 10-8; Dean Reynolds (England) beat Gauvreau 10-1; Rex Williams (England) beat F. Davis 10-6; Eugene Hughes (Rep. of Ireland) beat Newbury 10-6; Fagan beat Cliff Wilson (Wales) 10-9; John Parrott (England) beat Fowler 10-2; Edmonds beat Mark Wildman (England) 10-7; Mike Hallett (England) beat Chalmers 10-1; Joe Johnson (England) beat G. Foulds 10-6; Silvino Francisco (South Africa) beat Medati 10-7; John Campbell (Australia) beat Morra 10-9; W. Jones beat Graham Miles (England) 10-8; John Virgo (England) beat Wych 10-4; Murdo Macleod (Scotland) beat P. Francisco 10-7; T. Jones beat Eddie Sinclair (Scotland) 10-2

Competition Proper

First round: Steve Davis (England) beat N. Foulds 10-8; David Taylor (England) beat O'Kane 10-4; Alex Higgins (Northern Ireland) beat Reynolds 10-4; Terry Griffiths (Wales) beat Williams 10-3; Ray Reardon (Wales) beat E. Hughes 10-9; Fagan beat Willie Thorne (England) 10-6; Parrott beat John Spencer (England) 10-3; Kirk Stevens (Canada) beat Edmonds 10-8; Cliff Thorburn (Canada) beat Hallett 10-8; Bill Werbeniuk (Canada) beat Johnson 10-8; Dennis Taylor (Northern Ireland) beat S. Francisco 10-2; Eddie Charlton (Australia) beat Campbell 10-3; Jimmy White (England) beat W. Jones 10-4; T. Meo (England) beat Virgo 10-6; Doug Mountjoy (Wales) beat Macleod 10-5; Tony Knowles (England) beat T. Jones 10-8

Second round: S. Davis beat David Taylor 13-4; Griffiths beat Higgins 13-7; Reardon beat Fagan 13-9; Parrott beat Stevens 13-6; Thorburn beat Werbeniuk 13-3; Dennis Taylor beat Charlton 13-6; White beat Meo 13-11; Knowles beat Mountjoy 13-6

Quarter-finals: S. Davis beat Griffiths 13-6; Reardon beat Parrott 13-12; Dennis Taylor beat Thorburn 13-5; Knowles beat White 13-10

Semi-finals: S. Davis beat Reardon 16-5; Dennis Taylor beat Knowles 16-5

Final: Dennis Taylor beat S. Davis 18-17

World Championship Prize Money

Year (Sponsor)	No. of Entries	Total Prize Money £	First Prize £
1969 (Players No 6)	8	3,500	1,300
1970 (Players No 6)	9	not known	1,225
1971 (not sponsored)	9	not known	2,333
1972 (not sponsored)	16	not known	not known
1973 (Park Drive)	23	8,000	1,500
1974 (Park Drive)	31	10,000	2,000
1975 (not sponsored)	27	18,900	not known
1976 (Embassy)	27	15,300	6,000
1977 (Embassy)	24	17,000	6,000
1978 (Embassy)	28	24,000	7,500
1979 (Embassy)	35	35,000	10,000
1980 (Embassy)	49	60,000	15,000
1981 (Embassy)	46	75,000	20,000
1982 (Embassy)	67	110,000	25,000
1983 (Embassy)	74	130,000	30,000
1984 (Embassy)	84	200,000	44,000
1985 (Embassy)	103	300,000	60,000
1986 (Embassy)	113	350,000	70,000

The strain tells on Cliff Thorburn during his 1986 semi-final against Steve Davis

National Professional Championships

Stephen Hendry, Tony Meo and John Campbell all won their respective national professional championships for the first time in 1985-86.

Hendry, who had won the first of his two consecutive Scottish amateur titles at the age of 15, won the Canada Dry Scottish Professional Championship at Marco's Leisure, Edinburgh, at his first attempt.

Still only 17, Hendry eliminated the defending champion Murdo Macleod 6-5 on the final black of their quarter-final and went on to beat Ian Black 6-2 and Matt Gibson 10-5 for the £4,000 first prize.

For the first time the final received television coverage by BBC Scotland.

Meo won the Tolly Cobbold English Professional Championship at Ipswich by beating his fellow Londoner Neal Foulds 9-7 to win £18,500 and his first major individual title in Britain.

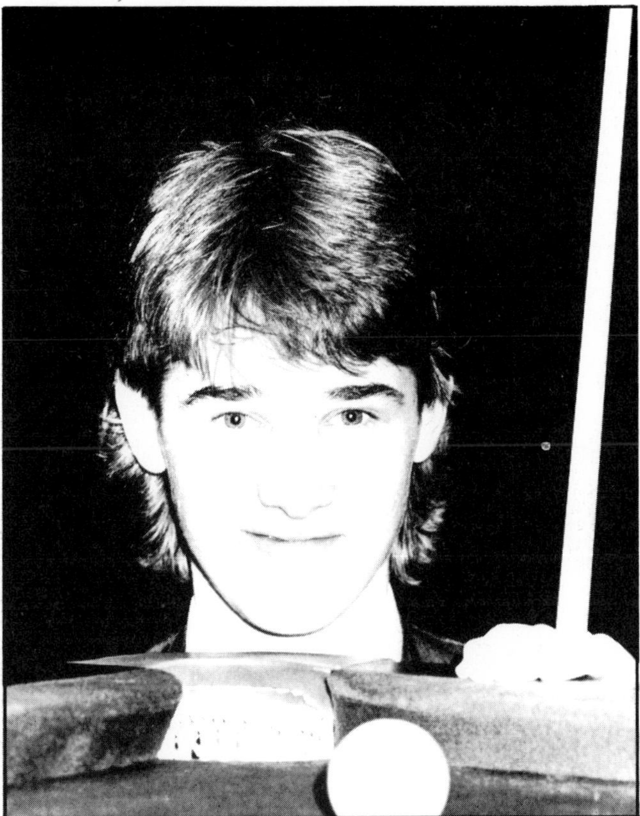

Stephen Hendry: Scottish champion

In the semi-finals, Meo achieved his first win over Steve Davis in eleven attempts as a professional, 9-7, thus bringing to an end a reign as English champion which had lasted since 1981.

Davis had won that inaugural event under the sponsorship of John Courage but it became impossible to stage the event under financial conditions which could realistically induce the leading players to enter until the WPBSA decided from 1984-85 onwards to donate £1,000 per entrant to the respective prize funds for the event.

In this way, the English Championship qualified for a grant of over £50,000 to which was added sponsorship from Tolly Cobbold, the brewers, who in 1985 transferred their support from an annual eight-man invitation event. Anglia television covered the English Championship (for transmission in their own area only) as they had the Tolly Cobbold Classic in the past.

In 1985, Davis had had to win the last two frames to beat Meo 9-8 in the semi-finals and a year later he led 7-6 before Meo won three frames in a row for the match.

In the other half of the draw, Foulds survived a 9-8 semi-final finish against Mike Hallett, who had earlier eliminated Joe Johnson.

Campbell became Australian champion at Orange RSL Club, some 125 miles from Sydney, by beating Eddie Charlton 10-7 for the £4,250 first prize.

Charlton had first won the title in 1964 and, apart from a defeat by Warren Simpson in 1968, had held it continuously until his defeat by Campbell although the event was not contested every year.

Cliff Thorburn took £3,000 for retaining the Canadian Professional Championship in Toronto with a 6-4 win over Robbie Chaperon; Terry Griffiths took £5,000 for retaining the Zetters Welsh Championship at Abertillery Leisure Centre, an event which has been annually covered by BBC Wales since 1980 and Dennis Taylor retained the Strongbow Irish Professional Championship by beating Alex Higgins 10-7 for the £8,000 first prize at Maysfield Leisure Centre, Belfast.

Higgins held the Irish title on a challenge basis since his 1972 victory over Jack Rea, withstanding subsequent challenges from Taylor and Patsy Fagan in 1978 and 1979.

On the same basis, Taylor held the title for two years after beating Higgins in 1980. The event was staged for the first time on a tournament basis in 1982 when Taylor won. Higgins regained the title in 1983 but, after it had fallen into abeyance for a year, Taylor won both in 1985 and 1986.

ENGLISH PROFESSIONAL CHAMPIONSHIP

1981 (sponsored by John Courage)

Qualifying: Edmonds beat Mike Hallett 9-3; Joe Johnson beat Tony Knowles 9-2; Mark Wildman beat Bernard Bennett 9-3; John Dunning beat David Greaves 9-4; Jim Meadowcroft beat John Barrie 9-3

First round: Edmonds beat Fred Davis 9-5; Tony Meo beat John Virgo 9-6; Graham Miles beat Sid Hood 9-1; Steve Davis beat Meadowcroft 9-2; John Spencer beat Pat Houlihan 9-1; Willie Thorne beat Wildman 9-2; Johnson w.o. John Pulman scr; Dunning beat David Taylor 9-8

Quarter-finals: Davis beat Spencer 9-7; Meo beat Miles 9-7; Thorne beat Dunning 9-0; Edmonds beat Johnson 9-5

Semi-finals: Davis beat Edmonds 9-0; Meo beat Thorne 9-8

Final: Davis beat Meo 9-3

1985 (sponsored by Tolly Cobbold)

Qualifying: Danny Fowler beat Bill Oliver 9-7; Malcolm Bradley beat Ian Williamson 9-8; Tony Jones beat Pat Houlihan 9-1; Les Dodd beat Roger Bales 9-5; Jack Fitzmaurice beat David Greaves 9-3; Mick Fisher beat Doug French 9-8; Steve Duggan beat Bob Harris 9-8; Dennis Hughes beat Mike Watterson 9-5; Dave Chalmers beat Jim Meadowcroft 9-3; Steve Longworth beat Ray Edmonds 9-4; Paul Medati beat John Hargreaves 9-8; Geoff Foulds beat Fred Davis 9-2; Graham Cripsey beat Bernard Bennett 9-0; George Scott beat Vic Harris 9-7

First round: Steve Davis beat Fowler 9-3; Mike Hallett beat Duggan 9-4; Joe Johnson beat Scott 9-1; Tony Meo beat Fisher 9-3; John Virgo beat Darrington 9-0; Dean Reynolds beat Fitzmaurice 9-2; Rex Williams beat T. Jones 9-6; Willie Thorne beat Dodd 9-1; Longworth beat Mark Wildman 9-3; Jimmy White beat Chalmers 9-5; Medati beat John Spencer 9-4; Neal Foulds beat D. Hughes 9-3; David Taylor beat Cripsey 9-5; John Parrott beat G. Foulds 9-4; Dave Martin beat Graham Miles 9-7; Tony Knowles beat Bradley 9-8

Second round: Virgo beat Johnson 9-4; Reynolds beat Thorne 9-6; Davis beat Williams 9-2; Meo beat Hallett 9-4; Knowles beat Martin 9-3; David Taylor beat Parrott 9-7; White beat N. Foulds 9-7; Longworth beat Medati 9-7

Quarter-finals: Meo beat Reynolds 9-4; Longworth beat White 9-5; Knowles beat David Taylor 9-2; Davis beat Virgo 9-2

Semi-finals: Knowles beat Longworth 9-6; Davis beat Meo 9-8

Final: Davis beat Knowles 9-2

1986 (sponsored by Tolly Cobbold)

First round: Dave Gilbert beat Barry West 9-8; Pat Houlihan beat John Hargreaves 9-5

Tony Meo: Tolly Cobbold English champion

Second round: Malcolm Bradley beat Gilbert 9-5; Fred Davis beat Dennis Hughes 9-6; Tony Jones beat Bob Harris 9-5; Bill Oliver beat Les Dodd 9-5; Paul Medati beat David Greaves 9-4; Steve Longworth beat Steve Duggan 9-4; Graham Cripsey beat Jim Meadowcroft 9-1; George Scott beat Bernard Bennett 9-1; Ian Williamson beat Mike Watterson 9-1; Ray Edmonds beat Mick Smith 9-8; Danny Fowler beat Mike Darrington 9-3; Houlihan w.o. John Dunning scr; Dave Chalmers beat Mick Fisher 9-2; Roger Bales beat Vic Harris 9-7

Third round: Steve Davis beat Bradley 9-3; Dave Martin beat F. Davis 9-8; John Virgo beat T. Jones 9-7; John Parrott beat Oliver 9-0; Willie Thorne beat Medati 9-2; Dean Reynolds beat Longworth 9-5; Mark Wildman beat Cripsey 9-5; Tony Meo beat Scott 9-1; Jimmy White beat Williamson 9-1; Rex Williams beat Miles 9-6; Neal Foulds beat Geoff Foulds 9-4; Edmonds beat David Taylor 9-6; Joe Johnson beat Fowler 9-7; John Spencer beat Houlihan 9-5; Mike Hallett beat Chalmers 9-1; Tony Knowles beat Bales 9-4

Fourth round: S. Davis beat Martin 9-4; Virgo beat Parrott 9-6; Reynolds beat Thorne 9-8; Meo beat Wildman 9-3; White beat Williams 9-5; N. Foulds beat Edmonds 9-4; Johnson beat Spencer 9-7; Hallett beat Knowles 9-5

Quarter-finals: S. Davis beat Virgo 9-2; Meo beat Reynolds 9-4; N. Foulds beat White 9-4; Hallett beat Johnson 9-6

Semi-finals: Meo beat S. Davis 9-7; N. Foulds beat Hallett 9-8

Final: Meo beat N. Foulds 9-7

IRISH PROFESSIONAL CHAMPIONSHIP

1982

First round: Eugene Hughes beat Dessie Sheehan 6-1

Quarter-finals: Hughes beat Jack Rea 6-0; Tommy Murphy beat Patsy Fagan 6-2

Semi-finals: Dennis Taylor beat Murphy 6-0; Alex Higgins beat Hughes 6-2

Final: Taylor beat Higgins 16-13

1983

First round: Dennis Taylor beat Billy Kelly 6-0; Patsy Fagan beat Tommy Murphy 6-4; Alex Higgins beat Jack Rea 6-3; Eugene Hughes beat Pascal Burke 6-2

Semi-finals: Higgins beat Hughes 6-2; Taylor beat Fagan 6-1

Final: Higgins beat Taylor 16-11

1985 (sponsored by Strongbow)

Preliminary round: Jack McLaughlin beat Dessie Sheehan 6-3

Qualifying: Pascal Burke beat Tony Kearney 6-4; Tommy Murphy beat Paddy Browne 6-3; Billy Kelly beat Paul Watchorn 6-2; Jack Rea beat McLaughlin 6-5

Quarter-finals: Patsy Fagan beat Murphy 6-2; Dennis Taylor beat Jack Rea 6-0; Alex Higgins beat Burke 6-0; Eugene Hughes beat Kelly 6-2

Semi-finals: Dennis Taylor beat Eugene Hughes 6-5; Higgins beat Fagan 6-3

Final: Dennis Taylor beat Higgins 10-5

1986 (sponsored by Strongbow)

First round: Billy Kelly beat Jack Rea 5-0; Tommy Murphy beat Joe O'Boye 5-0; Eugene Hughes beat Dessie Sheehan 5-0; Tony Kearney beat Patsy Fagan 5-0; Jack McLaughlin beat Paul Watchorn 5-0; Pascal Burke beat Paddy Browne 5-4

Quarter-finals: Dennis Taylor beat Kelly 6-1; Murphy beat Kearney 6-2; Alex Higgins beat McLaughlin 6-2; Hughes beat Burke 6-3

Semi-finals: Taylor beat Murphy 6-3; Higgins beat Hughes 6-2

Final: Taylor beat Higgins 10-7

SCOTTISH PROFESSIONAL CHAMPIONSHIP

1981

First round: Matt Gibson beat Bert Demarco 5-3; Jim Donnelly beat Eddie Sinclair 5-0; Eddie McLaughlin beat Chris Ross 5-3; Ian Black beat Murdo Macleod 5-4

Semi-finals: Gibson beat Donnelly 6-4; Black beat McLaughlin 6-3

Final: Black beat Gibson 11-7

1982

First round: Murdo Macleod beat Jim Donnelly 6-5

Quarter-finals: Chris Ross beat Bert Demarco 6-5; Matt Gibson beat Eddie McLaughlin 6-3; Ian Black beat Macleod 6-0; Eddie Sinclair beat John Phillips 6-3

Semi-finals: Black beat Ross 6-4; Sinclair beat Gibson 6-2

Final: Sinclair beat Black 11-7

1983

First round: Jim Donnelly beat Bert Demarco 6-4; Ian Black beat Eddie McLaughlin 6-4; Murdo Macleod beat Matt Gibson 6-5

Semi-finals: Eddie Sinclair beat Donnelly 6-5; Macleod beat Black 6-2

Final: Macleod beat Sinclair 11-9

1985

First round: Murdo Macleod beat Eddie McLaughlin 6-4; Matt Gibson beat Ian Black 6-2; John Rea beat Jim Donnelly 6-2; Eddie Sinclair beat Bert Demarco 6-3

Semi-finals: Macleod beat Gibson 6-4; Sinclair beat John Rea 6-2

Final: Macleod beat Sinclair 10-2

1986 (sponsored by Canada Dry)

First round: Stephen Hendry beat Bert Demarco 6-1

Quarter-finals: Hendry beat Murdo Macleod 6-5; Ian Black beat Eddie McLaughlin 6-4; John Rea beat Jim Donnelly 6-1; Matt Gibson beat Eddie Sinclair 6-4

Semi-finals: Hendry beat Black 6-2; Gibson beat John Rea 6-0;

Final: Hendry beat Gibson 10-5

WELSH PROFESSIONAL CHAMPIONSHIP

1980 (sponsored by Woodpecker)

First round: Doug Mountjoy beat Terry Griffiths 9-6; Ray Reardon beat Cliff Wilson 9-3

Final: Mountjoy beat Reardon 9-6

1981 (sponsored by Woodpecker)

Preliminary: Cliff Wilson beat Roy Andrewartha 6-5

First round: Wilson beat Doug Mountjoy 9-6; Ray Reardon beat Terry Griffiths 9-6

Final: Reardon beat Wilson 9-6

1982 (sponsored by Woodpecker)

First round: Cliff Wilson beat Marcus Owen 6-0; Terry Griffiths beat Colin Roscoe 6-2; Ray Reardon beat Clive Everton 6-1; Doug Mountjoy beat Roy Andrewartha 6-3

Semi-finals: Griffiths beat Wilson 9-6; Mountjoy beat Reardon 9-7

Final: Mountjoy beat Griffiths 9-8

1983 (sponsored by Woodpecker)

First round: Terry Griffiths beat Clive Everton 6-1; Ray Reardon beat Roy Andrewartha 6-2; Cliff Wilson beat Colin Roscoe 6-4; Doug Mountjoy beat Marcus Owen 6-0

Semi-finals: Reardon beat Griffiths 9-4; Mountjoy beat Wilson 9-3

Final: Reardon beat Mountjoy 9-1

1984 (sponsored by Strongbow)

First round: Doug Mountjoy beat Clive Everton 6-1; Terry Griffiths beat Roy Andrewartha 6-1; Ray Reardon beat Marcus Owen 6-1; Cliff Wilson beat Colin Roscoe 6-2

Semi-finals: Mountjoy beat Griffiths 9-5; Wilson beat Reardon 9-4

Final: Mountjoy beat Wilson 9-3

1985 (sponsored by BCE)

First round: Steve Newbury beat Wayne Jones 6-2; Tony Chappel beat Marcus Owen 6-0

Quarter-finals: Ray Reardon beat Clive Everton 6-2; Doug Mountjoy beat Newbury 6-5; Cliff Wilson beat Colin Roscoe 6-3; Terry Griffiths beat Chappel 6-0

Semi-finals: Griffiths beat Reardon 9-3; Mountjoy beat Wilson 9-2

Final: Griffiths beat Mountjoy 9-4

1986 (sponsored by Zetters)

First round: Tony Chappel w.o. Marcus Owen scr; Wayne Jones beat Clive Everton 6-2

Quarter-finals: Terry Griffiths beat Chappel 6-4; Cliff Wilson beat Steve Newbury 6-4; Doug Mountjoy beat Colin Roscoe 6-4; W. Jones beat Ray Reardon 6-4

Semi-finals: Griffiths beat Wilson 9-1; Mountjoy beat W. Jones 9-7

Final: Griffiths beat Mountjoy 9-3

Terry Griffiths: Zetters Welsh Professional champion

CANADIAN PROFESSIONAL CHAMPIONSHIP

1984

First round: Bernie Mikkelsen beat Paul Thornley 6-2; Gino Rigitano beat Joe Caggianello 6-3; Mario Morra beat Wayne Sanderson 6-4; Jim Wych beat Gerry Watson 6-1; Marcel Gauvreau beat Robert Chaperon 6-2

Quarter-finals: Morra beat Wych 6-4; Kirk Stevens beat Gauvreau 6-2; Frank Jonik beat Mikkelsen 6-3; Cliff Thorburn beat Rigitano 6-0

Semi-finals: Morra beat Stevens 7-6; Thorburn beat Jonik 7-3

Final: Thorburn beat Morra 9-2

1985

First round: Joe Caggianello beat Jim Bear 5-4; Robert Chaperon beat Paul Thornley 5-1; Bernie Mikkelsen beat Gerry Watson 5-3; John Bear beat Mario Morra 5-4; Jim Wych beat Wayne Sanderson 5-2

Quarter-finals: Chaperon beat Kirk Stevens 6-4; Frank Jonik beat Mikkelsen 6-4; Cliff Thorburn beat Caggianello 6-2; Wych beat Bear 6-3

Semi-finals: Chaperon beat Jonik 6-3; Thorburn beat Wych 6-5

Final: Thorburn beat Chaperon 6-4

AUSTRALIAN PROFESSIONAL CHAMPIONSHIP

1984

Qualifying round: Robbie Foldvari beat Jim Charlton 6-1; George Ganim beat Ian Anderson 6-5; James Giannaros beat Lou Condo 6-2

First round: Eddie Charlton beat Foldvari 6-4; Paddy Morgan beat Ganim 6-4; Warren King beat Giannaros 6-5; John Campbell beat Leon Heywood 6-2

Semi-finals: Charlton beat Morgan 9-2; King beat Campbell 9-6

Final: Charlton beat King 10-3

1985

First round: Glen Wilkinson beat Greg Jenkins 6-2; Lou Condo beat Edward Charlton 6-0

Second round: Wilkinson beat Leon Heywood 7-3; Robbie Foldvari beat Robinson 7-3; James Giannaros beat Condo 7-2

Quarter-finals: Eddie Charlton beat Wilkinson 8-2; Paddy Morgan beat Giannaros 8-4; Warren King beat Ian Anderson 8-2; John Campbell beat Foldvari 8-5

Semi-finals: Charlton beat Morgan 9-3; Campbell beat King 9-6

Final: Campbell beat Charlton 10-7

John Campbell: Australian champion

POT BLACK

The 17th series of *Pot Black,* which reached the end of its run on BBC2 in April 1986, was its last.

Pot Black, which was born in 1969 out of BBC2's desire for low budget programmes to which colour was intrinsic in order to stimulate sales of colour sets, immediately became one of the channel's most popular features.

It brought snooker and its leading players to a new public and outlined new possibilities for snooker as a television sport but its original format of sudden death one-frame matches was eventually to prove an element in its demise.

There was some doubt as to whether a television audience would accept snooker in more extended doses than BBC2's weekly 25 minutes but as the BBC began to cover the World Championship at greater length and, from 1978, on a daily basis, the public's response to the authentic Test Match version of snooker in all its complexity, tension and length, was overwhelming.

Pot Black, studio based and recorded for showing weeks later, was limited overs stuff in comparison.

A mere one-frame gave players little opportunity to get into their stride, for tension to develop or for the viewing public to become emotionally involved in an unfolding drama.

Worse still, the programme was committed to screening every frame, good, bad or indifferent, instead of being able to choose, as it does in major tournaments, from an abundance of riches.

Viewing figures for snooker remained excellent but there was always a danger of over-exposure. *Pot Black,* running 15 weeks, occupied more snooker air-time than its status, by the mid eighties, merited.

***Pot Black* winners**

1969	Ray Reardon	**1978**	Doug Mountjoy
1970	John Spencer	**1979**	Ray Reardon
1971	John Spencer	**1980**	Eddie Charlton
1972	Eddie Charlton	**1981**	Cliff Thorburn
1973	Eddie Charlton	**1982**	Steve Davis
1974	Graham Miles	**1983**	Steve Davis
1975	Graham Miles	**1984**	Terry Griffiths
1976	John Spencer	**1985**	Doug Mountjoy
1977	Perrie Mans	**1986**	Jimmy White

Jimmy White:
Pot Black*'s last champion*

Century Breaks

Alex Higgins: sixth in the century breakers list

When century breaks were rare, even professionals took great pride in recording each one they made in public. Joe Davis made his first in 1928 and his 687th and last in 1964.

In the Age of Joe, it was news if any amateur made a century but as standards improved in depth they grew more frequent. Just as a four-minute mile was no longer regarded as anything very special once a couple of dozen athletes had broken through this barrier, a century break at snooker no longer added much of a psychological dimension to its degree of technical difficulty.

In 1973, the lighter and livelier Super Crystalate ball superseded the Crystalate ball for the World Professional Championship and other professional tournaments. Concurrently, it began to be used for the overwhelming majority of amateur competitions.

In the last 15 years also, many more tables have had their pockets correctly undercut and another factor in making centuries so very much more common has been the enormous increase in the sheer volume of frames played. These days, not even 147s are all that uncommon in witnessed practice, even from players who have yet to make a substantial reputation in competition.

Few leading snooker players, amateur or professional, now keep count of their centuries any more than did the billiards players of old. There are simply too many of them. Nor do players invariably strive, in tournaments, to make a century when they have already done enough to be sure of winning that frame.

Nevertheless, there will always be a trace of distinction in making a tournament century so *Snooker Scene* decided to compile a list of centuries made in professional tournaments, starting arbitrarily with the November 1970 World Professional Championship in Australia as only from this date are detailed scores and breaks available from all matches.

Arbitrarily again, *Snooker Scene* decided to limit its researches to 'major tournaments', a term which has never been officially defined. The six ranking tournaments obviously had to be included. These comprise the Goya Trophy (formerly the Jameson International), the Rothmans Grand Prix (formerly the Professional Players Tournament), the Coral UK (to be sponsored by Tennents in 1986), the Mercantile Credit Classic (formerly the Lada Classic), the Dulux British Open and, of course, the Embassy World Championship. The centuries from these events are included even from those years in which they had not yet attained ranking status.

The Benson and Hedges Masters, snooker's oldest established sponsorship, and the Benson and Hedges Irish Masters have been given columns of their own; there is a special column for the player's own national 'closed' championship; and the 'others' section embraces the Langs Scottish Masters, the Carlsberg Challenge, the Hofmeister World Doubles, the World Cup (under various sponsors), the Norwich Union Open, the Yamaha International Masters, the Winfield Australian Masters, the BCE Canadian Masters and the BCE Belgian Classic.

This last category is the most arbitrary of all but is restricted to televised events which had or are intended to have a run of at least two years. One-offs have been excluded. On this basis, the 1985 Kit Kat tournament, which will not be repeated this year, and the 1979 Holsten tournament, in which John Spencer made his celebrated 147 with ITV on a meal-break, have been excluded.

Allowing any kind of blurring at the edges, however, it is clear that under any system Steve Davis would have topped the list by a considerable margin. This is all the more remarkable since he did not win his first major tournament, the Coral UK, until November 1980 while players like Alex Higgins (fifth) and Ray Reardon (sixth) were playing throughout the seventies.

A comparison of the order in which players appear in this list with their places in the world rankings reveals some interesting contrasts. Willie Thorne, seventh in the world rankings, is, to the surprise of none of those who admire his fluent break-building, second in the list of century breakers. John Virgo, outside the top 16 in the world rankings, is well within that category in century breakers in tenth place.

The high standings of John Spencer, Eddie Charlton and, for that matter, Ray Reardon in the century breakers list more accurately reflect past rather than current form.

	Total	Goya/ Jameson	PPT/ Rothmans	U.K. (Coral)	MCC/ Lada	Dulux	B & H	B & H Irish	World	National	Other
Steve Davis	72	5 (135)	7 (130)	12 (134)	6 (147)	4 (129)	2 (113)	4 (133)	18 (136)	4 (111)	10 (140)
Willie Thorne	37	2 (104)	5 (135)	9 (140)	4 (118)	4 (129)	1 (100)	1 (112)	8 (143)	—	3 (139)
Cliff Thorburn	34	2 (113)	4 (106)	4 (132)	3 (107)	—	2 (103)	—	9 (147)	—	10 (142)
Terry Griffiths	32	1 (107)	2 (119)	7 (131)	1 (137)	3 (110)	4 (136)	—	7 (121)	3 (119)	4 (121)
Jimmy White	32	2 (120)	—	5 (108)	2 (107)	—	3 (119)	3 (120)	8 (126)	2 (127)	7 (122)
Alex Higgins	29	3 (118)	—	12 (137)	1 (114)	2 (142)	1 (132)	—	8 (135)	2 (136)	—
Ray Reardon	24	—	2 (133)	4 (119)	1 (102)	—	2 (113)	1 (101)	10 (133)	1 (104)	3 (133)
Dennis Taylor	18	2 (134)	1 (112)	2 (135)	—	1 (100)	—	—	6 (135)	2 (128)	4 (120)
Tony Meo	18	—	—	4 (139)	—	1 (121)	2 (136)	1 (113)	3 (134)	1 (135)	5 (134)
John Virgo	18	—	1 (130)	6 (127)	—	—	—	—	6 (137)	1 (137)	4 (122)
Tony Knowles	17	1 (114)	2 (129)	3 (113)	—	—	—	—	4 (137)	2 (139)	5 (126)
John Spencer	16	—	1 (126)	1 (109)	—	—	—	—	13 (139)	1 (108)	—
Doug Mountjoy	15	—	—	2 (120)	3 (109)	—	2 (111)	—	8 (145)	—	—
Kirk Stevens	14	—	—	2 (120)	—	1 (108)	2 (147)	—	6 (139)	—	3 (120)
Eddie Charlton	13	—	—	1 (102)	—	—	2 (108)	1 (129)	9 (129)	—	—
Joe Johnson	12	1 (103)	3 (135)	2 (119)	1 (104)	—	—	—	3 (110)	—	1 (111)
Neal Foulds	10	2 (140)	—	3 (136)	1 (102)	—	—	—	3 (109)	1 (107)	—
John Campbell	9	—	2 (122)	1 (106)	—	—	—	—	—	3 (121)	3 (132)
Tony Jones	9	—	—	2 (113)	—	2 (112)	—	—	1 (104)	3 (102)	1 (101)
Graham Miles	9	3 (120)	—	1 (139)	1 (111)	—	—	—	4 (131)	—	—
Bill Werbeniuk	9	—	1 (101)	—	2 (118)	—	—	—	4 (143)	—	2 (108)
Rex Williams	6	—	—	2 (102)	2 (143)	—	—	—	2 (138)	—	—
Mario Morra	5	1 (100)	1 (105)	1 (130)	1 (125)	—	—	—	1 (104)	—	—
John Parrott	5	—	1 (118)	1 (101)	1 (102)	—	—	—	2 (114)	—	—
Tony Chappel	4	—	—	3 (119)	—	1 (101)	—	—	—	—	—
Fred Davis	4	—	—	—	—	—	—	—	4 (110)	—	—
Peter Francisco	4	—	1 (101)	3 (134)	—	—	—	—	—	—	—
Mike Hallett	4	1 (129)	—	—	—	—	—	—	1 (100)	2 (130)	—
Steve Longworth	4	—	—	—	—	—	—	—	2 (118)	2 (113)	—
Dave Martin	4	—	—	—	—	1 (145)	—	—	1 (127)	2 (106)	—
Tommy Murphy	4	2 (105)	—	—	—	—	—	—	2 (108)	—	—
Roger Bales	3	—	—	—	1 (103)	1 (104)	—	—	—	1 (101)	—
Ian Black	3	—	1 (113)	—	—	—	—	—	1 (108)	—	1 (108)
John Dunning	3	—	—	1 (101)	—	—	—	—	2 (132)	—	—
Robby Foldvari	3	—	—	1 (100)	—	1 (104)	—	—	1 (105)	—	—
Silvino Francisco	3	—	—	—	1 (111)	—	—	—	2 (128)	—	—
Eugene Hughes	3	—	2 (112)	—	—	—	—	—	—	1 (105)	—
Warren King	3	—	1 (101)	—	—	—	—	—	1 (100)	1 (130)	—
Steve Newbury	3	—	—	2 (122)	—	—	—	—	1 (134)	—	—
Dean Reynolds	3	—	1 (112)	—	—	—	—	—	2 (115)	—	—
Eddie Sinclair	3	—	—	1 (121)	—	—	—	—	2 (112)	—	—
David Taylor	3	1 (101)	—	—	—	—	—	—	—	1 (105)	1 (109)
Ian Williamson	3	1 (106)	—	—	—	—	—	—	2 (114)	—	—
Malcolm Bradley	2	—	—	1 (110)	—	1 (140)	—	—	—	—	—
Robbie Chaperon	2	—	—	—	—	—	—	—	2 (110)	—	—
Ray Edmonds	2	—	1 (101)	—	—	1 (121)	—	—	—	—	—
Danny Fowler	2	1 (107)	—	—	—	—	—	—	1 (137)	—	—
Vic Harris	2	—	—	—	—	—	—	—	1 (111)	1 (121)	—
Stephen Hendry	2	—	—	—	—	—	—	—	2 (141)	—	—
Pat Houlihan	2	—	—	1 (103)	—	—	—	—	1 (108)	—	—
Bernie Mikkelsen	2	—	—	—	—	—	—	—	2 (132)	—	—
Jack McLaughlin	2	1 (134)	—	1 (135)	—	—	—	—	—	—	—
Barry West	2	—	—	—	—	—	—	—	2 (112)	—	—
Mark Wildman	2	—	—	1 (115)	—	—	—	—	—	—	1 (110)
Cliff Wilson	2	1 (126)	—	1 (100)	—	—	—	—	—	—	—
O. B. Agrawal	1	—	1 (110)	—	—	—	—	—	—	—	—
Paddy Browne	1	—	—	1 (100)	—	—	—	—	—	—	—
Dave Chalmers	1	—	—	—	—	—	—	—	1 (107)	—	—
Graham Cripsey	1	—	—	1 (107)	—	—	—	—	—	—	—
Jim Donnelly	1	—	—	—	—	—	—	—	1 (112)	—	—
Tony Drago	1	—	—	—	—	—	—	—	1 (120)	—	—
Steve Duggan	1	—	—	—	—	1 (108)	—	—	—	—	—
Patsy Fagan	1	—	—	—	—	—	—	—	1 (105)	—	—
Doug French	1	—	—	—	—	—	—	—	1 (112)	—	—
Marcel Gauvreau	1	—	—	—	1 (129)	—	—	—	—	—	—
Wayne Jones	1	1 (102)	—	—	—	—	—	—	—	—	—
Murdo Macleod	1	—	—	—	—	—	—	—	—	1 (106)	—
Jim Meadowcroft	1	1 (100)	—	—	—	—	—	—	—	—	—
Paul Medati	1	—	—	1 (119)	—	—	—	—	—	—	—
Joe O'Boye	1	—	—	—	—	—	—	—	1 (118)	—	—
Marcus Owen	1	—	—	—	—	—	—	—	1 (102)	—	—
John Pulman	1	—	—	—	—	—	—	—	1 (119)	—	—
Gino Rigitano	1	—	—	—	—	—	—	—	1 (106)	—	—
Martin Smith	1	—	—	—	—	—	—	—	1 (108)	—	—
Paul Thornley	1	—	—	—	—	—	—	—	1 (126)	—	—
Mike Watterson	1	—	—	—	—	—	—	—	1 (107)	—	—

Overseas Circuit

Although there is no sign of a decline in British television audiences for snooker, there is general agreement on all sides that it would be unwise for the WPBSA to risk overexposure of the game by agreeing to more domestic television coverage.

Overseas, however, the situation is very different as snooker seeks to establish a tournament circuit during British summers.

Ironically, the two new overseas events which have been largely promoted by the WPBSA, the BCE Canadian Masters and the BCE Belgian Classic, both fall within the British winter.

Canada's winters and summers coincide with Britain's and there is therefore no market for a summer tournament there. The same applies to Belgium, of course, although the closer geographical proximity involved the players in no real problems of jetlag or other disruption.

The longest established overseas tournament is the Winfield Australian Masters, which has taken place in Sydney annually since 1979. It began with a sprint style *Pot Black* format but for three years, between 1983 and 1985, it was an authentic tournament with matches ranging in length from best of five to best of thirteen in the final.

These tournaments were won by Cliff Thorburn (1983), Tony Knowles (1984) and Tony Meo (1985).

In 1986 the event passed from Channel Ten to the Australian Broadcasting Commission who did not have the programme slots available to show the action on the 'same day' basis which is standard practice in Britain and had become so over the preceding three years in Australia.

There was therefore a reversion to a *Pot Black* style format in 1986 although there are high hopes that in 1987 it will be possible to schedule the most ambitious tournament ever staged in Australia. Ideally, this would be an event carrying world ranking points.

It may also be possible to resurrect the Winfield New Zealand Masters, a sprint style event which was staged for two years immediately after the Australian tournament until it lapsed in 1985.

The Far East circuit has been developed annually since 1983 by Barry Hearn, who has chiefly used the players he himself manages in a variety of four–eight man tournaments, mostly receiving television coverage in their respective countries, in Thailand, Malaysia, Singapore and Hong Kong.

Hearn has also ventured to Brazil where Steve Davis in 1985 and Davis and Tony Meo in 1986 played leading Brazilians at their own form of snooker – using an eight-foot table and only one red and all the colours – in front of huge live and television audiences.

Trips to the United States have also been made, notably to Dallas in 1984, but the country is so vast and the market so hard to conquer that snooker entrepreneurs may well leave it fairly low on their list of priorities.

Where new ground is broken or comparatively new ground more intensely cultivated, equipment concerns like Riley and BCE are likely to be involved with any new tournaments which are set up. How many of these there are will depend largely on the extent to which the sponsorship/television equation can be solved in each country.

China

Snooker, traditionally a game for past and present members of the Commonwealth, is expanding to new frontiers, particularly in the Far East. Janice Hale checked on the Hong Kong scene and went on professional snooker's first trip to China.

'I'm here to preach the gospel of snooker,' said Steve Davis in one of his countless television interviews after he had given the Peoples Republic of China its first taste of professional snooker.

The gospel has been preached so successfully in Britain that there is little further potential for domestic growth. Export markets are needed to continue the expansion of snooker the business as well as snooker the sport.

Barry Hearn was then a director of E. J. Riley, one of Britain's largest snooker equipment firms, and his players are still heavily involved with the company contractually. He then managed four leading players, Davis, Dennis Taylor, Terry Griffiths and Tony Meo, and now manages Willie Thorne and Neal Foulds as well. Hearn's troupe has made an annual tour of the Far East since 1983.

The results have been spectacular in Singapore and Thailand but most of all in Hong Kong where the number of tables in the colony has risen in ten years from 600 to 6,000.

Tables are manufactured in Hong Kong but British is still widely believed to be best in this field and most of the new ones have been shipped by the container load from Britain.

During the 1985 Camus Hong Kong Masters, Wong Hon, ten years ago a Vietnamese boat-person but now the owner of three clubs, placed an order for 300 tables to install, all on one floor, in what will be the largest snooker club in the world.

Ordinarily, the Hong Kong Masters would have been the end of the tour but in May 1985, just after Taylor had deprived Davis of the world title, an approach was made from China for these two players to play an exhibition match in Canton.

To fulfil this engagement the players had to abandon their first-class travel with Cathay Pacific to make a three-hour train journey, queueing in an egalitarian fashion at Customs and Immigration, although the hotel, the White Swan, was certainly equal to anything the opulent West could have provided.

The arena in the hotel's banqueting suite could have been that of any televised major tournament in Britain except that bottles of the tour sponsor's product – Camus cognac –

would never have been allowed to be so prominently displayed.

Prior to the match, perhaps sensing a British version of ping-pong diplomacy, television crews incestuously filmed each other. More important, the Chinese television service filmed the evening's play for later, edited transmission.

Originally, just Davis and Taylor were to play but the Chinese produced two players of their own and a tournament was organised. Snooker was banned for ten years during the Cultural Revolution but some 70 tables survived in Shanghai and it was from thence that these two players – out of the 2,000 China apparently has – were summoned.

The clash of cultures was epitomised by Davis's evening dress against Suen Luen Pak's casual trousers and open-necked shirt. The disparity in standard of play was swiftly established with Davis's break of 68 at his second visit to the table. The invited audience of 150 was already enthralled.

Anxious to do everything correctly, the Chinese misinterpreted a request for refreshment – only a jug of water and glasses were required – and suddenly the players' sitting-out table was groaning with a huge pot of coffee, a dozen cups and copious quantities of toast, butter and marmalade. I could tell Davis was moved by the way he raised a single eyebrow.

Yan Jin Jing did no better against Taylor than had his compatriot against Davis. Davis beat Taylor 2-1 in the final but the result was insignificant in comparison with the impression the British party hoped snooker would create with 350 million Chinese television viewers, among them, perhaps, China's venerable premier, Deng Xiao Ping, who was a devotee of a continental billiard game, Fourball, when he was working as a young man at the Renault plant in France.

One sure-fire winner, though, if the reaction of the live audience was anything to go by, was the trick-shot display culminating in referee Len Ganley – he who crushes the snooker ball in the Carling Black Label advert in the UK – hauling his vast bulk on to the table so that Taylor could pot the black he was holding in his mouth.

The matches played, the autographs signed, the niceties performed with showbiz aplomb, the Chinese banquet eaten, it was back to the train and home via Hong Kong to prepare for the rigours of the British season.

Are they going back? 'If they want us, we will,' said Hearn, content that his team can and do give snooker the right image, anywhere in the world.

Janice Hale

Barry Hearn and his Merry Men: Neal Foulds (left), Willie Thorne, Dennis Taylor, Steve Davis, Tony Meo and Terry Griffiths (right)

Barry Hearn

Barry Hearn quite enjoys it when the cynics query whether the 'H' in his name is silent. He is so far and away snooker's most successful manager that when Dennis Taylor realised on winning the 1985 world title last spring that he and his wife could not possibly cope with the extra demands his new status would place upon him, it was to Hearn he immediately turned.

Such an arrangement has obvious pitfalls. Hearn became a snooker manager when a gangling, ginger-haired teenager with nothing much about him except an eerie concentration and a developing snooker talent started playing in his snooker hall in Romford.

This was in 1976 and Hearn guided Steve Davis's career from this point. 'We had our first contract in 1978 but it wasn't until 1981 that I took any money off him,' Hearn recalls.

In fact, manager and player have been more like brothers and Hearn has never tried to convince any other player that he could offer them quite the same relationship. Tony Meo, Terry Griffiths and Taylor and, last season, Willie Thorne and Neal Foulds, all in turn accepted this position. Not one has ever regretted joining the stable even if all are well aware that, in certain ways, Davis will always be no 1 within it.

Hearn was born 37 years ago in Dagenham, Essex, the son of a bus driver. He has an instinctive understanding of what, for want of a better expression, may be called working-class pleasures and values. For all its popularity as a television entertainment, these are the sport's roots and this is why management figures who are more familiar with traditionally upmarket sports have never cut much ice in snooker.

On the other hand, those who know only snooker are ill-equipped to negotiate the political and commercial minefields which lie beneath its deceptively golden pastures. Above all, Hearn knows the world of finance. He was a chartered accountant at 21 and could add accountancy's highest qualification, FCA, to his name at 26.

As financial director, in his twenties, of Kensal House Investments, he was heavily involved in the world of fashion and textile design. 'Some business things I've seen work for Pierre Cardin and Yves St. Laurent I've adapted for my own scene.'

He talked Kensal House into buying a down-at-heel chain of snooker clubs, Lucania, which did, however, hold the freehold of all their operational sites. 'I built up my own holding from 5 per cent to 33⅓ per cent.' In June 1982, the clubs – indeed the whole of Kensal House Investments – was sold to Riley Leisure for £3.1m. Hearn himself retained for sentimental reasons and because of his need for a commercial base, the Romford club. Much refurbished, this is the epicentre of his Matchroom empire. While he deals in his office, Davis practises in the new exclusive three-table club, and the multi-table hall in which Hearn first set eyes on the youth who was to become Britain's highest paid sportsman goes on much as before.

Even while he was with Kensal House, Hearn maintained his own accountancy practice, dealt in stocks and shares and always had 'a dozen or twenty directorships' on the go. But increasingly in the late seventies and certainly since Matchroom commenced trading on 1 January 1982, his energies have been committed to snooker.

'There's a lot of bad sportsman management. I've seen sportsmen who have been allowed to over-indulge themselves. I've also seen some, particularly boxers, who have been very good and worked very hard but who've ended up with nothing.

'I don't think you can be a successful manager without understanding sportsmen. You must not only be aware but appreciative of the talents they have. To some extent, I'm a frustrated sportsman. I've played several sports without being really good at any of them. I've not had the ability and I've not been prepared to spend enough time either.

'But with business I can sit down and plan five years ahead. In fact, as a business, our strength is in our long-term contracts. Steve's John Courage contract is £1m for five years. That's a large amount of money and it's also a very emotive amount of money. The figure places the sport on a high level because it establishes beyond doubt that top snooker players do not come cheap.'

There is a five-year equipment contract with Riley, some sections of which, like under-sized tables, are for Davis alone though most are for the whole squad. It is probably worth about £1.5m in all.

Hearn takes particular pleasure in the Goya contract for the Matchroom range of men's toiletries. 'Goya only have 3 per cent of the UK market at the moment but it is growing. Since the Matchroom contract, the range had been sold in 25 countries as opposed to 10 beforehand. This includes Finland where they don't even play snooker.

'It's a straight 5 per cent royalty and this will be a lot of money. I like royalty arrangements because no one loses. If the product isn't successful we don't earn anything. If it is successful, no one can winge at anybody else.'

In the Far East, where summer tours by the Hearn troupe to Thailand, Hong Kong and Singapore have created an amazing explosion of interest in the game, there is a strong association with Camus cognac. 'I could probably get more money from a cigarette company but we wouldn't get the sport presented as well as we do now.' The troupe play exclusively on Riley tables in this part of the world and their guaranteed personal appearances on Riley tables sold to clubs there is a powerful sales factor.

While Hearn makes his financial killings, the game expands. Tournaments are created, publicity is generated, the snooker cake swells.

'The game has done so well in Britain, it can't grow any bigger. Standards have to be maintained, improved here and there, but the growth is now going to come overseas.'

The American market looms as the ultimate challenge but pool and the vested interests associated with it are still cagey about snooker and there is also the problem, as even soccer found with an enormous budget, of 'selling' a new game in commercial terms.

Meanwhile, Hearn built on Davis's successful trip to Brazil in 1985 with a return visit in June with Davis and Meo. Brazil plays its own version of snooker with only one red and the colours but Davis beat their national champion in front of a television audience of 40 million at both the British and Brazilian versions of the game.

Negotiations have reached an advanced stage with Nippon Television to give Japan its first taste of professional snooker and at some stage something will certainly accrue from the initial trip to China in summer 1985 when over 300 million viewers saw Davis play Taylor.

'I get a terrific buzz out of being involved with something like that. I actually quite like snooker as a game and to take it somewhere new in that kind of operation is a great feeling for me and the players.

'Europe is obviously going to be a big growth area. The money may not be all that wonderful to start with but it is something I want my players to be associated with from the outset. We haven't done that much in Australia and New Zealand, partly because the distance involved makes it difficult to exercise control that everything is being done properly. The first Canadian Masters went very well in November, particularly for Dennis as he won it, and I can see a few things happening there as CBC's viewing figures were quite good. It's all very exciting. Every day's a new highlight.'

Contracts have recently been signed for the group of six Matchroom players to endorse a range of Pirelli footwear and of Justwise luggage on a long-term basis. 'Snooker Loopy', the Chas and Dave single for which the Matchroom players acted as both subjects and backing group, reached fifth place in the charts and sold 200,000 copies in its first four weeks of sale. After that, anything seems possible.

Clive Everton

History of Snooker

In 1875 Colonel Sir Neville Chamberlain was a young subaltern with the Devonshire Regiment stationed at Jubbulpore. During the rainy season the officers' long afternoons were spent at the mess billiards table where the parent game was less popular than various round games which were better suited to more than two players and to which it was easier to add a modest gambling element.

'Pyramids', perhaps snooker's most obvious forerunner, was a game played with fifteen reds, initially placed in a triangle, with the apex red on what is now the pink spot but which was then known as the pyramid spot. Each time a player potted a red, all his opponents paid across the agreed stake money per ball.

In 'life pool', each player was given a cue-ball and an object-ball (e.g. white on red, red on yellow), the second player's object-ball being the first player's cue-ball and so on. The object was to pot one's specified object-ball three times. Each time a player's ball was potted, he lost a life and had to pay an agreed stake. When he had lost three 'lives' he paid an extra sum for a 'star' (or extra life) and when that was gone he was 'dead'. When only one player remained he scooped the kitty.

'Black pool' was a development of pool in that a black ball was added. When a player had potted his allocated ball, he could attempt the black. If he was successful, each of his opponents paid across an additional sum and he could then attempt the nearest ball. Joe Davis spent many of his youthful hours playing a similar game, 'pink pool'.

Black pool was the preferred game among the Devonshire officers but it was Chamberlain's inspiration gradually to add other coloured balls so that snooker came to be played with fifteen reds, yellow, green, pink and black. Blue and brown were added some years later.

These new colours produced a game whose variety (and variety of monetary forfeits) immediately caught on. The concept of break-building was much in the future and even the point values of the balls were not established until a little later; but it was in these casual and almost chance beginnings that the game undoubtedly had its origin.

When Compton Mackenzie, the novelist, interviewed him in 1938, Chamberlain recalled that the Devons one afternoon received a visit from a young subaltern who had been trained at the Royal Military Academy, Woolwich. In the course of conversation, the latter happened to remark that a first year cadet at Woolwich was referred to as a 'snooker' with the implication that this was the status of the lowest of the low. The original word for a cadet had been the French 'neux' which had been corrupted to 'snooker'.

Chamberlain said: 'The term was a new one to me but I soon had the opportunity of exploiting it when one of our party failed to hole a coloured ball which was close to a corner pocket. I called out to him: "Why, you're a regular snooker!"

'I had to explain to the company the definition of the word and to soothe the feelings of the culprit I added that we were all, so to speak, snookers at the game so it would be very appropriate to call the game snooker. The suggestion was adopted with enthusiasm and the game has been called snooker ever since.'

Thurston's original Billiard Room, 1814

Past Masters

John Spencer, three times World champion

Joe Davis

Joe Davis took snooker by the scruff of the neck in the twenties and thirties and by the sheer force of his skill and personality hauled it into position as the premier billiard table game.

Without him, snooker would never have had a World Professional Championship. Without him, it would never have graduated from its early venues – a billiard hall in Birmingham, the backroom of a pub in Nottingham – to Thurston's, the billiards holy of holies in Leicester Square, and from there to larger public venues such as the Horticultural Hall, Westminster, where the fortnight-long final, Joe Davis's last, in 1946 attracted over 20,000 spectators and grossed £12,000.

Without him, indeed, it would have been a different game; it was he who transformed it from a somewhat crude potting contest – 'The sort of game you play in corduroys and clogs' as Tom Reece acidly put it – into the present sophisticated mixture of break-building techniques and tactical complexities.

Originally, Joe was a billiards player. Born in 1901 in Whitwell, a Derbyshire village, he was 13 when he won the Chesterfield Championship, the only amateur event in which he ever competed; at 25 he reached his first professional billiards final; and the whole of Chesterfield turned out at the station to welcome him when he came home world champion in 1928.

It was, though, in the context of 'scraping and scratching to get a living' that he had approached the Billiards Association in 1926 to sanction a Professional Snooker Championship. He won the event (it rated only three paragraphs in *The Billiard Player* and earned him only £6.10s) and retained it until he abdicated in 1946, by which time snooker had overtaken billiards in popularity.

This was because Joe, the Australian Walter Lindrum, the New Zealander Clark McConachy and another Englishman, Tom Newman, had achieved between them a unique sporting distinction: they had become so good at their game that they had killed it as a public entertainment.

Through their total mastery, notoriously of nursery cannons, they achieved such a degree of perfection in their play that it no longer seemed to bear much resemblance to the game of billiards that amateurs enjoyed in their own clubs. Having exhausted one game, it was time to try another.

Even after his retirement from World Championship play, Joe continued to dominate the snooker scene. He was co-leaseholder of Leicester Square Hall which had succeeded Thurston's as the home of the professional game and he was chairman of the Professional Players Association: what he said, went.

He continued to play brilliantly. He made the game's first official 147 maximum in 1955 and was only beaten three times on level terms, on each occasion by his brother, Fred, in his entire career. He won many tournaments conceding substantial handicaps and was unquestionably accepted as no 1 long after he had ceased to play in the Championship.

During the Second World War, he toured theatres from the Palladium downwards with a variety act of intricate trick shots. Early television snooker revolved round him utterly and he was falling very little short of the incredibly high standards he invariably set himself when he ceased public play altogether in 1964.

It was always his priority to present snooker with a sense of dignity and status and no one took more pleasure than him in seeing the World Professional Championship become established at the Crucible Theatre, Sheffield, as one of sport's great annual spectacles. He died in July 1978, aged 77.

John Spencer

John Spencer may yet prove that he belongs in present rather than past masters but as his decline continued from 13th in the rankings in 1983-84 to 20th the following year and 34th going into the 1986-87 season, it does appear that his best days are behind him.

World professional champion at his first attempt in 1969 and champion again in 1970 and 1977, he was a prolific winner in the 1970s of events like the Park Drive 2000, the Norwich Union Open, the Wilsons Classic and the Holsten International which are no longer part of the scene.

It was in the Holsten in 1979 that he made the first 147 maximum in tournament history, but ITV, taking a meal-break at the time, did not record it and the pockets of the table on which it was made were found to be over-sized.

In some inexplicable way, his cue action lost its natural straightness and rhythm. Much of his energy was devoted to securing his business future with his two snooker clubs in Bolton and in the summer of 1984 the continuance of any sort of playing career was threatened by persistent double vision, a condition he now keeps in check only through a daily intake of prescribed steroids. He has become one of the BBC's most experienced summarisers and has always been one of the circuit's livelier practical jokers.

John Pulman

John Pulman, now chiefly known as a member of the ITV commentary team, was world champion from 1957 until his defeat in the quarter-final of the 1968-69 Championship by John Spencer. His peak years unfortunately coincided with professional snooker's greatest depression: when Pulman won the title in 1957 there were only four entries in the World Championship, and for the next seven years it was not contested because it was not considered a viable commercial proposition. When it was restored on a challenge basis in 1964, he made eight successful defences in four years. After the Championship was re-established with a tournament format, he reached the final in 1970 and the semi-finals in 1977.

John Pulman

Walter Donaldson

In style and doggedness Walter Donaldson was the Eddie Charlton of his day. An excellent long potter, he limited his range of positional possibilities by his reluctance to use side but nevertheless won two world titles. He left his native Scotland long before the war in order to manage billiard halls in Rotherham and Chesterfield, but made no great impact on the professional game before his five years' war service.

After the war, he immediately embarked on a relentless practice programme, shutting himself away for hours on end in the loft of a friend's house which contained a billiard table. Joe Davis retired in 1946 and to the surprise of most Donaldson succeeded him when he beat Fred Davis in the 1947 world final. He also beat the younger Davis in 1950 and was runner-up to him on six occasions before he retired in 1955.

Fred Davis

Even though he is now 72, it is still in one sense premature to describe Fred Davis as a past master because he was still good enough in the 1985-86 season to record wins over such notables as Bill Werbeniuk and Kirk Stevens. Even if his standard is two or three blacks worse than when he was in his prime, he enjoys the game as keenly as he ever did.

Still, his opponents find that they are not only playing the master tactician but are battling for the affection of the spectators as well. The warmth with which the audience greets Fred, when he arrives carrying the one cue he has used throughout his 54-year professional career, a twinkle as well as the glint of battle in his eye, makes him not just an opponent but part of a legend.

It is the Davis legend of how his elder brother, Joe, began professional snooker, developed it and, on his retirement, almost ended it; of how Fred was recognised by his peers as being hardly, if at times at all, inferior in skill, although he was unable in the public mind to disturb Joe's aura of invincibility.

Joe's retirement came in two stages. In 1946 he retired undefeated from World Championship play after holding the title for the 20 years since its inception. Fred then won the world professional crown eight times, only to find that the abdicated king was not after all in exile: Joe still ruled.

In his wily way, Joe had continued to play in all the other major tournaments, all of them handicapped, and in most of which he held a promotional interest. Fred, the official champion for the best part of a decade, was the only player who ever played Joe on level terms: he beat him three times. 'This made no impact whatsoever,' said Fred. 'Whatever I did, I was just Joe's younger brother.'

In 1964 Joe retired altogether, leaving behind only five active professionals. There was no championship at all between 1957 and 1964 and even when it was revived on a challenge basis it passed virtually unnoticed. 'I didn't play much. One season I didn't play at all. I wasn't interested because there wasn't anything to be interested in,' Fred recalls.

'It's different now. There's so much going on it's exciting just to be part of it.' Pension book and all, he intends to remain part of it as long as he can give 'a reasonable account of myself.'

With snooker reborn through television and sponsorship, Fred is the link with its previous incarnation, the younger brother who has become the game's elder statesman.

In 1980, a boyhood inner certainty that he would win the World Professional Billiards Championship – frustrated when snooker superseded billiards as a public entertainment – became reality when he successfully challenged Rex Williams for the title.

Billiards, on which Fred cut his teeth as a youngster in Chesterfield, calls for a vast knowledge of angles and the greatest delicacy of touch, qualities which Fred uses creatively in snooker in his safety play and close-in work around the reds and black. He dislikes hitting the ball hard and in fact lacks the cue power of younger players brought up solely on snooker. Fencing for openings and manoeuvring for position, rather than power shots and out-and-out potting, have always been his style.

Janice Hale

My Unfavourite Colour

Every player, even the greatest champion, misses key balls occasionally. 'Who missed what when' is the name of the game, and obviously the secret of success is to time your misses to coincide with quieter periods of play when a galumpher isn't going to be quite so costly.

This way, you also give less joy to the armchair sadists who only watch snooker in the hope of seeing a pro bowed over the table with small tufts of hair torn out of his head (Willie Thorne, for example, has given them ample satisfaction).

Spectators have varying reactions to crucial misses, according to whether or not the unfortunate player is in their favour. If they like you, they will let out various noises, such as 'ffff' (a sharp intake of breath to show it hurt them more than it hurt you), or 'ow' (a sigh of despair at having wasted their support on a mental defective), or, most popularly with female spectators, 'aaah' (as though a particularly ugly baby had just been lifted out of its pram for inspection).

If the public does *not* like the player in question, then there are Muffled Remarks. These include half-voiced expletives, oaths, apothegms and veiled references to Willie Wonka and natural fertilizer.

But naturally, the more simple and straightforward the ball missed, the more spectator behaviour tends to be exaggerated. An acquaintance of mine, seeing Steve Davis miss one on television, jumps out of his seat and holds his index fingers on either side of his forehead like horns, pointing them fiercely at the set. I have no idea of the significance of this stratagem.

Each ball has had its famous victims: men who went to pot when they themselves declined to do so, and if balls could tell stories of their conquests in bars, we may well imagine the sort of incidents they would refer to – dismal and degrading tales of human putrefaction over easy shots, of wavering courage and wobbling cues. Each ball could dine out on stories like these. What is significant is that no player, whatever his technical merits, can claim to have left no balls up in his wake.

Reds, because they are cheap and relatively cheerful, tend not to feature prominently in players' nightmares: in any case one is potting reds all the time, so a miss soon fades from memory. Still, there are odd occasions when a red has brought the flush to somebody's cheeks.

Eddie Charlton may well recall the time a red with the half-butt daunted his chances in the 1979 World Championship semi-final against Terry Griffiths. Eddie had been 48-0 in front in the fateful frame and the miss proved fatal, allowing Griffiths to snatch the frame 97-48 and the match by 19-17 after the ruinous red hit the top jaw.

Another crimson victim was Cliff Thorburn in his 1981 Masters semi-final duel with Alex Higgins when he went ahead 5-1 against a food-poisoned Alex affected by some West Country mustard the night before. Higgins, his shamrock-coloured visage puckered in woe, struggled to regain some control in the two following frames. At 5-3, 57-0, Thorburn seemed to be rolling home when a red suddenly failed to roll as he intended. Cliff saw red when press reports claimed he had missed a sitter: in fact there had been another ball slightly in his line of fire on that one.

But whatever the difficulty, Cliff's miss was like Milk of Magnesia to the Higgins stomach and a winning clearance put him right back in the match.

In any case, the reds had not quite finished with Thorburn. In the tenth frame, leading 52-34, Cliff's arm went slightly dead over a red along the cushion and the ball came to rest over the pocket. To make matters worse, the renewed Alex went on to fluke a long red en route to the Masters title.

Evidence of yellow ball peril is rather harder to find, but one especially ghastly one brought Tony Meo to consider an alternative career during the final of the English Professional Championship in 1981 against Steve Davis. The outcome of that match might easily have altered the fate of Mr Meo, if not Mr Davis, because although Tony was to lay the ghost of his defeat in 1986, it undoubtedly haunted him at various moments of his ten straight losses to his stablemate.

Going back to that original yellow that started all the trouble at the Haden Hill Leisure Centre, Sandwell, in March 1981, we find young Meo leading 2-1 and looking as though he is about to storm the barricades; 27 in front in the next frame and looking at an easy yellow, Tony took aim, fired and nearly fainted.

'I got a lot of stick about that,' he says, 'but I was trying to get onto the green, which is the natural thing, and in any case it was easier for me to pot yellow with screw back to get on the green than just jab it in.' With hindsight, it might have been better to jab.

But if that yellow made Meo sallow, it was the green that got Griffiths going in the qualifying section of the UK Championship against Rex Williams in Terry's first few months as a professional before his great world title win. That particular gangrenous ball resulted in what the Welshman called 'the most crushing defeat I have ever had.'

True, it was a very awkward green indeed. Griffiths led 8-3, poised for victory, and he felt like taking it on. It had to be cut back at quarter ball, across and against the nap, with the cue ball coming off three cushions for the brown. Perfect, if you could bring it off in a match-winning situation.

Griffiths looked at the green, the green looked at Griffiths, and the ball went sliding off on its own chosen path. That miss effectively gave the Welshman a slow puncture; he watched helplessly as Williams came roaring back to snatch the match 9-8. Few players ever forget this grim experience of being overhauled from well in front. They hear the footsteps coming from the rear for years.

Brown has been the unfavourite colour for some. Eddie Charlton, Mr Australian snooker, came within one good spit of the world title in 1975 against Ray Reardon and in front of his own people. A winning streak of eight frames put him

Steve Davis misses the final black in the 1985 Embassy World Championship

28-23 up and needing only three of the remaining ten frames for the Big Gong. You'd have put your money on Charlton.

He took aim at an available brown that would have put him 30-25 in front – within a frame of the Championship. Steady Eddie didn't miss browns like that, but he missed.

A brown was also the rogue ball for 1980 world finalist Cliff Thorburn. It was 'pretty well game ball' and would have put the Canadian 17-15 and virtually home free against Higgins. After it hit the corner of the baulk pocket 'from a foot or so,' Cliff said he almost died, 'because I was thinking if I pot this, I might win the Championship.'

Thorburn managed to put the miss behind him and finish the job. Not so Tony Meo, in the Pontins Open final that was to set Steve Davis on the glory road. Tony had gone 6-5 in front and needed only the clinching frame. He was about to clear up, with all the colours roughly on their spots, when a simple brown stopped him. 'I'd pot that nine times out of ten as well,' says Meo.

Other players have suffered a bad case of the blues. Rex Williams, in his 1972 World Championship semi-final, took a 20-point lead in the deciding frame against Higgins and was apparently coasting home when he hit a rebel blue which failed to sink. It wasn't easy: he was dead tight on the cushion and he needed position on a red. But that blue has haunted Rex ever since. 'I knew I'd lost the match,' he says.

Doug Mountjoy's nightmare blue came in the 1981 World Championship final, against the coming man Steve Davis. Having started badly, the Welshman had fought back to stand 11-13 down and looking dangerous.

When Davis could not seem to clinch the 25th frame, Mountjoy stepped up like a matador to put it away, needing only to the pink. A very ordinary blue into the middle pocket stayed out. Two shots later, when Doug had another go, it went down – but Mountjoy went in-off.

The blue had finished him. It also wasted Willie Thorne, of course. Everyone knows this sad tale: of how the certain-to-be 1985 Coral UK Champion allowed Davis to make what sportswriters fondly call 'a remarkable come-back.'

Davis had been reduced for much of the match to a mere spectator as Willie put on a potting display that included three century clearances and eight other big breaks to stand 13-8 and needing a frame-winning blue. The blue remained; it was Thorne who went down the plughole, dropping eight of the next nine frames to lose 16-14.

Worse was to come. In the Benson & Hedges Masters quarter-final, Willie was busy replying to Steve Davis's 61 with a seeming match-winning clearance in the decider when, lo and behold, it happened again. This time the blue got Thorne out of position and he missed the pink, but it was all the same to Willie: 'I don't know how many times getting on the wrong side of the blue is going to cost me a match,' he said.

The pink can be pretty shocking too. Ray Reardon got a surprise in the Masters final against John Spencer when a bevy of Benson & Hedges girls rose from their seats while Ray was negotiating the match-winning pink in that one, and a pink very nearly stopped Steve Davis in his tracks in the 1981 Yamaha Organs final.

Faced with a sitter at 8-2, 54-52, Steve's cue arm suddenly failed to act naturally. Seeing the pink ball still on the table, David Taylor, who till then had looked rather cadaverous, sprang from his seat and fought back to 6-8.

Davis eventually 'fell over the line,' saying 'I never could have believed potting a ball was so difficult.' It was one of those cases of the player far in front hearing the old footsteps coming.

Fred Davis, too, fell victim to the pink. Fred, who once quipped in the press room that snooker is 'no crueller than the gladiators,' was in the 1973 world quarter-final against Higgins needing only an inviting pink which would have put him one up with two to go. Failing to pot that ball, Fred gave Higgins the adrenalin he needed to fuel him to a spectacular 16-14 victory.

Five years later, the pink ball did for Fred again – this time in the semi-final against Perrie Mans after Davis had fought back to two frames behind and seemed about to repeat an earlier come-from-behind triumph over Reardon. The 64-year-old veteran, who first won this title in 1948, had a lot of support in the audience, not least from his brother Joe who, according to former women's champion Joyce Gardner sitting next to him, was 'playing every shot for Fred,' turning this way and that in his chair.

Fred Davis was looking good, doubling a blue into the middle pocket and squaring up to a pink that would make it 15-16. Amid pin-fall silence Fred fired – and missed. A groan went up in the auditorium.

Joe Davis, pale and shaken, was taken back to his hotel room and thence to St Mary's Hospital where he underwent massive heart surgery from which he was never to recover. The pink was with some justification described as 'the ball that killed Joe Davis.'

The black, because of its significance on the table, is often the deciding ball in a match; so many nightmares may be recounted involving slight miscues and accidents around the black spot. Here is a pressure ball, pure and simple. Steve Davis missed the last black of the 1985 World Championship. If from his whole career he could play one shot anew it would be that.

Alex Higgins would recall his 1979 World Championship quarter-final with Terry Griffiths when he stood 55-0 up with the score at 11-11.

Especially poignant in this story is the fact that, to reach this happy advantage, Alex had been potting death or glory balls of great technical merit throughout the match and the black on its spot which he was now scenting, nostrils flared in determination, seemed to present no problems whatsoever.

How terrible then to Irish sensibilities must the following sequence of events have been as the black shot off, hit the back of the jaw and threw itself back upon the table like a bomb refusing to leave the bay in a stricken Heinkel.

Higgins did not have another chance, Griffiths went on to triumph and female adulation. And Alex, whatever his subsequent successes in the Championship, never forgot, or forgave. He may still occasionally be observed sporting a black eye, the badge of a much deeper mark upon his psyche.

Angela Patmore

Snooker Wives

This is the scenario. Nice young man marries nice young girl. The nice young man (perhaps he works as a postman or a coal miner) turns out to be a genius at snooker. Two years on, the nice young girl finds she's married to a millionaire.

The story sounds like it should have a happy ending – fade out on a shot of the couple kissing under crossed cues. But in the real world, this is often not the case. The divorce rate among professional snooker players is high. (Alex Higgins, Silvino Francisco, David Taylor, Eddie Charlton and now, it seems, Ray Reardon are among the victims, though some are happily remarried.)

Along with the money comes a life which would strain the happiest of marriages. The sport takes husbands away from home for long periods of time. Free drink is thrust upon players at every tournament and they are constantly surrounded by groupies. All too often, the wife is left at home in her gilded cage with nothing better to do than iron another hand-made shirt and read about the exploits of her superstar husband in the newspapers.

But in spite of the pressure on these marriages, some do survive. Margot Spencer, wife of John Spencer for the last 17 years, says the secret is simple. 'It's no use sitting around waiting for the old man to come home. The wife must make her own life.'

In recent years, Margot has certainly practised what she preaches. In Bolton, she manages a bar and the luxurious John Spencer Snooker Centre in Manchester Road. Not bad for a woman who, when she first met her husband, had never seen a game of snooker. She says:

'When we met, John had just turned professional, but I didn't even know what that meant. I'd never even seen the game. Our first date was nearly our last when he yelled at me as I got in his car "Don't put your feet on my balls." '

The first time John entered the World Championship, he had to borrow £100 from his bank manager. 'In those days £100 was an awful lot of money,' says Margot. It was a terrible risk, but we both had faith in his skill. John is a gambler by nature and I don't care for the form some of his gambling takes, but I've never objected to him gambling on himself. I've always supported him in that.'

To earn some steady money, Margot devised a scheme for sending John out to challenge club players. 'If he lost, we paid them £25. If they lost, they paid us. We sent letters explaining the scheme to as many clubs as we could find. We could barely afford the stamps. But the response was

Terry and Annette Griffiths

John and Margot Spencer

terrific. Soon we were earning £25 a night – more than most people earned in a week in those days.'

Margot thinks that the marriages of today's players suffer because they make it to the top too quickly. 'They can become millionaires in a couple of years. It doesn't give their marriages time to adjust. It doesn't give couples anything to achieve together. In some respects, I'm glad John and I had those hungry years.'

In 1969, when John won the World Championship, the Spencers moved into the big time although the real boom was to come later on as television became interested in the game.

'There is no doubt that John's success did put a strain on our marriage. He had to be away from home for months at a time. But I travelled with him quite a lot. We decided against having a family so that I could do this.'

As far as other women are concerned, Margot says: 'I believe that what you don't know can't hurt you, but if I ever found out, I wouldn't put up with it.'

With an eye to the future and the knowledge that no one stays at the top for ever, the Spencers opened a bar with a few snooker tables. Margot stayed at home to run it while John went on the road. It was so successful that they decided to open the John Spencer Snooker Centre last year.

'We've put everything we own into it. It's our biggest gamble to date. I lost one and a half stone worrying about whether we had got it right. I'm glad to say that it seems as if we have. It's doing very well.

'So you see, I've had just as much a career out of snooker as John has and I would recommend it to the wife of any top player. You have to get some independence – financial and emotional.'

When Annette Griffiths married Terry Griffiths in 1969, she married a bus conductor. She'd no idea that, nine years later, he would be World Snooker Champion. She says: 'When we met, Terry played as an amateur. During our two-year courtship, he gave it up for a season because we weren't seeing enough of each other. Soon after we were married, I came to realise how much snooker meant to him. When he decided to go professional, I backed him up. He packed in his job, but I was working in a car factory, so it was okay.'

1979 was the year that Terry came from nowhere to win the World Championship. Annette says: 'I knew he'd won a lot of money and that I wouldn't be going back to the car factory, but I didn't realise what a difference it was going to make to our lives. The phone never stopped ringing. People wanted to give us things for nothing. The press camped out on our doorstep. The first couple of months were terrible for both of us. We didn't know how to handle it. Terry was away most of the time. I was at home with young children [Darren was born in '72 and Wayne in '79]. But slowly we both adjusted to it. There was a time when I thought I'd never get used to the life, but I've surprised myself. The last two years have been marvellous for me. Now the kids are older, I can get away to the tournaments more. I travel with Terry two or three days a week.'

Annette now has only one regret. Before Terry became a snooker superstar, she persuaded him to have a vasectomy. 'At the time, I thought I'd always have to keep on working. I thought we couldn't afford another child. Now, of course, money isn't a problem and we regret having done it. I have two boys and I would have loved a girl. But that's nothing you can blame on snooker. Just one of those sad things.'

Fiona Thorne met Willie in 1978 when he was already an established player. Last year they married and they now have 9-month-old twins, Kieran and Tristan. She says: 'You couldn't say I rushed into marriage. We'd known each other eight years. I went into it with my eyes open knowing full well what a life married to a top snooker player would mean.'

For Fiona, tied to the home with two babies, marriage to Willie means a great deal of time spent at home on her own. 'In the season, I'm on my own practically every night. If he gets home, it's 1 or 2 a.m. and he's out of the house by mid morning the next day to get to the next game. May to September are off season months, but he goes away on tours, he goes to the club to practise and he likes to play golf and go horse racing.'

Fiona says her solution to this is to lead a very independent life. 'I have my own lifestyle while he is away based around the children, my friends, shopping and keeping fit at the gym. I think any woman married to a successful man must make her own life, have her own interests and friends.'

When the twins are older, she hopes to be able to accompany Willie to major tournaments. 'I get a great thrill out of seeing him play and I love the atmosphere at the big events.'

Meanwhile, stuck at home with the babies, she says: 'I believe we have a good marriage. We have a mature understanding and I think we are both very happy with the way things are.'

Jane Ennis

Willie and Fiona Thorne on their wedding day

Professional Billiards

World Professional Billiards Championship

1870	William Cook beat John Roberts Jr	1200-1083
	John Roberts Jr beat William Cook	1000-522
	John Roberts Jr beat A. Bowles	1000-759
	Joseph Bennett beat John Roberts Jr	1000-905
1871	John Roberts Jr beat Joseph Bennett	1000-637
	William Cook beat Joseph Bennett	1000-942
1872	William Cook beat John Roberts Jr	1000-799
1874	William Cook beat John Roberts Jr	1000-784
1875	John Roberts Jr beat William Cook	1000-837
	John Roberts Jr beat William Cook	1000-865
1877	John Roberts Jr beat William Cook	1000-779
1880	Joseph Bennett beat William Cook	1000-949
1881	Joseph Bennett beat Tom Taylor	1000-910
1885	John Roberts Jr beat William Cook	3000-2908
	John Roberts Jr beat Joseph Bennett	3000-1360
1889	Charles Dawson beat Joe North	9000-4715
1900	Charles Dawson beat H. W. Stevenson	9000-6775
1901	H. W. Stevenson beat Charles Dawson	9000-6406
	Charles Dawson beat H.W. Stevenson	9000-5796
	H.W. Stevenson (declared champion)	
1903	Charles Dawson beat H.W. Stevenson	9000-8700
1908	Melbourne Inman (declared champion)	
1909	Melbourne Inman beat Albert Williams	9000-7662

Billiards Control Club Rules

1909	H.W. Stevenson (declared champion)	
1910	H.W. Stevenson led Melbourne Inman (match abandoned)	13370-13212
	H.W. Stevenson beat Melbourne Inman	18000-16907
1911	H.W. Stevenson beat Melbourne Inman	18000-16914
1912	Melbourne Inman beat Tom Reece	18000-9675
1913	Melbourne Inman beat Tom Reece	18000-16627
1914	Melbourne Inman beat Tom Reece	18000-12826
1919	Melbourne Inman beat H.W. Stevenson	16000-9468
1920	Willie Smith beat Claude Falkiner	16000-14500
1921	Tom Newman beat Tom Reece	16000-10744
1922	Tom Newman beat Claude Falkiner	16000-15167
1923	Willie Smith beat Tom Newman	16000-15180
1924	Tom Newman beat Tom Reece	16000-14845
1925	Tom Newman beat Tom Reece	16000-10092
1926	Tom Newman beat Joe Davis	16000-9505
1927	Tom Newman beat Joe Davis	16000-14763
1928	Joe Davis beat Tom Newman	16000-14874
1929	Joe Davis beat Tom Newman	18000-17219
1930	Joe Davis beat Tom Newman	20198-20117
1932	Joe Davis beat Clark McConachy	25161-19259
1933	Walter Lindrum beat Joe Davis	21815-21121
1934	Walter Lindrum beat Joe Davis	23553-22678
1951	Clark McConachy beat John Barrie	9294-6691
1968	Rex Williams beat Clark McConachy	5499-5234

In 1971, the World Professional Billiards and Snooker Association declared its autonomy in running professional championships after the Billiards and Snooker Control Council had stripped Williams of his title and declared that Lesley Driffield and Jack Karnehm, the only two professionals not then recognising the WPBSA, should play for the vacant championship. When this match took place, Driffield beat Karnehm, but the WPBSA continued to recognise Williams as champion.

1971	Rex Williams beat Bernard Bennett	9250-4058
1973	Rex Williams beat Jack Karnehm	8340-4336
1974	Rex Williams beat Eddie Charlton	7017-4916
1976	Rex Williams beat Eddie Charlton	9015-5149
1980 (June)	Fred Davis beat Rex Williams	5978-4452

The June 1980 title match between Davis and Williams was the last to be held on a challenge basis; in November that year a tournament format was introduced.

1980 (November)*	Fred Davis beat Mark Wildman	3037-2064
1982*	Rex Williams beat Mark Wildman	3000-1785
1983*	Rex Williams beat Fred Davis	1500-605
1984	Mark Wildman beat Eddie Charlton	1045-1012
1985**	Ray Edmonds beat Norman Dagley	3-1
1986**	Robbie Foldvari beat Norman Dagley	3-1

* Matches played to a points target rather than over a specified duration.
** Matches best of five games 400 up.

Robbie Foldvari: Monarflex World Professional Billiards champion

Robbie Foldvari

(Australia)

BORN: 2.6.60
HOME: SYDNEY/NORTHAMPTON

One Australian, Walter Lindrum, dominated billiards so thoroughly that he sent the World Professional Championship into limbo for 17 years.

At Romiley Forum, Stockport, in March 1986, another Australian, Robbie Foldvari, captured that title under conditions which the billiards fraternity hope will further stimulate the modest revival the three-ball game has enjoyed in the past few years.

In the age of Lindrum, championship matches lasted a fortnight, four hours play each day. Eddie Charlton, the greatest snooker player Australia has produced, was a schoolboy when he played the great Lindrum. 'He could make a thousand break as easily as I could drink a cup of tea,' Charlton is fond of recalling.

Robbie Foldvari in play

The record books confirm just how good Lindrum was. His highest break was 4,137 and he mastered the skills of the game so thoroughly that he killed it off as a public entertainment and paved the way for snooker to take over.

The greatest of his many specialities was to group the three balls together near a cushion and run off lengthy series of delicate nursery cannons. It was consummately skilful but, through endless repetition, infinitely boring. The other leading players of the day, trying to match him, also made their contributions to the long hibernation of professional billiards.

What now helps make billiards a more attractive spectacle is that the level of skill has deteriorated so markedly from the inhuman perfection shown by the great players of the thirties.

Such rule changes as a limitation of 75 consecutive cannons, which would have made the game more varied in Lindrum's day, are actually superfluous today because no one is skilful enough regularly to reach the limit anyway.

Foldvari, an economics graduate from Melbourne University, who stands 69th in snooker's world rankings, provides a link between the two ages of billiards.

His coach was Murt O'Donoghue, a New Zealander who, at Griffith, New South Wales, in 1934, achieved the first recorded 147 snooker maximum. O'Donoghue hustled throughout the 1920s in New Zealand and Australia before building up a chain of 27 snooker clubs. He never pursued either game competitively but even in his seventies, with poor eyesight, he could rattle off long runs of nursery cannons and show anyone who wished to learn, like young Foldvari, the intricacies of the game.

The old-timers would have been aghast at the current formula adopted for billiards – the best of five games of 400 up – but to get billiards on television, recurrent crises and climaxes have to be on offer, much as they are in snooker.

Foldvari's 3-1 world final victory over Norman Dagley was achieved with some solid all-round play. His highest breaks were 182 in the third game and 193 in the fourth, peanuts by Lindrum's standards but made in a very different context and good enough anyway to help him regain the title for Australia 35 years after Lindrum, unchallenged for 17 years, had relinquished it.

More important for the game, the BBC's coverage of the final attracted sufficiently strong viewing figures for there to be reasonable hope that not only the final but the semi-finals will be covered in 1987.

Janice Hale

Norman Dagley

(England)

BORN: 27.6.30
HOME: EARL SHILTON

If he had played any other game, Norman Dagley would have become a household name. But through playing billiards, snooker's elder but for years almost moribund elder brother, it was only to the three-ball game's hard core of aficionados that he became a superstar.

Dagley, 56, won two world and fifteen English amateur titles but did not consider it worthwhile turning professional until the 1984-85 season.

He does not play snooker and it was taking the professional billiards fraternity all its efforts to stage an annual world championship without worrying too much about prize money.

So for years, Dagley preferred to stay amateur in order to enjoy the biennial overseas trips afforded by the World Amateur Championship.

He won his first amateur title at the Malta Hilton in 1971. 'The only way I could eat here would be to do it through a building society,' he said, relishing a lifestyle billiards could only periodically bring him.

Eye trouble stopped him defending in Bombay in 1973 but he won in Auckland in 1975, lost in the semi-finals in Melbourne in 1977, the 1979 and 1981 finals in Colombo and Delhi and the 1983 semi-finals back in Malta.

For a decade and a half his rivalry with a Bombay lawyer, Michael Ferreira, who has won the world amateur title three times, was like Tom and Jerry's but in India Ferreira's billiards achievements have made him a national celebrity.

Dagley spends much of his life serving behind the bar and occasionally doing some coaching at a Nuneaton snooker centre just down the road from the Leicestershire village of Earl Shilton where he learnt to play.

This sleepy outpost of middle England oddly produced two top-rate amateur players, the Wright brothers, Jack and Reg, both of whom reached the English Amateur Championship final in their day. Reg was Dagley's mentor.

'He used to thrash me night after night at Earl Shilton Institute. He never spared me. But it was the best training in the world. And even when I started to overtake Reg he continued to help me,' said Dagley.

In 1984-85 billiards achieved two breakthroughs: Channel 4 ran a seven-week series which drew high viewing figures and the World Professional Billiards and Snooker Association, flush with money from the snooker boom, voted £20,000 rising to £30,000 by 1990 into the annual prize fund for the world championship.

These developments persuaded Dagley to turn professional. To the surprise of the billiards world he failed to win the world title at his first attempt, losing 3-1 to Ray Edmonds in the final as he was to lose 3-1 to Robbie Foldvari in the final a year later. It was ironic that he should produce, in the televised 1986 final, one of the worst competitive performances of his career in front of – through television – his largest ever audience, but he has always risen above setbacks in his career and can be expected to do so again.

Janice Hale

Norman Dagley, 15 times English Amateur Billiards champion

Amateur Status

The original concept of amateurism has disappeared from modern snooker, and with it many of the old hypocrisies.

It used to be the case that anyone, man or woman, who so much as served a cup of tea in a snooker hall was designated a professional, regardless of playing ability.

The moneyed, ruling classes enforced gentlemen and players categorisation in snooker, as they did in most sports. This distinction was gradually eroded by a mixture of commercial pressures and changes in social thinking.

For a while, 'shamateurism' ruled – a system of indirect or even illicit payments, sometimes in the form of sinecures. The governing classes still governed and appearances were preserved.

Official definitions of amateurism were modified, but the façade remained until 1971 when the Billiards and Snooker Control Council, who had been recognised as the official governing body for both the professional and amateur sides of the game, abolished the term 'amateur'.

This, though, was a little too late in the day, for earlier that year the World Professional Billiards and Snooker Association had disassociated itself from the B & SCC and declared itself the sole governing body for the professional game. In effect, this meant that as the WPBSA designated all its members professionals, everyone else was automatically regarded as an amateur.

The International Billiards and Snooker Federation (IBSF), the one-nation, one-vote body for regulating the World Amateur Championships that had come into being in 1971, recognised that 'player' or 'non-professional' were terms either too vague or too negative to be in the title of their events so the term 'amateur' remained.

The definition of amateurism adopted by the IBSF in 1972 defined professionals simply as members of the WPBSA, those who 'declare themselves professional' or those who endorse products connected with the game. All limitations on amateurs receiving prize money or exhibition fees were abolished.

Since 1972, therefore, snooker and billiards have effectively been professional through and through, save that one group of players acknowledges the WPBSA as their controlling and governing body, while the rest acknowledge their own, domestic amateur associations and the IBSF.

Quite openly and properly, many amateurs began to play full-time. Many others welcomed any prize money they could earn in amateur tournaments as a supplement to the income they derived from their regular occupations. It often happens that a top-class amateur earns more from snooker than a middle-ranked professional.

Applications for professional status used to be judged by a sub-committee of the WPBSA and ratified by the WPBSA's main board. However, the WPBSA introduced, in the summer of 1985, with the co-operation of amateur governing bodies, a system of qualifying tournaments for professional status.

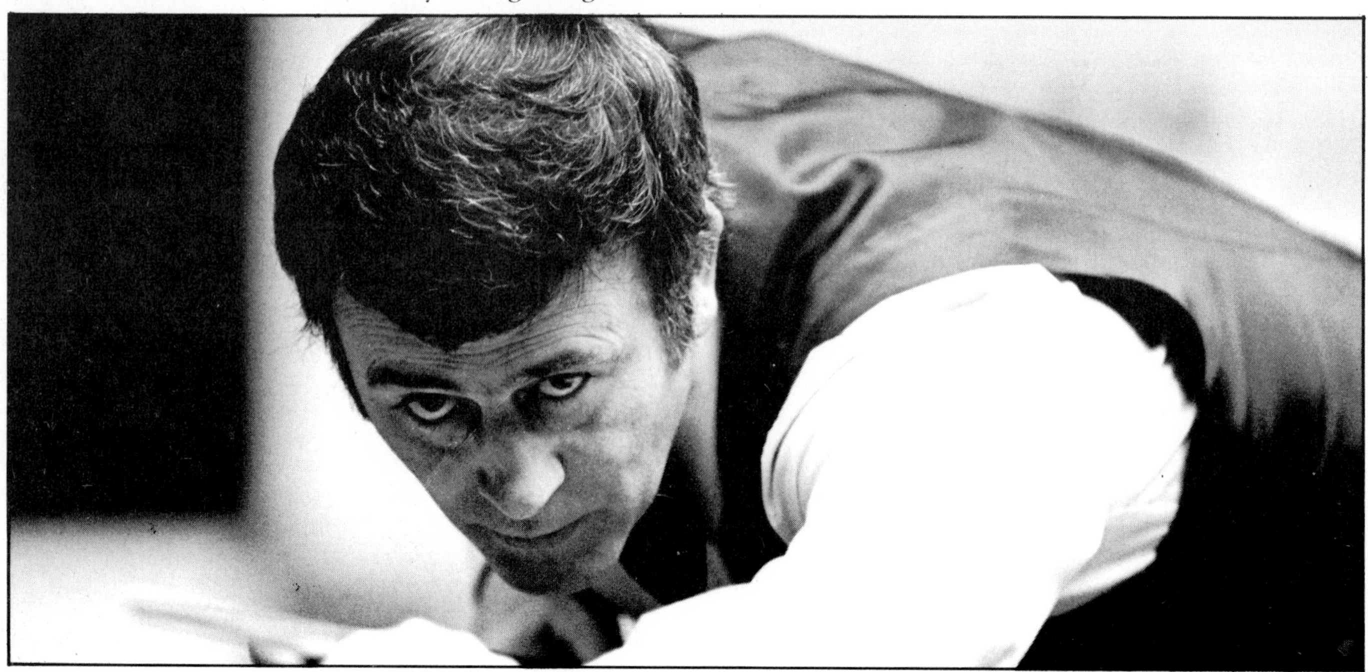

Doug Mountjoy, who won the 1976 World Amateur Snooker Championship before embarking on a successful professional career

World Amateur Championships

The pinnacle of amateur snooker is the World Amateur Championship which in 1985 became an annual event, instead of alternating with the World Amateur Billiards Championship. The latter will still be held every two years.

The World Amateur Billiards Championship, originally the British Empire Championship, was grudgingly instituted by the B & SCC (then the Billiards Association and Control Council) under pressure from overseas countries. The BA & CC thought that the Amateur Championship – essentially an English event though its title did not reflect that – was quite sufficient.

It was held eight times before the war and was revived in 1951 as the World Amateur Championship, the Empire having by then diminished, although the same countries, by and large, were represented. The World Amateur Snooker Championship, first mooted in 1952, was instituted in 1963.

Entry to these Championships is made through official national associations. Host nations determine whether one or two competitors per country are accepted. In addition, the defending champion's country is entitled to nominate him; the host country is also entitled to an extra representative and to fill any late vacancies.

A record 23 countries were represented in the 1985 World Amateur Snooker Championship at the Tower Ballroom, Blackpool, as the Billiards and Snooker Control Council celebrated its centenary with the fullest ever gathering of the world's snooker clans.

The initial event in 1963 took place with only five competitors from four countries. The introduction of Sports Council grants accounted for a sharp increase in the number of entrants in the early seventies but in recent years the increase has been a reflection of the spread of the game itself.

Snooker's main growth areas have been the Far East, which was represented in Blackpool by Hong Kong, Singapore and Thailand, and Europe, with Belgium, Sweden and Iceland all competing for the second time. Mauritius, Egypt and Zimbabwe could also be counted among the newly emerging snooker nations and Kenya made its international debut.

Omprakesh Agrawal, the young Indian who in Dublin in 1984 had broken the Anglo-Welsh monopoly of the title, turned professional and thus did not defend. His compatriot, Geet Sethi, who won the World Amateur Billiards Championship in Delhi in July, attempted to become the first player to hold both world amateur titles simultaneously but lost in the quarter-finals as the title went to the 38-year-old Maltese Paul Mifsud.

The event was financed through sponsorship of £30,000 from BCE, the table manufacturers, a gift of £20,000 from the World Professional Billiards and Snooker Association and a grant of £17,500 from the Sports Council.

Paul Mifsud became the first player to win World Amateur Championships at both billiards and snooker by clinching the latter title at Blackpool in 1985 with an 11-6 victory in the final over the former Cardiff City football goalkeeper, Dilwyn John.

Paul Mifsud, the only player to win World Amateur titles at both billiards and snooker

Mifsud won the billiards title in Colombo in 1979 and was runner-up in the snooker to Doug Mountjoy in Johannesburg in 1976 before losing to two other players who have also become leading professionals, Kirk Stevens in the 1978 quarter-finals in Malta and Jimmy White in the 1980 semi-finals in Tasmania.

He turned professional but Malta's isolated geographical location requires either constant expenditure on airfares or a semi-permanent move to Britain to make playing the circuit a realistic proposition. He therefore resigned his professional status after the 1983–84 season when he stood 49th in the world rankings.

WORLD AMATEUR SNOOKER CHAMPIONSHIP

Year	Venue	Winner	Runner-up
1963	Calcutta	G. Owen (England)	F. Harris (Australia)
1966	Karachi	G. Owen (England)	J. Spencer (England)
1968	Melbourne	D. Taylor (England)	M. Williams (Australia)
1970	Edinburgh	J. Barron (England)	S. Hood (England)
1972	Cardiff	R. Edmonds (England)	M. Francisco (South Africa)
1974	Dublin	R. Edmonds (England)	G. Thomas (Wales)
1976	Johannesburg	D. Mountjoy (Wales)	P. Mifsud (Malta)
1978	Malta	C. Wilson (Wales)	J. Johnson (England)
1980	Launceston	J. White (England)	R. Atkins (Australia)
1982	Calgary	T. Parsons (Wales)	Jim Bear (Canada)
1984	Dublin	O.B. Agrawal (India)	T. Parsons (Wales)
1985	Blackpool	P. Mifsud (Malta)	D. John (Wales)

WORLD AMATEUR BILLIARDS CHAMPIONSHIP

1926	London	J. Earlam (England)	G.Shailer (Australia)
1927	London	A. Prior (South Africa)	H. Coles (Wales)
1929	Johannesburg	L. Hayes (Australia)	A. Prior (South Africa)
1931	Sydney	L. Steeples (England)	S. Lee (England)
1933	London	S. Lee (England)	T. Jones (Wales)
1935	London	H. Coles (Wales)	J. McGhee (Scotland)
1936	Johannesburg	R. Marshall (Australia)	A. Prior (South Africa)
1938	Melbourne	R. Marshall (Australia)	K. Kennerley (England)
1951	London	R. Marshall (Australia)	F. Edwards (England)
1952	Calcutta	L. Driffield (England)	R. Marshall (Australia)
1954	Sydney	T. Cleary (Australia)	R. Marshall (Australia)
1958	Calcutta	W. Jones (India)	L. Driffield (England)
1960	Edinburgh	J. H. Beetham (England)	J. Long (Australia)
1962	Perth	R. Marshall (Australia)	W. Jones (India)
1964	Pukekohe	W. Jones (India)	J. Karnehm (England)
1967	Colombo	L. Driffield (England)	M. J. M. Lafir (Sri Lanka)
1969	London	J. Karnehm (England)	M. Ferreira (India) M. Francisco (South Africa) M. J. M. Lafir (Sri Lanka)
1971	Malta	N. Dagley (England)	M. Francisco (South Africa)
1973	Bombay	M. J. M. Lafir (Sri Lanka)	S. Mohan (India)
1975	Auckland	N. Dagley (England)	M. Ferreira (India)
1977	Melbourne	M. Ferreira (India)	R. Close (England)
1979	Colombo	P. Mifsud (Malta)	N. Dagley (England)
1981	Delhi	M. Ferreira (India)	N. Dagley (England)
1983	Malta	M. Ferreira (India)	S. Agrawal (India)
1985	Delhi	G. Sethi (India)	R. Marshall (Australia)

National Amateur Championships

The English Amateur Billiards Championship, instituted in 1888, and the English Amateur Snooker Championship, in 1916, are the two senior national amateur championships. Indeed, the latter is the oldest snooker championship, amateur or professional. 'The English' has enjoyed a slightly higher status than other national championships, partly through its seniority and partly because it accepts entries from players qualified to represent other countries, a legacy of the days when the event was known simply as 'The Amateur Championship'.

In the modern game, this has created confusion and possibly injustice as several Welshmen and a few Irishmen have figured prominently in the championships, eliminating players qualified to represent England in the process.

National associations ordinarily use their national championships to select their representatives for the World Amateur Championship, but the open nature of the English Championship has left the B & SCC, which represents the English game, without quite the clearcut method of selection enjoyed by other countries.

ENGLISH AMATEUR SNOOKER CHAMPIONSHIP

1916	C. N. Jacques
1917	C. N. Jacques
1918	T. N. Palmer
1919	S. H. Fry
1920	A. R. Wisdom
1921	M. J. Vaughan
1922	J. McGlynn
1923	W. Coupe
1924	W. Coupe
1925	J. McGlynn
1926	W. Nash
1927	O. T. Jackson
1928	P. H. Matthews
1929	L. Steeples
1930	L. Steeples
1931	P. H. Matthews
1932	W. E. Bach
1933	E. Bedford
1934	C. H. Beavis
1935	C. H. Beavis
1936	P. H. Matthews
1937	K. Kennerley
1938	P. H. Matthews
1939	P. Bendon
1940	K. Kennerley
1941-45	No contests
1946	H. J. Pulman
1947	H. Morris
1948	S. Battye
1949	T. C. Gordon
1950	A. Nolan
1951	R. Williams
1952	C. Downey
1953	T. C. Gordon
1954	G. Thompson
1955	M. Parkin
1956	T. C. Gordon
1957	R. Gross
1958	M. Owen
1959	M. Owen
1960	R. Gross
1961	A. Barnett
1962	R. Gross
1963	G. Owen
1964	R. Reardon
1965	P. Houlihan
1966	J. Spencer
1967	M. Owen
1968	D. Taylor
1969	R. Edmonds
1970	J. Barron
1971	J. Barron
1972	J. Barron
1973	M. Owen
1974	R. Edmonds
1975	S. Hood
1976	C. Ross
1977	T. Griffiths
1978	T. Griffiths
1979	J. White
1980	J. O'Boye
1981	V. Harris
1982	D. Chalmers
1983	T. Jones
1984	S. Longworth
1985	T. Whitthread
1986	A. Harris

ENGLISH AMATEUR BILLIARDS CHAMPIONSHIP

1888	H. A. O. Lonsdale A. P. Gaskell
1889	A. P. Gaskell A. P. Gaskell
1890	A. P. Gaskell A. P. Gaskell W. D. Courtney
1891	W. D. Courtney A. P. Gaskell
1892	A. R. Wisdom S. S. Christey
1893	A. R. Wisdom S.H. Fry A. H. Vahid
1894	H. Mitchell W. T. Maughan
1896	S. H. Fry
1899	A. R. Wisdom
1900	S. H. Fry
1901	S. S. Christey
1902	A. W. T. Good A. W. T. Good
1903	A. R. Wisdom S. S. Christey
1904	W. A. Lovejoy
1905	A. W. T. Good
1906	E. C. Breed
1907	H. C. Virr
1908	H. C. Virr
1909	Major Fleming
1910	H. A. O. Lonsdale
1911	H. C. Virr
1912	H. C. Virr
1913	H. C. Virr
1914	H. C. Virr
1915	A. W. T. Good
1916	S. H. Fry
1917	J. Graham-Symes
1918	J. Graham-Symes
1919	S. H. Fry
1920	S. H. Fry
1921	S. H. Fry
1922	J. Graham-Symes
1923	W. P. McLeod
1924	W. P. McLeod
1925	S. H. Fry
1926	J. Earlam
1927	L. Steeples
1928	A. Wardle
1929	H. F. E. Coles
1930	L. Steeples
1931	S. Lee

1932 S. Lee
1933 S. Lee
1934 S. Lee
1935 H. F. E. Coles
1936 J. Thompson
1937 K. Kennerley
1938 K. Kennerley
1939 K. Kennerley
1940 K. Kennerley
1941-45 No contests
1946 M. Showman
1947 J. Thompson
1948 J. Thompson
1949 F. Edwards
1950 F. Edwards
1951 F. Edwards
1952 A. L. Driffield
1953 A. L. Driffield
1954 A. L. Driffield
1955 F. Edwards
1956 F. Edwards
1957 A. L. Driffield
1958 A. L. Driffield
1959 A. L. Driffield
1960 J. H. Beetham
1961 J. H. Beetham
1962 A. L. Driffield
1963 J. H. Beetham
1964 A. Nolan
1965 N. Dagley
1966 N. Dagley
1967 A. L. Driffield
1968 M. Wildman
1969 J. Karnehm
1970 N. Dagley
1971 N. Dagley
1972 N. Dagley
1973 N. Dagley
1974 N. Dagley
1975 N. Dagley
1976 R. Close
1977 R. Close
1978 N. Dagley
1979 N. Dagley
1980 N. Dagley
1981 N. Dagley
1982 N. Dagley
1983 N. Dagley
1984 N. Dagley
1985 R. Close
1986 K. Shirley

NORTHERN IRELAND

SNOOKER

1927 G. Barron
1928 J. Perry
1929 W. Lyttle
1930 J. Luney
1931 J. McNally
1932 Capt. J. Ross
1933 J. French
1934 Capt. J. Ross
1935 W. Agnew
1936 W. Lowe
1937 J. Chambers
1938 J. McNally
1939 J. McNally
1941 J. McNally
1945 J. McNally
1946 J. McNally
1947 J. Rea
1948 J. Bates
1949 J. Bates
1950 J. Bates
1951 J. Stevenson
1952 J. Stevenson
1953 J. Stevenson
1954 W. Seeds
1955 J. Stevenson
1956 S. Brooks
1957 M. Gill
1958 W. Agnew
1959 W. Hanna
1960 M. Gill
1961 D. Anderson
1962 S. McMahon
1963 D. Anderson
1964 P. Morgan
1965 M. Gill
1966 S. Crothers
1967 D. Anderson
1968 A. Higgins
1969 D. Anderson
1970 J. Clint
1971 S. Crothers
1972 P. Donnelly
1973 J. Clint
1974 P. Donnelly
1975 J. Clint
1976 E. Swaffield
1977 D. McVeigh
1978 D. McVeigh
1979 R. Burke
1980 S. Clarke
1981 T. Murphy
1982 S. Pavis
1983 J. McLaughlin Jr
1984 J. McLaughlin Jr
1985 S. Pavis
1986 C. Sewell

BILLIARDS

1925 T. McCluney
1926 T. McCluney
1927 J. Sloan
1928 A. Davison
1929 J. Blackburn
1930 J. Blackburn
1931 J. Blackburn
1932 W. Lowe
1933 W. Mills
1934 W. Lowe
1935 W. Morrison
1936 J. Blackburn
1937 J. Blackburn
1938 W. Lowe
1939 W. Lowe
1940 No contest
1941 E. Haslem
1942-44 No contests
1945 E. Haslem
1946 J. Holness
1947 J. Bates
1948 J. Bates
1949 J. Bates
1950 J. Bates
1951 E. Haslem
1952 R. Taylor
1953 W. Scanlon
1954 W. Scanlon
1955 D. Turley
1956 J.Stevenson
1957 W. Scanlon
1958 W. Hanna
1959 W. Hanna
1960 W. Dennison
1961 R. Hanna
1962 N. McQuay
1963 W. Hanna
1964 D. Anderson / D. Turley } joint
1965 W. Ashe
1966 D. Anderson
1967 W. Loughan
1968 D. Anderson
1969 W. Loughan
1970 S. Crothers
1971 J. Bates
1972-73 No contests
1974 P. Donnelly
1975 P. Donnelly
1976 P. Donnelly
1977 T. Taylor
1978 W. Loughan
1979 J. Bates
1980 S. Clarke
1981 W. Loughan
1982 P. Donnelly
1985 S. Clarke
1986 D. Elliott

REPUBLIC OF IRELAND

SNOOKER

1931 J. Ayres
1933 S. Fenning
1935 S. Fenning
1937 P. J. O'Connor
1940 P. Merrigan
1942 P. J. O'Connor
1944 S. Fenning
1947 C. Downey
1948 P. Merrigan
1949 S. Fenning
1952 W. Brown
1953 S. Brooks
1954 S. Fenning
1955 S. Fenning
1956 W. Brown
1957 J. Connolly
1958 G. Gibson
1959-60 No contests
1961 W. Brown
1962 J. Weber
1963 J. Rogers
1964 J. Rogers
1965 W. Fields
1966 G. Hanway
1967 P. Morgan
1968 G. Hanway
1969 D. Dally
1970 D. Sheehan
1971 D. Sheehan
1972 J. Rogers
1973 F. Murphy
1974 P. Burke
1975 F. Nathan
1976 P. Burke
1977 J. Clusker
1978 E. Hughes
1979 E. Hughes
1980 D. Sheehan
1981 A. Kearney
1982 P. Browne
1983 J. Long
1984 P. Ennis
1985 G. Burns
1986 G. Burns

BILLIARDS

1931 J. Ayres
1933 J. Ayres
1934 S. Fenning
1935 S. Fenning
1936 S. Fenning
1937 T. O'Brien
1938-41 No contests
1942 S. Fenning
1943 No contest
1944 S. Fenning
1945-47 No contests
1948 W. Brown
1949 S. Fenning
1950-51 No contests
1952 M. Nolan
1953 D. Turley
1954 M. Nolan
1955 M. Nolan
1956 M. Nolan
1957 M. Nolan
1958 W. Dennison
1959-60 No contests
1961 K. Smyth
1962 K. Smyth
1963 J. Bates
1964 J. Bates
1965 L. Codd
1966 L. Codd
1967 P. Morgan
1968 P. Morgan
1969 J. Rogers
1970 L. Drennan
1971 L. Codd
1972 L. Codd
1973 T. Martin
1974 T. Doyle
1975 P. Fenelon
1976 J. Rogers
1977 E. Hughes
1978 E. Hughes
1979 L. Drennan
1980 P. Burke
1981 P. Burke
1982 D. Elliott
1984 A. Murphy
1985 A. Roache

SCOTLAND

SNOOKER

1931 G. Brown
1946 J. Levey
1947 J. Levey
1948 I. Wexelstein
1949 W. Ramage
1950 W. Ramage
1951 A. Wilson
1952 D. Emerson
1953 P. Spence
1954 D. Edmond
1955 L. U. Demarco
1956 W. Barrie
1957 T. Paul
1958 J. Phillips
1959 J. Phillips
1960 E. Sinclair
1961 J. Phillips
1962 A. Kennedy
1963 E. Sinclair
1964 J. Phillips
1965 L. U. Demarco
1966 L. U. Demarco
1967 E. Sinclair
1968 E. Sinclair
1969 A. Kennedy
1970 D. Sneddon
1971 J. Phillips
1972 D. Sneddon
1973 E. Sinclair
1974 D. Sneddon
1975 E. Sinclair
1976 E. Sinclair
1977 R. Miller
1978 J. Donnelly
1979 S. Nivison
1980 M. Gibson
1981 R. Lane
1982 P. Kippie
1982 G. Carnegie
1984 S. Hendry
1985 S. Hendry
1986 S. Muir

BILLIARDS

1913 Captain Croneen
1914-21 No contests
1922 H. L. Fleming
1923 M. Smith

1924 No contest
1925 W. D. Greenlees
1926 M. Smith
1927 M. Smith
1928 M. Smith
1929 J. McGhee
1930 M. Smith
1933 A. Ramage
1934 N. Canney
1935 H. King
1936 N. Canney
1937 J. McGhee
1938 J. McGhee
1939 No contest
1940 W. McCann
1941-45 No contests
1946 J. Levey
1947 A. Ramage
1948 W. Ramage
1949 W. Ramage
1950 A. Ramage
1951 W. Ramage
1952 J. Murray
1953 J. Bates
1954 J. Bates
1955 W. Ramage
1956 W. Ramage
1957 W. Ramage
1958 W. Ramage
1959 W. Ramage
1960 A. Ramage
1961 P. Spence
1962 W. Ramage
1963 W. Ramage
1964 W. Ramage
1965 W. Ramage
1966 W. Ramage
1967 W. Ramage
1968 A. Kennedy
1969 A. Kennedy
1970 D. Sneddon
1971 D. Sneddon
1972 L. U. Demarco
1973 D. Sneddon
1974 D. Sneddon
1975 D. Sneddon
1976 D. Sneddon
1977 J. Nugent
1978 D. Sneddon
1979 H. Nimmo
1980 D. Sneddon
1981 D. Sneddon
1982 W. Kelly
1983 H. Nimmo

WALES

SNOOKER

1930 T. Jones
1931 T. Jones
1932 T. Jones
1933 T. Jones
1934 T. Jones
1935 T. Jones
1936 T. Jones
1937 G. Howells
1938 B. Gravenor
1939 W. E. James
1947 T. Jones
1948 R. Smith
1949 A. J. Ford
1950 R. Reardon
1951 R. Reardon
1952 R. Reardon
1953 R. Reardon
1954 R. Reardon
1955 R. Reardon
1956 C. Wilson
1957 R. D. Meredith
1958 A. Kemp
1959 J. R. Price
1960 L. Luker
1961 T. Parsons
1962 A. J. Ford
1963 R. D. Meredith
1964 M. L. Berni
1965 T. Parsons
1966 L. L. O'Neill
1967 L. L. O'Neill
1968 D. Mountjoy
1969 T. Parsons
1970 D. T. May
1971 D. T. May
1972 G. Thomas
1973 A. Lloyd
1974 A. Lloyd
1975 T. Griffiths
1976 D. Mountjoy
1977 C. Wilson
1978 A. Lloyd
1979 C. Wilson
1980 S. Newbury
1981 C. Roscoe
1982 T. Parsons
1983 W. Jones
1984 T. Parsons
1985 M. Bennett
1986 K. Jones

BILLIARDS

1920 H. F. E. Coles
1921 H. F. E. Coles
1922 H. F. E. Coles
1923 H. F. E. Coles
1924 H. F. E. Coles
1925 Unknown
1926 Unknown
1927 Unknown
1928 G. Moore
1929 J. Tregoning
1930 Unknown
1931 L. Prosser
1932 T. Jones
1933 T. Jones
1934 Unknown
1935 I. Edwards
1936 J. Tregoning
1937 B. Gravenor
1938 J. Tregoning
1939 B. Gravenor
1940-46 No contests
1946 T. G. Rees
1947 T. C. Morse
1948 J. Tregoning
1949 I. Edwards
1950 W. Pierce
1951 W. Pierce
1952 J. Tregoning
1953 B. Sainsbury
1954 R. Smith
1955 J. Tregoning
1956 A. J. Ford
1957 R. Smith
1958 R. W. Oriel
1959 A. J. Ford
1960 C. Everton
1961 R. W. Oriel
1962 R. W. Oriel
1963 R. W. Oriel
1964 R. W. Oriel
1965 R. W. Oriel
1966 R. W. Oriel
1967 R. W. Oriel
1968 D. E. Edwards
1969 R. W. Oriel
1970 R. W. Oriel
1971 R. W. Oriel
1972 C. Everton
1973 C. Everton
1974 R. W. Oriel
1975 R. W. Oriel
1976 C. Everton
1977 C. Everton
1978 R. W. Oriel
1979 R. W. Oriel
No further contests

AUSTRALIA

SNOOKER

1953 W. Simpson
1954 W. Simpson
1955 E. Pickett
1956 R. Marshall
1957 W. Simpson
1958 F. Harris
1959 K. Burles
1960 K. Burles
1961 M. Williams
1962 W. Barrie
1963 F. Harris
1964 W. Barrie
1965 W. Barrie
1966 M. Williams
1967 M. Williams
1968 M. Williams
1969 W. Barrie
1970 M. Williams
1971 M. Williams
1972 M. Williams
1973 M. Williams
1974 L. Condo
1975 R. Atkins
1976 R. Atkins
1977 R. Atkins
1978 K. Burles
1979 J. Campbell
1980 W. King
1981 W. King
1982 J. Giannaros
1983 G. Lackenby
1984 G. Wilkinson
1985 J. Bonner

BILLIARDS

1913 G. B. Shailer
1914-19 No contests
1920 J. R. Hooper
1921 G. B. Shailer
1922 G. B. Shailer
1923 G. B. Shailer
1924 E. Eccles
1925 G. B. Shailer
1926 L. W. Hayes
1927 L. W. Hayes
1928 L. W. Hayes
1929 A. H. Hearndon
1930 S. Ryan
1931 H. L. Goldsmith
1932 A. Sakzewski
1933 L. W. Hayes
1934 L. W. Hayes
1935 L. W. Hayes
1936 R. Marshall
1937 R. Marshall
1938 R. Marshall
1939 R. Marshall
1940-45 No contests
1946 R. Marshall
1947 T. Cleary
1948 R. Marshall
1949 R. Marshall
1950 T. Cleary
1951 R. Marshall
1952 R. Marshall
1953 R. Marshall
1954 R. Marshall
1955 R. Marshall
1956 J. Long
1957 R. Marshall
1958 T. Cleary
1959 R. Marshall
1960 J. Long
1961 R. Marshall
1962 R. Marshall
1963 R. Marshall
1964 J. Long
1965 T. Cleary
1966 T. Cleary
1967 J. Long
1968 J. Long
1969 R. Marshall
1970 R. Marshall
1971 M. Williams
1972 P. Tarrant
1973 P. Tarrant
1974 J. Reece
1975 J. Long
1976 G. Ganim Jr
1977 G. Ganim Jr
1978 G. Ganim Jr
1979 G. Ganim Jr
1980 G. Ganim Jr
1981 G. Ganim Jr
1982 R. Foldvari
1983 R. Foldvari
1984 F. Humphreys
1985 R. Marshall

CANADA

SNOOKER

1979 J. Wych
1980 Jim Bear
1981 R. Chaperon
1983 A. Robidoux
1984 T. Finstad
1985 A. Robidoux

BILLIARDS

1979 E. Fisher
1980 S. Holden
1981 R. Chaperon
1982 R. Chaperon

INDIA

SNOOKER

1939 P. K. Deb
1940 P. K. Deb
1941 V. R. Freer
1942 P. K. Deb
1943-45 No contests
1946 T. A. Selvaraj
1947 T. Sadler
1948 W. Jones
1949 T. A. Selvaraj
1950 F. Edwards (Eng)
1951 T. A. Selvaraj
1952 W. Jones
1953 A. L. Driffield (Eng)
1954 W. Jones
1955 T. A. Selvaraj
1956 M. J. M. Lafir
1957 M. J. M. Lafir
1958 W. Jones
1959 M. J. M. Lafir
1960 W. Jones
1961 M. J. M. Lafir
1962 R. Marshall (Aust)
1963 M. J. M. Lafir
1964 S. Shroff
1965 S. Shroff
1966 T. Monteiro
1967 S. Shroff
1968 S. Mohan
1969 S. Shroff
1970 S. Shroff
1971 T. Monteiro
1972 S. Shroff

1973 S. Shroff
1974 M. J. M. Lafir
1975 M. J. M. Lafir
1976 A. Savur
1977 M. J. M. Lafir
1978 A. Savur
1979 A. Savur
1980 J. White (Eng)
1981 G. Parikh
1984 G. Sethi
1985 G. Sethi

BILLIARDS

1931 M. M. Begg
1932 P. K. Deb
1933 Major Meade
1934 Mg Ba Sin
1935 P. K. Deb
1936 P. K. Deb
1937 M. M. Begg
1938 P. K. Deb
1939 P. K. Deb
1940 S. H. Lyth
1941 V. R. Freer
1942 V. R. Freer
1943-45 No contests
1946 C. Hirjee
1947 C. Hirjee
1948 V. R. Freer
1949 T. A. Selvaraj
1950 W. Jones
1951 W. Jones
1952 W. Jones
1953 L. Driffield (Eng)
1954 W. Jones
1955 W. Jones
1956 C. Hirjee
1957 W. Jones
1958 C. Hirjee
1959 T. Cleary (Aust)
1960 W. Jones
1961 W. Jones
1962 R. Marshall (Aust)
1963 W. Jones
1964 W. Jones
1965 W. Jones
1966 W. Jones
1967 A. Savur
1968 S. Mohan
1969 M. Ferreira
1970 S. Mohan
1971 S. Mohan
1972 S. Mohan
1973 S. Mohan
1974 M. Ferreira
1975 G. C. Parikh
1976 M. Ferreira
1977 M. J. M. Lafir
1978 M. Ferreira
1979 M. Ferreira
1980 M. Ferreira
1981 G. Sethi
1982 M. Ferreira
1983 F. Agrawal
1984 G. Sethi
1985 M. Ferreira

MALTA

SNOOKER

1947 L. Galea
1948 T. B. Oliver
1949 L. Galea
1950 W. Asciak
1951 W. Asciak
1952 A. Borg
1953 A. Borg
1954 W. Asciak
1955 A. Borg
1956 W. Asciak
1957 W. Asciak
1958 W. Asciak
1959 A. Borg
1960 A. Borg
1961 A. Borg
1962 A. Borg
1963 M. Tonna
1964 A. Borg
1965 A. Borg
1966 A. Borg
1967 A. Borg
1968 P. Mifsud
1969 P. Mifsud
1970 P. Mifsud
1971 P. Mifsud
1972 P. Mifsud
1973 A. Borg
1974 A. Borg
1975 P. Mifsud
1976 P. Mifsud
1977 A. Borg
1978 P. Mifsud
1979 P. Mifsud
1980 J. Grech
1981 J. Grech
1982 P. Mifsud
1983 P. Mifsud
1984 T. Drago
1985 P. Mifsud

BILLIARDS

1947 V. Micallef
1948 No contest
1949 E. Bartolo
1950 W. Asciak
1951 W. Asciak
1952 W. Asciak
1953 W. Asciak
1954 W. Asciak
1955 W. Asciak
1956 A. Asciak
1957 A. Asciak
1958 A. Asciak
1959 A. Asciak
1960 A. Asciak
1961 A. Borg
1962 J. Bartolo
1963 J. Bartolo
1964 W. Asciak
1965 A. Asciak
1966 A. Asciak
1967 A. Asciak
1969 P. Mifsud
1970 W. Asciak
1971 P. Mifsud
1972 W. Asciak
1973 P. Mifsud
1974 P. Mifsud
1975 P. Mifsud
1976 P. Mifsud
1977 P. Mifsud
1978 J. Grech
1979 P. Mifsud
1980 J. Grech
1981 No contest
1982 V. Ellul
1983 J. Grech

NEW ZEALAND

SNOOKER

1945 S. Moses
1946 J. Munro
1947 W. Thompson
1948 L. Stout
1949 L. Stout
1950 L. Stout
1951 N. Lewis
1952 L. Stout
1953 L. Stout
1954 R. Franks
1955 L. Stout
1956 L. Stout
1957 W. Harcourt
1958 W. Harcourt
1959 W. Thomas
1960 T. Yesberg
1961 F. Franks
1962 K. Murphy
1963 W. Harcourt
1964 T. Yesberg
1965 L. Napper
1966 L. Napper
1967 R. Flutey
1968 L. Napper
1969 L. Glozier
1970 K. Tristram
1971 B. J. Bennett
1972 N. Stockman
1973 W. Hill
1974 K. Tristram
1975 K. Tristram
1976 D. Kwok
1977 D. Meredith
1978 D. Meredith
1979 D. Meredith
1980 D. O'Kane
1981 G. Kwok
1982 D. Kwok
1983 D. Kwok
1984 G. Kwok
1985 P. De Groot

BILLIARDS

1908 J. Ryan
1909 No contest
1910 F. Lovelock
1911 F. Lovelock
1912 H. Valentine
1913 H. Valentine
1914 N. Lynch
1915 W. E. Warren
1916 H. Siedeberg
1917 H. Siedeberg
1918 W. E. Warren
1919 H. Siedeberg
1920 W. E. Warren
1921 H. Siedeberg
1922 E. V. Roberts
1923 E. V. Roberts
1924 R. Fredotovich
1925 C. Mason
1926 E. V. Roberts
1927 E. V. Roberts
1928 A. Bowie
1929 L. Stout
1930 W. E. Hackett
1931 A. Duncan
1932 C. Mason
1933 A. Albertson
1934 H. McLean
1935 L. Holdsworth
1936 S. Moses
1937 S. Moses
1938 L. Holdsworth
1939 R. Carrick
1940 S. Moses
1941 R. Carrick
1942 R. Carrick
1943 A. Albertson
1944 S. Moses
1945 J. Shepherd
1946 R. Carrick
1947 C. Peek
1948 R. Carrick
1949 R. Carrick
1950 R. Carrick
1951 R. Carrick
1952 L. Stout
1953 A. Twohill
1954 A. Twohill
1955 A. Twohill
1956 A. Twohill
1957 A. Twohill
1958 A. Albertson
1959 A. Twohill
1960 W. Harcourt
1961 A. Albertson
1962 W. Harcourt
1963 H. C. Robinson
1964 T. Yesberg
1965 L. Napper
1966 A. Twohill
1967 A. Twohill
1968 A. Twohill
1969 E. Simmons
1970 L. Napper
1971 W. Harcourt
1972 B. Kirkness
1973 H. C. Robinson
1974 H. C. Robinson
1975 T. Yesberg
1976 H. C. Robinson
1977 B. Kirkness
1978 B. Kirkness
1979 R. Adams
1980 D. Meredith
1981 D. Meredith
1982 D. Meredith
1983 D. Meredith
1984 D. Meredith
1985 D. Meredith

SOUTH AFRICA

SNOOKER

1937 A. Prior
1938 A. H. Ashby
1939 A. Prior
1940-45 No contests
1946 F. Walker
1947 No contest
1948 F. Walker
1949 E. Kerr
1950 T. G. Rees
1951 T. G. Rees
1952 T. G. Rees
1953 J. van Rensburg
1954 J. van Rensburg
1955 J. van Rensburg
1956 F. Walker
1957 J. van Rensburg
1958 R. Walker
1959 M. Francisco
1960 P. Mans Jr
1961 J. van Rensburg
1962 J. van Rensburg
1963 J. van Rensburg
1964 M. Francisco
1965 M. Francisco
1966 M. Francisco
1967 J. van Rensburg
1968 S. Francisco
1969 S. Francisco
1970 J. van Rensburg
1971 M. Francisco
1972 J. van Rensberg
1973 J. van Rensburg
1974 S. Francisco
1975 M. Francisco
1976 No contest
1977 S. Francisco
1978 J. van Nickerk
1979 F. Ellis
1980 F. Ellis
1981 P. Francisco
1982 P. Francisco
1983 P. Francisco

BILLIARDS

1920 Sgt. Bruyns

1921 A. Prior
1922 A. Prior
1923 No contest
1924 A. Prior
1925 P. Rutledge
1926 A. Prior
1927 A. Percival
1928 P. Rutledge
1929-30 No contests
1931 A. Prior
1932-36 No contests
1937 A. M. Burke
1938 A. Prior
1939 A. Prior
1940-45 No contests
1946 P. G. Kempen
1947 No contest
1948 P. G. Kempen
1949 T. G. Rees
1950 T. G. Rees
1951 I. Drapin
1952 T. G. Rees
1953 T. G. Rees
1954 F. Walker
1955 F. Walker
1956 G. Povall
1957 F. Walker
1958 F. Walker
1959 M. Francisco
1960 R. Walker
1961 M. Francisco
1962 M. Francisco
1963 M. Francisco
1964 M. Francisco
1965 M. Francisco
1966 M. Francisco
1967 J. van Rensburg
1968 M. Francisco
1969 M. Francisco
1970 M. Francisco
1971 M. Francisco
1972 S. Francisco
1973 S. Francisco
1974 M. Francisco
1975 S. Francisco
1976 No contest
1977 M. Francisco
1978 C. van Dijk
1979 C. van Dijk
1980 C. van Dijk
1981 P. Spence
1983 P. Francisco

SRI LANKA
SNOOKER

1948 M. J. M. Lafir
1949 M. M. Faiz
1950 M. J. M. Lafir
1951 M. S. A. Hassan
1952 M. J. M. Lafir
1953 M. J. M. Lafir
1954 M. J. M. Lafir
1955 M. J. M. Lafir
1956 M. J. M. Lafir
1957 M. J. M. Lafir
1958 M. J. M. Lafir
1959 M. J. M. Lafir
1960 M. J. M. Lafir
1961 M. J. M. Lafir
1962 M. J. M. Lafir
1963 M. J. M. Izzath
1964 M. J. M. Lafir
1965 M. J. M. Lafir
1966 M. J. M. Lafir
1967 N. J. Rahim
1968 No contest
1969 M. J. M. Lafir
1970 N. J. Rahim
1971 No contest
1972 N. J. Rahim
1973 M. J. M. Lafir
1974 Abandoned
1975 N. A. Rahim
1976 M. S. U. Mohideen
1977 M. S. U. Mohideen
1978 N. A. Rahim
1981 H. Boteju
1982 J. A. Wahid
1983 H. Boteju
1984 K. Sirisoma
1985 H. Boteju

BILLIARDS

1948 A. C. Cambal
1949 M. J. M. Lafir
1950 M. J. M. Lafir
1951 M. J. M. Lafir
1952 M. J. M. Lafir
1953 M. J. M. Lafir
1954 A. C. Cambal
1955 T. A. Selvaraj
1956 T. A. Selvaraj
1957 M. J. M. Lafir
1959 M. J. M. Lafir
1960 M. J. M. Lafir
1961 M. J. M. Lafir
1962 M. J. M. Lafir
1963 M. H. M. Mujahid
1964 M. J. M. Lafir
1966 M. J. M. Lafir
1967 J. K. Bakshani
1969 M. J. M. Lafir
1970 M. J. M. Lafir
1972 M. J. M. Lafir
1973 M. J. M. Lafir
1974 S. Shaharwardi
1975 M. S. U. Mohideen
1976 W. Weerasinghe
1977 W. Weerasinghe
1978 J. W. H. Boteju
1979 W. Weerasinghe
1981 J. W. H. Boteju
1982 H. Boteju
1983 W. Weerasinghe
1984 H. Boteju
1985 K. Sirisoma

ZIMBABWE
SNOOKER

1981 A. Thomson
1982 A. Thomson
1983 J. Daly
1984 J. Daly
1985 A. Thomson

BRITISH JUNIOR CHAMPIONSHIPS
SNOOKER (under 16)

1944 G. Owen
1945 R. Baker
1946 D. Thomas
1947 M. Knapp
1948 R. Williams
1949 R. Williams
D. Lewis
1950 M. Owen
1951 M. Owen
1952 M. Wildman
1953 J. Board
1954 D. Bond
1955 P. Shelley
1956 A. Hart
1957 P. Shelley
1958 D. Bend
1959 J. Doyle
1960 N. Cripps
1961 No contest
1962 J. Virgo
1963 J. Hollis
1964 D. Clinton
1965 No contest
1966 J. Terry
1967 No contest
1968 E. Stone
1969 P. Hughes
1970 W. Thorne
1971 J. Mills
1972 J. Mills
1973 P. Bardsley
1974 S. Holroyd
1975 M. Hallett
1976 W. Jones
1977 J. White
1978 D. Adds
1979 A. Pyle
1980 T. Whitthread
1981 C. Hamson
1982 S. Ventham
1983 S. Hendry
1984 B. Morgan
1985 B. Bunn
1986 D. Grimwood

SNOOKER (under 19)

1949 A. Kemp
1950 J. Carney
1951 R. Williams
1952 C. Wilson
1953 C. Wilson
1954 M. Wildman
1955 W. McGivern
1956 E. Sinclair
1957 H. Burns
1958 W. West
1959 D. Root
1960 D. Bend
1961 I. Rees
1962 A. Matthews
1963 A. Matthews
1964 J. Fisher
1965 J. Virgo
1966 J. Hollis
1967 No contest
1968 J. Maughan
1969 J. Terry
1970 J. Terry
1971 J. Johnson
1972 A. Knowles
1973 W. Thorne
1974 A. Knowles
1975 E. Hughes
1976 I. Williamson
1977 I. Williamson
1978 T. Meo
1979 J. O'Boye
1980 T. Murphy
1981 D. Reynolds
1982 N. Foulds
1983 M. Thompson
1984 M. Clark
1985 W. Rendle
1986 B. Pinches

BILLIARDS (under 16)

1922 W. Donaldson
1923 W. Leigh
1924 L. Steeples
1925 S. Lee
1926 R. Gartland
1927 R. Gartland
1928 R. L. Bennett
1929 F. Davis
1930 H. J. Bennett
1931 C. Desbottes
1932 D. Hawkes
1933 Unknown
1934 W. Swinhoe
1935 D. Cruikshank
1936 D. Cruikshank
1937 D. Curson
1938 J. Hamilton
1939 R. Smith
1940 B. Smith
1941-47 No contests
1948 R. Williams
1949 R. Williams
1950 M. Owen
1951 E. Parry
1952 M. Wildman
1953 C. Everton
1954 H. Burns
1955 D. Deakes
1956 C. Dean
1957 P. Shelley
1958 P. Morgan
1959 P. Morgan
1960 A. Matthews
1961 B. Whitehead
1962-67 No contests
1968 C. Williamson
1969 P. Bardsley
1970 W. Thorne
1971 P. Bardsley
1972 P. Bardsley
1973 T. Wells
1974 P. Allan
1975 S. McNamara
1976 D. Bonney
1977 D. Bonney
1978 K. Walsh
1979 A. Pyle
1980 K. Walsh
1981 D. Presgrave
1982 S. Naisby
1983 P. Gilchrist
1984 C. Rowntree
1985 M. Russell
1986 L. Connor

BILLIARDS (under 19)

1949 G. Toner
1950 R. Williams
1951 R. Williams
1952 J. Sinclair
1953 M. Wildman
1954 M. Wildman
1955 D. Scott
1956 C. Everton
1957 C. Myers
1958 C. Marks
1959 P. Morgan
1960 D. Bend
1961 P. Morgan
1962 A. Matthews
1963 A. Matthews
1964-67 No contests
1968 D. Taylor
1969 D. Burgess
1970 J. Terry
1971 W. Thorne
1972 W. Thorne
1973 W. Thorne
1974 T. Wells
1975 E. Hughes
1976 S. Davis
1977 I. Williamson
1978 I. Williamson
1979 M. Garvey
1980 G. Charville
1981 S. Hawkins
1982 R. Marshall
1983 S. Naisby
1984 S. Naisby
1985 S. Naisby
1986 M. Russell

Amateur Home International Championship

The first official amateur home international, a challenge match between Wales and England, was staged at the Afan Lido, Port Talbot, in 1969. In 1970, the Republic of Ireland joined to make a triangular series and Scotland made it quandrangular in 1971.

Matches were played either home or away until 1978 when Pontins offered to sponsor the event at its annual Autumn Festival of Snooker at Prestatyn. The Isle of Man joined the competition that year and Northern Ireland competed for the first time in 1979.

Only England (seven wins) and Wales (seven – including the last six) have won the series, within which each match consists of six three-frame contests.

Home International Snooker Championships

1969

England beat Wales *Port Talbot* 10-8

1970-1

England beat Wales *Harringay* 14-4
England beat Rep. of Ireland *Dublin* 14-4
Wales beat Rep. of Ireland *Port Talbot* 17-1

	W	D	L	For	Agst	Pts
England	2	0	0	28	8	4
Wales	1	0	1	21	15	2
Rep. of Ireland	0	0	2	5	31	0

Friendly:
Wales beat Scotland *Neath* 10-8

1971-2

England beat Scotland *Newcastle* 10-8
England beat Rep. of Ireland *Harringay* 14-4
England drew with Wales *Neath* 9-9
Scotland drew with Wales *Edinburgh* 9-9
Scotland beat Rep. of Ireland *Dublin* 12-6
Wales beat Rep. of Ireland *Dublin* 13-5

	W	D	L	For	Agst	Pts
England	2	1	0	33	21	5
Wales	1	2	0	31	23	4
Scotland	1	1	1	29	25	3
Rep. of Ireland	0	0	3	15	39	0

1972-3

England beat Scotland *Edinburgh* 16-2
England beat Rep. of Ireland *Dublin* 13-5
England drew with Wales *Hull* 9-9
Wales beat Rep. of Ireland *Pontygwaith* 15-3
Wales beat Scotland *Llay* 10-8
Scotland beat Rep. of Ireland *Dublin* 13-5

	W	D	L	For	Agst	Pts
England	2	1	0	38	16	5
Wales	2	1	0	32	22	5
Scotland	1	0	2	23	31	2
Rep. of Ireland	0	0	3	15	41	0

1973-4

England beat Wales *Garnant* 14-4
England beat Scotland *Carlisle* 11-7
England drew with Rep. of Ireland *Bolton* 9-9
Wales beat Rep. of Ireland *Dublin* 11-7
Wales beat Scotland *Dublin* 9-9

	W	D	L	For	Agst	Pts
England	2	1	0	34	20	5
Wales	2	0	1	29	25	4
Rep. of Ireland	0	2	1	25	29	2
Scotland	0	1	2	20	34	1

1974-5

Wales beat Rep. of Ireland *Neath* 12-6
Wales beat Scotland *Maerdy* 14-4
Wales beat England *Exeter* 10-8
England beat Scotland *Edinburgh* 12-6
England beat Rep. of Ireland *Glasnevin* 11-7
Scotland beat Rep. of Ireland *Dundee* 12-6

	W	D	L	For	Agst	Pts
Wales	3	0	0	36	18	6
England	2	0	1	31	23	4
Scotland	1	0	2	22	32	2
Rep. of Ireland	0	0	3	19	35	0

1975-6

Wales beat Rep. of Ireland *Dublin* 13-5
Wales beat Scotland *Edinburgh* 11-7
Wales beat England *Merthyr* 11-7
England beat Rep. of Ireland *Grimsby* 13-5
England beat Scotland *Southport* 12-6
Scotland beat Rep. of Ireland *Dunloaghaire* 12-6

	W	D	L	For	Agst	Pts
Wales	3	0	0	35	19	6
England	2	0	1	32	22	4
Scotland	1	0	2	25	29	2
Rep. of Ireland	0	0	3	16	38	0

1976-7

England beat Rep. of Ireland *Dublin* 13-5
England beat Wales *Doncaster* 12-6
England beat Scotland *Glasgow* 11-7
Wales beat Scotland *Trealaw* 14-4
Wales beat Rep. of Ireland *Cardiff* 13-5
Scotland beat Rep. of Ireland *Edinburgh* 12-6

	W	D	L	For	Agst	Pts
England	3	0	0	36	18	6
Wales	2	0	1	33	21	4
Scotland	1	0	2	23	31	2
Rep. of Ireland	0	0	3	16	38	0

1977-8

Wales beat England *Caerphilly* 10-8
Wales beat Scotland *Dublin* 12-6
Wales beat Rep. of Ireland *Dublin* 15-3
England beat Scotland *Doncaster* 10-8
England beat Rep. of Ireland *Portsmouth* 11-7
Scotland beat Rep. of Ireland *Dublin* 12-6

	W	D	L	For	Agst	Pts
Wales	3	0	0	37	17	6
England	2	0	1	29	25	4
Scotland	1	0	2	26	28	2
Rep. of Ireland	0	0	3	16	38	0

1978

England beat Isle of Man *Prestatyn* 15-3
England beat Rep. of Ireland 14-4
England beat Scotland 16-2
England beat Wales 10-7
Wales beat Isle of Man 16-2
Wales beat Rep. of Ireland 11-7
Wales drew with Scotland 9-9
Scotland beat Isle of Man 15-3
Scotland drew with Rep. of Ireland 9-9
Rep. of Ireland beat Isle of Man 15-3

	W	D	L	For	Agst	Pts
England	4	0	0	55	16	8
Wales	2	1	1	43	28	5
Scotland	1	2	1	35	37	4
Rep. of Ireland	1	1	2	34	38	3
Isle of Man	0	0	4	12	60	0

1979

England beat Northern Ireland *Prestatyn* 16-2
England beat Isle of Man 16-2
England beat Rep. of Ireland 11-7
England beat Scotland 10-8
England beat Wales 10-7
Wales beat Northern Ireland 12-6
Wales beat Isle of Man 16-2
Wales beat Scotland 11-7
Wales drew with Rep. of Ireland 9-9
Rep. of Ireland beat Scotland 10-8
Rep. of Ireland drew with Northern Ireland 9-9
Rep. of Ireland drew with Wales 9-9
Rep. of Ireland beat Isle of Man 12-6
Scotland beat Isle of Man 13-5
Scotland beat Northern Ireland 10-8
Northern Ireland drew with Rep. of Ireland 9-9
Northern Ireland beat Isle of Man 14-4

	W	D	L	For	Agst	Pts
England	5	0	0	63	26	10
Wales	3	1	1	55	34	7
Rep. of Ireland	2	2	1	47	43	6
Scotland	2	0	3	46	44	4
Northern Ireland	1	1	3	39	51	3
Isle of Man	0	0	5	19	71	0

1980

England beat Northern Ireland *Prestatyn* 15-3
Scotland beat Isle of Man 14-4
Wales beat Northern Ireland 10-8
England beat Isle of Man 15-3
Wales beat Scotland 12-6
Rep. of Ireland beat Northern Ireland 11-7
Northern Ireland beat Isle of Man 12-6
Wales beat Rep. of Ireland 14-4
Rep. of Ireland drew with Scotland 9-9
Wales beat Isle of Man 15-3
England beat Rep. of Ireland 12-6
Scotland drew with Northern Ireland 9-9
England beat Scotland 14-4
Wales beat England 10-7

	W	D	L	For	Agst	Pts
Wales	5	0	0	61	28	10
England	4	0	1	63	26	8
Rep. of Ireland	2	1	2	43	47	5
Scotland	1	2	2	42	48	4
Northern Ireland	1	1	3	39	51	3
Isle of Man	0	0	5	21	69	0

1981

Northern Ireland drew with
Rep. of Ireland *Prestatyn* 9-9
Scotland beat Isle of Man 13-5
England beat Isle of Man 17-1
Wales beat Northern Ireland 11-7
England beat Rep. of Ireland 11-7
Wales beat Scotland 13-5
Wales beat Rep. of Ireland 12-6
England beat Northern Ireland 10-8
Rep. of Ireland drew with Isle of Man 9-9
Scotland beat Northern Ireland 19-8
Wales beat Isle of Man 15-3
Rep. of Ireland beat Scotland 10-8
Scotland beat England 10-8
Northern Ireland beat Isle of Man 10-8
England led Wales 9-7 (match abandoned)

	W	D	L	A	For	Agst
Wales	4	–	–	1	58	29
England	3	–	1	1	54	33
Scotland	3	–	2	–	46	44
Rep. of Ireland	1	2	2	–	41	49
Northern Ireland	1	1	3	–	42	48
Isle of Man	–	1	4	–	26	64

The Wales v England match was abandoned at the point when Wales was assured of retaining the championship

1982

Wales beat Isle of Man *Prestatyn* 16-2
England drew with Scotland 9-9
Rep. of Ireland drew with Northern Ireland 9-9
Isle of Man drew with Scotland 9-9
England beat Isle of Man 12-6
Wales beat Northern Ireland 10-8
Wales beat Scotland 12-6
England beat Rep. of Ireland 11-7
Rep. of Ireland beat Isle of Man 15-3
Northern Ireland beat Scotland 12-6
England beat Northern Ireland 14-4
Wales beat Rep. of Ireland 11-7
Scotland beat Rep. of Ireland 11-7
Northern Ireland beat Isle of Man 15-3
Wales led England 9-8 (match abandoned)

	W	D	L	For	Agst	Pts
Wales*	4	0	0	49	23	8
England*	3	1	0	46	26	7
Northern Ireland	2	1	2	53	37	5
Scotland	1	2	2	41	49	4
Rep. of Ireland	1	1	3	44	46	3
Isle of Man	0	1	4	26	66	1

*** Not including Wales v England match which was curtailed when Wales led 9-8 at which point they could not be overtaken.**

1983

Wales beat Scotland *Prestatyn* 13-5
England beat Rep. of Ireland 13-5
Wales beat Northern Ireland 13-5
Scotland beat Isle of Man 11-7
Isle of Man beat Rep. of Ireland 11-7
Scotland drew with Northern Ireland 9-9
Rep. of Ireland beat Northern Ireland 10-8
England beat Isle of Man 14-4
England beat Northern Ireland 13-5
Wales beat Isle of Man 10-8
Wales beat Rep. of Ireland 14-4
England beat Scotland 11-7
Northern Ireland beat Isle of Man 13-5
Scotland beat Rep. of Ireland 10-8
Wales beat England 10-7

	W	D	L	For	Agst	Pts
Wales	5	0	0	60	29	10
England	4	0	1	58	31	8
Scotland	2	1	2	42	48	5
Northern Ireland	1	1	3	40	50	3
Isle of Man	1	0	4	35	55	2
Rep. of Ireland	1	0	4	34	56	2

1984

Rep. of Ireland drew with Scotland 9-9
England beat Northern Ireland 13-5
Wales beat Isle of Man 15-3
England drew with Scotland 9-9
Northern Ireland beat Rep. of Ireland 12-6
Scotland drew with Wales 9-9
Northern Ireland beat Isle of Man 11-7
England beat Isle of Man 12-6
England beat Rep. of Ireland 11-7
Scotland beat Isle of Man 15-3
Wales beat Northern Ireland 11-7
Wales beat England 10-8
Rep. of Ireland beat Isle of Man 12-6
Scotland beat Northern Ireland 10-8
Wales beat Rep. of Ireland 14-4

	W	D	L	For	Agst	Pts
Wales	4	1	0	59	31	9
England	3	1	1	53	37	7
Scotland	2	3	0	52	38	7
Northern Ireland	2	0	3	37	67	4
Rep. of Ireland	1	1	3	38	52	3
Isle of Man	0	0	5	25	53	0

1985

Wales beat Rep. of Ireland 11-7
Wales beat Northern Ireland 13-5
Wales beat Isle of Man 15-3
Wales beat Scotland 11-7
Wales beat England 8-7
England beat Isle of Man 16-2
England beat Rep. of Ireland 10-8
England beat Northern Ireland 14-4
Northern Ireland beat Isle of Man 14-5
Northern Ireland beat Scotland 10-8
Northern Ireland beat Rep. of Ireland 11-7
Rep. of Ireland beat Isle of Man 12-6
Rep. of Ireland beat Scotland 12-6
Scotland beat Isle of Man 12-6
Scotland beat England 12-6

	W	D	L	For	Agst	Pts
Wales	5	0	0	58	29	10
England	3	0	2	53	34	6
Northern Ireland	3	0	2	43	47	6
Rep. of Ireland	2	0	3	46	44	4
Scotland	2	0	3	45	45	4
Isle of Man	0	0	5	22	68	0

Individual performances in the home internationals

ENGLAND

R. Andrewartha

1974–5
v Rep. of Ireland *Glasnevin* beat P. Miley 2-1
v Wales *Exeter* lost to M. Berni 1-2
v Scotland *Edinburgh* beat I. Wallace 3-0
1975–6
v Scotland *Southport* beat S. Nivison 3-0
v Wales *Merthyr* lost to T. Parsons 0-3

C. Archer

1984
v Northern Ireland *Prestatyn* beat S. Pavis 2-1
v Scotland beat D. Sneddon 2-1
v Isle of Man lost to P. Partington 1-2
v Wales beat G. Thomas 2-1

J. Barron

1969
v Wales *Port Talbot* beat D. Mountjoy 3-0
1970–1
v Wales *Harringay* beat D. May 2-1
v Rep. of Ireland *Dublin* beat J. Weber 2-1
1971–2
v Scotland *Newcastle* beat J. Phillips 2-1
v Rep. of Ireland *Harringay* beat D. Sheehan 3-0
v Wales *Neath* beat D. May 2-1
1972–3
v Scotland *Edinburgh* beat D. Sneddon 3-0
v Wales *Hull* lost to G. Thomas 1-2

M. Bradley

1982
v Isle of Man *Prestatyn* beat P. Reynolds 2-1
v Scotland beat J. Allan 3-0
v Rep. of Ireland beat M. Ralph 3-0
v Wales lost to W. Jones 1-2
1983
v Rep. of Ireland *Prestatyn* beat M. Kane 2-1
v Northern Ireland beat A. Sharpe 3-0
v Scotland lost to G. Carnegie 1-2
v Wales lost to W. Jones 1-2

D. Chalmers

1982
v Isle of Man *Prestatyn* lost to C. Cooper 1-2
v Scotland lost to K. Baird 0-3
1983
v Rep. of Ireland *Prestatyn* lost to M. Ralph 1-2
v Scotland lost to K. Baird 1-2

J. Chambers

1985
v Scotland lost to B. Kelly 0-3
v Rep. of Ireland lost to R. Nolan 1-2

G. Cripsey

1981
v Isle of Man *Prestatyn* beat P. Reynolds 3-0
v Northern Ireland beat P. Donnelly 2-1
v Scotland lost to R. Lane 0-3

M. Darrington

1980
v Northern Ireland *Prestatyn* beat T. Murphy 2-1
v Isle of Man beat K. Kinrade 3-0
v Rep. of Ireland beat P. Watchorn 2-1
1981
v Isle of Man *Prestatyn* beat J. Kinrade 3-0
v Rep. of Ireland beat G. Sutton 3-0
v Northern Ireland beat D. McVeigh 3-0
v Scotland beat J. Zonfrillo 3-0
v Wales lost to A. Lloyd 1-2

S. Davis

1977–8
v Scotland *Doncaster* beat D. Sneddon 3-0
v Wales *Caerphilly* beat T. Parsons 2-1

L. Dodd

1981
v Rep. of Ireland *Prestatyn* beat M. Kane 2-1
v Northern Ireland lost to E. Swaffield 1-2
v Scotland lost to J. Rankeillor 0-3

S. Duggan

1982
v Isle of Man *Prestatyn* beat R. Crowley 2-1
v Scotland lost to R. Land 0-3
v Northern Ireland beat A. Sharpe 2-1
v Wales lost to T. Parsons 1-2

R. Edmonds

1969
v Wales *Port Talbot* beat T. Parsons 3-0
1970–1
v Wales *Harringay* beat D. Mountjoy 2-1
v Rep. of Ireland *Dublin* beat F. Murphy 2-1
1971–2
v Scotland *Newcastle* lost to D. Sneddon 1-2
v Rep. of Ireland *Harringay* beat J. Weber 3-0
v Wales *Neath* lost to M. Berni 1-2
1972–3
v Scotland *Edinburgh* beat B. Demarco 3-0

v Wales *Hull* lost to D. May 1-2
1973–4
v Wales *Garnant* beat A. Lloyd 3-0
v Rep. of Ireland *Bolton* lost to D. Sheehan 1-2
1974–5
v Rep. of Ireland *Glasnevin* lost to P. Burke 1-2
v Wales *Exeter* beat A. Lloyd 2-1
1975–6
v Rep. of Ireland *Grimsby* beat E. Hughes 2-1
v Scotland *Southport* lost to J. Zonfrillo 1-2
v Wales *Merthyr* beat M. Berni 3-0
1976–7
v Rep. of Ireland *Dublin* beat P. Burke 2-1
v Wales *Doncaster* beat J. Prosser 2-1
v Scotland *Glasgow* beat E. McLaughlin 2-1
1977–8
v Rep. of Ireland *Portsmouth* lost to P. Burke 1-2
v Scotland *Doncaster* lost to E. Sinclair 1-2
v Wales *Caerphilly* beat C. Wilson 2-1

G. Filtness

1985
v Wales beat R. Jones 2-1
v Scotland beat J. Allen 2-1
v Rep. of Ireland beat J. Long 2-1
v Northern Ireland beat S. McClarey 3-0

J. Fitzmaurice

1972–3
v Rep. of Ireland *Dublin* beat G. Hanway 3-0
1975–6
v Rep. of Ireland *Grimsby* beat N. Clarke 3-0
v Scotland *Southport* lost to M. McLeod 1-2
v Wales *Merthyr* lost to J. Selby 1-2
1976–7
v Rep. of Ireland *Dublin* lost to G. Sutton 1-2

G. Foulds

1976–7
v Rep. of Ireland *Dublin* lost to R. Brennan 1-2
v Scotland *Glasgow* beat B. Demarco 2-1
1977–8
v Rep. of Ireland *Portsmouth* beat T. Langan 3-0
v Scotland *Doncaster* lost to E. McLaughlin 0-3
v Wales *Caerphilly* beat G. Thomas 2-1
1978
v Isle of Man *Prestatyn* beat P. Reynolds 2-1
v Scotland beat J. Halcrow 3-0
v Wales lost to C. Everton 1-2
1979
v Isle of Man *Prestatyn* beat C. Cooper 3-0
v Scotland lost to J. Halcrow 0-3

N. Foulds

1982
v Isle of Man *Prestatyn* beat M. Colquitt 3-0
v Rep. of Ireland lost to J. Long 0-3
v Northern Ireland beat J. McLaughlin 2-1
v Wales lost to S. Newbury 0-3

D. Fowler

1983
v Rep. of Ireland *Prestatyn* beat G. Gibson 2-1
v Northern Ireland beat J. McLaughlin 3-0
v Scotland beat R. Lane 2-1
v Isle of Man beat T. Wilson 2-1
v Wales lost to T. Parsons 1-2

D. French

1971–2
v Wales *Neath* lost to D. Meredith 1-2
1972–3
v Rep. of Ireland *Dublin* beat F. Nathan 2-1
v Rep. of Ireland *Bolton* lost to D. Lenehan 1-2
v Scotland *Carlisle* beat D. Sneddon 2-1

P. Gibson

1985
v Isle of Man beat M. Colquitt 3-0
v Scotland lost to J. McNellan 1-2
v Northern Ireland lost to H. Morgan 1-2

T. Graham

1972–3
v Rep. of Ireland *Dublin* beat R. Brennan 2-1
1973–4
v Scotland *Carlisle* lost to B. Demarco 1-2

M. Hallett

1978
v Isle of Man *Prestatyn* beat R. Cowley 3-0
v Rep. of Ireland beat J. Rogers 2-1
v Scotland beat D. Sneddon 2-1
v Wales lost to C. Wilson 0-3

J. Hargreaves

1974–5
v Scotland *Edinburgh* beat J. Zonfrillo 2-1
1975–6
v Scotland *Southport* beat E. McLaughlin 3-0
1976–7
v Rep. of Ireland *Dublin* beat J. Clusker 3-0
v Scotland *Glasgow* beat D. Sneddon 2-1
v Wales *Doncaster* beat S. Newbury 2-1
1977–8
v Rep. of Ireland *Portsmouth* beat D. Wilson 2-1
v Scotland *Doncaster* beat R. Cadman 3-0
v Wales *Caerphilly* lost to T. Griffiths 0-3
1978
v Isle of Man *Prestatyn* beat J. Radcliffe 3-0
v Scotland beat M. Gibson 3-0
v Wales beat T. Parsons 2-1
1979
v Northern Ireland *Prestatyn* beat R. Burke 3-0
v Isle of Man beat P. Partington 3-0
v Rep. of Ireland lost to D. Sheehan 1-2
v Scotland lost to M. Gibson 1-2
v Wales beat J. Selby 3-0
1980
v Northern Ireland *Prestatyn* beat D. McVeigh 2-1
v Scotland beat P. Kippie 3-0
v England lost to J. Selby 0-2
1981
v Isle of Man *Prestatyn* beat R. Cowley 2-1
v Rep. of Ireland beat M. Ralph 2-1
v Northern Ireland lost to A. Sharpe 0-3
v Wales beat T. Parsons 2-1
1982
v Scotland *Prestatyn* J. Zonfrillo 2-1
v Rep. of Ireland beat P. Ennis 2-1
v Northern Ireland beat E. Swaffield 2-1
v Wales beat T. Chappel 2-0

B. Harris

1981
v Isle of Man *Prestatyn* beat C. Cooper 3-0
v Rep. of Ireland beat P. Watchorn 2-1
v Scotland beat J. McNellan 2-1
v Wales beat D. May 2-1

V. Harris

1980
v Northern Ireland *Prestatyn* beat S. Clarke 3-0
v Rep. of Ireland beat G. Sutton 3-0
v Scotland beat J. Donnelly 3-0
v Wales lost to D. John 0-3

S. Hood

1969
v Wales *Port Talbot* lost to J. Ford 1-2
1970–1
v Wales *Harringay* beat J. Ford 2-1
v Rep. of Ireland *Dublin* lost to A. Roche 1-2
1971–2
v Scotland *Newcastle* beat E. Sinclair 2-1
v Rep. of Ireland *Harringay* beat F. Byrne 2-1
v Wales *Neath* beat D. John 2-1
1972–3
v Scotland *Edinburgh* beat J. Phillips 2-1
v Wales *Hull* beat D. Mountjoy 2-1
1973–4
v Wales *Garnant* beat D. May 3-0
v Rep. of Ireland *Bolton* lost to P. Miley 1-2
v Scotland *Carlisle* beat J. Phillips 2-1

1974–5
v Wales *Exeter* beat G. Thomas 2-1
v Scotland *Edinburgh* lost to E. Sinclair 1-2
v Rep. of Ireland *Glasnevin* beat N. Clarke 2-1
1975–6
v Rep. of Ireland *Grimsby* beat F. Nathan 3-0
v Scotland *Southport* beat E. Sinclair 2-1
v Wales *Merthyr* lost to T. Griffiths 1-2
1976–7
v Rep. of Ireland *Dublin* beat E. Hughes 3-0
v Scotland *Glasgow* lost to E. Sinclair 1-2
v Wales *Doncaster* beat D. Thomas 2-1
1977–8
v Rep. of Ireland *Portsmouth* lost to J. Clusker 1-2
1978
v Rep. of Ireland *Prestatyn* beat D. Wilson 2-1

P. Houlihan

1969
v Wales *Port Talbot* lost to M. Berni 0-3

D. Hughes

1979
v Northern Ireland *Prestatyn* beat J. Begley 3-0
v Rep. of Ireland lost to G. Sutton 0-3

R. Jarmak

1983
v Northern Ireland *Prestatyn* beat E. Swaffield 2-1
v Isle of Man beat C. Cooper 2-1
v Wales drew with R. Jones 1-1

J. Johnson

1976–7
v Rep. of Ireland *Dublin* beat D. Sheehan 3-0
v Scotland *Glasgow* beat R. Miller 2-1
v Wales *Doncaster* lost to T. Griffiths 1-2
1977–8
v Rep. of Ireland *Portsmouth* beat R. Brennan 2-1
v Scotland *Doncaster* beat R. Miller 2-1
v Wales *Caerphilly* lost to A. Lloyd 1-2
1978
v Isle of Man *Prestatyn* beat C. Cooper 2-1
v Rep. of Ireland beat P. Burke 3-0
v Scotland beat J. Zonfrillo 2-1
v Wales beat J. Selby 3-0

A. Knowles

1978
v Isle of Man *Prestatyn* beat M. Quine 3-0
v Rep. of Ireland beat F. Nathan 2-1
v Scotland beat J. Donnelly 3-0
v Wales beat A. Lloyd 2-0
1979
v Northern Ireland *Prestatyn* beat D. McVeigh 3-0
v Isle of Man beat J. Radcliffe 2-1
v Rep. of Ireland beat T. Langan 3-0
v Scotland beat I. Wallace 3-0
v Wales beat T. Parsons 2-1

S. Longworth

1983
v Rep. of Ireland *Prestatyn* beat J. Long 2-1
v Scotland beat J. Rankeillor 3-0
v Isle of Man beat P. Reynolds 2-1
v Wales beat S. Newbury 3-0

R. Marshall

1984
v Scotland *Prestatyn* lost to S. Hendry 0-3
v Isle of Man beat R. Cowley 3-0
v Rep. of Ireland beat G. Burns 2-1
1985
v Wales drew with D. John 1-1
v Isle of Man beat M. Quine 2-1
v Rep. of Ireland lost to K. Doherty 1-2
v Northern Ireland beat K. McAlinden 3-0

D. Martin

1979
v Northern Ireland *Prestatyn* beat S. Pavis 2-1
v Isle of Man beat A. Christian 3-0

v Rep. of Ireland beat P. Miley 3-0
v Scotland lost to M. McLeod 1-2
v Wales lost to A. Lloyd 1-2
1980
v Northern Ireland *Prestatyn* beat P. Donnelly 3-0
v Isle of Man beat P. Reynolds 2-1
v Rep. of Ireland lost to D. Sheehan 1-2
v Wales beat D. May 3-0

T. Meo

1978
v Isle of Man *Prestatyn* beat W. Craig 2-1
v Rep. of Ireland beat E. Hughes 2-1
v Scotland beat E. Sinclair 3-0
v Wales beat S. Newbury 2-1

J. O'Boye

1980
v Northern Ireland *Prestatyn* J. Begley 3-0
v Isle of Man beat C. Cooper 2-1
v Rep. of Ireland lost to P. Burke 1-2
v Scotland beat I. Black 2-1
v Wales beat A. Lloyd 2-1
1984
v Northern Ireland beat A. Sharpe 3-0
v Scotland beat S. Muir 2-1
v Rep. of Ireland beat J. Long 3-0
v Wales beat M. Bennett 2-1

B. Oliver

1982
v Isle of Man *Prestatyn* lost to T. Wilson 1-2
v Northern Ireland beat S. Pavis 2-1

K. Owers

1985
v Wales lost to G. Heycock 0-1
v Isle of Man beat C. Cooper 3-0
v Rep. of Ireland beat R. Brennan 2-1
v Northern Ireland beat S. Parvis 2-1

J. Parrott

1982
v Scotland *Prestatyn* beat J. Rea 2-1
v Rep. of Ireland beat P. Browne 2-1
v Northern Ireland beat F. Cahoon 3-0
v Wales beat A. Lloyd 2-1

D. Roe

1985
v Wales lost to N. Davies 1-2
v Isle of Man beat T. Wilson 2-1
v Scotland lost to S. Muir 1-2
v Rep. of Ireland lost to G. Burns 1-2

C. Ross

1969
v Wales *Port Talbot* beat A. Kemp 2-1
1970-1
v Wales *Harringay* beat E. Richards 3-0
v Rep. of Ireland *Dublin* beat R. Dunne 3-0
1971-2
v Scotland *Newcastle* B. Demarco 2-1
v Rep. of Ireland *Harringay* beat A. Roche 3-0
v Wales *Neath* beat D. Thomas 2-1
1972-3
v Scotland *Edinburgh* beat E. Sinclair 2-1
v Wales *Hull* lost to A. Lloyd 1-2
v Rep. of Ireland *Dublin* lost to J. Rogers 1-2
1973-4
v Wales *Garnant* beat M. Berni 2-1
1974-5
v Rep. of Ireland *Glasnevin* lost to F. Nathan 1-2
v Wales *Exeter* lost to D. Mountjoy 1-2
1975-6
v Rep. of Ireland *Grimsby* beat J. Rogers 2-1
v Wales *Merthyr* lost to A. Lloyd 1-2

G. Scott

1974-5
v Scotland *Edinburgh* beat M. Gibson 3-0
1976-7
v Scotland *Glasgow* beat J. Phillips 2-1
v Wales *Doncaster* beat T. Parsons 2-1
1977-8
v Rep. of Ireland *Portsmouth* beat P. Watchorn 2-1
v Scotland *Doncaster* lost to M. Gibson 1-2
v Wales *Caerphilly* lost to S. Newbury 1-2
1978
v Rep. of Ireland *Prestatyn* beat R. Brennan 3-0
1979
v Isle of Man *Prestatyn* beat R. Cowley 2-1
v Rep. of Ireland beat P. Burke 2-1
v Wales drew with C. Everton 1-1

M. Smith

1983
v Northern Ireland *Prestatyn* lost to W. Walker 0-3
1984
v Scotland beat J. Rankeillor 2-1
v Isle of Man lost to T. Wilson 1-2
v Rep. of Ireland beat M. Ralph 2-1
v Wales beat A. Lloyd 2-1

D. Taylor

1971-2
v Wales *Neath* lost to R. Oriel 1-2

G. Thompson

1969
v Wales *Port Talbot* lost to A. Lloyd 1-2

W. Thorne

1972-3
v Rep. of Ireland *Dublin* beat F. Murphy 2-1
1973-4
v Wales *Garnant* beat J. Prosser 2-1
v Rep. of Ireland *Bolton* beat F. Byrne 3-0
v Scotland *Carlisle* beat J. Zonfrillo 2-1
1974-5
v Wales *Exeter* beat T. Griffiths 2-1
v Scotland *Edinburgh* lost to W. McKerron 1-2
v Rep. of Ireland *Glasnevin* beat L. Kenna 2-1
1975-6
v Rep. of Ireland *Grimsby* lost to P. Fagan 1-2

S. Ventham

1983
v Scotland *Prestatyn* beat J. Rea 2-1
v Isle of Man beat R. Cowley 3-0
1984
v Northern Ireland lost to E. Swaffield 1-2
v Isle of Man beat M. Colquitt 2-1
v Wales lost to D. John 1-2

J. Virgo

1970-1
v Wales *Harringay* beat G. Thomas 3-0
v Rep. of Ireland *Dublin* beat M. Lowth 3-0
1971-2
v Scotland *Newcastle* beat G. Carnegie 2-1
v Rep. of Ireland *Harringay* beat F. Murphy 2-1
1972-3
v Scotland *Edinburgh* beat J. Wilson 3-0
v Wales *Hull* lost to M. Berni 1-2
v Rep. of Ireland *Dublin* beat F. Byrne 3-0
1973-4
v Wales *Garnant* beat G. Thomas 2-1
v Rep. of Ireland *Bolton* beat P. Burke 2-1
v Scotland *Carlisle* beat E. Sinclair 2-1
1974-5
v Rep. of Ireland *Glasnevin* beat D. Sheehan 3-0
v Scotland *Edinburgh* beat J. Phillips 2-1
1975-6
v Rep. of Ireland *Grimsby* beat P. Burke 2-1
v Scotland *Southport* beat D. Sneddon 2-1
v Wales *Merthyr* lost to D. Mountjoy 1-2

M. Watterson

1979
v Northern Ireland *Prestatyn* beat P. Donnelly 2-1
v Scotland beat S. Nevison 3-0
v Wales lost to S. Newbury 0-3
1980
v Isle of Man *Prestatyn* beat J. Radcliffe 3-0
v Scotland beat M. Gibson 3-0
v Wales beat C. Roscoe 2-1

B. West

1981
v Rep. of Ireland *Prestatyn* beat P. Ennis 2-1
v Northern Ireland beat S. Pavis 3-0
v Wales beat D. John 2-1
1982
v Scotland beat *Prestatyn* J. Rankeillor 2-1
v Rep. of Ireland beat R. Brennan 3-0
v Northern Ireland beat K. Erwin 3-0
v Wales beat J. Selby 2-1
1983
v Rep. of Ireland *Prestatyn* beat R. Brennan 3-0
v Northern Ireland beat J. McLaughlin 3-0
v Scotland beat J. Halcrow 2-1
v Isle of Man beat M. Colquitt 3-0
v Wales lost to A. Lloyd 1-2
1984
v Northern Ireland beat K. Erwin 2-1
v Scotland beat J. Halcrow 2-1
v Rep. of Ireland beat M. Kane 2-1
v Wales lost to N. Davies 1-2

J. White

1979
v Northern Ireland *Prestatyn* beat E. Swaffield 3-0
v Isle of Man beat P. Reynolds 3-0
v Rep. of Ireland beat E. Hughes 2-1
v Scotland beat E. McLaughlin 2-1
v Wales beat G. Thomas 3-0
1980
v Northern Ireland *Prestatyn* beat S. Pavis 2-1
v Isle of Man beat W. Craig 3-0
v Rep. of Ireland beat M. Kane 2-1
v Scotland beat E. McLaughlin 2-1
v Wales lost to S. Newbury 0-3

T. Whitthread

1984
v Isle of Man beat P. Reynolds 3-0
v Rep. of Ireland beat P. Ennis 2-1
v Wales beat R. Jones 3-0
1985
v Wales lost to R. Welch 0-3
v Isle of Man beat L. Gale 3-0
v Scotland lost to R. Lane 1-2
v Northern Ireland beat K. Erwin 2-1

M. Wildman

1970-1
v Wales *Harringay* beat M. Berni 2-1
v Rep. of Ireland *Dublin* beat G. Hanway 3-0
1971-2
v Scotland *Newcastle* lost to W. McKerron 1-2
v Rep. of Ireland *Harringay* lost to J. Rogers 1-2
1972-3
v Scotland *Edinburgh* beat W. McKerron 3-0
v Wales *Hull* beat T. Parsons 3-0
1973-4
v Wales *Garnant* beat D. Mountjoy 2-1
v Rep. of Ireland *Bolton* lost to J. Weber 1-2
v Scotland *Carlisle* beat R. Eprile 2-1
1974-5
v Wales *Exeter* lost to T. Parsons 0-3

I. Williamson

1981
v Isle of Man *Prestatyn* beat M. Quine 3-0
v Northern Ireland lost to S. Clarke 1-2
v Scotland lost to J. Rea 1-2
v Wales beat J. Selby 1-0

G. Wood

1980
v Isle of Man *Prestatyn* beat M. Quine 2-1
v Rep. of Ireland beat E. Hughes 3-0
v Scotland lost to J. McNellan 1-2

1981
v Isle of Man *Prestatyn* beat J. Radcliffe 3-0
v Rep. of Ireland lost to P. Burke 0-3
v Scotland beat K. Baird 2-1
v Wales lost to S. Newbury 0-2
1982
v Isle of Man *Prestatyn* beat M. Clinton 3-0
v Rep. of Ireland lost to G. Gibson 1-2
1983
v Rep. of Ireland *Prestatyn* beat P. Ennis 3-0
v Northern Ireland beat S. Pavis 2-1
v Isle of Man beat M. Clinton 2-1
v Wales lost to T. Chappel 0-3
1984
v Northern Ireland beat H. Morgan 2-1
v Isle of Man lost to C. Cooper 1-2

J. Wright
1984
v Northern Ireland *Prestatyn* beat S. McClarey 3-0
v Scotland lost to R. Lane 1-2
v Rep. of Ireland lost to D. McKiernan 0-3
1985
v Wales beat M. Bennett 3-0
v Isle of Man beat P. Reynolds 3-0
v Scotland lost to K. McIntosh 1-2
v Rep. of Ireland beat R. McAuley 3-0
v Northern Ireland beat W. Mills 3-0

ISLE OF MAN

A. Christian
1979
v England *Prestatyn* lost to D. Martin 0-3

M. Clinton
1981
v Rep. of Ireland *Prestatyn* lost to P. Watchorn 1-2
v Wales lost to J. Selby 0-3
1982
v Scotland lost to J. Zonfrillo 1-2
v Wales lost to A. Lloyd 1-2
v England lost to G. Wood 0-3
v Rep. of Ireland lost to P. Browne 1-2
v Northern Ireland lost to F. Cahoon 0-3
1983
v Scotland lost to R. Lane 1-2
v England lost to G. Wood 1-2
1985
v Wales lost to R. Dorkins 1-2
v Rep. of Ireland lost to R. McAuley 0-3
v Scotland lost to B. Blues 0-3

M. Colquitt
1982
v Scotland lost to J. Rankeillor 1-2
v Wales lost to S. Newbury 0-3
v England lost to N. Foulds 0-3
v Northern Ireland lost to J. McLaughlin 1-2
1983
v Rep. of Ireland beat R. McCrum 2-1
v Wales lost to J. Selby 1-2
v Scotland lost to J. McNellan 1-2
v England lost B. West 0-3
v Northern Ireland lost to S. Pavis 1-2
1984
v Wales lost to M. Bennett 1-3
v Northern Ireland beat E. Swaffield 2-1
v England lost to S. Ventham 1-2
v Scotland lost to D. Sneddon 1-2
v Rep. of Ireland beat K. Doherty 3-0
1985
v Wales lost to G. Thomas 1-2
v Rep. of Ireland lost to P. Miley 0-3
v Scotland lost to S. Nivison 1-2
v England lost to P. Gibson 0-3
v Northern Ireland beat E. Swaffield 2-1

C. Cooper
1978
v England *Prestatyn* lost to J. Johnson 1-2
v Wales lost to A. Lloyd 0-3
v Rep. of Ireland lost to P. Burke 0-3
v Scotland lost to J. Zonfrillo 1-2
1979
v Scotland *Prestatyn* lost to S. Nivison 1-2
v England lost to G. Foulds 0-3
v Wales lost to C. Everton 0-3
v Northern Ireland lost to B. Harvey 0-3
v Rep. of Ireland beat J. Long 3-0
1980
v Scotland *Prestatyn* lost to P. Kippie 1-2
v England lost to J. O'Boye 1-2
v Northern Ireland lost to J. Begley 1-2
v Wales lost to R. Welch 1-2
v Rep. of Ireland lost to P. Burke 1-2
1981
v Scotland *Prestatyn* lost to K. Baird 1-2
v England lost to B. Harris 0-3
v Rep. of Ireland beat G. Sutton 3-0
v Wales lost to A. Lloyd 0-3
v Northern Ireland lost to S. Pavis 1-2
1982
v Scotland *Prestatyn* beat J. Rea 2-1
v Wales lost to T. Parsons 0-3
v England beat D. Chalmers 2-1
v Rep. of Ireland lost to P. Ennis 0-3
v Northern Ireland lost to S. Pavis 1-2
1983
v Rep. of Ireland *Prestatyn* lost to D. Cranley 1-2
v Wales beat W. Jones 3-0
v Scotland lost to J. Halcrow 1-2
v England lost to R. Jarmak 1-2
v Northern Ireland lost to E. Swaffield 0-3
1984
v Wales lost to D. John 0-3
v Northern Ireland lost to A. Sharpe 1-2
v England beat G. Wood 2-1
v Scotland lost to G. Carnegie 1-2
1985
v Wales lost to M. Hendra 1-2
v Rep. of Ireland beat R. Brennan 2-1
v Scotland beat W. Kelly 2-1
v England lost to K. Owers 0-3
v Northern Ireland lost to S. McClarey 0-3

R. Cowley
1978
v England *Prestatyn* lost to M. Hallett 0-3
v Wales lost to G. Thomas 1-2
v Rep. of Ireland beat J. Rogers 2-1
v Scotland lost to J. Donnelly 0-3
1979
v Scotland *Prestatyn* lost to I. Wallace 0-3
v England lost to G. Scott 1-2
v Wales lost to T. Parsons 1-2
v Northern Ireland lost to J. Begley 1-2
v Rep. of Ireland lost to E. Hughes 0-3
1981
v Scotland *Prestatyn* beat R. Miller 2-1
v England lost to J. Hargreaves 0-3
v Rep. of Ireland lost to M. Ralph 1-2
v Wales lost to D. May 1-2
v Northern Ireland beat J. McLaughlin 2-1
1982
v Scotland *Prestatyn* beat G. Carnegie 3-1
v Wales lost to W. Jones 0-3
v England lost to S. Duggan 1-2
v Rep. of Ireland lost to P. Watchorn 0-3
v Northern Ireland lost to E. Swaffield 0-3
1983
v Rep. of Ireland *Prestatyn* beat M. Kane 3-0
v Wales lost to T. Parsons 0-3
v Scotland beat G. Carnegie 3-0
v England lost to S. Ventham 0-3
v Northern Ireland lost to J. McLaughlin 1-2
1984
v Wales lost to N. Davies 1-2
v Northern Ireland lost to K. Erwin 1-2
v England lost to R. Marshall 0-3
v Scotland lost to S. Hendry 0-3
v Rep. of Ireland lost to M. Ralph 1-2

W. Craig
1978
v England *Prestatyn* lost to T. Meo 1-2
v Wales lost to J. Selby 1-2
v Rep. of Ireland beat J. Langan 2-1
v Scotland lost to J. Halcrow 1-2
1979
v Scotland *Prestatyn* lost to J. Donnelly 0-3
v Wales lost to V. Rosser 0-3
v Northern Ireland lost to D. McVeigh 0-3
1980
v Scotland *Prestatyn* lost to M. Gibson 0-3
v England lost to J. White 0-3
v Wales lost to C. Roscoe 0-3

L. Gale
1985
v Rep. of Ireland lost to K. Doherty 1-2
v England lost to T. Whitthread 0-3
v Northern Ireland lost to A. Sharpe 0-3

J. Kinrade
1978
v Rep. of Ireland *Prestatyn* lost to E. Hughes 0-3
1981
v Scotland *Prestatyn* lost to R. Lane 1-2
v England lost to M. Darrington 3-0
v Rep. of Ireland lost to M. Kane 0-3
v Wales lost to W. Jones 0-3

K. Kinrade
1978
v Wales *Prestatyn* lost to T. Parsons 0-3
1980
v Scotland *Prestatyn* lost to M. McLeod 1-2
v England lost to M. Darrington 0-3
v Northern Ireland lost to T. Murphy 1-2
v Wales lost to A. Lloyd 1-2
v Rep. of Ireland lost to E. Hughes 0-3
1983
v Northern Ireland *Prestatyn* lost to A. Sharpe 0-3

P. Partington
1979
v Scotland *Prestatyn* lost to M. McLeod 1-2
v England lost to J. Hargreaves 0-3
v Rep. of Ireland lost to P. Burke 1-2
1980
v Scotland *Prestatyn* lost to I. Black 0-3
v Northern Ireland lost to G. Sharpe 0-3
v Rep. of Ireland beat G. Sutton 2-1
1981
v Rep. of Ireland *Prestatyn* beat P. Browne 2-1
v Wales lost to T. Parsons 1-2
v Northern Ireland lost to A. Sharpe 1-2
1983
v Rep. of Ireland *Prestatyn* beat P. McNally 2-1
v Wales lost to S. Newbury 0-3
1984
v Wales lost to R. Jones 1-2
v Northern Ireland lost to H. Morgan 1-2
v England beat C. Archer 2-1

M. Quine
1978
v England *Prestatyn* lost to A. Knowles 0-3
v Wales lost to C. Everton 0-3
v Scotland lost to D. Sneddon 0-3
1979
v Wales *Prestatyn* lost to S. Newbury 0-3
v Northern Ireland lost to D. McVeigh 1-2
v Rep. of Ireland beat T. Langan 2-1
1980
v England *Prestatyn* lost to G. Wood 1-2
v Northern Ireland lost to S. Pavis 1-2
v Wales lost to S. Newbury 0-3
v Rep. of Ireland lost to D. Sheehan 1-2
1981
v Scotland *Prestatyn* lost to J. Zonfrillo 0-3
v England lost to I. Williamson 0-3
v Northern Ireland lost to E. Swaffield 1-2

1982
v Rep. of Ireland *Prestatyn* lost to G. Gibson 1-2
1984
v Rep. of Ireland lost to D. McKiernan 0-3
1985
v Wales lost to R. Jones 0-3
v Scotland lost to M. Kerry 0-3
v England lost to R. Marshall 1-2
v Northern Ireland lost to S. Pavis 1-2

J. Radcliffe

1978
v England *Prestatyn* lost to J. Hargreaves 0-3
v Scotland lost to E. McLaughlin 0-3
1979
v Scotland *Prestatyn* lost to E. McLaughlin 1-2
v England lost to A. Knowles 1-2
v Wales lost to A. Lloyd 0-3
v Northern Ireland lost to S. Pavis 1-2
v Rep. of Ireland lost to G. Sutton 0-3
1980
v Scotland *Prestatyn* lost to E. McLaughlin 0-3
v England lost to M. Watterson 0-3
v Northern Ireland lost to E. Swaffield 1-2
v Wales lost to D. May 0-3
v Rep. of Ireland lost to M. Kane 0-3
1981
v Scotland *Prestatyn* lost to J. Rea 0-3
v England lost to G. Wood 0-3
v Northern Ireland lost to D. McVeigh 1-2

N. Radcliffe

1978
v Rep. of Ireland *Prestatyn* lost to J. Clusker 0-3

P. Reynolds

1978
v England *Prestatyn* lost to G. Foulds 1-2
v Wales lost to C. Wilson 0-3
v Rep. of Ireland lost to G. Sutton 0-3
v Scotland lost to R. Miller 1-2
1979
v Scotland *Prestatyn* beat J. Phillips 2-1
v England lost to J. White 0-3
v Wales lost to J. Selby 1-2
v Northern Ireland lost to P. Donnelly 1-2
v Rep. of Ireland lost to D. Sheehan 0-3
1980
v Scotland *Prestatyn* beat J. Donnelly 2-1
v England lost to D. Martin 1-2
v Northern Ireland beat S. Clarke 2-1
v Wales lost to J. Selby 1-2
v Rep. of Ireland lost to M. Ralph 1-2
1981
v Scotland *Prestatyn* lost to J. Halcrow 1-2
v England lost to G. Cripsey 0-3
v Rep. of Ireland beat A. Kearney 2-1
v Wales lost to M. Bennett 1-2
v Northern Ireland beat P. Donnelly 2-1
1982
v Scotland *Prestatyn* lost to D. Sneddon 1-2
v Wales lost to J. Terry 1-2
v England lost to M. Bradley 1-2
v Rep. of Ireland lost to J. Long 1-2
v Northern Ireland lost to A. Sharpe 1-2
1983
v Rep. of Ireland *Prestatyn* beat J. Long 2-1
v Wales lost to R. Jones 1-2
v Scotland lost to S. Muir 0-3
v England lost to S. Longworth 1-2
v Northern Ireland beat S. McClarey 2-1
1984
v Wales lost to G. Thomas 1-2
v Northern Ireland lost to S. Pavis 1-2
v England lost to T. Whitthread 0-3
v Scotland lost to S. Muir 0-3
v Rep. of Ireland lost to J. Long 0-3
1985
v Wales lost to M. Bennett 0-3
v Rep. of Ireland beat G. Burns 2-1
v Scotland beat K. McIntosh 2-1
v England lost to J. Wright 0-3
v Northern Ireland lost to K. Erwin 1-2

P. Smethurst

1984
v Scotland lost to K. McIntosh 0-3

T. Wilson

1982
v Scotland *Prestatyn* lost to J. Allan 1-2
v Wales lost to J. Selby 0-3
v England beat B. Oliver 2-1
v Rep. of Ireland lost to M. Kane 0-3
v Northern Ireland lost to S. Clarke 0-3
1983
v Rep. of Ireland *Prestatyn* lost to M. Ralph 1-2
v Wales beat J. Griffiths 3-0
v Scotland lost to K. Baird 1-2
v England lost to D. Fowler 1-2
v Northern Ireland lost to K. Erwin 1-2
1984
v Wales lost to A. Lloyd 0-3
v England beat M. Smith 2-1
v Scotland lost to R. Lane 1-2
v Rep. of Ireland beat G. Burns 2-1
v Northern Ireland lost to S. McClarey 1-2
1985
v Wales lost to G. Heycock 0-3
v Rep. of Ireland lost to J. Long 1-2
v Scotland lost to R. Lane 1-2
v England lost to D. Roe 1-2
v Northern Ireland lost to H. Morgan 1-2

NORTHERN IRELAND

J. Begley

1979
v England *Prestatyn* lost to D. Hughes 0-3
v Wales lost to J. Terry 1-2
v Scotland lost to M. Gibson 1-2
v Rep. of Ireland beat E. Hughes 2-1
v Isle of Man beat R. Cowley 2-1
1980
v England *Prestatyn* lost to J. O'Boye 0-3
v Isle of Man beat C. Cooper 2-1

R. Burke

1979
v England *Prestatyn* lost to J. Hargreaves 0-3
v Scotland lost to E. McLaughlin 0-3

F. Cahoon

1982
v England *Prestatyn* lost to J. Parrott 0-3
v Isle of Man beat M. Clinton 3-0

S. Clarke

1980
v England *Prestatyn* lost to V. Harris 0-3
v Rep. of Ireland lost to M. Kane 1-2
v Isle of Man lost to P. Reynolds 1-2
1981
v Rep. of Ireland *Prestatyn* lost to P. Ennis 1-2
v Wales lost to W. Jones 1-2
v England beat I. Williamson 2-1
v Scotland lost to J. Rankeillor 0-3
1982
v Scotland *Prestatyn* lost to J. Rankeillor 1-2
v Isle of Man beat T. Wilson 3-0
1984
v Wales beat R. Jones 2-1
v Scotland lost to J. McNellan 0-3

F. Connolly

1982
v Rep. of Ireland *Prestatyn* lost to G. Gibson 1-2

P. Donnelly

1979
v England *Prestatyn* lost to M. Watterson 1-2
v Wales beat A. Lloyd 2-1
v Scotland beat J. Phillips 3-0
v Rep. of Ireland beat D. Sheehan 2-1
v Isle of Man beat P. Reynolds 2-1
1980
v England *Prestatyn* lost to J. O'Boye 0-3
v Wales lost to A. Lloyd 1-2
v Rep. of Ireland lost to G. Sutton 1-2
v Scotland lost to E. McLaughlin 1-2
1981
v Rep. of Ireland *Prestatyn* lost to M. Kane 1-2
v Wales lost to S. Newbury 1-2
v England lost to G. Cripsey 1-2
v Isle of Man lost to P. Reynolds 1-2
1982
v Scotland *Prestatyn* beat R. Lane 2-1
v Wales lost to S. Newbury 0-3

K. Erwin

1982
v Wales *Prestatyn* beat J. Griffiths 2-1
v Rep. of Ireland lost to P. Watchorn 1-2
v England lost to B. West 0-3
1983
v Wales *Prestatyn* lost to R. Jones 0-3
v Isle of Man beat T. Wilson 2-1
v Scotland lost to R. Lane 0-3
1984
v England lost to B. West 1-2
v Rep of Ireland beat P. Ennis 3-0
v Isle of Man beat R. Cowley 2-1
v Wales lost to A. Lloyd 1-2
v Scotland lost to S. Hendry 1-2
1985
v Wales beat M. Hendra 2-1
v Rep. of Ireland beat D. Cranley 3-0
v England lost to T. Whitthread 1-2
v Isle of Man beat P. Reynolds 2-1
v Scotland beat K. McIntosh 3-1

B. Harvey

1979
v Wales *Prestatyn* lost to J. Terry 1-2
v Isle of Man beat C. Cooper 3-0

K. McAlinden

1985
v Rep. of Ireland beat G. Sutton 3-0
v England lost to R. Marshall 0-3
v Scotland beat J. Allen 2-1

S. McClarey

1983
v Rep. of Ireland *Prestatyn* lost to P. Ennis 1-2
v Isle of Man lost to P. Reynolds 1-2
v Scotland lost to J. Rea 1-2
1984
v England lost to J. Wright 0-3
v Rep. of Ireland lost to M. Nolan 1-2
v Isle of Man beat T. Wilson 2-1
v Wales lost to M. Bennett 1-2
1985
v Wales lost to M. Bennett 1-2
v Rep. of Ireland lost to G. Burns 1-2
v England lost to G. Filtness 0-3
v Isle of Man beat C. Cooper 3-0
v Scotland lost to R. Lane 1-2

Jim McLaughlin

1983
v England *Prestatyn* lost to D. Fowler 0-3
v Rep. of Ireland lost to M. Kane 0-3
1984
v Wales lost to N. Davis 0-3

John McLaughlin

1979
v Rep. of Ireland *Prestatyn* lost to T. Langan 0-3
v Isle of Man beat M. Quine 2-1
1981
v Rep. of Ireland *Prestatyn* lost to M. Ralph 1-2
v Scotland lost to J. Rea 1-2
v Isle of Man lost to R. Cowley 1-2
1982
v Scotland *Prestatyn* beat J. Zonfrillo 3-0
v Wales lost to A. Lloyd 1-2

v Rep. of Ireland lost to P. Browne	1-2
v England lost to N. Foulds	1-2
v Isle of Man beat M. Colquitt	2-1
1983	
v England *Prestatyn* lost to B. West	0-3
v Wales beat A. Lloyd	3-0
v Rep. of Ireland lost to R. Brennan	1-2
v Isle of Man beat R. Cowley	2-1
v Scotland beat J. Laidlaw	3-0

D. McVeigh

1979	
v England *Prestatyn* lost to A. Knowles	0-3
v Wales lost to T. Parsons	0-3
v Scotland beat J. Donnelly	2-1
v Rep. of Ireland beat G. Sutton	3-0
v Isle of Man beat W. Craig	3-0
1980	
v England *Prestatyn* lost to J. Hargreaves	1-2
v Wales lost to D. John	1-2
v Rep. of Ireland lost to D. Sheehan	0-3
v Scotland beat J. Halcrow	2-1
1981	
v Rep. of Ireland *Prestatyn* lost to G. Sutton	1-2
v Wales lost to A. Lloyd	1-2
v England lost to M. Darrington	0-3
v Scotland lost to J. Zonfrillo	1-2
v Isle of Man beat J. Radcliffe	2-1
1985	
v Rep. of Ireland lost to J. Long	0-3

W. Mills

1985	
v Rep. of Ireland beat R. Nolan	2-1
v England lost to J. Wright	0-3

H. Morgan

1984	
v England lost to G. Wood	1-2
v Rep. of Ireland beat J. Long	2-1
v Isle of Man beat P. Partington	2-1
v Scotland beat K. McIntosh	2-1
1985	
v Wales lost to N. Davies	0-3
v Rep. of Ireland beat K. Doherty	2-1
v England beat P. Gibson	2-1
v Isle of Man beat T. Wilson	2-1
v Scotland lost to S. Muir	0-3

T. Murphy

1980	
v England *Prestatyn* lost to M. Darrington	1-2
v Wales beat V. Rosser	3-0
v Rep. of Ireland beat P. Burke	2-1
v Isle of Man beat K. Kinrade	2-1
v Scotland beat P. Kippie	2-1

S. Pavis

1979	
v England *Prestatyn* lost to D. Martin	1-2
v Wales lost to S. Newbury	0-3
v Scotland lost to S. Nivison	1-2
v Rep. of Ireland lost to P. Burke	1-2
v Isle of Man beat J. Radcliffe	2-1
1980	
v England *Prestatyn* lost to J. White	1-2
v Wales lost to D. May	1-2
v Isle of Man beat M. Quine	2-1
v Rep. of Ireland lost to E. Hughes	1-2
v Scotland lost to J. Donnelly	1-2
1981	
v Rep. of Ireland *Prestatyn* beat A. Kearney	3-0
v Wales lost to T. Parsons	0-3
v England lost to B. West	0-3
v Scotland beat J. McNellan	2-1
v Isle of Man beat C. Cooper	2-1
1982	
v Scotland *Prestatyn* beat D. Sneddon	3-0
v Wales lost to T. Parsons	1-2
v Rep. of Ireland beat M. Kane	3-0
v England lost to B. Oliver	1-2
v Isle of Man beat C. Cooper	2-1
1983	
v England *Prestatyn* lost to G. Wood	1-2
v Wales lost to T. Parsons	0-3
v Rep. of Ireland beat R. McCrum	3-0
v Isle of Man beat M. Colquitt	2-1
v Scotland lost to J. Halcrow	1-2
1984	
v England lost to C. Archer	1-2
v Rep. of Ireland beat D. McKiernan	2-1
v Isle of Man beat P. Reynolds	2-1
v Wales lost to D. John	0-3
v Scotland lost to S. Muir	1-2
1985	
v Wales lost to D. John	1-2
v England lost to K. Owers	1-2
v Isle of Man beat M. Quine	2-1
v Scotland beat J. McNellan	3-0

A. Sharpe

1980	
v Wales *Prestatyn* lost to S. Newbury	1-2
v Isle of Man beat P. Partington	3-0
v Scotland lost to I. Black	1-2
1981	
v Rep. of Ireland *Prestatyn* beat P. Burke	2-1
v Wales beat D. John	2-1
v England beat J. Hargreaves	3-0
v Scotland beat K. Baird	2-1
v Isle of Man beat P. Partington	2-1
1982	
v Scotland *Prestatyn* beat J. Rea	2-1
v Wales beat T. Chappel	2-1
v Rep. of Ireland lost to P. Ennis	1-2
v England lost to S. Duggan	1-2
v Isle of Man beat R. Reynolds	2-1
1983	
v England *Prestatyn* lost to M. Bradley	0-3
v Wales lost to T. Chappel	1-2
v Rep. of Ireland beat D. Cranley	2-1
v Isle of Man beat K. Kinrade	3-0
v Scotland beat J. McNellan	3-0
1984	
v England lost to J. O'Boye	0-3
v Rep. of Ireland beat M. Kane	2-1
v Isle of Man beat C. Cooper	2-1
v Scotland beat G. Carnegie	3-0
1985	
v Wales lost to G. Thomas	1-2
v Isle of Man beat L. Gale	3-0
v Scotland beat B. Kelly	2-1

E. Swaffield

1979	
v England *Prestatyn* lost to J. White	0-3
v Wales beat J. Selby	2-1
v Scotland lost to J. Halcrow	1-2
v Rep. of Ireland lost to P. Miley	1-2
1980	
v Wales *Prestatyn* lost to C. Roscoe	1-2
v Rep. of Ireland beat P. Watchorn	2-1
v Isle of Man beat J. Radcliffe	2-1
v Scotland beat M. Macleod	2-1
1981	
v Wales *Prestatyn* beat D. May	2-1
v England beat L. Dodd	2-1
v Scotland beat R. Miller	2-1
v Isle of Man beat M. Quine	2-1
1982	
v Scotland *Prestatyn* lost to K. Baird	1-2
v Wales beat W. Jones	2-1
v Rep. of Ireland beat A. Kearney	2-1
v England lost to J. Hargreaves	1-2
v Isle of Man beat R. Cowley	3-0
1983	
v England *Prestatyn* lost to R. Jarmak	1-2
v Wales lost to S. Newbury	1-2
v Rep. of Ireland lost to M. Ralph	1-2
v Isle of Man beat C. Cooper	3-0
v Scotland lost to G. Carnegie	1-2
1984	
England beat S. Ventham	2-1
v Rep. of Ireland beat G. Burns	2-1
v Isle of Man lost to M. Colquitt	1-2
v Wales beat G. Thomas	3-0
v Scotland lost to D. Sneddon	1-2
1985	
v Wales lost to R. Welch	0-3
v Isle of Man lost to M. Colquitt	1-2

W. Walker

1983	
v England *Prestatyn* beat M. Smith	3-0
v Wales lost to W. Jones	0-3

REPUBLIC OF IRELAND

R. Brennan

1971-2	
v Wales *Dublin* lost to R. Oriel	0-3
1972-3	
v England *Dublin* lost to T. Graham	1-2
1976-7	
v Wales *Cardiff* lost to T. Griffiths	0-3
v Scotland *Edinburgh* beat R. Cadman	2-1
v England *Dublin* beat G. Foulds	2-1
1977-8	
v Scotland *Dublin* beat W. McKerron	3-0
v England *Portsmouth* lost to J. Johnson	1-2
1978	
v England *Prestatyn* lost to G. Scott	0-3
v Scotland lost to D. Sneddon	1-2
1982	
v England *Prestatyn* lost to B. West	0-3
1983	
v England *Prestatyn* lost to B. West	0-3
v Northern Ireland beat J. McLaughlin	2-1
v Scotland beat J. McNellan	2-1
1985	
v Isle of Man lost to C. Cooper	1-2
v Scotland beat S. Nivison	2-1
v England lost to K. Owers	1-2

P. Browne

1981	
v Isle of Man *Prestatyn* lost to P. Partington	1-2
1982	
v Northern Ireland *Prestatyn* beat J. McLaughlin	2-1
v Isle of Man beat M. Clinton	2-1
v Scotland lost to J. Allan	1-2
v England lost to J. Parrott	1-2
v Wales beat W. Jones	2-1

P. Burke

1973-4	
v Scotland *Dublin* D. Sneddon	2-1
v England *Bolton* lost to J. Virgo	1-2
v Wales *Dublin* lost to T. Griffiths	1-2
1974-5	
v Wales *Neath* lost to D. Mountjoy	1-2
v England *Glasnevin* beat R. Edmonds	2-1
v Scotland *Dundee* beat E. Sinclair	2-1
1975-6	
v England *Grimsby* lost to J. Virgo	1-2
v Wales *Dublin* beat G. Thomas	2-1
v Scotland *Dunlaoghaire* lost to E. Sinclair	0-3
1976-7	
v Wales *Cardiff* lost to T. Parsons	0-2
v Scotland *Edinburgh* lost to E. Sinclair	0-3
v England *Dublin* lost to R. Edmonds	1-2
1977-8	
v Wales *Dublin* lost to T. Parsons	1-2
v Scotland *Dublin* lost to E. Sinclair	1-2
v England *Portsmouth* beat R. Edmonds	2-1
1978	
v England *Prestatyn* lost to J. Johnson	0-3
v Isle of Man beat C. Cooper	3-0
v Wales beat A. Lloyd	2-1
v Scotland beat J. Zonfrillo	2-1
1979	
v Scotland *Prestatyn* beat J. Donnelly	2-1
v England lost to G. Scott	1-2
v Northern Ireland beat S. Pavis	2-1
v Wales beat J. Terry	2-1

v Isle of Man beat P. Partington 2-1
1980
v Northern Ireland *Prestatyn* lost to T. Murphy 1-2
v Wales lost to A. Lloyd 0-3
v Scotland beat J. McNellan 2-1
v England beat J. O'Boye 2-1
v Isle of Man beat C. Cooper 2-1
1981
v Northern Ireland *Prestatyn* lost to A. Sharpe 1-2
v England beat G. Wood 3-0
v Wales lost to T. Parsons 0-3
v Scotland beat J. Rea 3-0

G. Burns

1984
v Scotland beat R. Lane 2-1
v Northern Ireland lost to E. Swaffield 1-2
v England lost to R. Marshall 1-2
v Isle of Man lost to T. Wilson 1-2
v Wales lost to R. Jones 0-3
1985
v Northern Ireland beat S. McClarey 2-1
v Isle of Man lost to P. Reynolds 1-2
v Scotland beat B. Blues 3-0
v England beat D. Roe 2-1

F. Byrne

1971-2
v England *Harringay* lost to S. Hood 1-2
1972-3
v Wales *Pontygwaith* lost to M. Berni 1-2
v England *Dublin* lost to J. Virgo 0-3
1973-4
v Scotland *Dublin* lost to B. Demarco 1-2
v England *Bolton* lost to W. Thorne 0-3
v Wales *Dublin* lost to J. Selby 1-2
1975-6
v Scotland *Dunlaoghaire* beat B. Demarco 2-1

N. Clarke

1973-4
v Wales *Dublin* lost to M. Berni 0-3
1974-5
v England *Glasnevin* lost to S. Hood 1-2
v Scotland *Dundee* lost to B. Demarco 1-2
v Wales *Neath* lost to M. Berni 0-3
1975-6
v England *Grimsby* lost to J. Fitzmaurice 0-3
1977-8
v Scotland *Dublin* lost to M. Gibson 0-3

J. Clusker

1976-7
v Wales *Cardiff* lost to C. Wilson 1-2
v England *Dublin* lost to J. Hargreaves 0-3
1977-8
v Wales *Dublin* beat C. Wilson 2-1
v Scotland *Dublin* lost to R. Miller 1-2
v England *Portsmouth* beat S. Hood 2-1
1978
v Isle of Man *Prestatyn* beat N. Radcliffe 3-0
v Wales lost to C. Everton 1-2

D. Cranley

1983
v Isle of Man *Prestatyn* beat C. Cooper 2-1
v Wales lost to W. Jones 1-2
v Northern Ireland lost to A. Sharpe 1-2
v Scotland lost to J. Rea 1-2
1985
v Wales lost to M. Bennett 1-2
v Northern Ireland lost to K. Erwin 0-3

K. Doherty

1984
v Isle of Man lost to M. Colquitt 0-3
v Wales lost to G. Thomas 0-3
1985
v Wales beat R. Jones 2-1
v Northern Ireland lost to H. Morgan 1-2
v Isle of Man beat L. Gale 2-1
v Scotland beat J. Allan 2-1

v England beat R. Marshall 2-1

R. Dunne

1970-1
v England *Dublin* lost to C. Ross 0-3

P. Ennis

1981
v Northern Ireland *Prestatyn* beat S. Clarke 2-1
v England lost to B. West 1-2
v Wales lost to D. John 0-3
v Scotland beat K. Baird 2-1
1982
v Northern Ireland *Prestatyn* beat A. Sharpe 2-1
v Isle of Man beat C. Cooper 3-0
v Scotland beat R. Lane 2-1
v England lost to J. Hargreaves 1-2
v Wales lost to T. Parsons 1-2
1983
v England *Prestatyn* lost to G. Wood 0-3
v Wales lost to T. Parsons 0-3
v Northern Ireland beat S. McClarey 2-1
v Scotland beat S. Muir 3-0
1984
v Scotland beat G. Carnegie 3-0
v Northern Ireland lost to K. Erwin 0-3
v England lost to T. Whitthread 1-2
v Wales beat A. Lloyd 2-1

P. Fagan

1975-6
v England *Grimsby* beat W. Thorne 2-1
v Wales *Dublin* lost to D. Mountjoy 1-2
v Scotland *Dunlaoghaire* beat J. Phillips 2-1

G. Gibson

1982
v England *Prestatyn* beat G. Wood 2-1
v Wales lost to J. Terry 0-3
v Scotland lost to J. Rea 1-2
1983
v England *Prestatyn* lost to D. Fowler 1-2
v Wales lost to A. Lloyd 0-3

J. Grace

1970-1
v Wales *Port Talbot* lost to G. Thomas 1-2
1972-3
v Wales *Pontygwaith* lost to D. Mountjoy 0-3

G. Hanway

1970-1
v England *Dublin* lost to M. Wildman 0-3
v Wales *Port Talbot* lost to J. Ford 0-3
1971-2
v Scotland *Dublin* beat C. Brown 2-1
1972-3
v Scotland *Dublin* lost to G. Hadden 1-2
v Wales *Pontygwaith* lost to T. Parsons 1-2
v England *Dublin* lost to J. Fitzmaurice 0-3
1973-4
v Scotland *Dublin* lost to J. Phillips 0-3

E. Hughes

1974-5
v Scotland *Dundee* lost to I. Wallace 1-2
1975-6
v England *Grimsby* lost to R. Edmonds 1-2
v Wales *Dublin* lost to M. Berni 0-3
v Scotland *Dunlaoghaire* lost to M. Macleod 1-2
1976-7
v Scotland *Edinburgh* lost to E. McLaughlin 1-2
v England *Dublin* lost to S. Hood 0-3
1978
v England *Prestatyn* lost to T. Meo 1-2
v Isle of Man beat J. Kinrade 3-0
v Wales beat J. Selby 2-1
v Scotland beat J. Donnelly 2-1
1979
v Scotland *Prestatyn* lost to S. Nivison 1-2
v England lost to J. White 1-2
v Northern Ireland lost to J. Begley 1-2

v Isle of Man beat R. Cowley 3-0
v Wales beat T. Parsons 3-0
1980
v Northern Ireland *Prestatyn* beat S. Pavis 2-1
v Wales lost to D. May 1-2
v Scotland lost to E. McLaughlin 1-2
v England lost to G. Wood 0-3
v Isle of Man beat K. Kinrade 3-0

M. Kane

1977-8
v Scotland *Dublin* lost to D. Sneddon 0-3
1980
v Northern Ireland *Prestatyn* beat S. Clarke 2-1
v Wales beat C. Roscoe 2-1
v Scotland lost to J. Halcrow 1-2
v England lost to J. White 1-2
v Isle of Man beat J. Radcliffe 3-0
1981
v Northern Ireland *Prestatyn* beat P. Donnelly 2-1
v England lost to L. Dodd 1-2
v Wales beat J. Selby 2-1
v Isle of Man beat J. Kinrade 3-0
v Scotland lost to R. Lane 1-2
1982
v Northern Ireland *Prestatyn* lost to S. Pavis 0-3
v Isle of Man beat T. Wilson 3-0
v Scotland lost to G. Carnegie 1-2
v Wales lost to S. Newbury 0-3
1983
v England *Prestatyn* lost to M. Bradley 1-2
v Isle of Man lost to R. Cowley 0-3
v Northern Ireland beat J. McLaughlin 3-0
1984
v Scotland lost to S. Muir 1-2
v Northern Ireland lost to A. Sharpe 1-2
v Rep. of Ireland lost to B. West 1-2
v Wales lost to M. Bennett 0-3

A. Kearney

1981
v Northern Ireland *Prestatyn* lost to S. Pavis 0-3
v Wales lost to S. Newbury 1-2
v Isle of Man lost to P. Reynolds 1-2
v Scotland lost to J. McNellan 1-2
1982
v Northern Ireland *Prestatyn* lost to E. Swaffield 1-2

L. Kenna

1970-1
v Wales *Port Talbot* lost to D. Mountjoy 0-3
1974-5
v England *Glasnevin* lost to W. Thorne 1-2
1975-6
v Wales *Dublin* lost to J. Selby 0-3
1976-7
v Wales *Cardiff* beat S. Newbury 3-0
v Scotland *Edinburgh* lost to J. Phillips 0-3
1977-8
v Wales *Dublin* lost to S. Newbury 0-3

T. Langan

1977-8
v England *Portsmouth* lost to G. Foulds 0-3
1978
v Isle of Man *Prestatyn* lost to W. Craig 1-2
1979
v Scotland *Prestatyn* lost to M. Gibson 1-2
v England lost to A. Knowles 0-3
v Northern Ireland beat J. McLaughlin 3-0
v Wales lost to S. Newbury 1-2
v Isle of Man lost to M. Quine 1-2

D. Lenehan

1973-4
v Scotland *Dublin* beat E. Sinclair 2-1
v England *Bolton* beat D. French 2-1
v Wales *Dublin* beat C. Wilson 2-1

J. Long

1979
v Isle of Man *Prestatyn* lost to C. Cooper 0-3

1982
v Isle of Man *Prestatyn* beat P. Reynolds 2-1
v Scotland beat J. Rankeillor 2-1
v England beat N. Foulds 3-0
v Wales beat T. Griffiths 2-1
1983
v England *Prestatyn* lost to S. Longworth 1-2
v Isle of Man lost to P. Reynolds 1-2
v Wales lost to S. Newbury 1-2
v Scotland lost to J. Laidlaw 0-3
1984
v Scotland beat S. Hendry 2-1
v Northern Ireland lost to H. Morgan 1-2
v England lost to J. O'Boye 0-3
v Isle of Man beat P. Reynolds 3-0
v Wales lost to D. John 0-3
1986
v Wales beat G. Heycock 2-1
v Northern Ireland beat D. McVeigh 3-0
v Scotland lost to S. Muir 1-2
v England lost to G. Filtness 1-2
v Isle of Man beat T. Wilson 2-1

M. Lowth

1970-1
v England *Dublin* lost to J. Virgo 0-3

R. McAuley

1985
v Isle of Man beat M. Clinton 3-0
v Scotland beat K. McIntosh 2-1
v England lost to J. Wright 0-3

R. McCrum

1983
v Isle of Man *Prestatyn* lost to M. Colquitt 1-2
v Northern Ireland lost to S. Pavis 0-3

D. McKiernan

1984
v Scotland lost to J. Rankeillor 1-2
v Northern Ireland lost to S. Pavis 1-2
v England beat J. Wright 3-0
v Isle of Man beat M. Quine 3-0

P. McNally

1983
v Isle of Man *Prestatyn* lost to P. Partington 1-2
v Wales lost to P. Jones 1-2
v Scotland beat K. Baird 2-1

P. Miley

1973-4
v England *Bolton* beat S. Hood 2-1
v Wales *Dublin* lost to G. Thomas 0-3
1974-5
v England *Glasnevin* lost to R. Andrewartha 1-2
1979
v Scotland *Prestatyn* lost to J. Halcrow 1-2
v England lost to D.Martin 0-3
v Northern Ireland beat E. Swaffield 2-1
v Wales lost to A. Lloyd 0-3
1985
v Wales lost to D. John 0-3
v Isle of Man beat M. Colquitt 3-0

F. Murphy

1970-1
v England *Dublin* lost to R. Edmonds 1-2
1971-2
v England *Harringay* lost to J. Virgo 1-2
v Scotland *Dublin* lost to W. McKerron 1-2
1972-3
v England *Dublin* lost to W. Thorne 1-2
1976-7
v Wales *Cardiff* lost to A. Lloyd 0-3

F. Nathan

1972-3
v England *Dublin* lost to D. French 1-2
1974-5
v England *Glasnevin* beat C. Ross 2-1
v Scotland *Dundee* lost to J. Phillips 1-2
v Wales *Neath* lost to A. Lloyd 1-2
1975-6
v England *Grimsby* lost to S. Hood 0-3
1978
v England *Prestatyn* lost to A. Knowles 1-2
v Wales lost to S. Newbury 0-3
v Scotland lost to E. McLaughlin 0-3

M. Nolan

1984
v Northern Ireland beat S. McClarey 2-1
v Wales beat A. Issitt 2-1

R. Nolan

1985
v Wales lost to N. Davies 1-2
v Northern Ireland lost to W. Mills 1-2
v Scotland beat J. McNellan 2-1
v England beat J. Chambers 2-1

M. Ralph

1980
v Isle of Man *Prestatyn* beat P. Reynolds 2-1
1981
v Northern Ireland *Prestatyn* beat J. McLaughlin 2-1
v England lost to J. Hargreaves 1-2
v Wales lost to A. Lloyd 1-2
v Isle of Man beat R. Cowley 2-1
v Scotland lost to J. Rankeillor 1-2
1982
v England *Prestatyn* lost to M. Bradley 0-3
1983
v England *Prestatyn* beat D. Chalmers 2-1
v Isle of Man beat T. Wilson 2-1
v Wales lost to R. Jones 1-2
v Northern Ireland beat E. Swaffield 2-1
v Scotland lost to J. Halcrow 0-3
1984
v Scotland lost to D. Sneddon 0-3
v England lost to M. Smith 1-2
v Isle of Man beat R. Cowley 2-1

A. Roche

1970-1
v England *Dublin* beat S. Hood 2-1
1971-2
v England *Harringay* lost to C. Ross 0-3
v Scotland *Dublin* lost to J. Phillips 1-2
v Wales *Dublin* beat M. Berni 2-1
1972-3
v Wales *Pontygwaith* lost to D. May 0-3
v Scotland *Dublin* lost to B. Demarco 1-2

J. Rogers

1970-1
v Wales *Port Talbot* lost to M. Berni 0-3
1971-2
v England *Harringay* beat M. Wildman 2-1
v Scotland *Dublin* lost to D. Sneddon 1-2
v Wales *Dublin* lost to D. May 1-2
1972-3
v Scotland *Dublin* lost to J. Phillips 0-3
v England *Dublin* beat C. Ross 2-1
1974-5
v Wales *Neath* beat G. Thomas 2-1
1975-6
v England *Grimsby* lost to C. Ross 1-2
v Wales *Dublin* lost to T. Griffiths 0-3
1977-8
v Wales *Dublin* lost to T. Griffiths 0-3
1978
v England *Prestatyn* lost to M. Hallett 1-2
v Isle of Man lost to R. Cowley 1-2
v Wales lost to T. Parsons 0-3

D. Sheehan

1970-1
v Wales *Port Talbot* lost to D. May 0-3
1971-2
v England *Harringay* lost to J. Barron 0-3
v Wales *Dublin* lost to D. Meredith 0-3
1973-4
v Scotland *Dublin* beat J. Zonfrillo 2-1
v England *Bolton* beat R. Edmonds 2-1
v Wales *Dublin* lost to D. Mountjoy 0-3
1974-5
v England *Glasnevin* lost to J. Virgo 0-3
v Scotland *Dundee* lost to D. Sneddon 0-3
v Wales *Neath* lost to T. Parsons 1-2
1975-6
v Wales *Dublin* beat J. Prosser 2-1
v Scotland *Dunlaoghaire* lost to J. Zonfrillo 1-2
1976-7
v England *Dublin* lost to J. Johnson 0-3
v Scotland *Edinburgh* lost to D. Sneddon 1-2
v Wales *Dublin* lost to G. Thomas 0-3
1979
v Scotland *Prestatyn* beat I. Wallace 3-0
v England beat J. Hargreaves 2-1
v Northern Ireland lost to P. Donnelly 1-2
v Wales beat V. Rosser 2-1
v Isle of Man beat P. Reynolds 3-0
1980
v Northern Ireland *Prestatyn* beat D. McVeigh 3-0
v Wales lost to D. John 0-3
v Scotland lost to I. Black 1-2
v England beat D. Martin 2-1
v Isle of Man beat M. Quine 2-1

G. Sutton

1976-7
v England *Dublin* beat J. Fitzmaurice 2-1
v Scotland *Edinburgh* beat J. Zonfrillo 2-1
v Wales *Cardiff* lost to D. Thomas 1-2
1977-8
v Wales *Dublin* lost to A. Lloyd 0-3
v Scotland *Dublin* lost to R. Cadman 0-3
1978
v Wales *Prestatyn* beat C. Wilson 2-1
v Isle of Man beat P. Reynolds 3-0
v Scotland beat M. Gibson 3-0
1979
v Scotland *Prestatyn* beat E. McLaughlin 2-1
v England beat D. Hughes 3-0
v Northern Ireland lost to D. McVeigh 0-3
v Wales lost to J. Selby 1-2
v Isle of Man beat J. Radcliffe 3-0
1980
v Northern Ireland *Prestatyn* beat P. Donnelly 2-1
v Wales lost to J. Selby 1-2
v Scotland beat M. Macleod 2-1
v England lost to V. Harris 0-3
v Isle of Man lost to P. Partington 1-2
1981
v Northern Ireland *Prestatyn* beat D. McVeigh 2-1
v England lost to M. Darrington 0-3
v Isle of Man lost to C. Cooper 0-3
1985
v Wales lost to R. Welch 1-2
v Northern Ireland lost to K. McAlinden 0-3

P. Thornton

1970-1
v Wales *Port Talbot* lost to E. Richards 0-3
1971-2
v Scotland *Dublin* lost to E. Sinclair 0-3
1972-3
v Scotland *Dublin* lost to E. Sinclair 1-2

P. Watchorn

1977-8
v England *Portsmouth* lost to G. Scott 1-2
1980
v Northern Ireland *Prestatyn* lost to E. Swaffield 1-2
v Wales lost to S. Newbury 0-3
v Scotland beat M. Gibson 2-1
v England lost to M. Darrington 1-2
1981
v England *Prestatyn* lost to V. Harris 1-2
v Wales beat D. May 2-1
v Isle of Man beat M. Clinton 2-1
v Scotland beat J. Zonfrillo 2-1

1982
v Northern Ireland *Prestatyn* beat K. Erwin 2-1
v Isle of Man beat R. Cowley 3-0
v Scotland lost to K. Baird 0-3
v Wales beat A. Lloyd 2-1

L. Watson
1972-3
v Wales *Pontygwaith* lost to A. Lloyd 0-3
1975-6
v Scotland *Dunlaoghaire* lost to W. McKerron 0-3

J. Weber
1970-1
v England *Dublin* lost to J. Barron 1-2
1971-2
v England *Harringay* lost to R. Edmonds 0-3
v Scotland *Dublin* lost to B. Demarco 1-2
v Wales *Dublin* beat D. Mountjoy 2-1
1972-3
v Scotland *Dublin* lost to D. Sneddon 1-2
v Wales *Pontygwaith* lost to G. Thomas 1-2
1973-4
v Scotland *Dublin* beat W. McKerron 2-1
v England *Bolton* beat M. Wildman 2-1
1974-5
v Wales *Neath* lost to T. Griffiths 1-2
v Scotland *Dundee* lost to J. Zonfrillo 1-2

N. Wills
1971-2
v Wales *Dublin* lost to D. John 0-3

D. Wilson
1977-8
v England *Portsmouth* lost to J. Hargreaves 1-2
1978
v England *Prestatyn* lost to S. Hood 1-2
v Scotland lost to E. Sinclair 1-2

G. Wilson
1982
v Northern Ireland *Prestatyn* beat F. Connolly 2-1
v Isle of Man beat M. Quine 2-1
v Scotland lost to J. Rea 1-2

SCOTLAND

J. Allan
1982
v England *Prestatyn* lost to M. Bradley 0-3
v Wales lost to T. Chappel 1-2
v Isle of Man beat T. Wilson 2-1
v Rep. of Ireland beat P. Browne 2-1
1985
v Rep. of Ireland lost to K. Doherty 1-2
v England lost to G. Filtness 1-2
v Northern Ireland lost to K. McAlinden 1-2

K. Baird
1981
v Isle of Man *Prestatyn* beat C. Cooper 2-1
v Northern Ireland lost to A. Sharpe 1-2
v Rep. of Ireland lost to P. Ennis 1-2
v England lost to G. Wood 1-2
1982
v England *Prestatyn* beat D. Chalmers 3-0
v Wales lost to W. Jones 1-2
v Northern Ireland beat E. Swaffield 2-1
v Rep. of Ireland beat P. Watchorn 3-0
1983
v Wales *Prestatyn* lost to S. Newbury 0-3
v England beat D. Chalmers 2-1
v Isle of Man beat T. Wilson 2-1
v Rep. of Ireland lost to P. McNally 1-2

I. Black
1980
v Wales *Prestatyn* lost to A. Lloyd 0-3
v Isle of Man beat P. Partington 3-0
v Rep. of Ireland beat D. Sheehan 2-1
v Northern Ireland beat A. Sharpe 2-1
v England lost to J. O'Boye 1-2

B. Blues
1985
v Rep. of Ireland lost to G. Burns 0-3
v Isle of Man beat M. Clinton 3-0

C. Brown
1971-2
v Wales *Edinburgh* lost to D. Mountjoy 0-3
v Rep. of Ireland *Dublin* lost to G. Hanway 1-2

R. Cadman
1976-7
v Rep. of Ireland *Edinburgh* lost to D. Brennan 1-2
1977-8
v Rep. of Ireland *Dublin* beat G. Sutton 3-0
v England *Doncaster* lost to J. Hargreaves 0-3

G. Carnegie
1971-2
v England *Newcastle* lost to to J. Virgo 1-2
1982
v Isle of Man *Prestatyn* lost to R. Cowley 0-3
v Rep. of Ireland beat M. Kane 2-1
1983
v Wales *Prestatyn* lost to W. Jones 1-2
v Northern Ireland beat E. Swaffield 2-1
v England beat M. Bradley 2-1
v Isle of Man lost to R. Cowley 0-3
1984
v Rep. of Ireland lost to P. Ennis 0-3
v Isle of Man beat C. Cooper 2-1
v Northern Ireland lost to A. Sharpe 0-3

B. Demarco
1971-2
v England *Newcastle* lost to C. Ross 1-2
v Wales *Edinburgh* beat J. Terry 3-0
v Rep. of Ireland *Dublin* beat J. Weber 2-1
1972-3
v Rep. of Ireland *Dublin* beat A. Roche 2-1
v England *Edinburgh* lost to R. Edmonds 0-3
v Wales *Llay* beat J. Prosser 2-1
1973-4
v Rep. of Ireland *Dublin* beat F. Byrne 2-1
v England *Carlisle* beat T. Graham 2-1
v Wales *Edinburgh* lost to J. Selby 1-2
1974-5
v Wales *Maerdy* beat D. Mountjoy 2-1
v Rep. of Ireland *Dundee* beat N. Clarke 2-1
1975-6
v Wales *Edinburgh* lost to J. Selby 1-2
v Rep. of Ireland *Dunlaoghaire* lost to F. Byrne 1-2
1976-7
v Wales *Trealaw* lost to J. Selby 1-2
v England *Glasgow* lost to G. Foulds 1-2
1977-8
v Wales *Dublin* beat T. Parsons 2-1

J. Donnelly
1978
v Wales *Prestatyn* beat S. Newbury 3-0
v England lost to A. Knowles 0-3
v Isle of Man beat R. Cowley 3-0
v Rep. of Ireland lost to E. Hughes 1-2
1979
v Isle of Man *Prestatyn* beat W. Craig 3-0
v Rep. of Ireland lost to P. Burke 1-2
v Northern Ireland lost to D. McVeigh 1-2
v Wales lost to S. Newbury 0-3
1980
v Isle of Man *Prestatyn* lost to P. Reynolds 1-2
v Wales lost to D. John 1-2
v Northern Ireland beat S. Pavis 2-1
v England lost to V. Harris 0-3

R. Eprile
1973-4
v England *Carlisle* lost to M. Wildman 1-2

M. Gibson
1974-5
v England *Edinburgh* lost to G. Scott 0-3
v Wales *Maerdy* lost to T. Parsons 0-3
1977-8
v Rep. of Ireland *Dublin* beat N. Clarke 2-1
v England *Doncaster* beat G. Scott 2-1
1978
v Wales *Prestatyn* lost to A. Lloyd 1-2
v England lost to J. Hargreaves 0-3
v Rep. of Ireland lost to G. Sutton 0-3
1979
v England *Prestatyn* beat J. Hargreaves 2-1
v Rep. of Ireland beat T. Langan 2-1
v Northern Ireland beat J. Begley 2-1
v Wales beat T. Parsons 2-1
1980
v Isle of Man *Prestatyn* beat W. Craig 3-0
v Wales beat J. Selby 2-1
v Rep. of Ireland lost to P. Watchorn 1-2
v England lost to M. Watterson 0-3

G. Hadden
1972-3
v Rep. of Ireland *Dublin* beat G. Hanway 2-1
v Wales *Llay* lost to A. Lloyd 0-3

J. Halcrow
1978
v England *Prestatyn* lost to G. Foulds 0-3
v Isle of Man beat W. Craig 2-1
1979
v England *Prestatyn* beat G. Foulds 3-0
v Rep. of Ireland beat P. Miley 2-1
v Northern Ireland beat E. Swaffield 2-1
v Wales beat J. Terry 2-1
1980
v Rep. of Ireland *Prestatyn* beat M. Kane 2-1
v Northern Ireland lost to D. McVeigh 1-2
1981
v Isle of Man *Prestatyn* beat P. Reynolds 2-1
v Wales lost to S. Newbury 0-3
1983
v Northern Ireland *Prestatyn* beat S. Pavis 2-1
v England lost to B. West 1-2
v Isle of Man beat C. Cooper 2-1
v Rep. of Ireland beat M. Ralph 3-0
1984
v England lost to B. West 1-2
v Wales lost to D. John 0-3

S. Hendry
1984
v Rep. of Ireland lost to J. Long 1-2
v England beat R. Marshall 3-0
v Wales beat I. Tilley 3-0
v Isle of Man beat R. Cowley 3-0
v Northern Ireland beat K. Erwin 2-1

B. Kelly
1985
v Wales beat D. John 2-1
v Isle of Man lost to C. Cooper 1-2
v England beat J. Chambers 3-0
v Northern Ireland lost to A. Sharpe 1-2

M. Kerr
1985
v Wales lost to N. Davies 0-3
v Isle of Man beat M. Quine 3-0

P. Kippie
1980
v Isle of Man *Prestatyn* beat C. Cooper 2-1
v Wales lost to S. Newbury 1-2
v Northern Ireland lost to T. Murphy 1-2
v England lost to J. Hargreaves 0-3

J. Laidlaw
1983
v Northern Ireland *Prestatyn* lost to J. McLaughlin 0-3

v Rep. of Ireland beat J. Long 3-0

R. Lane

1981
v Isle of Man *Prestatyn* beat J. Kinrade 2-1
v Wales lost to T. Parsons 1-2
v Rep. of Ireland beat M. Kane 2-1
v England beat G. Cripsey 3-0
1982
v England *Prestatyn* beat S. Duggan 3-0
v Wales lost to A. Lloyd 1-2
v Northern Ireland lost to P. Donnelly 1-2
v Rep. of Ireland lost to P. Ennis 1-2
1983
v Wales *Prestatyn* lost to A. Lloyd 1-2
v Northern Ireland beat K. Erwin 3-0
v England lost to D. Fowler 1-2
v Isle of Man beat M. Clinton 2-1
1984
v Rep of Ireland lost to G. Burns 1-2
v England beat J. Wright 2-1
v Isle of Man beat T. Wilson 2-1
1985
v Wales lost to R. Jones 0-3
v Isle of Man beat T. Wilson 2-1
v England beat T. Whitthread 2-1
v Northern Ireland beat S. McClarey 2-1

M. Macleod

1975-6
v Wales *Edinburgh* lost to D. Mountjoy 0-3
v England *Southport* beat J. Fitzmaurice 2-1
v Rep. of Ireland *Dunlaoghaire* beat E. Hughes 2-1
1976-7
v Wales *Trealaw* lost to T. Griffiths 0-3
1979
v Isle of Man *Prestatyn* beat P. Partington 2-1
v Wales lost to G. Thomas 1-2
v England beat D. Martin 2-1
1980
v Isle of Man *Prestatyn* beat K. Kinrade 2-1
v Wales lost to C. Roscoe 0-3
v Rep. of Ireland lost to G. Sutton 1-2
v Northern Ireland lost to E. Swaffield 1-2

K. McIntosh

1984
v Isle of Man beat P. Smethurst 3-0
v Northern Ireland lost to H. Morgan 1-2
1985
v Wales beat G. Thomas 3-0
v Rep. of Ireland lost to R. McAuley 1-2
v Isle of Man lost to P. Reynolds 1-2
v England beat J. Wright 2-1
v Northern Ireland lost to K. Erwin 1-3

W. McKerron

1971-2
v England *Newcastle* beat M. Wildman 2-1
v Wales *Edinburgh* lost to R. Oriel 1-2
v Rep. of Ireland *Dublin* beat F. Murphy 2-1
1972-3
v England *Edinburgh* lost to M. Wildman 0-3
v Wales *Llay* lost to R. Oriel 1-2
1973-4
v Rep. of Ireland *Dublin* lost to J. Weber 1-2
v Wales *Edinburgh* lost to C. Wilson 1-2
1974-5
v England *Edinburgh* beat W. Thorne 2-1
v Wales *Maerdy* lost to M. Berni 0-3
1975-6
v Wales *Edinburgh* lost to A. Lloyd 0-3
v Rep. of Ireland *Dunlaoghaire* beat L. Watson 3-0
1976-7
v Wales *Trealaw* lost to S. Newbury 1-2
v Rep. of Ireland *Dublin* lost to R. Brennan 0-3

E. McLaughlin

1975-6
v England *Southport* lost to J. Hargreaves 0-3
1976-7
v Rep. of Ireland *Edinburgh* beat E. Hughes 2-1
v England *Glasgow* lost to R. Edmonds 1-2
1977-8
v Wales *Dublin* beat A. Lloyd 2-1
v England *Doncaster* beat G. Foulds 3-0
1978
v Wales *Prestatyn* lost to C. Wilson 1-2
v Isle of Man beat J. Radcliffe 3-0
v Rep. of Ireland beat F. Nathan 3-0
1979
v England *Prestatyn* lost to J. White 1-2
v Wales beat C. Everton 2-1
v Northern Ireland beat R. Burke 3-0
v Rep. of Ireland lost to G. Sutton 2-1
v Isle of Man beat J. Radcliffe 2-1
1980
v Isle of Man *Prestatyn* beat J. Radcliffe 3-0
v Wales beat R. Welch 2-1
v Rep. of Ireland beat E. Hughes 2-1
v Northern Ireland beat P. Donnelly 2-1
v England lost to J. White 1-2

J. McNellan

1980
v Rep. of Ireland *Prestatyn* lost to P. Burke 1-2
v England beat G. Wood 2-1
1981
v Wales *Prestatyn* lost to D. May 0-3
v Northern Ireland lost to S. Pavis 1-2
v Rep. of Ireland beat A. Kearney 2-1
v England lost to B. Harris 1-2
1983
v Wales *Prestatyn* beat R. Jones 2-1
v Northern Ireland lost to A. Sharpe 0-3
v Isle of Man beat M. Colquitt 2-1
v Rep. of Ireland lost to R. Brennan 1-2
1984
v Wales lost to R. Jones 0-3
v Northern Ireland beat S. Clarke 3-0
1985
v Wales lost to R. Welch 1-2
v Rep. of Ireland lost to R. Nolan 1-2
v England beat P. Gibson 2-1
v Northern Ireland lost to S. Pavis 0-3

R. Miller

1976-7
v England *Glasgow* lost to J. Johnson 1-2
1977-8
v Wales *Dublin* lost to C. Wilson 0-3
v Rep. of Ireland *Dublin* beat J. Clusker 2-1
v England *Doncaster* lost to J. Johnson 1-2
1978
v Wales *Prestatyn* beat D. John 2-1
v Isle of Man beat P. Reynolds 2-1
1981
v Isle of Man *Prestatyn* lost to R. Cowley 1-2
v Northern Ireland lost to E. Swaffield 1-2

S. Muir

1983
v Isle of Man *Prestatyn* beat P. Reynolds 3-0
v Rep. of Ireland lost to P. Ennis 0-3
1984
v Rep. of Ireland beat M. Kane 2-1
v England lost to J. O'Boye 1-2
v Wales beat G. Thomas 2-1
v Isle of Man beat P. Reynolds 3-0
v Northern Ireland beat S. Pavis 2-1
1985
v Wales lost to M. Bennett 1-2
v Rep. of Ireland beat J. Long 2-1
v England beat D. Roe 2-1
v Northern Ireland beat H. Morgan 3-0

S. Nivison

1975-6
v England *Southport* lost to R. Andrewartha 0-3
1979
v England *Prestatyn* lost to M. Watterson 0-3
v Wales lost to A. Lloyd 0-3
v Northern Ireland beat S. Pavis 2-1
v Rep. of Ireland beat E. Hughes 2-1
v Isle of Man beat C. Cooper 2-1
1985
v Rep. of Ireland lost to R. Brennan 1-2
v Isle of Man beat M. Colquitt 2-1

J. Phillips

1971-2
v England *Newcastle* lost to J. Barron 1-2
v Wales *Edinburgh* beat M. Berni 2-1
v Rep. of Ireland *Dublin* beat A. Roche 2-1
1972-3
v Rep. of Ireland *Dublin* beat J. Rogers 3-0
v England *Edinburgh* lost to S. Hood 1-2
v Wales *Llay* beat M. Berni 2-1
1973-4
v Rep. of Ireland *Dublin* beat G. Hanway 3-0
v England *Carlisle* lost to S. Hood 1-2
v Wales *Edinburgh* T. Griffiths 0-3
1974-5
v Rep. of Ireland *Dundee* beat F. Nathan 2-1
v Wales *Maerdy* lost to T. Griffiths 0-3
v England *Edinburgh* lost to J. Virgo 1-2
1975-6
v Wales *Edinburgh* lost to T. Parsons 1-2
v Rep. of Ireland *Dunlaoghaire* lost to P. Fagan 1-2
1976-7
v Wales *Trealaw* lost to T. Parsons 0-3
v Rep. of Ireland *Edinburgh* beat L. Kenna 3-0
v England *Glasgow* lost to G. Scott 1-2
1977-8
v Wales *Dublin* lost to G. Thomas 1-2
1979
v Isle of Man *Prestatyn* lost to P. Reynolds 1-2
v Northern Ireland lost to P. Donnelly 0-3

J. Rankeillor

1981
v Wales *Prestatyn* lost to J. Selby 1-2
v Northern Ireland beat S. Clarke 3-0
v Rep. of Ireland beat M. Ralph 2-1
v England beat L. Dodd 3-0
1982
v England *Prestatyn* lost to B. West 1-2
v Wales beat J. Selby 2-1
v Isle of Man beat M. Colquitt 2-1
v Northern Ireland beat S. Clarke 2-1
v Rep. of Ireland lost to J. Long 1-2
1983
v Wales *Prestatyn* lost to T. Chappel 0-3
v England lost to S. Longworth 0-3
1984
v Rep. of Ireland beat D. McKiernan 2-1
v England lost to M. Smith 1-2
v Wales beat J. Selby 2-1

J. Rea

1981
v Isle of Man *Prestatyn* beat J. Radcliffe 3-0
v Wales lost to A. Lloyd 1-2
v Northern Ireland beat J. McLaughlin 2-1
v Rep. of Ireland lost to P. Burke 0-3
v England beat I. Williamson 2-1
1982
v England *Prestatyn* lost to J. Parrott 1-2
v Isle of Man lost to C. Cooper 1-2
v Northern Ireland lost to A. Sharpe 1-2
v Rep. of Ireland beat G. Gibson 2-1
1983
v Wales *Prestatyn* lost to T. Parsons 1-2
v Northern Ireland beat S. McClarey 2-1
v England lost to S. Ventham 1-2
v Rep. of Ireland beat D. Cranley 2-1

E. Sinclair

1971-2
v England *Newcastle* lost to S. Hood 1-2
v Wales *Edinburgh* beat G. Thomas 2-1
v Rep. of Ireland *Dublin* beat P. Thornton 3-0
1972-3
v Rep. of Ireland *Dublin* lost to P. Thornton 2-1
v England *Edinburgh* lost to C. Ross 1-2
v Wales *Llay* beat D. May 2-1

1973-4
v Rep. of Ireland *Dublin* lost to D. Lenehan 1-2
v England *Carlisle* lost to J. Virgo 1-2
v Wales *Edinburgh* lost to A. Lloyd 0-3
1974-5
v England *Edinburgh* beat S. Hood 2-1
v Wales *Maerdy* lost to G. Thomas 1-2
v Rep. of Ireland *Dundee* lost to P. Burke 1-2
1975-6
v Wales *Edinburgh* beat T. Griffiths 3-0
v England *Southport* lost to S. Hood 1-2
v Rep. of Ireland *Dunlaoghaire* beat P. Burke 3-0
1976-7
v Wales *Trealaw* lost to A. Lloyd 1-2
v Rep. of Ireland *Edinburgh* beat P. Burke 3-0
v England *Glasgow* beat S. Hood 2-1
1977-8
v Wales *Dublin* lost to T. Griffiths 0-3
v Rep. of Ireland *Dublin* lost to P. Burke 2-1
v England *Doncaster* beat R. Edmonds 2-1
1978
v Wales *Prestatyn* lost to T. Parsons 0-3
v England lost to T. Meo 0-3
v Rep. of Ireland beat D. Wilson 2-1

D.Sneddon
1971-2
v England *Newcastle* beat R. Edmonds 2-1
v Wales *Edinburgh* lost to D. May 1-2
v Rep. of Ireland *Dublin* beat J. Rogers 2-1
1972-3
v Rep. of Ireland *Dublin* beat J. Weber 2-1
v England *Edinburgh* lost to J. Barron 0-3
v Wales *Llay* lost to G. Thomas 1-2
1973-4
v Rep. of Ireland *Dublin* lost to P. Burke 1-2
v England *Carlisle* lost to D. French 1-2
v Wales *Edinburgh* lost to D. Mountjoy 0-3
1974-5
v Rep. of Ireland *Dundee* beat D. Sheehan 3-0
v Wales *Maerdy* lost to A. Lloyd 1-2
1975-6
v Wales *Edinburgh* beat M. Berni 2-1
v England *Southport* lost to J. Virgo 1-2
1976-7
v Wales *Trealaw* lost to J. Prosser 1-2
v Rep. of Ireland *Edinburgh* beat D. Sheehan 2-1
v England *Glasgow* lost to J. Hargreaves 1-2
1977-8
v Wales *Dublin* lost to S. Newbury 1-2
v Rep. of Ireland *Dublin* beat M. Kane 3-0
v England *Doncaster* lost to S. Davis 0-3
1978
v England *Prestatyn* lost to M. Hallett 1-2
v Isle of Man beat M. Quine 3-0
v Rep. of Ireland beat R. Brennan 2-1
1982
v Wales *Prestatyn* lost to T. Parsons 0-3
v Isle of Man beat P. Reynolds 2-1
v Northern Ireland lost to S. Pavis 0-3
1984
v Rep. of Ireland beat M. Ralph 3-0
v England lost to C. Archer 1-2
v Wales beat M. Bennett 2-1
v Isle of Man beat M. Colquitt 2-1
v Northern Ireland beat E. Swaffield 2-1

I. Wallace
1974-5
v Rep. of Ireland *Dundee* beat E. Hughes 2-1
v England *Edinburgh* lost to R. Andrewartha 0-3
1979
v England *Prestatyn* lost to A. Knowles 0-3
v Rep. of Ireland lost to D. Sheehan 0-3
v Isle of Man beat R. Cowley 3-0

J. Wilson
1972-3
v England *Edinburgh* lost to J. Virgo 0-3

J. Zonfrillo
1973-4
v Rep. of Ireland *Dublin* lost to D. Sheehan 1-2
v England *Carlisle* lost to W. Thorne 1-2
v Wales *Edinburgh* beat G. Thomas 2-1
1974-5
v England *Edinburgh* lost to J. Hargreaves 1-2
v Rep. of Ireland *Dundee* beat J. Weber 2-1
1975-6
v England *Southport* beat R. Edmonds 2-1
v Rep. of Ireland *Dunlaoghaire* lost to D. Sheehan 2-1
1976-7
v Rep. of Ireland *Edinburgh* lost to G. Sutton 1-2
1978
v Wales *Prestatyn* beat J. Selby 2-1
v England lost to J. Johnson 1-2
v Isle of Man beat C. Cooper 2-1
v Rep. of Ireland lost to P. Burke 1-2
1981
v Rep. of Ireland *Prestatyn* beat M. Quine 3-0
v Wales beat D. John 2-1
v Northern Ireland beat D. McVeigh 2-1
v Rep. of Ireland lost to P. Watchorn 1-2
v England lost to M. Darrington 0-3
1982
v England *Prestatyn* lost to J. Hargreaves 1-2
v Wales lost to S. Newbury 1-2
v Isle of Man beat M. Clinton 2-1
v Northern Ireland lost to J. McLaughlin 0-3

WALES

M. Bennett
1981
v Isle of Man *Prestatyn* beat P. Reynolds 2-1
1984
v Isle of Man beat M. Colquitt 3-1
v Scotland lost to D. Sneddon 2-1
v Northern Ireland beat S. McClarey 2-1
v England lost to J. O'Boye 1-2
v Rep. of Ireland beat M. Kane 3-0
1985
v Rep.of Ireland beat D. Cranley 2-1
v Northern Ireland beat S. McClarey 2-1
v Isle of Man beat P. Reynolds 3-0
v Scotland beat S. Muir 2-1
v England lost to J. Wright 0-3

M. Berni
1969
v England *Port Talbot* beat P. Houlihan 3-0
1970-1
v England *Harringay* lost to M. Wildman 1-2
v Rep. of Ireland *Port Talbot* beat J. Rogers 3-0
1971-2
v England *Neath* beat R. Edmonds 2-1
v Scotland *Edinburgh* lost to J. Phillips 1-2
v Rep. of Ireland *Dublin* lost to A. Roche 1-2
1972-3
v Rep. of Ireland *Pontygwaith* beat F. Byrne 2-1
v England *Hull* beat J. Virgo 2-1
v Scotland *Llay* lost to J. Phillips 1-2
1973-4
v England *Garnant* lost to C. Ross 1-2
v Rep. of Ireland *Dublin* lost to N. Clarke 0-3
1974-5
v Scotland *Maerdy* beat W. McKerron 3-0
v England *Exeter* beat R. Andrewartha 2-1
v Rep. of Ireland *Neath* beat N. Clarke 3-0
1975-6
v Scotland *Edinburgh* lost to D. Sneddon 2-1
v Rep. of Ireland *Dublin* beat E. Hughes 3-0
v England *Merthyr* lost to R. Edmonds 0-3

T. Chappel
1982
v Northern Ireland *Prestatyn* lost to A. Sharpe 1-2
v Scotland beat J. Allan 2-1
v England lost to J. Hargreaves 0-2
1983
v Scotland *Prestatyn* beat J. Rankeillor 3-0
v Northern Ireland beat A. Sharpe 2-1
v England beat G. Wood 3-0

N. Davies
1984
v Isle of Man beat R. Cowley 2-1
v Northern Ireland beat Jim McLaughlin 3-0
v England beat B. West 2-1
1985
v Rep. of Ireland beat R. Nolan 2-1
v Northern Ireland beat H. Morgan 3-0
v Scotland beat M. Kerr 3-0
v England beat D. Roe 2-1

R. Dorkings
1985
v Isle of Man beat M. Clinton 2-1

C. Everton
1978
v Isle of Man *Prestatyn* beat M. Quine 3-0
v Rep. of Ireland beat J. Clusker 2-1
v England beat G. Foulds 2-1
1979
v Isle of Man *Prestatyn* beat C. Cooper 3-0
v Scotland lost to E. McLaughlin 1-2
v England drew with G. Scott 1-1

J. Ford
1969
v England *Port Talbot* beat S. Hood 2-1
1970-1
v England *Harringay* lost to S. Hood 1-2
v Rep. of Ireland *Port Talbot* beat G. Hanway 3-0

J. Griffiths
1982
v Northern Ireland *Prestatyn* lost to K. Erwin 1-2
v Rep. of Ireland lost to J. Lang 1-2
1983
v Isle of Man *Prestatyn* beat M. Colquitt 2-1

T. Griffiths
1973-4
v Rep. of Ireland *Dublin* beat P. Burke 2-1
v Scotland *Edinburgh* beat J. Phillips 3-0

1974-5
v Scotland *Maerdy* beat J. Phillips 3-0
v England *Exeter* lost to W. Thorne 1-2
v Rep. of Ireland *Neath* beat J. Weber 2-1
1975-6
v Scotland *Edinburgh* lost to E. Sinclair 0-3
v Rep. of Ireland *Dublin* beat J. Rogers 3-0
v England *Merthyr* beat S. Hood 2-1
1976-7
v Scotland *Trealaw* beat M. Macleod 3-0
v England *Doncaster* beat J. Johnson 2-1
v Rep. of Ireland *Cardiff* beat R. Brennan 3-0
1977-8
v Scotland *Dublin* beat E. Sinclair 3-0
v Rep. of Ireland *Dublin* beat J. Rogers 3-0
v England *Caerphilly* beat J. Hargreaves 3-0

M. Hendra

1985
v Northern Ireland lost to K. Erwin 1-2
v Isle of Man beat C. Cooper 2-1

G. Heycock

1985
v Rep.of Ireland lost to J. Long 1-2
v Isle of Man beat T. Wilson 3-0
v England beat K. Owers 1-0

A. Issitt

1984
v Rep. of Ireland lost to M. Nolan 1-2

D. John

1971-2
v England *Neath* lost to S. Hood 1-2
v Rep. of Ireland *Dublin* beat N. Wills 3-0
1978
v Scotland *Prestatyn* lost to R. Miller 1-2
1980
v Northern Ireland *Prestatyn* beat D. McVeigh 2-1
v Scotland beat J. Donnelly 2-1
v Rep. of Ireland beat D. Sheehan 3-0
v England beat V. Harris 3-0
1981
v Northern Ireland *Prestatyn* lost to A. Sharpe 1-2
v Scotland lost to J. Zonfrillo 1-2
v Rep. of Ireland beat P. Ennis 3-0
v England lost to B. West 1-2
1984
v Isle of Man beat C. Cooper 3-0
v Scotland beat J. Halcrow 3-0
v Northern Ireland beat S.Pavis 3-0
v England beat S. Ventham 2-1
v Rep. of Ireland beat J. Long 3-0
1985
v Rep. of Ireland beat P. Miley 3-0
v Northern Ireland beat S. Pavis 2-1
v Scotland lost to B. Kelly 1-2
v England drew with R. Marshall 1-1

P. Jones

1983
v Rep. of Ireland *Prestatyn* beat P. McNally 2-1

R. Jones

1983
v Scotland *Prestatyn* lost to J. McNellan 1-2
v Isle of Man beat P. Reynolds 2-1
v Rep. of Ireland beat M. Ralph 2-1
v Northern Ireland beat K. Erwin 3-0
v England drew with R. Jarmak 1-1
1984
v Isle of Man beat P. Partington 2-1
v Scotland beat J. McNellan 3-0
v Northern Ireland lost to S. Clarke 1-2
v England lost to T. Whitthread 0-3
v Rep. of Ireland beat G. Burns 3-0
1985
v Rep. of Ireland lost to K. Doherty 1-2
v Isle of Man beat M. Quine 3-0
v Scotland beat R. Lane 3-0
v England lost to G. Filtness 1-2

W. Jones

1981
v Northern Ireland *Prestatyn* beat S. Clarke 2-1
v Isle of Man beat J. Kinrade 3-0
1982
v Isle of Man *Prestatyn* beat R. Cowley 3-0
v Northern Ireland lost to E. Swaffield 1-2
v Scotland beat K. Baird 2-1
v Rep. of Ireland lost to P. Browne 1-2
v England beat M. Bradley 2-1
1983
v Scotland *Prestatyn* beat G. Carnegie 2-1
v Isle of Man lost to C. Cooper 0-3
v Rep. of Ireland beat D. Cranley 2-1
v Northern Ireland beat W. Walker 3-0
v England beat M. Bradley 2-1

A. Kemp

1969
v England *Port Talbot* lost to C. Ross 1-2

A. Lloyd

1969
v England *Port Talbot* beat G. Thompson 2-1
1972-3
v Rep. of Ireland *Pontygwaith* beat L. Watson 3-0
v England *Hull* beat C. Ross 2-1
v Scotland *Llay* beat G. Hatton 3-0
1973-4
v England *Garnant* lost to R. Edmonds 0-3
v Scotland *Edinburgh* beat E.Sinclair 3-0
1974-5
v Scotland *Maerdy* beat D. Sneddon 2-1
v England *Exeter* lost to R. Edmonds 1-2
v Rep. of Ireland *Neath* beat F. Nathan 2-1
1975-6
v Scotland *Edinburgh* beat W. McKerron 3-0
v England *Merthyr* beat C. Ross 2-1
1976-7
v Scotland *Trealaw* beat E. Sinclair 2-1
v Rep. of Ireland *Cardiff* beat F. Murphy 3-0
1977-8
v Scotland *Dublin* lost to E. McLaughlin 1-2
v Rep. of Ireland *Dublin* beat G. Sutton 3-0
v England *Caerphilly* beat J. Johnson 2-1
1978
v Scotland *Prestatyn* beat M. Gibson 2-1
v Isle of Man beat C. Cooper 3-0
v Rep. of Ireland lost to P. Burke 1-2
v England lost to A. Knowles 0-2
1979
v Northern Ireland lost to P. Donnelly 1-2
v Isle of Man beat J. Radcliffe 3-0
v Rep. of Ireland beat P. Miley 3-0
v England beat D. Martin 2-1
1980
v Northern Ireland *Prestatyn* beat P. Donnelly 2-1
v Scotland beat I. Black 3-0
v Rep. of Ireland beat P. Burke 3-0
v Isle of Man beat K. Kinrade 2-1
v England lost to J. O'Boye 1-2
1981
v Northern Ireland *Prestatyn* beat D. McVeigh 2-1
v Scotland beat J. Rea 2-1
v Rep. of Ireland beat M. Ralph 2-1
v Isle of Man beat C. Cooper 3-0
v England beat M. Darrington 2-1
1982
v Isle of Man *Prestatyn* beat M. Clinton 2-1
v Scotland beat R. Lane 2-1
v Northern Ireland beat J. McLaughlin 2-1
v Rep. of Ireland lost to P. Watchorn 1-2
v England beat J. Parrott 1-2
1983
v Scotland *Prestatyn* beat R. Lane 2-1
v Rep. of Ireland beat G. Gibson 3-0
v Northern Ireland lost to J. McLaughlin 0-3
v England beat B. West 2-1
1984
v Isle of Man beat T. Wilson 3-0
v Northern Ireland beat K. Erwin 2-1
v England lost to M. Smith 1-2
v Rep. of Ireland lost to P. Ennis 1-2

D. May

1970-1
v England *Harringay* lost to J. Barron 1-2
v Rep. of Ireland *Port Talbot* beat D. Sheehan 3-0
1971-2
v England *Neath* lost to J. Barron 1-2
v Scotland *Edinburgh* beat D. Sneddon 2-1
v Rep. of Ireland *Dublin* beat J. Rogers 2-1
1972-3
v Rep. of Ireland *Pontygwaith* beat A. Roche 3-0
v England *Hull* beat R. Edmonds 2-1
v Scotland *Llay* lost to E. Sinclair 1-2
1973-4
v England *Garnant* lost to S. Hood 0-3
1980
v Northern Ireland *Prestatyn* beat S. Pavis 2-1
v Rep. of Ireland beat E. Hughes 2-1
v Isle of Man beat J. Radcliffe 3-0
v England lost to D. Martin 0-3
1981
v Northern Ireland *Prestatyn* lost to E. Swaffield 1-2
v Scotland beat J. McNellan 3-0
v Rep. of Ireland lost to P. Watchorn 1-2
v Isle of Man beat R. Cowley 2-1
v England lost to B. Harris 1-2

D. Meredith

1971-2
v England *Neath* beat D. French 2-1
v Rep. of Ireland *Dublin* beat D. Sheehan 3-0

D. Mountjoy

1969
v England *Port Talbot* lost to J. Barron 0-3
1970-1
v England *Harringay* lost to R. Edmonds 1-2
v Rep. of Ireland *Port Talbot* beat L. Kenna 3-0
1971-2
v Scotland *Edinburgh* beat C. Brown 3-0
v Rep. of Ireland *Dublin* lost to J. Weber 1-2
1972-3
v Rep. of Ireland *Pontygwaith* beat J. Grace 3-0
v England *Hull* lost to S. Hood 1-2
1973-4
v England *Garnant* lost to M. Wildman 1-2
v Rep. of Ireland *Dublin* beat D. Sheehan 3-0
v Scotland *Edinburgh* beat D. Sneddon 3-0
1974-5
v Scotland *Maerdy* lost to B. Demarco 1-2
v England *Exeter* beat C. Ross 2-1
v Rep. of Ireland *Neath* beat P. Burke 2-1
1975-6
v Scotland *Edinburgh* beat M. Macleod 3-0
v Rep. of Ireland *Dublin* beat P. Fagan 2-1
v England *Merthyr* beat J. Virgo 2-1

S. Newbury

1976-7
v Scotland *Trealaw* beat W. McKerron 2-1
v England *Doncaster* lost to J. Hargreaves 1-2
v Rep. of Ireland *Cardiff* lost to L. Kenna 0-3
1977-8
v Scotland *Dublin* beat D. Sneddon 2-1
v Rep. of Ireland *Dublin* beat L. Kenna 3-0
v England *Caerphilly* beat G. Scott 2-1
1978
v Scotland *Prestatyn* lost to J. Donnelly 0-3
v Rep. of Ireland beat F. Nathan 3-0
v England lost to T. Meo 1-2
1979
v Northern Ireland *Prestatyn* beat S. Pavis 3-0

v Isle of Man beat M. Quine 3-0
v Scotland beat J. Donnelly 3-0
v Rep. of Ireland beat T. Langan 2-1
v England beat M. Watterson 3-0
1980
v Northern Ireland *Prestatyn* beat A. Sharpe 2-1
v Scotland beat P. Kippie 2-1
v Rep. of Ireland beat P. Watchorn 3-0
v Isle of Man beat M. Quine 3-0
v England beat J. White 3-0
1981
v Northern Ireland *Prestatyn* beat P. Donnelly 2-1
v Scotland beat J. Halcrow 3-0
v Rep. of Ireland beat A. Kearney 2-1
v England beat G. Wood 2-0
1982
v Isle of Man *Prestatyn* beat M. Colquitt 3-0
v Northern Ireland beat P. Donnelly 3-0
v Scotland beat J. Zonfrillo 2-1
v Rep. of Ireland beat M. Kane 3-0
v England beat N. Foulds 3-0
1983
v Scotland *Prestatyn* beat K. Baird 3-0
v Isle of Man beat P. Partington 3-0
v Rep. of Ireland beat J. Long 2-1
v Northern Ireland beat E. Swaffield 2-1
v England lost to S. Longworth 0-3

R. Oriel

1971-2
v England *Neath* beat D. Taylor 2-1
v Scotland *Edinburgh* beat W. McKerron 2-1
v Rep. of Ireland *Dublin* beat R. Brennan 3-0
1972-3
v Scotland *Llay* beat W. McKerron 2-1

T. Parsons

1969
v England *Port Talbot* lost to R. Edmonds 0-3
1972-3
v Rep. of Ireland *Pontygwaith* beat G. Hanway 2-1
v England *Hull* lost to M. Wildman 0-3
1974-5
v Scotland *Maerdy* beat M. Gibson 3-0
v England *Exeter* beat M. Wildman 3-0
v Rep. of Ireland *Neath* beat D. Sheehan 2-1
1975-6
v Scotland *Edinburgh* beat J. Phillips 2-1
v England *Merthyr* beat R. Andrewartha 3-0
1976-7
v Scotland *Trealaw* beat J. Phillips 3-0
v England *Doncaster* lost to G. Scott 1-2
v Rep. of Ireland *Cardiff* beat P. Burke 3-0
1977-8
v Scotland *Dublin* lost to B. Demarco 1-2
v Rep. of Ireland *Dublin* beat P. Burke 2-1
v England *Caerphilly* lost to S. Davis 1-2
1978
v Scotland *Prestatyn* beat E. Sinclair 3-0
v Isle of Man beat K. Kinrade 3-0
v Rep. of Ireland beat J. Rogers 3-0
v England lost to J. Hargreaves 1-2
1979
v Northern Ireland *Prestatyn* beat D. McVeigh 3-0
v Isle of Man beat R. Cowley 2-1
v Scotland lost to M. Gibson 1-2
v England lost to A. Knowles 1-2
1981
v Northern Ireland *Prestatyn* beat S. Pavis 3-0
v Scotland beat R. Lane 2-1
v Rep. of Ireland beat P. Burke 3-0
v Isle of Man beat P. Partington 2-1
v England lost to J. Hargreaves 1-2
1982
v Isle of Man *Prestatyn* beat C. Cooper 3-0
v Northern Ireland beat S. Pavis 2-1
v Scotland beat D. Sneddon 3-0
v Rep. of Ireland beat P. Ennis 2-1
v England beat S. Duggan 2-1
1983
v Scotland *Prestatyn* beat J. Rea 2-1
v Rep. of Ireland beat P. Ennis 3-0
v Isle of Man beat R. Cowley 3-0
v Northern Ireland beat S. Pavis 3-0
v England beat D. Fowler 2-1

J. Prosser

1972-3
v Scotland *Llay* lost to B. Demarco 1-2
1973-4
v England *Garnant* lost to W. Thorne 1-2
1975-6
v Rep. of Ireland *Dublin* lost to D. Sheehan 1-2
1976-7
v Scotland *Trealaw* beat D. Sneddon 2-1
v England *Doncaster* lost to R. Edmonds 1-2

E. Richards

1970-1
v England *Harringay* lost to C. Ross 0-3
v Rep. of Ireland *Port Talbot* beat P. Thornton 3-0

C. Roscoe

1980
v Northern Ireland *Prestatyn* beat E. Swaffield 2-1
v Scotland beat M. Macleod 3-0
v Rep. of Ireland lost to M. Kane 1-2
v Isle of Man beat W. Craig 3-0
v England lost to M. Watterson 1-2

V. Rosser

1979
v Isle of Man *Prestatyn* beat W. Craig 3-0
v Rep. of Ireland lost to D. Sheehan 1-2
1980
v Northern Ireland *Prestatyn* lost to T. Murphy 0-3

J. Selby

1973-4
v Rep. of Ireland *Dublin* beat F. Byrne 2-1
v Scotland *Edinburgh* beat B. Demarco 2-1
1975-6
v Scotland *Edinburgh* beat B. Demarco 2-1
v Rep. of Ireland *Dublin* beat L. Kenna 3-0
v England *Merthyr* beat J. Fitzmaurice 2-1
1976-7
v Scotland *Trealaw* beat B. Demarco 2-1
v England *Doncaster* lost to G. Foulds 0-3
1978
v Scotland *Prestatyn* lost to J. Zonfrillo 1-2
v Isle of Man beat W. Craig 2-1
v Rep. of Ireland lost to E. Hughes 1-2
v England lost to J. Johnson 0-3
1979
v Northern Ireland *Prestatyn* lost to E. Swaffield 1-2
v Isle of Man beat P. Reynolds 2-1
v Rep. of Ireland beat G. Sutton 2-1
v England lost to J. Hargreaves 0-3
1980
v Scotland *Prestatyn* lost to M. Gibson 1-2
v Rep. of Ireland beat G. Sutton 2-1
v Isle of Man beat P. Reynolds 2-1
v England beat J. Hargreaves 2-1
1981
v Scotland *Prestatyn* beat J. Rankeillor 2-1
v Rep. of Ireland lost to M. Kane 1-2
v Isle of Man beat M. Clinton 3-0
v England lost to I. Williamson 0-1
1982
v Isle of Man *Prestatyn* beat T. Wilson 3-0
v Scotland lost to J. Rankeillor 1-2
v England lost to B. West 1-2
1983
v Isle of Man *Prestatyn* beat M. Colquitt 2-1

J. Terry

1971-2
v Scotland *Edinburgh* lost to B. Demarco 0-3
1979
v Northern Ireland *Prestatyn* beat B. Harvey 2-1
v Scotland lost to J. Halcrow 1-2
v Rep. of Ireland lost to P. Burke 1-2
1982
v Isle of Man *Prestatyn* beat P. Reynolds 2-1
v Rep. of Ireland beat G. Gibson 3-0

D. Thomas

1971-2
v England *Neath* lost to C. Ross 1-2
1976-7
v England *Doncaster* lost to S. Hood 1-2
v Rep. of Ireland *Cardiff* beat G. Sutton 2-1

G. Thomas

1970-1
v England *Harringay* lost to J. Virgo 0-3
v Rep. of Ireland *Port Talbot* beat J. Grace 2-1
1971-2
v Scotland *Edinburgh* lost to E. Sinclair 1-2
1972-3
v Rep. of Ireland *Pontygwaith* beat J. Weber 2-1
v England *Hull* beat J. Barron 2-1
v Scotland *Llay* beat D. Sneddon 2-1
1973-4
v England *Garnant* lost to J. Virgo 1-2
v Rep. of Ireland *Dublin* beat P. Miley 3-0
v Scotland *Edinburgh* lost to J. Zonfrillo 1-2
1974-5
v Scotland *Maerdy* beat E. Sinclair 2-1
v England *Exeter* lost to S. Hood 1-2
v Rep. of Ireland *Neath* lost to J. Rogers 1-2
1975-6
v Rep. of Ireland *Dublin* lost to P. Burke 1-2
1977-8
v Scotland *Dublin* beat J. Phillips 2-1
v Rep. of Ireland *Dublin* beat D. Sheehan 3-0
v England *Caerphilly* lost to G. Foulds 1-2
1978
v Isle of Man *Prestatyn* beat R. Cowley 2-1
1979
v Northern Ireland *Prestatyn* beat J. Begley 2-1
v Scotland beat M. Macleod 2-1
v England lost to J. White 0-3
1984
v Isle of Man beat P. Reynolds 2-1
v Scotland lost to S. Muir 1-2
v Northern Ireland lost to E. Swaffield 0-3
v England lost to C. Archer 1-2
v Rep. of Ireland beat K. Doherty 3-0
1985
v Northern Ireland beat A. Sharpe 2-1
v Isle of Man beat M. Colquitt 2-1
v Scotland lost to K. McIntosh 0-3

I. Tilley

1984
v Scotland lost to S. Hendry 0-3

R. Welch

1980
v Scotland *Prestatyn* lost to E. McLaughlin 1-2
v Isle of Man beat C. Cooper 2-1
1985
v Rep. of Ireland beat G. Sutton 2-1
v Northern Ireland beat E. Swaffield 3-0
v Scotland beat J. McNellan 2-1
v England beat T. Whitthread 3-0

C. Wilson

1973-4
v Rep. of Ireland *Dublin* lost to D. Lenehan 1-2
v Scotland *Edinburgh* beat W. McKerron 2-1
1976-7
v Rep. of Ireland *Cardiff* beat J. Clusker 2-1
1977-8
v Scotland *Dublin* beat R. Miller 3-0
v Rep. of Ireland *Dublin* lost to J. Clusker 1-2
v England *Caerphilly* lost to R. Edmonds 1-2
1978
v Scotland *Prestatyn* beat E. McLaughlin 2-1
v Isle of Man beat P. Reynolds 3-0
v Rep. of Ireland lost to G. Sutton 1-2
v England beat M. Hallett 3-0

Women's Snooker

Allison Fisher, 18, confirmed the opinion of those who believe that she is by far the best player women's snooker has ever seen by going through an entire year's competition undefeated by another woman.

Now a player of 100 break standard, she also emphasised in various open events her capacity to compete on equal terms with the best male amateurs.

At the Hastings Snooker Festival in April, she was beaten only 4-3 by Terry Whitthread, the 1985 English Amateur Champion, in a special challenge match covered by the cable television company Screensport after she had been within only two colours of victory when leading 3-1.

She emphatically avenged her defeat in the 1984 Women's World Amateur Championship semi-finals by her closest rival, Stacey Hillyard, 16, by beating her 5-1 to take the £1,250 first prize in the 1985 event at Breaks, Solihull.

Allison Fisher, the best player the women's game has ever produced

Mandy Fisher, one of the leading women players

But for Hillyard winning the fifth frame of the final, she would have won the title without losing a frame in the entire 78-entry competition which was chiefly sponsored by First Leisure, the leisure and entertainment group and the Midland brewers, Mitchells and Butlers.

After a premature attempt to promote professional women's snooker as a public entertainment had failed in 1983-84, all distinctions between amateur and professional status in the women's game were abolished on 1 January 1986. This provided for all women's tournaments to be open but for any player to declare herself a professional for coaching or other purposes if she so desired.

One of the many positive consequences of this decision is that there will be no third women's world amateur championship but that a women's world open with a fully international field will be held in the corresponding dates slot 9-12 October in 1986.

Of the four women's opens held before the game split temporarily into professional and amateur sections, Vera Selby (England) won in 1976 and 1981, Lesley McIlrath (Australia) in 1980 and Sue Foster (England) in 1983.

A professional circuit was organised in 1984, sponsored by National Express, on which Mandy Fisher (England) won two of the five tournaments and the overall snowball prize. Sue Foster and Sue LeMaich (Canada) won the two other first prizes.

The women's professional scene broke up in acrimony and disarray. The World Ladies Billiards and Snooker Association elected a new administration which in the last two years has made substantial progress in building up a circuit of one-day tournaments with modest prize money, widening the base of participation and generally making itself more credible.

Standards noticeably rose not only at the top but at the levels immediately beneath it. The Tuborg UK Championship, which was held at the Willie Thorne Snooker Centre, Leicester, in 1986, was the first tournament to be staged since the women's game had gone open.

Most of the professionals, with very few competitive opportunities following the break-up of their own circuit, clearly suffered from their lack of recent competition and it was also clear that their standards had been matched and in many cases overtaken by the younger players coming through the ranks.

Vera Selby, twice Women's World champion

Allison Fisher predictably took the £175 first prize by beating Stacey Hillyard 4-2 in the final, after reaching it without dropping a single frame.

Hillyard, who in January 1985 had become the first woman to make a century break in bona fide competition with an effort of 114 in the Bournemouth League, took the break prize with 82 and made other breaks of 65, 53 and 54 during the day. Other breaks included 64 and 61 by Georgina Aplin and 59 by Angela Jones.

As recently as 1984, Mandy Fisher's 62 had been the highest ever made by a woman in competition.

WOMEN'S WORLD AMATEUR 1984

Semi-finals: S. Hillyard beat A. Fisher 4-3; N. Stelmach beat C. Walch 4-0

Final: Hillyard beat Stelmach 4-1

B & SCC WOMEN'S AMATEUR

1984
Final: S. Hillyard beat M. Tart 4-3

1985
Final: S. Hillyard beat C. Walch 4-2

TUBORG UK WOMEN'S AMATEUR 1985

Final: A. Fisher beat C. Walch 3-0

WOMEN'S WORLD AMATEUR 1985

Semi-finals: S. Hillyard beat C. Walch 4-2; A. Fisher beat J. Dowen 4-0

Final: Fisher beat Hillyard 5-1

B & SCC WOMEN'S AMATEUR

1986
Final: A. Fisher beat C. Walch 4-0

TUBORG UK WOMEN'S CHAMPIONSHIP 1986

Final: A. Fisher beat S. Hillyard 4-2

Lesley McIlrath, Women's World champion 1980

The Basic Rules of Snooker

Snooker is played with 22 balls which are positioned at the start of the frame (or game) as shown in the diagram. The cue-ball, which is used alternately by both players, can be placed anywhere in the 'D' for the first stroke but must thereafter be played from where it comes to rest, except after an in-off or if it is forced off the table, in which cases the next player must again play from the 'D'.

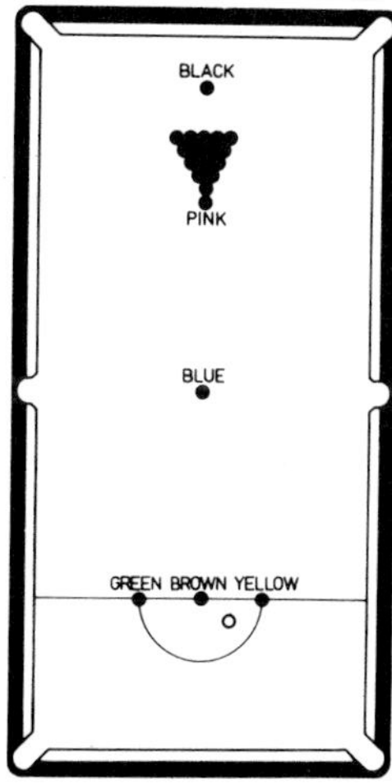

Points are scored by potting and by receiving penalties from foul strokes. Each player must first attempt to strike a red (value 1). When he pots a red he must then play at a colour, the values of which are: black (7), pink (6), blue (5), brown (4), green (3), yellow (2).

The player should nominate the colour he is attempting, although the letter of this rule is not enforced in cases where this is obvious.

If a colour is potted, it is replaced on its own spot, another red is then attempted and so on until all the reds have been potted.

The colours are then taken in ascending order of value until only the cue-ball remains on the table.

Failure to strike a red involves a penalty of four points (the minimum penalty for any foul) but the penalty is increased to 5, 6 or 7 if, instead of a red, the cue-ball strikes blue, pink or black. An in-off is a foul carrying a penalty of four points, or more if the ball which the cue-ball initially strikes before entering a pocket is of higher value.

Failure to strike a nominated colour also carries a four point penalty, or more if the ball involved is of higher value. If, for example, green is nominated but pink is struck, the penalty is 6. If pink is nominated and green is struck the penalty is also 6.

Penalties often result, not from incompetence or chance, but from snookers. A snooker occurs when the balls are so placed that a player cannot strike the ball he is due to play without hitting a cushion or making the cue-ball swerve.

If a player is snookered on the reds after a foul shot by his opponent he may nominate any coloured ball as a red. This is known as a free ball. If he pots it he scores one and can then nominate a colour in the usual way.

If no red remains, a free ball is valued at a number of points equal to that of the lowest value colour remaining and the colours are then taken in sequence.

For the purpose of this rule, a player is deemed to be snookered if he cannot directly hit both extremities of the object-ball he is due to play. (The exception to this rule is when one or more reds are preventing a player striking a particular red.)

FOUL SHOTS

After any foul shot, whether he is entitled to a free ball or not, a player can ask his opponent to play again. A foul is committed in both billiards and snooker if:

(a) a player's cue-tip strikes the cue-ball more than once in the same stroke
(b) a ball is forced off the table
(c) a player plays with both feet off the floor
(d) a player plays before all the balls have come to rest
(e) a player strikes or touches a ball other than with the tip of the cue
(f) the cue-ball jumps over an intervening ball
(g) the balls are wrongly spotted when the player takes his shot.

If at the end of a frame the scores are level, the black is replaced on its spot and the player winning the toss of a coin has the choice of whether he or his opponent takes first shot at it from anywhere within the 'D'.

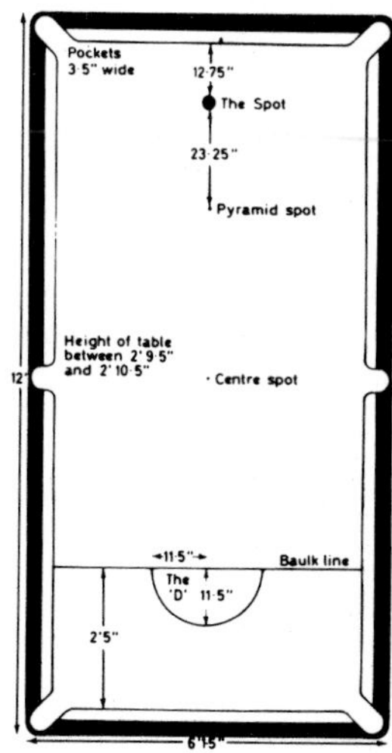

Snooker Glossary

Break: A sequence of scoring shots.

Break off: The first shot of a frame in which the striker plays at the unbroken triangle of reds.

Clear the table: A sequence of shots in which a player pots all the balls left on the table.

Double: A shot by which a ball enters a pocket after striking one or more cushions.

Free ball: If a player is snookered after a foul shot by his opponent he may nominate any coloured ball as a red. If it is potted, he scores one and can then nominate a colour in the usual way. If all the reds have left the table, the free ball is valued at the same number of points as the lowest-valued ball on the table and the colours are then taken in sequence. (*N.B.* For the purpose of this rule a player is deemed to be snookered if he cannot hit both extremities of the object-ball.)

Maximum break: A sequence of shots in which a player takes all fifteen reds, fifteen blacks and all the colours to score 147.

Plant: A position in which the first object-ball is played on to the second object-ball in such a way as to make the second ball enter the pocket.

Safety shot: A shot in which a player makes no attempt to score but intends to leave his opponent unable to score.

Screw: Reverse spin. This is applied by striking the cue-ball well below centre.

Set: A position in which two object-balls are touching in such a way that the second ball is certain to be potted however the first object-ball is struck.

Shot to nothing: A shot in which a player attempts a pot in such a way as to leave himself in position to continue his break if successful but to leave the cue-ball in a safe position for his opponent if unsuccessful.

Side: Side spin. This is applied by striking the cue-ball to either the right or left of centre.

Snooker: A position in which the cue-ball cannot hit an object-ball because of an intervening ball.

Stun: A shot in which the cue-ball is stopped dead (if the pot is straight) by striking the cue-ball just below centre. If the pot is not straight, the stun shot is used to widen the angle the cue-ball takes after potting the object-ball.

Billiards Glossary

Coup: Striking the cue-ball into a pocket without contacting another ball.

Cue-ball: The ball struck with the cue.

Full-ball shot: A contact in which the cue-tip, the centre of the cue-ball and the centre of the object-ball form a straight line.

Half-ball shot: A contact in which half the cue-ball covers half the object-ball at the moment of impact.

Hazard: A pot, in-off, or combination of the two.

In hand: The situation wherein a player, having scored an in-off, can place the cue-ball by hand in the D for his next shot.

Miss: Failing to strike any object-ball.

Natural angle: Any angle which the cue-ball may take after striking an object-ball at medium pace without side or screw.

Pot: Propelling the cue-ball on to an object-ball to send the object-ball into a pocket.

Safe position: When the balls are so situated that a scoring stroke looks very unlikely.

Swing: When the cue-ball follows a wide arc after contacting an object-ball at about half-ball with considerable force; a shot usually employed to widen the angle taken by the cue-ball to achieve an in-off or cannon.

Stringing: A practice sometimes adopted to decide which player shall begin the game or have choice of ball. Each player plays a white from the baulk line to the top cushion to bring it back as near as possible to the baulk cushion. The player whose ball finishes nearest the baulk cushion has the choice of both ball and order of play.